D0722480

How to Write and Sell Confessions

How to Write and Sell Confessions

by
Susan C. Feldhake

Publishers   THE WRITER, INC.   Boston

Library of Congress Cataloging in Publication Data

Feldhake, Susan C.
How to Write and Sell Confessions

1. Confession stories—Authorship. I. Title.
PN3377.5.C6F44   808 '.025   79-25354
ISBN 0-87116-123-0

Printed in the United States of America

To My Parents
ARVID *and* MILLIE CHRISTIANSEN
and SYLVIA KAUFFMAN
who gave me love, and encouraged me
to make all my dreams become reality

CONTENTS

INTRODUCTION

Confession magazines (in which the stories are really fictional) have been with us a long time. Many of the magazines currently on the stands have been around—and buying stories from writers—since 1919, when *True Confessions* was launched. Probably no one market has bought more short stories than the confession magazines.

There is a large demand for *fictional* personal-experience stories that make up what are commonly known as "true confession" magazines. These stories are *not* true—although they could have happened easily. The loyal readership of the confession magazines look to them for guidance and solutions to everyday problems, as well as for entertainment and escape.

Other magazines use personal-experience confessions. In fact, many of the major women's magazines publish nonfiction personal-experience material closely related to the traditional fictional confession story. For example, "My Problem and How I Solved It" (*Good Housekeeping*), "Young Mother's Story" (*Redbook*), and "It's Not Easy to Be a Woman Today" (*Ladies' Home Journal*) are regular features in these magazines and pay exceptionally well for true-life accounts dealing with a problem or a conflict and offering a satisfying resolution.

Religious magazines—*Guideposts, Faith at Work,* and *Christian Home*—also use personal-experience stories and accounts to inspire their readers and present them with effective ways to solve problems and live more fulfilling lives.

The formulas for all confessions—whether fact or fiction—are strikingly similar. What differentiates the various confessions and determines the kind of magazine a story would be best suited for are style, content, vocabulary, focus, and factuality. All these aspects of writing confessions will be covered here so that beginning writers can learn the techniques and procedures.

With a record of selling 95% of the manuscripts I have submitted to the confessions—many of them bought on the first submission—I recommend to other writers techniques that I use for plotting stories, and developing my nonfiction ideas.

Fictional confessions (which may be short-short or novelette length) and how to write them will be covered first and in greatest detail, since that market is much larger than the market for factual confessions found in other types of magazines.

The skills and techniques for writing successful fictional confession stories also apply to the factual confessions and the nonfiction articles. The special editorial requirements, style, and topics for factual confessions will be discussed in a separate chapter.

If you learn to recognize a salable personal experience—yours or someone else's—and to turn it effectively into a fictional or factual confession, you are on your way to success in the confession field. And you may receive added satisfaction from knowing that your published work gave comfort and courage to readers searching for solutions to the same problems.

SUSAN C. FELDHAKE

How to Write and Sell Confessions

I

THE CONFESSION FIELD

A GLANCE at the magazine stand reveals approximately thirty different confession magazine titles that are distributed nationwide. These magazines allot more space to short stories than any other group of publications. With more and more slick magazines opting for reportorial articles over fiction, the confession field may be the last bastion of the short story.

In the past decade, many new confession magazines have been launched. These fictional confessions are written with no by-line, usually from a woman's point of view, in first person, and are aimed at the blue-collar or working-class reader. The contents of the magazines may range from wholesome to racy to pornographic, depending on magazine policy and readership. All confession magazines, however, use about ten stories in every issue, in contrast with the token short story or two used in women's magazines, who reject literally hundreds of stories for each one selected.

If you sell a short story to a major women's magazine, it may be the only one they will accept from you for at least a year, unless you are already a selling author. These national magazines do not use an unknown writer's work too often. Because confession magazines do not use by-lines on the stories they publish, writers can sell stories to the same magazine month after month. Multiply the number of confession magazines published each month by ten stories per issue and you can quickly see why the confession field is insatiable and has a constant need for new stories. Fresh stories. Good stories. Timely stories. Helpful stories.

Many writers begin writing confessions as a source of a steady income; others, to gain writing experience and editorial guidance. Still others write confessions to relax after working on "serious" writing. And there are house-wives who write confessions to supplement the family income.

Confession writers come from all segments of society, and because they vary so widely in their individual life styles, and view problems in such different ways, their stories are as unique as they are.

You need no special qualifications or background to "confess" personal experiences—whether in fact or fiction form. You need a sensitivity to emotional reac-tions, a talent for solving problems, a love for people, and the determination and insight to make even a common problem exciting and dramatic enough to hold reader attention.

You needn't have a degree in psychology or any other special educational background. One of the country's most prolific confession writers lacks even a high-school diploma, but her capacity and insight for analyzing personal experiences and offering sound solutions more than make up for that lack.

To get started writing confessions you need paper, carbon, envelopes, and a typewriter. You must also have a knowledge of good grammar and language usage, determination, drive and discipline—which can not be bought, but can be learned. If you have the talent and the right attitude, success can be yours.

As in any other field, however, you must plot well and write your best, but you can also be assured that because there is more demand for material than can be met, your chances of having a confession story accepted are that much greater.

While confession publishers are always looking for stories, they demand quality. Usually the first stories that a beginning confession writer produces are rejected. These initial efforts should be viewed as apprenticeship.

Confession magazine editors are generous with help and praise and often give a fledgling writer a start. Since they constantly need to attract new writers, they carefully look at each new writer in the "slush pile" (unsolicited manuscripts) as a possible addition to their list of regular writers.

An editor who gets submissions regularly from a new writer reads them and will note the writer's improvement. When the stories get close to acceptable quality, the editor will often start to buy from the writer, doing essential editorial work to improve the story. If the writers continue to submit stories, in time they will learn to create polished confessions that can be used with little editorial revision.

With hard work it is possible to become a regular with an editor. Typically, confessions editors sort through their incoming mail. The stack of submissions is divided into two piles: in one goes the work of writers they know can be counted on for good material; the other, the envelopes with unfamiliar names, or the names of writers who have not shown much promise in the past.

The first pile is read quickly and the percentage of stories bought is high. The second pile of stories is read as time allows, and the acceptances are proportionately smaller. A story that stands out from the slow pile—even if a diamond-in-the-rough—will catch the editor's eye. That writer's name will be remembered, and that writer can usually count on a faster reading on subsequent submissions.

II

WHAT IS THERE TO CONFESS?

THERE IS almost an unlimited number of subjects for confession stories, if you keep in mind that the "real you" isn't confessing, but the countless fictional narrators in your imagination are.

Rarely does a beginning confession writer make a sale with the first story or two written for the field. Usually the early attempts are too hackneyed and are rejected on the grounds that they are "contrived," "lacking in motivation," the characters "don't seem real," the subject matter is "old hat," or the plots have been "written into the ground" by previous writers, who, in the beginning seemed instinctively to select the same ideas and story lines for *their* first efforts.

Some of the first-time ideas to avoid (unless you can give them a truly unique twist) are:

The husband, suspected by his wife of having an affair, is really using his secretary or the woman neighbor to help him concoct a wonderful surprise (like a mink coat) for his suspicious wife.

A teen-age girl has an unmotivated affair with her stepfather that gets no one in the story anywhere . . . but into bed.

A husband and wife want a baby . . . The wife is raped—through her own careless actions—and she conceals the rape from her husband. When she finds herself pregnant, she doesn't know who the real father is—until after the birth some physical family trait is revealed, proving the baby was fathered by the woman's husband and not the rapist.

A town's "bad girl" reforms, and no longer puts out for the fellows, so they rape her for her new upright behavior.

A tear-jerker in which a wife begs her dying husband (who is so sick that making love would be a major feat for him) to give her a baby.

A housewife gets into debt through her credit cards and can't admit the folly to her husband, so works as an escort while her husband is at his job.

Or the interracial stories in which the writer hopes that the shock of interracial sex will sell the story. (It won't.)

These are some of the plots and situations that are routinely returned with pointed rejections. If the quality of the writing warrants some encouragement, it will usually come as a scrawled note on the form rejection and read: "Unbelievable!" "Too predictable." "Contrived." "Couldn't have happened—but try again."

Those particular story situations are considered commonplace by many editors, unless the treatment is unusual.

Here is a short sample list of subjects a writer may want to "confess":

I was a hand-me-down wife.
Men won't marry a tramp like me.
I was a mail-order bride.
I didn't want to die a virgin.
My boyfriend called me "jailbait."
My body made promises I couldn't keep.

I went from country girl to call girl.
My husband called me a sex martyr.
I'm the only one my little boy wants in bed.
My boyfriend gave me an abortion.
I hired a man to make love to me.
My brother-in-law made me pregnant.
I was a sex surrogate.
I was a porn star.
I was pregnant and a virgin.
I had a sex-change operation.
We played spin-the-bottle for sex partners.
I sold my body to the highest bidder.
I was blackmailed by a sex pervert.

The list could go on and on with numerous problems suitable for confession writing, some trivial, others complex.

Perhaps you feel you've lived a tame life and that nothing exciting or shocking has ever happened to you. You may be absolutely right. But it won't prevent you from writing salable confession stories!

What about the people around you? The town "bad girl"? Or your classmates from high school? Borrow their problems and the errors they made in the process of living. Change them and rearrange them. Live the problem in your imagination. Write it and sell it to the confessions.

Even with a circle of interesting friends and acquaintances who are having, or have had, unusual and exciting experiences that may spark story ideas, confession writers who want to remain in the field must constantly come up with new, fresh twists for their stories.

I know of two prolific confession writers, one from a city in the South and the other from a small farming community in the North, who became friends by mail. When they discovered they had both done stories on the same topic, they swapped these printed stories and were surprised by their totally different handling of the same topic. As a result these two writers swap ideas with regularity. Both sell the stories written as a result of their shared ideas—and often to the same editor, much to their amusement.

While not all confession writers are lucky enough to have contact with another writer in the field so willing— or even able—to share, there are a lot of places to find ideas.

Medical columns carried by most daily newspapers are an excellent source of material. Such startling things as pseudocyesis (false pregnancy), allergy to sperm, frightening strains of resistant gonorrhea, medical breakthroughs in repairing vasectomies, or implantation of embryos in the wombs of infertile women are topics that have been covered in medical columns and make timely sources for a modern confession story.

Often information gleaned from a medical column, or from listening to a person list symptoms of an ailment, gives a confession writer enough information on a disease to write about it. Many times this information is sufficient to allow the writer to plot the story with the more intricate details left out or glossed over because they are not necessary to the success of the story. But, if the story *hinges* on a medical subject it is important to ensure accuracy.

Talk to your family doctor or a friend who is a nurse and ask a few questions. Most people are eager to help a writer do research for a story. Another place to check up on medical information to make sure it is correct is in textbooks at the public library. Be sure to use technical terms and names in your stories. Using precise medical terms in your manuscript *immediately* gives the story believability.

You can get good story ideas at public meetings, family reunions, and parties. These are not in fully-developed story form, but the ideas may make an excellent basis for a salable story. Be a good listener and people will open up to you and share their problems.

At a party, a young woman who had been married for several years almost burst into tears when she remarked that her mother-in-law accused her of taking birth control pills to keep from bearing a child. This was not true, and the young wife was crushed by such a cruel accusation. A story idea was planted—and took root—and months later I wrote the story in quite a different form: a young wife elopes with a man who wants many children. When she returns home, her mother tells her the truth about her heredity—that her real father was a retarded street-cleaner, who had raped her mother. The young wife secretly takes contraceptives, because she is terrified of bearing a retarded baby. She doesn't yet feel secure enough in her husband's love to tell him the truth, and the dark secret stays hidden; her deception is revealed much later, and amends are made. It sold as a confession story called "I'm Haunted By My Mother's Past."

Similar ideas *when changed* will make interesting situations and problems for confession stories. But if experiences and problems of relatives or friends are the basis for a story, be sure to change the details and camouflage the real-life plot, places, and people.

Underground newspapers and other periodicals that carry "personal" ads in the classified section—*New York Magazine, Saturday Review,* etc.—are often good sources for ideas, as are question-and-answer advice columns and letters to the editors of newspapers and major magazines and publications for women, such as *Good Housekeeping, McCall's, Cosmopolitan, Ladies' Home Journal,* and *Ms.*

Newspapers are good places to locate timely ideas. Not from the front-page headlines, but, rather, in the often tiny accounts buried near the middle of the paper, such as the one about a young man who sued his pregnant teen-age girlfriend for custody of the unborn baby she planned to place for adoption—and won his case.

A writer will have less competition using a short news item than one which has been given wide national coverage. Minor human-interest items will not become overdone almost overnight.

The advice columns, such as "Dear Abby," "Ann Landers," and others of this type where people can bare their souls, present their most intimate problems, air pet peeves, ask for advice, or warn others about dangerous situations, are excellent sources for story material. These are problems that beset average Americans and are what confession readers will relate to.

Teen columns are also good places to find what problems modern young people are concerned with. These columns can help keep a confession writer in tune with the times. By listening to teen-agers voice their hopes, dreams, and fears, the writer gains valuable insight into what makes them laugh or cry. As a result, stories tailored to that age group will be relevant, entertaining, inspiring, and informative.

Television talk shows, too, are ideal for spotting timely topics and controversies. The questions raised by the audience or host—and then comments and solutions—often go right to the heart of the kind of problem confession readers are interested in.

Other sources of ideas include the men's magazines (*Playboy, Oui, Penthouse*, and others) that carry columns in which readers ask for information or advice, and the magazine often has experts in the field give accurate information and answers to these provocative questions. These magazines also invite readers to comment and publish surveys on many interesting and timely topics. Even if sometimes a bit bizarre, these "answers" can be adapted and altered to fit into the confession field.

I know one confession writer who has written stories about female sex surrogates but never gave much thought to the fact that there were male sex surrogates, until in *Oui* she read a letter from a professional woman who hired the services of a male sex surrogate at a sex therapy center. Why? So that the male sex surrogate could teach her how to use her body correctly to give her greater sexual fulfillment in her love affairs.

It was a provocative idea. The writer wrote the story from the viewpoint of a woman who hires a sex surrogate for the purpose described, and the story sold.

The *Ladies' Home Journal* feature "Can This Marriage Be Saved?" offers sound ideas for confession stories dealing with marital problems. The problems presented in the real "case" marriage are usually universal and therefore suitable for confession stories—provided the writer uses only the topic and of course *not* the complete plot and events from the published piece.

Even cartoons dealing with marital situations can spark story ideas. Cartoons have humorous appeal because they depict a situation common to many people. Look behind the laughter and find the serious theme that you can turn into a convincing confession story.

Probably one of the best places to get confession ideas is from the confession magazines. While confession writers don't always take the time to read the magazines they write for, after they learn the craft and sell regularly, they always read the covers.

Go to the newsstand with a notebook. Look through the month's confession magazines. Jot down story blurbs and titles that appeal to you. Ideas for stories may come to you from these blurbs right away, or in a month or two. When you glance at the title or blurb, a whole plot may take shape. Filtered through your perceptions and imagination, it will be a completely different, new story. On a lazy day when you don't feel like writing, make up your own list of provocative titles and blurbs (as if you were an editor). Or read some published confession stories and try to figure out what is going to happen and how. You will quickly realize that your ideas are not what actually happens in the published version at all. And, while reading a story—you will have developed a plot of your own. All that is left to do is . . . write it!

III

SHAPING THE IDEA INTO A THEME

THERE MAY seem to be innumerable salable ideas for confessions, yet actually they are all variations on a limited number of basic ways to "sin." You discover this quickly when you begin to write confession stories.

For example, although the situation of pregnancy out of wedlock is common, each young woman and her boyfriend are unique individuals, and it is their uniqueness and their methods of coping with the problem that make each story different.

As a confession writer you must not put aside a theme permanently when you have written one story on that topic. Not if you want to continue writing confessions! Instead, try to view it from yet another angle, and a different story may develop . . . and another . . . and another.

Occasionally, there are new confession ideas that grow out of changed laws, in such areas as abortion, support of unmarried mate and child, open homosexual relations and the effect on families, and so on. Or, fresh ideas may emerge from discoveries in science, such as male contraception, test-tube babies, cloning, vasectomy repair, and similar medical advances. All of these when thought about in terms of particular invented characters can help writers produce timely new confessions.

Few persons are totally insulated from life today. With modern communications, even if an event or scientific case does not take place in our immediate locale, we learn of it from newspaper stories, and radio or television broadcasts. And, usually through these news releases, and often detailed feature newspaper and magazine articles, a writer can acquire enough basic knowledge of the situation or theory to write a confession story about the topic intelligently and persuasively. Or, she can at least get enough accurate information to aid in researching the topic further at the public library.

As important as having an interesting, provocative idea to write about is having something *worth* writing about. The story you write must have a theme and make a point. Readers of confession magazines want stories in which the characters have intense, cliff-hanging problems. If the problem is so trivial that the reader won't care if it is solved or not, the story has no valid reason for being told. And, it certainly won't be purchased or published, *no matter how good the writing is.*

Confession writers with vivid imaginations find insight and understanding invaluable professional aids to ferret out the traits and motivations that make each individual character react differently to the same stimulus or problem. As a result, story problems will be solved in a particular way by a certain character and in quite another way by a different person, because of individual emotional structure, background, environment, temperament, peer pressure, values, relationships, parental attitudes or other formative factors.

Half a dozen sixteen-year-old girls all faced with an unwanted pregnancy would solve their problem in six different ways. This makes it possible to develop the basic idea into six story solutions, or plots. For instance:

1) Marriage
2) Abortion
3) Adoption
4) Single parenthood
5) Selling the baby on the black market
6) Allowing parents to raise the baby as a sibling

How the narrator *arrives* at the decision, how she *grows* from it, and what she *learns* from the experience all bear out the theme.

Think about the basic idea of a new wife who finds out that sex is not all it is touted to be. She endures but does not enjoy her husband's advances. How might she solve her problem?

1) Suffer in silence
2) Encourage her husband to seek fulfillment elsewhere
3) Alienate him so he'll leave her alone
4) Seek professional counseling
5) Hire a sex surrogate to teach her to be responsive
6) Get a divorce so she can live alone
7) Take a female companion

At the other end of the scale, what about the nymphomaniac who marries, hoping it will solve her problem, only to find she is still driven by her desires? How might she cope with her problem?

1) Seek satisfaction with other men
2) Make unreasonable physical demands on her husband
3) Buy a sex machine

4) Keep her desire secret
5) Get professional counseling
6) Purchase a "chastity belt"

The options for developing an idea into a distinct theme are many. By selecting an unusual message or point to get across, you may make even the most over-worked idea into a unique and fresh story.

Relaxed social behavior and attitudes toward sex in the 1970's produced new topics that would not even have been hinted at a few years ago. Now these subjects and themes find their way into issue after issue of confession magazines.

For instance, the climax scene of a story dealing with a pregnant teen-ager can prove—or disprove—that abortion is the answer; that forced marriages start out with a handicap; or that giving a child up for adoption is the answer to give the baby and the girl a new start in life. Single parenthood may have some good facets, but the drawbacks could be proved as well. Solving the problem by selling the baby on the black market would no doubt cause painful repercussions. Having a baby raised as a younger brother or sister would also cause problems to surface in the future.

For an exercise in ways to shape the same idea into a different theme and develop several confession stories, try jotting down your own list of possible solutions (give at least two) for each of the following examples:

1) What could happen if an ex-husband has embarrassing nude pictures of his former wife and after she remarries decides to blackmail her?

2) What about a wife who learns her husband is gay and has no inclination to go straight?

3) What options are open to a woman still in love with a husband who is permanently impotent?

4) What about a young girl who has been known as a confirmed liar in the past, so that no one believes her when her stepfather sexually molests her?

5) What could happen to a teen-age runaway far from home and out of money?

6) What about the wife who learns her out-of-work husband brings home money he earns as a male hooker, though he claims to have won the money playing poker?

7) What if a husband developed a heart problem, kept it a secret from his wife, and blamed her for his sudden disinterest in sex?

The basic situation remains the same, but each writer's theme, plot, and climax or solution can make a different but satisfying confession story.

IV

KNOW YOUR READER—THE EDITOR DOES

BEFORE plotting and writing a confession story it is imperative that the writer understand the special confession market and the readership which comprises the field, so that the stories will appeal to the average confession reader.

Periodically editors of confession magazines offer free magazine subscriptions to the first number of readers who enter a "contest" by telling which stories they liked best in a particular issue. Confession readers are quick to enter these "contests," which some editors consider an "opinion poll."

For the cost of a few free subscriptions, editors gain valuable information from their readers that helps them to continue to buy stories with the reasonable assurance they will please the reading audience.

Readers of one or more confession magazines per month are almost all women, ranging in age from approximately thirteen to retirement, with the heaviest representation in the late teens to early thirties group.

While many of the readers are married and have one or more children at home, just as many are single, dating, and hope eventually to get married, settle down, and raise a family.

Most buyers of or subscribers to confessions work at blue-collar jobs, which is why editors of confession magazines often state in market listings in writers periodicals that they want "blue-collar stories." The reader wants the narrator and her cohorts to live the same kind of life she, the reader, lives, understands, and easily relates to.

Of course, not all women who regularly read confessions are young mothers or work as waitresses, typists, checkout clerks, or at other routine, unglamorous jobs. However, the readers who take confession stories *seriously* and believe them to be true *do* fit the blue-collar work pattern. For this reason editors do not want to chance alienating this particular readership by having heroines in stories performing unusual, glamorous, elitist or "snobbish" jobs.

In fact, unless her job has real purpose or point in the story (such as working as a sex surrogate), the narrator's occupation does not have to be specifically named. Writing "at the office," or "taking a coffee break between customers" suffices. The specifics of the narrator's work are not often important to the story line. What is important is to make the job so commonplace that the confession reader could easily picture herself holding it.

Readers of confession stories like to dream. Vicariously, as they read, they fall in love with the male character right along with the narrator. Instead of having the narrator love a salesman, factory worker, or a garage mechanic, make the hero the factory *foreman*, or the service station *owner*. This indicates a higher salary, and more power and responsibility, and hints that the man is the aggressive type whom a bright woman with an eye to the future would want for a boyfriend or husband.

And, if the "hero" is an architect who comes to town to do business with the company in which the narrator is in the typing pool, or if he is an advertising executive or a handsome rancher with a thousand-acre spread in Colorado, it makes for more exciting dreaming. This type of work makes the man a "catch" to narrator and reader alike. It's just as easy to love a rich man as a poor man, they reason. Maybe easier.

Although readers like stories in which the narrators may have rich and powerful boyfriends (proof that a poor girl can "make good"), in real life readers often have limited funds to live on and little opportunity to meet such men.

Many positions held by confession readers and their husbands or boyfriends are such ordinary bread-and-butter jobs as store clerks, sanitation service haulers, mechanics, factory workers, file clerks, meat cutters, shop clerks, truck drivers, farmers, hotel maids, food service workers, salespeople, construction workers, and laborers who make up the majority of the work force of our country.

Some earn well above the minimum wage. Others do not. In general they must watch a budget. They look for value and bargains in consumer purchases because they must make their money go farther than those in higher-income brackets.

You must not, therefore, have your story heroine spending money carelessly, or living too posh a life (unless, of course, that is the source of her problem or "sin"). This could cause the budget-conscious reader to view her as a spendthrift. Or it could cause readers to dislike the narrator for living in such luxury that the readers' lot would seem all the more miserable. These are small points, but important ones.

Always keep in mind that the confession reader may have to save her money for weeks, months, or even years to buy something that a person in a high-income bracket takes for granted. A confession reader will have more natural empathy for a narrator who resorts to buying items on a lay-away plan than one who whips out an American Express Card for expensive purchases.

In writing stories in which a character who did not finish school is integral to the plot, show that the character values education by having her attend night school, make plans for an equivalency test, or even take a correspondence course.

The confession reader may be found anywhere. She may live in a rural area, in a small town, or in a large, impersonal city. Where she lives doesn't matter: her basic, human traits, desires and emotions will make her identify with confession-story characters.

Writers may have more money and education than their readers, but they can use universal emotions and desires to bridge the differences in life styles and educational and economic backgrounds.

Confession readers are as interested in new things as anyone else, but will probably pay more attention to news of a test-tube baby, a public figure's messy divorce, or a "palimony" suit than to a missile launching or Presidential speech.

They are trusting and tend to be somewhat unsophisticated. They talk to people in the doctor's waiting room, strike up a conversation with a stranger at the lunch counter, or chat with other passengers while waiting at the bus stop. They have good friends whom they chat with often and intimately, sharing secrets and exchanging confidences.

The reader views the story heroine as a friend who is sharing her most private thoughts and personal problems via the story. Upon finishing the story, the reader feels that she personally knows the narrator and even regards her as a new friend.

As they read the stories, confession readers laugh, cry, suffer and rejoice over the narrator and her situation. Some readers get so emotionally involved in fictional personal experience in a confession magazine that they write to the editor offering advice for her to pass along to the narrator, telling her how she could have better solved the dilemma. Or, the reader may write to the editor, confiding that she had the same problem, and go on to tell how *she* solved *hers*.

Occasionally, a story is published in which the narrator is *not* liked by the readers. When this happens the vocal readership write irate letters to complain that the narrator is spoiled, immature, selfish, and doesn't deserve the good life and the happiness she got at the end of the story.

A cardinal rule for confession writers is *know your readers*. Then create a character and story they will relate to, like and remember.

V

VIEWPOINT: MALE OR FEMALE?

No MATTER how much the plots of confessions may differ from one another, the stories all have one thing in common: they are written in first-person viewpoint, and usually—though not always—told by a female narrator, who may be given a name, but goes by "I" for the duration of the story.

For example, in my story "I Auctioned My Body to the Highest Bidder," published in *Exciting Confessions,* Mindy, my teen-age narrator, begins telling her story:

> All evening long snow had been falling. The temperature was just below freezing and snow came down in big, gentle flakes with no wind to whip them into drifts. They created a soft blanket of snow on the ground.
>
> I had been sitting at my upstairs window, looking down over the street when I heard the whoosh of air brakes and turned to see one of the McKnelly rigs pull up our street, round the corner, then go to the warehouses at the back of their property.
>
> Within ten minutes another eighteen-wheeler rounded the corner, and flipped the amber rig lights on and off. When the driver got right in front of our house, he beeped the

diesel's horn, almost rattling the windows out of our house. I knew then Chuck McKnelly, my boyfriend, was in off the road.

Confession stories are always written from first-person viewpoint, because a person can confess only to those things she has done herself. First-person viewpoint is used also so that the "I" in the story will draw the reader fully into the action. The reader lives the story vicariously as she reads it, which makes her believe it. The use of "I/me" completely embraces the reader so she shares the sensory perceptions, emotional reactions, and thoughts of the narrator.

Using third-person viewpoint—the detached "she/he" popular in slick-magazine fiction—would put up a barrier that would separate the reader from the story characters.

Mastering first-person viewpoint is a *must* for anyone hoping to succeed in the confession-story field. For some writers, writing in the third person seems to "come naturally"; others claim to write more easily in first person. *Either* viewpoint *can* be learned.

The biggest problem most aspiring writers have with using the first-person viewpoint—particularly in the confession field—is their initial feeling of guilt or embarrassment. Inexperienced writers often cannot dissociate the "I-character" from the "I-self." Subconsciously, they are afraid that readers will attribute the wrongdoings of the "I-character" to the "I-self" behind the typewriter.

The first few paragraphs, when self-consciousness and embarrassment are most acute, are the most difficult to write. But, after a few pages are written, the "I-charac-ter" completely takes over. In the writer's mind, the point has been driven home: the "I" behind the typewriter and the "I" on paper are separate entities, and the self-consciousness and embarrassment fade.

Writing from the first-person viewpoint is not difficult; using this viewpoint can even be fun. Many confession writers are surprised by what the "I-characters" reveal about themselves. It's the characters who take over to tell their own stories that are loved and remembered by confession readers. These story heroines are the ones whom editors and readers view as real, flesh-and-blood people.

While writers may try for days to get to know the third-person character in their story, when they write in the first-person, their knowledge of and identification with the character are immediate. You are "in" on all the narrator's thoughts and actions, past and present, and are aware of her hopes for the future.

When you set out to write a confession story, you can choose to write from either a female or a male viewpoint. Since the majority of confessions have female narrators, reading several stories can give the interested writer a "feel" for the feminine viewpoint.

A few men read confession magazines regularly, but most editors do not cater to them; however, some editors may include an occasional male-viewpoint story in an issue if it is exceptionally well done and believable.

If the confession story is in the male viewpoint, this should be shown *at the outset*, so the reader will not assume that the narrator is a female. For example, a male-narrator confession story might begin by having the male narrator identified by name:

I parked the car at Baylor Lake, and reached for my girl, Janie.

"Gary . . ." she murmured and pulled away from me. She

clenched her hands in her lap. Then her fingers picked wildly at the heavy ID bracelet of mine I'd placed on her wrist six months before. "I feel awful, Gary," she went on in a squeaky voice. "But-but, I've found someone else. A guy I met at camp this summer." She paused. Her chin was determined. "Take your bracelet back."

I held out my hand. She dropped the metal chain-link bracelet that was still warm from her skin into my outstretched palm. I stared at it.

"Well," I said, and my voice came out a whistle. "I guess there's not much to say, huh?"

"Nothing except . . . Gary, I'm really sorry."

"Yeah. Me too," I said tightly. I reached for the ignition. "It was fun while it lasted. And I'll always think you're the greatest, Janie."

Things were stiff. We were both trying too hard to act like nothing was wrong. But it was. When Janie slammed the door behind her, it was like something inside me died.

A few years ago it was popular for women to write male-viewpoint confessions. Some stories sold, since editors seemed to buy more male-viewpoint stories then. The astute reader could often spot a few clues to suggest the story was the work of a woman, though, as men and women do *not* view things the same way. A detail that a man would overlook might be something that no woman could miss or resist commenting on. Male confession writers, for some reason, seem to be able to make the shift to female thinking more easily than most women can "enter" the macho mind of a male confession narrator, and they do it more convincingly.

A confession writer who uses the male viewpoint has a distinct handicap since over ninety percent of published confession stories tell the woman's side of things. That means that the writer's male-viewpoint material must be exceptional to sell.

A male-viewpoint fictional "confession"—particularly if it is a personal-experience account of an unusual relationship, or unique sexual episode—can sometimes be placed with the men's magazines.

Playboy, Oui, Penthouse, and other top-selling men's magazines which cater to readers with high income and education, rarely use an actual confession story. Some of the lesser-known men's magazines—*Cavalcade, Dude, Gent, Nugget* and others—are slanted to the blue-collar worker between the ages of 18 and 35. These magazines actively seek male confession stories. These stories are personal-experience confessions, but they differ from the traditional female-confession story: The story often presents no problem, and a solution is not sought. These stories may be confessions of a lurid sexual episode, or another provocative experience. Naturally, these magazines are read largely by men, and the stories are written from the male viewpoint so that men readers will identify with the stories.

Anyone interested in writing male-viewpoint stories for confession magazines should obtain copies of magazines which do publish stories from the male viewpoint, and see how writers have successfully handled telling a man's story. Reading the men's magazines to study the male-viewpoint confession experiences they publish is a valuable aid for those who wish to be successful in this field.

When it comes to writing the male-viewpoint story for the female confession magazines, some writers will try, and a few talented story tellers will succeed. But, for most confession writers—who happen to be women—trying to beat those odds may not be worthwhile.

VI

PATTERNS FOR PLOTTING

No ONE has come up with the exact rules of how to plot. Plotting can, however, be made easier by following certain guidelines. Many writers, for instance, are helped by knowing before they start to write a story how it will begin and how it will end.

For decades—since the earliest days of the confession magazines in the 1920's—the story "formula" for the confession field was "sin-suffer-repent." *Every* story that was written and bought was plotted to this pattern. As a result the stories were very often predictable. The reader always knew that the narrator would make a mistake, it would cause her a lot of anguish, then she would repent and berate herself for her sins, and the story would end on a note of reform and happiness. Frequently the stories became very "preachy" when putting the point across at the climax.

In recent years, as a result of the sexual revolution, readers no longer want to be preached at; they no longer care to read that their actions that do not seem shameful to them are sin, sin, sin!

But, the old "sin-suffer-repent" formula is still salable if the narrator does not get too righteous and preachy, and if in the end she stresses that her decision was right for her. She must, however, make it clear that what was right for *her* may not be right for *everyone*.

There are some new, loosely structured patterns for plotting confessions today that writers use successfully as they plan stories:

One confession writer I know rarely writes confessions that fit into the "sin-suffer-repent" pattern: she has her own formula: "don't-knock-it-until-you've-tried-it." Using this formula, she boldly leads the narrator and the reader into many situations in which the narrator is confronted with a decision that the reader may be currently facing also, or will face in the near future. Seeing how the narrator handles it, the reader can decide if it is a way she would handle a similar situation, and if such a solution would satisfy her.

"You-always-hurt-the-one-you-love" is a popular formula, in which the narrator thinks her actions will affect no one but herself. Later she learns that she not only affects others, but also hurts the one she loves; this realization is more painful to her than if she had been injured by her actions. She works to make it up to the person she hurts, succeeds in her effort to do so, and stresses at the conclusion of the story that she is going to think before acting in the future, so she won't harm others by her actions.

The "girl-meets-boy, girl-loses-boy-through-foolish-action, girl-gets-boy-back-when-she-learns-her-lesson" is a basic formula for romantic love stories often found in the confession magazines.

In addition to these tried-and-true formula confessions, there is a new freedom for writers to use in plotting salable confession stories. The endings are more surprising, varied, and less judgmental. They let readers react without bias—theirs or the author's—and reach personal decisions in terms of modern sexual trends and life styles now common and acceptable.

When the writer has selected the problem (idea), and knows the ending, developing the plot is like working an algebra equation in which $x + ? = y$. Given two known quantities, it's possible to calculate the unknown. In other words, know the beginning and the end, and the middle will take care of itself.

Some confession writers recommend naming the narrator, then writing one sentence after another until an idea and plot line begin to surface. Too often, those who rely on this "sit-down-and-write-without-a goal" method find that after ten or twelve pages, they are bogged down and can't think the narrator out of her problem. Or, worse still, they haven't yet managed to think the narrator *into* a worthwhile conflict.

There are some writers, on the other hand, who prefer to start with a theme or situation, then find an ending that will illustrate the theme, and finally go back and decide how the story line (or plot) will advance. They carefully fit the narrator to the story, adding the traits, motivations, and story twists necessary to create an entertaining and believable tale. But it is wise to have a general direction or goal in mind before starting the story.

As you mull over the possible endings, the first one you select is probably not the right one for your story, and it may be an overfamiliar solution that has been used by other confession writers handling the same problem over the years. To avoid this, write down the first ending you think of. Then, view the problem from a different angle, and decide how the direction of the story could be changed. The result may be an unorthodox ending, not one generally accepted by the average reader. If so, terrific. *It is the unusual solution which makes a story salable.*

If, however, you cannot immediately think of a unique way to solve the problem, note the story idea in your journal so you won't forget it, and let your subconscious do the work for you. If the idea has been planted and your subconscious has had time to absorb it sufficiently, you may at some future time reread the entry in your journal and a complete story line will reveal itself to you.

When buying stories for their magazines, confession magazine editors constantly consider the background of their average readers. Here are some typical comments made by editors in rejecting some stories:

"The plot is thin, familiar, and predictable."

"Capably written, but the plot is mind-boggling, with too many twists and turns to be believable."

"The story is well-written but difficult to follow. Too much happens in this story to make it readable. It would not be easily followed or understood by our average reader."

"There is no serious conflict for the narrator in this plot. Sorry we have to pass it up."

These editorial comments sum up most confession editors' requirements: there should be enough plot . . . but not too much.

Because plotting can be a drawn-out process, you can accomplish it with less agony and frustration if you work it out when you are away from the typewriter. Sitting before a blank sheet of paper can make the process of plotting seem formidable. It is therefore much easier to map out a story in your mind while driving to work, doing the dishes, mowing the grass, vacuuming the carpet, or performing other mundane chores that do not require full concentration. By the time your task or trip or whatever is completed, you will often have worked out your story line and will be free and ready to sit down at the typewriter and get the story down on paper.

Once you settle upon the idea or situation for the story and work out the ending, ask yourself (and the narrator within you) these questions: *Why? What? How?*

As you question the life, actions, and basic decisions of your narrator, the middle of the story will usually emerge to fill in the period between the beginning and ending with a suitable plot.

Here is an illustration of how I applied my plotting method to an idea and developed it into a successful confession story:

Several years ago while reading one of the major men's magazines I saw a provocative article about a happily married man, "Fearless Fred," who had an unusual way of bringing home the bacon. Fearless Fred worked as a male prostitute in a large city.

Fred didn't streetwalk. Instead, he drove a small van outfitted with the latest in sex equipment, and set up appointments with sexually frustrated persons. He was handsomely rewarded for his efforts. The startling fact was that Fred's wife knew of his business venture and was openly supportive!

This article was one of the first accounts of male prostitution to appear in print. Later, I learned through newscasts and television specials dealing with runaways that male prostitution was on the increase. I decided it would make a timely story idea.

As the working title, I chose "I Hired a Man to Love Me," because I wanted the story from the woman's point of view. The ending would be the startling revelation that the male hooker was someone well-known to the narrator. It seemed to me that though a single woman hiring a man for sex could be dramatic, it would be even more dramatic if a married woman were to pay for the services of a male hooker.

To keep reader sympathy the narrator would have to have a very compelling reason to go out and hire what she couldn't get at home. This would have to be plotted into the story line.

I asked myself the basic questions: *Why*? *What*? *How*? *Why* wasn't the narrator getting sex at home? The answer—the narrator's husband was too tired for sex and seemed preoccupied and strained from the pressure of the new traveling salesman job he'd taken after being unemployed for six months when a factory closed.

What happens when a husband ignores his wife's needs? Frustration!

How long will the narrator put up with it? Only as long as it takes her to realize she has a problem that needs a solution.

How would this solution come to an innocent wife and mother who lives in a lovely ranch home in a friendly suburban neighborhood? Ordinarily . . . it wouldn't.

By *what* means can a shocking solution be suggested to her? This was answered by including in the plot the arrival in the mail of a sample copy of an "underground" newspaper. Later in the day, the narrator's savvy next-door neighbor drops in, sees the paper, and reads the personal classified ads together with the narrator. The knowing neighbor points out those ads that are really cleverly worded fronts for male hookers. Thus, the solution has been planted in the narrator's mind.

But, she can't write or call the hooker at this point in the story. *Why*? Because the reader would never go along with that. In order to keep reader sympathy, the narrator must be driven to cheat.

How can this best be accomplished? Through failure. The narrator plans a big seduction of her tired husband. When the seduction fails, she is hurt, frustrated and desperate, and she feels free to solve her problems with any solution she sees fit to employ.

To move the story along, I have the narrator make an appointment with a male hooker. She goes to a sleazy hotel, undresses, and awaits her hired lover. By this time the narrator is having second thoughts. She goes through a brief period of self-recrimination when she thinks of her poor, tired husband, working so hard on his sales route while she revels in an afternoon rendezvous at his expense.

What does the narrator decide to do? Go home, face her husband, and solve the problem by talking to him about it (which is exactly what the reader wants her to do).

The climax of the story comes more quickly than she planned: she opens the hotel room door to rush away from the scene—and is confronted by the male hooker she hired—*her husband*! The climax is shattering, totally unexpected, but logical and believable because of careful plotting and motivation.

During the plotting of this story, I thought of many twists — and rejected them, because they didn't "balance" with other parts of the story. This plot, which sold to *Modern Love Confessions* ("I Went to a Male Prostitute"), took me several hours to plan, from the known beginning (idea) to the chosen goal at the end.

Here is another example of this method of plotting:

What would happen if a man who had divorced his wife because she refused to have children told his girlfriend that he would marry her only if she became pregnant first? In my story, "I'm Having a Phantom Baby"

(*Personal Romances*), the narrator wants to marry her boyfriend and becomes desperate to conceive. Finally, she becomes pregnant and they marry. The drama increases when the narrator's mother-in-law comes to visit, hates her pregnant daughter-in-law on sight, and starts saying that her daughter-in-law is an adulteress.

After a heated argument, the young couple ask the mother-in-law to leave. She starts to say something, but restrains herself, and leaves immediately. Relations are severed. Two months later, when the narrator goes for a pre-natal check, the doctor tells her that she is not pregnant, but is suffering from pseudocyesis—false pregnancy. When she failed to conceive, her mind tricked her body into imitating pregnancy.

The ironic ending—*carefully planned before the middle of the story was plotted*—is revealed: the narrator's husband was left sterile following a bout with mumps during early adolescence.

In another story, my narrator found herself penniless, alone, and desperate in the big city. She answers an ad for a sex surrogate and promises herself she'll look for "respectable work" in a few weeks—after she has saved a nest egg. Greed keeps her on the job at the sex clinic for months. After a series of twists, the ending—*worked out before the story was plotted*—is revealed: Her "doctor" boss is a phony; the clinic is more accurately termed a "brothel," and the narrator is arrested as a prostitute. The story, called, "I Was a Sex Surrogate," was published in *Hip*.

In all confession stories, no matter how good the beginning, how unexpected the end, and how clever the middle, the writer's effort is lost if the narrator cannot gain reader sympathy. This is best done by opening the story with a scene showing the narrator as desperate, sad, humiliated, or facing a problem that leads directly to the conflict. Editors and readers don't like to wade through pages of prose to discover the problem; it should be spelled out on the first page—if possible—and certainly no later than the first five hundred words of the story.

The problem must be so serious that the reader will feel compassion when the narrator takes some action— anything—to try to solve the problem, even if what she does is morally wrong.

It is essential that the reader feel empathy and forgiveness toward the narrator. Each time the narrator is defeated, the reader should feel the sting of setback, too. This will evoke reader sympathy and sustain it. Humiliation, tragedy, bad luck, hurt feelings, misunderstandings, and misfortune should be worked into the plot to keep the reader feeling pity for the beset, desperate narrator, so that when she makes mistakes, the reader feels they are justified *under the circumstances*.

Make your reader not only pity the narrator, but like her, in spite of her misguided actions. If you *as the writer* can't like and sympathize with your narrator, don't expect the editor and readers to.

In another one of my stories, "I Begged My Guy to Love Me" (published in *Intimate Story*), a divorcée entering the job market for the first time wants to impress her potential boss. Instead, she makes him laugh at her:

"Do you know how to run office machines?" Mr. Marshton asked with a glance at the copier and invoice machines.

"No," I admitted. "But I learn quickly!" I added when a frown came to his face. I glanced determinedly at the machines. "Th-they can't be any harder to use than learning to run a washer or dryer for the first time."

Mr. Marshton laughed. My face burned when I realized how stupid the words sounded. It was just the kind of nervous remark I'd promised myself I wouldn't blurt out. But after nine years of being a housewife this was the only world I knew.

And so, the narrator in this story shows her humanness; she is embarrassed, and wins sympathy and understanding from her readers—all on page one of the story.

Teen-age readers of my story "Tired of Being a Virgin—I Sold My Body to the Highest Bidder" (In *Exciting Confessions*) would understand and sympathize with Mindy, my narrator, when she offered herself to her older boyfriend, was refused, and had him make light of her offer of love.

"You'd better get dressed before I change my mind and decide to hunt San Quentin Quail without a license. I can get sex any time I want it," Chuck said. "I'm not going to lower myself to stealing it from a trusting kid. Get dressed!"

Chuck kept his eyes averted from my bare breasts and exposed body as he clasped his clothes to him and headed into the adjoining room. A moment later he came out, not glancing in my direction.

"I'm going to take another toboggan ride down the hill to cool off. I suggest you take a hike in the woods. And don't go near the snowman we made. As hot as you are you'll melt him!" Chuck turned and walked out the door, laughing at his own joke. I wanted to die when I realized how foolish I looked, begging him to make love to me. Tears of humiliation welled in my eyes, and I fumbled for my clothes.

Story patterns and plots are extremely valuable for writers of confession stories. But many confessions that do not follow a plot or formula are still satisfying and salable. The writer need not be concerned with having a story fit into any conventional formula or plot pattern. If the story does not, just allow it to move along naturally. Write—and let your own formula pattern emerge. To keep your stories fresh, unique and salable, follow your story-telling instincts and intuition.

VII

CHARACTERIZATION

CHARACTERIZATION is a stumbling block for many beginning writers. Almost as bad as the rejection slips saying that the plot is too thin and weak are the ones that say:

"Your characters don't come across as flesh-and-blood people."

"Your characters are made of cardboard."

"Breathe some life into your people!"

"Don't use stereotypes! Make real characters."

Real characters are not "born"—they are created. One method is to make a data sheet, on which the writer lists all the physical and emotional attributes of a given character—color of hair and eyes, occupation, place of birth, family tree, disposition—before choosing the plot or theme of the story.

I have found, however, that for confessions, this too often leads to flat stereotypes rather than characters whom readers can identify with, because particularly in confessions it is the intangible emotional reactions and interrelationships that make characters convincing and believable. The situation and the problem are more important in confession stories.

The confession writer may use a data sheet as a kind of checklist for consistency in referring to age, hair color, etc., of characters while writing a story draft. Many writers keep such a log, as a reminder.

Whether you start with theme and plot (as most confession writers do) or with a *few selected* character and personality traits, it is important that you know the physical and emotional makeup of your narrator. The narrator must act in keeping with these traits unless an event in the story makes her behave out of character.

Confession characters are composites of traits that may be categorized as *universal, physical*, and *emotional.*

Universal. The ability to think, cry, breathe, smell, sneeze, and other natural emotions and reactions the reader will assume your characters possess, unless informed otherwise. Unless a character is an amputee, blind, deaf, or has a handicap integral to the plot, you can let the reader assume that your characters possess *all* the common universal traits.

Physical. Short or tall, homely or beautiful, swarthy or fair, graceful or awkward, plump or svelte.

Emotional. I consider these the most important for the confession writer to use in characterizing a person and giving him or her credibility. They include anger, lust, jealousy, resentment, shame, guilt—and must be conveyed through dialogue, action, or narration to give depth and reality to your confession characters.

Because confession readers consider themselves to be "average" people and identify with an "average" narrator, I prefer not to describe the narrator in all physical details. Readers will not immediately relate to a narrator who is described as too fat, too thin, too homely, or too beautiful—unless the trait has direct bearing on the story, as in the following example, from my story, "Too

Homely to Date—But Not to Rape" (*True Romantic Confessions*).

The narrator's opinion of herself and the way she views her physical attributes are her problem. On page one of the story, she states that she knows she's plain, presents her problem, explains her feelings about herself (and others), supplies a hint about her personal background, introduces supporting characters and immediately gains reader sympathy—all in one scene.

I'd always known I was plain. Well, maybe not *always*. But I'd been aware of it since the summer ten years before when I was five and my cousin came to visit Gram for two weeks. Uncle Harley, Gram's bachelor brother, held Gerilynn on his lap and dunked sugar cookies in his coffee while she took dainty bites. I slouched in my chair, wriggling my toes in the holes of my tennis shoes and slopped crumbs and milk on Gram's red checked oilcloth that covered the kitchen table. Gram smiled and smoothed my tangled braids as she went by.

Uncle Harley tucked Gerilynn's blond curls in place as she slowly chewed her cookies. He looked over her head and murmured to Gram that compared to Gerilynn, I looked like "seven miles of mud roads." Gram frowned. Uncle Harley chuckled.

"Some were meant to be pretty, and some just weren't," he said philosophically and reached across the table, winking as he tweaked my nose. I tried to smile at him. Maybe Uncle Harley didn't think a five year old could understand what he said, but I did.

I swallowed at the dry lump stuck in my throat and hurriedly excused myself. I ran out and hid in Gram's hen house, crying while the chickens fluttered and clucked around, coming close as they waited for me to feed them corn. Instead, I cried harder. I never felt so ugly in my life.

Through emotions, observations and comparison, Gerilynn's beauty is contrasted with the narrator's slouching, disheveled appearance. Add to this Uncle Harley's tactless remark, and the reader understands perfectly why the narrator feels unattractive. The reader accepts the narrator's opinion, and there is no need to enlarge upon, or list, the specifics regarding her physical blemishes.

In most confession stories, the readers will relate to the narrator and her feelings. Because they identify with her—homely or not—they live the story vicariously as they read it, and subconsciously transfer their own physical traits to her. Readers come to feel that they know the narrator, not by her flaxen hair, high cheekbones, indigo-blue eyes, or slim legs, but because of how she reveals her emotions to them. Physical description of the narrator is, therefore, unimportant, unless it is required by the plot and can be worked in naturally. The writer risks making the narrator seem vain—and, therefore, unsympathetic—if she comments on her own good looks.

A narrator may describe herself in a complimentary way without sounding like an egomaniac by comparing herself with another character, either showing her similarity to or difference from this person. This technique is perfect for describing two characters in a short space, and the information can be dispersed a bit at a time to prevent slowing the story's pace, as in this example:

"You—you—you're just like your mother!" Calvin sputtered angrily. He hurled the words at me like rocks. His face was ashen with fury. He snorted, shook his head disgustedly, and stomped from the house, slamming the door behind him for emphasis.

I felt deflated, like the wind had been knocked out of me by our fight. I turned away from the door, numb, and my eyes caught my image in the sparkling clean kitchen window above the sink, backed by the shadowy darkness of night. There, I saw myself reflected: neat, clean, modestly dressed, my face and figure reasonably attractive.

Cal's words rang in my ears. Our fight had been so awful. And so stupid! Tears of hurt and confusion welled in my eyes when I remembered it. Had Cal said what he had simply because he knew that comparing me with Mom was guaranteed to hurt? Or...was I *really* more like her than I wanted to admit? Like mother like daughter? I wondered, and shuddered at the thought.

The last time I'd accidentally run into Mom had been on Main Street, three months before. She'd been blowsy and pale, her bleached hair tangled. Her eyes were faded and red. Her face was heavily made up—as usual—but no make up could hide the brittle harshness in her features that was proof of the life she lived, flitting from bar to bar, man to man.

I thought of the way I'd worked so hard to leave my past behind, to become Cal's wife, and be a good mother to our children. I was a respected member of the community, was active in school affairs. And I was a decent person!

"I'm not like her!" I whispered, and my voice cracked. "You're wrong, Cal!" I murmured as I looked toward the inky darkness. I wasn't like my mother—and I never would be. I'd die before I'd make my kids ashamed of me for the way I lived and the things I did. I never wanted them to be ashamed of me, the way I'd always been ashamed of Mom...

When the narrator fails to see herself as the rest of the world views her, it may be necessary to describe her appearance more fully. My story, "Men Won't Marry a Tramp Like Me" (*Intimate Story*), for example, deals with a narrator who had one conception of herself until it was rudely pointed out to her by a drunken cowboy that other people saw her quite differently.

Aggie-Anne Carson, the heroine, is nicknamed Bubbles. As the story progresses, she begins to dream that she has a future with Mark, a clean-cut rodeo rider she dates during the summer when he follows the circuit to earn money for veterinary school. Out of curiosity, Mark's partner comes to the concession stand where Aggie-Anne works to see what the girl Mark loves is like. He humiliates Bubbles by giving her a glimpse of what the world sees when they look at her.

When I turned away in the bathroom of the small trailer, I met my eyes in the filmy bathroom mirror over the basin. I saw what the drunken cowboy had seen. Me—with a bright red mouth and hardened eyes with too much makeup, and brassy blond hair that was dark at the roots. I shook my head sadly. The drunken cowboy was right. We'd make some pair—a tramp like me—and Mark's sweet little church-going Mama back in Texas.

Although it is rarely necessary for the writer to describe the narrator, the man that the narrator loves, on the other hand, should be described in minute detail, from the color of his hair and eyes to such details as a manly, rugged physique, broad shoulders, narrow hips, a handsome face, probing eyes, and a smile that's "like a warm caress." Use any images you find appropriate to draw the reader a mental portrait of the hero so she may fully appreciate the narrator's romantic feelings for him.

Here is an example from my story, "Too Hot to Wait for the Right Man" (*Intimate Story*). The narrator, Myra, a wealthy rancher's daughter, has a crush on her father's foreman.

Clete had changed from the wild and woolly rodeo bum he'd been when he came to the ranch five years before when he was twenty-two and I was going-on-thirteen. Since then, Clete had calmed down, mellowed, I guess you could say. He seemed content to wear himself out working on the ranch during the day, and reading late into the night out in the bunkhouse, when he wasn't playing checkers with me after supper.

Often I wondered about the bright lights, noise, and excitement of the rodeo circuit. But when I asked him, Clete smiled slowly, and his gray eyes became distant—then he changed the subject. He never talked about it. But the ornate silver championship belt buckle he always wore, the trophies lined up on a shelf in the bunk house, and the slight limp of his left leg—that got worse when he was tired—were proof that Clete had been a top rodeo rider. And he got out while the getting was good.

My heart pounded when I realized that Clete saw me in a different way, too. He'd been treating me like . . . a woman, not a pain-in-the-neck kid.

My heart skipped a beat when he towered over me, so tall and handsome with his sunstreaked brown hair that was striking against his coppery tan. His steel gray eyes grew soft with love as he looked down at me.

My body trembled with sudden fear. I didn't know how to treat this new Clete, the Clete who was so unfamiliar to me!

Supporting characters may be described in some depth, or, to prevent the story from dragging, they may be given a simple "character tag" to help the reader remember them. This key to their personalities may include a nervous habit, a superstition, an irritating quirk, a rigid routine, or another such mannerism.

Here is an example, from my story, "We Got Beat at Our Own Sex Games" (*Bronze Thrills*). Angie, the narrator, is at a party where her husband Rick is showering Judi, a recent divorcée, with attention. Angie's worries are underscored when the hostess Marla comments on the situation. In that dialogue she gives a hint of description for both Judi and Angie without actually listing their physical attributes.

"I'm sure Rick doesn't mean anything by a little flirting," I said stiffly, more to console myself than to convince Marla.

She glanced at me sharply. "Maybe Rick doesn't," she said with a careful pause for emphasis. "But Judi does . . ."

Marla smiled at me sympathetically. "Never mind. All men like to flirt. Rick couldn't possibly take Judi seriously. There's more to you than meets the eye—and Rick knows it. Why, you're twice the person Judi could ever hope to be!" Marla said with a sniff. "All she happens to be is a pretty face and a sexy body." She shoved the tray of fancy sandwiches into my hands. "Come on and help me serve sandwiches. And quit worrying!"

I followed her into the crowded room. Nervously I glanced at Judi. She was so slim and tanned. Her curvy body was poured into a hot pink dress with a slit up to the thigh. Her black hair was beauty-shop perfect.

Sighing, I turned away and caught my image in the mirror above Marla's sofa. Even when I sucked in my breath the fifteen pounds I'd gained since Rick and I got married was evident on my hips and around my waist. I felt plump, dowdy, and unattractive with the haircut Marla had given me two weeks before.

Ugly thoughts burned in my mind. Rick was so handsome he could've married any girl. But he chose me. Sometimes I still couldn't believe he'd chosen me. After two years of marriage, I couldn't help but wonder if maybe he regretted it. If he was bored with me. If he was—next to a beautiful sexpot like Judi—a "nice girl" like me didn't have a prayer!

There are a number of techniques the confession writer can draw on to create real characters. Emotional traits are often the deciding factor between a good characterization and a great one. They should be subtly slipped into a story, to make the greatest impact on readers. These traits—often deep psychological qualities—may be shown through dialogue, narration, comparison, or a combination, to develop and present to the reader a total personality.

In the following example, the narrator in my story, "My Guy's Man Enough to Love Me—But Am I Woman Enough to Let Him?" (in *True Life Secrets*), is a student working at a café to earn her way through college. She is characterized through her reactions and emotions—insecurity, sensitivity—when a group of servicemen play a trick on her:

Sometimes the soldiers acted more like spoiled brats than grown men, I thought to myself as I reached for the upside down glasses two at a time and placed them in the plastic tub on the bus cart. I collected the silverware and wadded napkins. Then, I reached for the last upside down glass with the fifty cent tip underneath. Too late I realized they'd pulled a trick on me and it was full of water that was trapped between the table and the glass. I tried to leap out of the way, but water sloshed all over me, drenching my thin uniform. The glass shattered on the floor.

The soldiers laughed like hyenas. I stared at them hard. It was tiring enough waiting tables at Tom's Café after a day of classes only to face a long night of studying. It was discouraging to work so long and hard for so little pay, without having to put up with all the soldiers' thoughtless pranks.

Tears filled my eyes as they elbowed each other and laughed, hooting as they teased me. Instead of having a snappy reply like one of the other waitresses would've popped up with, for me, it was the last straw. I burst into tears. The more I tried to stop crying, the harder I sobbed.

Jobs and occupational references round out a story character—male or female. A clerk in a fashion boutique may be viewed as an avant-garde person. A clerk in a bookstore may be regarded as more intellectual. A female clerk in a hardware store may automatically be seen as less feminine in her interests than a clerk in a lingerie store.

For men, such jobs as truck driver, rodeo rider, electric lineman, lumberjack, wildcat oil-well driller, plainclothes policeman, or any other occupation that requires physical strength and stamina, immediately give the character a manly, rugged image. Sedentary jobs—librarian, druggist, accountant, lawyer, male secretary—suggest a less "macho" male.

Careful selection of your characters' names can help you highlight their personality. Bubbles quickly presents a picture of a frivolous, voluptuous, scatterbrained sexpot. The name says it so well that you almost don't need to describe her. Names like Cookie, Goldie, and even a character's citizens'-band radio "handle," can also also indicate character.

Perky, unusual names can give female characters an aura of romance and glamor without a word of physical description. Modern names like Kenna, Gayla, Lori, Krista, Jodi, Shawna, Lesli, Shannon, Terri, Karmen, Debi and Karin, are appropriate for lively young narrators. Names like Ellen, Dorothy, Agnes, Alice, Frannie, Grace, Louise, Betty, and Catharine, may be viewed as old-fashioned and evoke in the reader the concept of a staid, reliable, sensible woman who will be able to offer logical advice to the troubled narrator.

For the male character, manly names suggest a rugged, competent or romantic image worthy of the narrator's love: Clay, Derek, Guy, Frank, Ron, Hugh, Rick,

Jordan, Brad, Brett, Eric, Mitch. On the other hand, names like Morris, Horace, Cyril, Owen, Curtis, Gale, Doran, Lloyd, or Henry, might suggest a less aggressive and romantic male, at least, for confession readers. A look through the telephone directory or a book for naming a baby may turn up many interesting, unusual first and last names. Names vary from one region of the country to another—a name common in your area might be rarely used in another state.

You should avoid overusing the same names in stories, especially unusual ones, like Saranell, or Suebeth. A good way to prevent this is to keep a log of names you have used in your stories. This can help you discover the beauty of names, and how they may complement and add dimension to your characters' personalities.

It is also a good idea to keep a record of occupations you give your characters, particularly men. This will ensure use of unusual and varying jobs which can add interest to the story and more depth to characters.

By understanding your characters' universal, physical and emotional traits, you can make the people in your stories come alive. And, once they live on the page, let them take over and tell the story. You will have no trouble convincing your reader of your characters' reality and successfully transforming them from a figment of your imagination into flesh-and-blood "people" who will be loved and remembered by your readers.

VIII

MOTIVATION: KNOW IT AND SHOW IT

THE DIFFERENCE between a rejected and an accepted story is often a matter of motivation. Motivation is one aspect of story creation all too often ignored by beginning writers. They don't give their characters strong enough reasons for behaving as they do, particularly if an action may seem out of character.

When people in real life react to pressures by behaving in strange ways, we can accept their quirks. Out-of-character behavior on the part of a confession character, however, is not allowed—unless you can offer a sound, logical reason that motivates the character to abandon behavior in keeping with what is previously known of him or her *in favor of actions totally unexpected*.

The importance of giving a reason for a character to behave in a certain way was proved to me by a spate of rejection slips from confession editors, reading:

"This is too farfetched for me. Where's your motivation?"

"An amusing story, but it's one our readers would never believe without the right motivation."

"Well-written, but not believable. The narrator had no reason to follow through as she did in the story. It didn't really make sense and led nowhere."

The rejections were painful, but the editors' comments were justified, and they brought home to me the importance of motivation, if a story is to be accepted.

A confession narrator can't do something on impulse, simply because she feels like it, but can't explain it, or doesn't know why she did it. *You* must know why—and show why—so that the motivation is clear, and the groundwork is laid perhaps before the narrator comes to realize why she reacts as she does.

As the creator of the story, you probably know your narrator's reason for reacting as she does, but you must share this special knowledge with the reader. Motivation may be shown through narrative, dialogue, or an observation on the part of another character who spots the motivation of the narrator before she herself is aware of why she reacts as she does. It isn't important *how* the motivation is shown—only that it *is*.

There are many things about your narrator you will know—and won't bother revealing—for fear of boring the readers with more than they care or need to know. But it is *imperative* that motivation be shown for things the narrator does that would be frowned on by the average reader. The motivation will help elicit reader sympathy.

The reason the narrator has for doing something ordinarily unacceptable may be as simple as seeking revenge for an old injustice. Or the narrator could be trying to save face, or protect her husband or child.

What kind of narrator would marry one brother if she knew she was pregnant by the other? Not your average narrator. But, what if there were extenuating circumstances?

In my story, "Hand-Me-Down Wife" (in *Intimate Story*), the narrator is desperate. Her unborn baby's father has just been sentenced to prison. The problem is presented to the readers on page one. Also shown is the fact that Jenna is an orphan and has no one to turn to. This helps foreshadow the motivation scene in which she makes a decision: Her lover's younger, very decent brother, Clay, takes her home so she won't be alone in her grief, they get drunk, end up in bed. He feels he must "do right" by her, and he mumbles he loves her and asks her to marry him.

Her answer? Jenna, who has been around, instinctively starts to turn down his proposal—*until her pregnancy motivates her into a different answer:*

> Suddenly I remembered the tiny life growing inside me and I bit back my words and brought my lips to Clay's instead.
> "Yes! We'll get married. It will work out," I whispered. And it would! Perfectly. I'd have a father for my baby. I'd have a husband. And I'd let Clay think that the baby was his and was born prematurely.

Sometimes motivation must be shown in a story for other characters, not just the narrator. They may have reactions that must involve the narrator in order to fulfill the requirements of the story line. To be satisfying, the story must reveal their motivation as well.

What kind of fellow would *insist* that his girlfriend become pregnant before he would think about marrying her? Not the average young man who enjoys his freedom. But, Tony, the "hero" in my story, "I'm Having a Phantom Baby," is not an average fellow.

Tony's background included a brief, bitter marriage which ended in divorce when his wife, after tricking him into marriage, refused to give him the children he wanted. This incident is the motivation for his future behavior:

> "The next time I get married it's going to be on *my* terms," Tony said firmly. Then he took me into his arms and kissed me brutally, his lips hurting mine. "I want kids," he murmured huskily. "And I don't intend to beg and plead with my wife to give them to me. I'll marry you—*when I have to*. Now you know my...terms."
>
> My blood raced through my veins as I took the wallet from Tony's hand.
>
> "Don't use one," I whispered bravely. I pulled him into my arms, kissing him as we pressed close. "Make me pregnant tonight!" I begged.

How can you maneuver a small child into the parental bed to disrupt a husband and wife's sex life and make chaos of the marriage? Through motivation!

Most adults are aware that doctors recommend children not be allowed in bed with adults. But, there are few mothers who would banish a sick, frightened, or tearful child. In my story, "I Sleep With My Husband and My Son" (in *Intimate Story*), the little boy's real father is killed in a bulldozer accident. Here is an excerpt from the scene that followed:

> After the funeral Timmy started sleeping poorly. Almost every night he woke up with a bad dream, tummy ache, or just plain scared and lonely. When he came crawling into bed with me it seemed natural and right to hold and cuddle him. I let him stay where he felt safe and protected.
>
> Before I knew it, Timmy slept with me every night. I never said anything or tried to force him back to his own room. I figured after he quit having nightmares and was ready, he'd go back to his own room.

Unfortunately the little boy, who became jealous of his stepfather, made it a point not to return to his room, and he almost broke up his mother's new marriage. The little boy's constant appearance in the marital bed was believable because it had been well-motivated in the story.

What reason can a man have for becoming a male hooker, especially if he's married? The reason had better be good. For Stan, the married hooker in "I Went to a Male Prostitute" (in *Modern Love Confessions*), the reason was valid.

Stan and his wife bought a new home that cost more than they could really afford. When the factory closed down, five hundred men were out of work. With no high school diploma, Stan had a rougher time than others did finding work. Finally, he got a job as a salesman. His motivation was financial: the need to protect and provide for his loved ones...*in any way he could*, even if it meant "selling" his own body. Here is the scene that reveals his motivation:

> "Calm down, Kris! It was just business!" Stan shook my shoulders. "The women—they didn't mean anything to me! You've got to believe that. It's you I love. It was just a job! For God's sake do you think I could have gone through with it and lived in hell if I wasn't desperate to provide for you and the kids?"
>
> Stan's voice was hoarse as he explained his worries and frustrations as he saw our savings account evaporate, and the equity in our home slip away like sand through an hourglass.

The desperation of his situation and his motivation make him a prime candidate for forgiveness and understanding from his wife—and sympathy and acceptance from the reader.

Why would a young girl get kicks from sex only when she is beaten up and forced into it? This is the subject of my story, "Sex Scars Are a Brand of My Sick Needs," published by *Hip*.

The narrator is the eldest child of a straight-laced, hell-fire-and-brimstone preacher who equates sex with evil, and pleasure with sin. The girl grows up hearing and believing these things. As a result she rebuffs all advances from men, and most boys respect her wishes. One doesn't. He rapes her violently, and in spite of herself, she is aroused and enjoys it. Subconsciously she allowed herself to accept the pleasure because the pain was her punishment.

"I'll make you enjoy sex whether you want to or not. I'll make you do it," Lonnie said, panting. I cried from pain. "You're going to like it!" he ordered.

"Never!" I whispered, my voice hoarse with defiance.

Lonnie held me a prisoner to him until I was overcome by the awful, degrading feelings. My body shuddered helplessly and a shivering tingle throbbed through me.

"How'd you like it?" he asked. His voice was smug and jeering.

I pulled my rumpled clothes into place. "I didn't," I spat. "I hated it. I hated the things you *forced* me to do. And I hate you!"

But it was all a lie . . . I liked the way Lonnie made me feel!

Because of the narrator's background she believed she could enjoy sex only when it was forced upon her and not of her own free choice. As a result, tender lovers turn her off. She subconsciously sought out rough men to reaffirm her opinion of herself, and looked for professional help at a mental-health clinic only after she was brutally battered by a man she casually picked up for sex.

As these examples show, it doesn't matter *how* motivation is shown in the confession story—only that it *is*.

IX

PLAUSIBILITY AND PLANTS

IT IS NOT always easy to make an unusual confession story believable and to convince editors and readers that it really happened. Perhaps confession editors are born a bit dubious, possibly because of reading—and rejecting— so many contrived stories.

So here is a guideline:

Truth is too strange for fiction.

Remember that the next time an editor rejects a story based on a real-life incident. A story that is too strange will not sell. Just because a "strange" story really happened to someone you know, don't expect the editor to believe it or to buy it.

Motivation can help to make a story convincing. But you cannot count on coincidence or luck to carry the rest of the load. Coincidences often occur in real life—but *not* in confession stories, *unless you can make the coincidence in your story seem not only likely, but probable.*

To make unlikely events seem logical, you must pave the way through the skillful use of writing tricks known as "plants." Plants are hints or clues dropped so casually into the story that the reader is aware of them only after they become important later in the plot.

In "I Went to a Male Prostitute," it seemed implausible for a wife not to know exactly what her husband did for a living. To explain the narrator's acceptance of her husband's vagueness about his job as a "salesman," the wife is shown as not having "a good head for business," thus explaining her ready acceptance of what he has told her. The reader and the narrator don't even suspect the husband is being deliberately vague about his job until what he *really* does for a living is discovered.

Another story, "I Begged My Man to Love Me" (in *Intimate Story*), deals with impotence caused by sugar diabetes. When Curt's impotence is revealed, the climax comes as a surprise but not an unbelievable one, because of a careful plant near the beginning of the story:

> I set the tray on the table and put the coffee pot on a trivet. I offered Curt the sugar and cream, but he brushed them away.
> "I take mine black. No sugar. Doctor's orders," he explained. "Nice kids you've got," he went on. "How long were you married?"

Later, his impotence resulting from sugar diabetes is revealed. It is accepted by the reader who recalls the carefully planted phrase.

In another story, "God Gave Us This Child to Teach Us How to Love" (in *Personal Romances*), a young mother delivers her baby after long, difficult labor. On the second page of the story this is what takes place:

> They gave me a shot and everything faded away. Words took forever to be spoken.
> "Oh . . . *no!*" Don said from somewhere in the room. I tried to sit up. Someone pushed me back down.
> "Is our baby dead?" I cried.

A moment later Don leaned over me. I fought to open my eyes and focus them on his face. The sedative kept pulling me down.

"The baby is alive, Marny. It's a girl. Everything will be fine," he said gently. "Rest now." I nodded and groggily sank into oblivion.

Because of the hard delivery, the young mother was kept sedated all day long. When a new nurse comes on duty that evening and finds Marny awake, she asks if Marny would like to have her baby brought to her. Of course, Marny does. The nurse brings the baby, and Marny discovers her infant daughter is pitifully deformed.

A surprise? At first. But immediately both Marny and the reader will remember the carefully planted "Oh . . . no!"

In many stories, the narrator is saved, not through her own ingenuity and efforts, but through the actions of another character. In such cases, it is vitally important to use plants to show that the supporting character would have the necessary knowledge or the means needed to save the situation.

In "I Set Myself Up for Rape," for example (in *Personal Romances*), the narrator, teen-age Missy, goes from being a popular student in a small-town school to being a nobody in a large-city school. Her new stepbrother, David, who is very intelligent, doesn't care if he is popular or not, and he is an object of Missy's scorn.

One day Missy finally manages to get asked out by the school's most popular boy. She is excited and happy, until David comes home and bursts her bubble.

"Are you going someplace tonight?" David asked when he saw me in curlers.

"Yeah," I said coolly. "Chip Arnold asked me out."

"Oh?" David asked, frowning. Then he started to mumble that he didn't think Chip was the kind of guy I should be dating and there were nicer boys for me to go out with.

"What are you trying to do? Play big brother?" I asked. "Well, bug off, David! It's about time someone in this rotten city realized I'm alive and didn't figure that I'm a boring nobody just because I live in the same house you do!"

David looked hurt—and like he wanted to say more—but instead he gave me a disgusted look, dropped into the chair and clamped his mouth shut as he stared straight ahead at the television set.

At the story's end, the reader and Missy realize that David *did* know more than Missy gave him a chance to say. I had planted the fact that as the team's water boy, David had a chance to overhear Chip's plan to take advantage of Missy's eagerness to date the team. David follows Chip and Missy on the date and intervenes before Chip's planned gang-rape can take place. His showing up to save his young stepsister is believable because the fact that he seemed to know more than he was telling was subtly planted when Missy tells him she is going out with Chip.

The best plants are those slipped in so unobtrusively that the reader is not aware of them until the climax of the story when the plants are remembered, making the solution to the story problem acceptable. If the plant is too obvious it may give the story away prematurely. Work your plants in early so your story will be satisfying and believable.

X

SEX: LOVE OR LUST?

SEX—described or implied—has always been integral to the confession story. What was sexually taboo in the 1940's became commonplace in the 1950's. What wasn't mentioned in the 1950's was coyly hinted at in the 1960's. What was merely hinted at in the 1960's became the main topic of conversation at social gatherings, has filled the pages of magazines, and became the theme of best-selling books in the 1970's. The 1980's may push the boundaries of explicit sex in fiction even further, but in any case, there will probably be no turning back.

In the 1950's a story dealing with an unwed mother (which implied an illicit sex act) was risqué enough almost to guarantee a sale. By the 1960's sexual mores had changed—but not much. Unwed mothers were still good for selling stories, as were such plots as seducing the pillar of the community, getting your parents unwittingly high at a pot party, or running off to live in a hippie commune where (presumably) free love flourished.

Actual sex scenes in the confession stories of the 1960's, however, were rare. If a sex scene did take place in a story, it was covered in only a sentence or two. More often the sex act was implied, and most of the intimate details were left to the reader's imagination. All publications changed radically during the last decade. Sex scenes in stories today are not only permissible but encouraged by many confession editors. Stories may describe sex that previously titles only hinted at, and the story itself did not deliver.

At first glance, the covers of the confession magazines appear similar. Close inspection of the covers and the wording of the titles and blurbs, however, points out the vitally important differences among the confession magazines on the newsstands today. Generally speaking, there are three types of confession magazines: *wholesome, racy,* and *pornographic.* Story topics may be identical in all of these magazines, but the treatment, emphasis, language limits, and handling of sex are poles apart.

In the "wholesome" confession magazines, for example, the story topic may seem nonsexual, but sex is usually implied. "Racy" confession magazines consider sex a staple for an acceptable story. In the "pornographic" magazines, it's a "must" for stories to be based on a provocative sexual experience or problem.

Topics such as child and male prostitution, battered wives, gay husbands, parents facing a child's admission of homosexuality, unwed mothers, sex-change operations, impotence, frigidity, child molesters, exhibitionists, as well as stories with explicit medical details, are used in all the confession magazines, but in a style appropriate for the particular type of publication.

The "wholesome" magazines, often referred to as "The Trues" by the editors, include: *True Story, True Love, True Experience, True Confessions, True Romance, Secrets,* and *Modern Romances.* The titles of the stories in these magazines only hint of sex. A story called

"Sex Wars," for example, instead of pertaining to a brazen bedroom battle is really about a liberated woman who confronts a male chauvinist in a fight about rights and equality. If a sex scene is included in the "wholesome" story, it will be very brief, low-key, and presented with details glossed over using high-flown language. The characters may go as far as a kiss, or, maybe, a caress—nothing more. These magazines emphasize that sex is only one part of the narrator's total makeup and life. Stories dealing with sexual problems in the wholesome magazines usually illustrate how sex affects the narrator as a person and adversely influences other areas in her life.

In the "wholesome" magazine stories, sordid, shocking or clearly titillating aspects of sex are not mentioned. When a narrator in a wholesome story makes a sexual mistake, it is always because *love* was foremost in her mind and emotions at the moment.

Some stories written for the "wholesome" group, if they fail to be accepted by a confession magazine, can sometimes with minor revision be submitted to the regular women's magazines. And stories that have not made the grade in the women's magazines can sometimes be rewritten as confessions for submission to "wholesome" confession publications.

The "wholesome" magazines constitute about one-fifth of the total number of confession magazines. The competition is keen in this group because they pay top rates. It is difficult for a novice writer to break in quickly. If a writer decides to try "racy" confession stories, however, the chances of selling improve greatly, because many more of these magazines exist. A sampling of titles: *Daring Romances, Personal Romances, Exciting Confessions, Intimate Story* (plus the "albums" by these names), *Modern Love Confessions, Real Story, True Life Secrets,* and so on.

Sex is important to the "racy" confession story, and editors realize that sex sells their magazines. Here are some examples of stories that have appeared in "racy" confessions:

> "I Went From High-School Girl—To Hooker!"—about a runaway who gets into the clutches of a big-city pimp.
>
> "I Was Blackmailed By a Sex Pervert"—about a girl who keeps a fantasy diary, which is found by the school janitor (a pervert), who blackmails her into helping him satisfy his abnormal sexual desire.
>
> "My Man Does Things No Woman Can Tolerate"— about a frigid woman raised in a puritanical home; she suspects her husband of being the culprit in a child molestation crime, because he asks her to do things that "no woman can tolerate," and is frustrated by her refusals.
>
> "My Husband Could Win First Prize in a Kinky Sex Contest"—about a young wife who gets turned off by her husband's request that she try the weird things he reads about in the men's magazines.

Editors want such stories with sex scenes, provided the action fits naturally and believably, and that the writing is handled tastefully, using permissible language.

The "racy" story contains one or more often two sex scenes, described in detail, and the sex in these stories is stressed. The narrator may have love in mind when she enters a sexual situation, but she also has lust in her heart. However, sex scenes are written without referring to specific sexual terms, or to the anatomy or body functions. No clinical or vulgar "street" terms are used. Instead, euphemistic words—vocabulary similar to that used in "wholesome" stories—are selected to convey the sexual ideas in an inoffensive way. "Wholesome" and "racy" magazines use basically the same language. Sex in the "racy" confessions is portrayed realistically. If the scene is tender, loving, and romantic, sex is described accordingly. If the act is violent, humiliating, and degrading, sex is shown as a brutal assault. But the language is always in good taste. Unusual sexual acts are carefully written so that the action is somewhat vague, but the wording allows the astute, sophisticated reader to understand exactly what is going on.

"Pornographic" confession magazines use detailed sex scenes that are blatant, with slang, four-letter words, gutter language and bawdy euphemisms, often resulting in scenes that are quite "smutty."

Two or three years ago, there were four to five "pornographic" magazines in the confession field. Now, these magazines are published only sporadically. Though at first they paid writers, soon they developed a reputation for not paying. I do not list the titles of these magazines, as they come and go, surface and resurface, as the titles are sold or change hands. The blurbs on the covers of the "pornographic" confessions describe the sexual experience depicted in the pages of the magazine.

The same event, written for each of the three types of confessions, would read quite differently. Here is an illustration of a story about rape:

In a "wholesome" confession story on rape, there would be a description of the attacker grabbing the narrator and beginning the assault. Then everything blurs for the victim, and she wakes up later in a hospital bed, or regains consciousness in the park under a bush, or comes to in the back alley and examines the scrapes and bruises she received in the sexual attack. The details of the actual rape are omitted.

The "racy" and "pornographic" stories will show the rape without omitting anything from the sequence of events. But though the rape scene in these two types of magazine will have approximately the same sexual content, the words used to describe the action will differ. The "racy" magazine will use more gentle words, while the "pornographic" magazine will use crude, gutter language.

As another illustration, consider a story dealing with impotency. The "wholesome" magazine would be likely to show the anguished narrator puzzled and hurt by an attempt at sex which failed. No real details would be given. The failure would be implied.

In the "racy" and "pornographic" stories, the sex scene would begin with kisses to caresses, and build in urgency to the point when the male was unable to perform, and the story would explode with trauma, shock, shame, and unsatisfied desires. Again, the difference between "racy" and "pornographic" would be the words used in the telling of the story.

The subject of frigidity would be shown in the "wholesome" story by the narrator berating herself in narrative, or confiding to a neighbor in an exchange of dialogue that she can't seem to be a "real woman" to her husband, even though she loves him.

The story of a frigid wife in the "racy" and "pornographic" confession magazines would begin with a scene showing her husband's first caress, which makes her skin crawl as she fights down the urge to push him away. It would continue to his last effort at tender lovemaking, which makes the narrator shudder with repulsion, as she feels trapped, and obligated to perform sexually. As before, the words chosen to describe the actual sex scenes would be the real difference between these two stories.

Sex is in the confessions to stay, but some sexual perversions will probably never be accepted or viewed with sympathy by confession readers in any of the three types of confession magazines, even though some of the more sophisticated men's and women's magazines have already introduced these aspects of sex into their pages. Some of these taboos include bestiality, incest-for-fun, child molestation portrayed as an acceptable sexual outlet, and sadism to the extent of personal injury. These perversions will probably always be too extreme to be included in the confession stories because the buying audience wishes to believe in basic goodness, love, family ties, and personal decency.

It is imperative that writers study various confession magazines to see how much sex is allowable, and then be prepared to write and submit stories in that style.

Confession writing is very commercial. Sex is a commodity that the majority of the confession editors are in the market to buy. It is harder to break in if you choose not to write about sex—realistically or suggestively—and your success in the confession field will be limited until you do so.

XI

POLISHING THE ROUGH DRAFT

WHEN you have written a complete but still rough draft of your confession story, it's time to begin cutting and polishing, the hard work that is required to turn the rough story—which is probably loose and choppy—into a smooth, fast-paced, salable confession, ready for submission. Some writers scoff at revision. If you feel this way about your work, get out of the confession field!

Even when a confession story has been written at one sitting and the pace is brisk, there are almost always sections in which the writer's imagination and the narration slow down and the story slides from overdrive into neutral and rolls to a stop.

The problem can be corrected by giving these areas a thorough going-over. If you used ten sentences to convey an idea where one or two would have put your point across, rewrite and revise. When the passage in the story zips along in high gear again, you'll know you've succeeded. It is important to delete nonessentials from a story and add the telling details that bring the story events to life.

As you wrote the rough draft of the story, you "lived" it through your narrator. When reading over the script, you are in effect "reliving" it. With this in mind, recall the subtle details that will add drama, depth, and believability. Then edit the dialogue and narrative to make the greatest impact on your reader.

All too often writers have no idea of the style acceptable in the confession field, and they submit manuscripts that are in stream-of-consciousness style, or read like newspaper accounts, or are all narrative or all dialogue. Occasionally, even a story in third-person or multi-person viewpoint will be submitted by would-be confession writers who haven't bothered to look between the covers of a confession magazine before sending in their work for consideration. The best style to aim for is a "spoken" one that gives the confession story the readability and the intimacy it needs to have a ring of truth.

Purple prose is one of the most glaring faults in the work of beginning confession writers. When they are unsure of how to show emotion—through actions and dialogue—they attempt to do it by using grandiose and florid adjectives. As a result, the story narrative sounds artificial, and rarely will be purchased, even if the plot is good.

Authors who write in genres outside the confession field should keep in mind that the average confession reader may not have a large enough vocabulary to understand certain words, and therefore, these must not be used. The manuscript may still be purchased if it contains some words that a confession reader might not comprehend, and these words may be taken out by the editor, unless, of course, the editor has under consideration by another writer a story that needs *no* such editing.

For example, if you have a character "grimace," the editor will probably change it to "frown," a word more universally and quickly understood and used. Don't have your character "imbibe"; most readers "drink." Your narrator's husband will never come home "intoxicated," but he might come home at two in the morning "drunk." He will likewise not become "infuriated," but he may "fly off the handle."

Most persons have in their memories vivid sensory recollections, such as the creamy *taste* of chocolate fudge, the harsh *smell* of ammonia, the acrid *stench* of burning hair, the *odor* of a wet dog, the *texture* or *feel* of burlap, the *sound* of a wailing police siren, or the *sight* of a flaming pink sky at sunset. These are all stimuli that were perceived by our senses (touch, smell, sight, sound, taste) and recorded in our memories.

With these sensory perceptions "on file," the reader instantly recalls the experience whenever he sees a phrase or word that connotes it, and goes on to the next sentence without realizing that a vivid recollection was just evoked and re-experienced.

After reading a story that makes use of the five senses in a skillful way, a reader feels that she has lived through the experience because the sensory stimulation was so acute. Here is an example of effective sensory writing from "Men Won't Marry a Tramp Like Me" (published by *Intimate Story*), with the particular sense noted in italics:

> When the rodeo announcer's voice echoed over the public address system the crowd roared. (*Sound*) I ran to the wooden fence and clawed my way up the rough, splintered planks. (*Touch*) A Brahman bull thrashed in the chute before he bucked into the arena. The huge bull twisted and spun. Mark's legs flew in the air. A patch of daylight appeared between Mark and the bull. (*Sight*) My mouth went dry and metallic with fear. (*Taste*) A powerful hind leg crashed down and landed on Mark's pelvis and slid off.

(*Sight*) Mark screamed in agony (*Sound*) and clutched himself as he writhed in pain. The bull whirled away, kicking and lunging around the corral (*Sight*) in a cloud of choking dust that mingled with the musky scent of animal sweat. (*Smell*)

Showing the scene through sensory description is much more effective than having the narrator, Bubbles, say: "I climbed the rungs of the corral in time to see Mark thrown off the bull and trampled." The tension that sensory writing brings to a story is worth working to achieve.

Dialogue is another aspect of confession writing you must master. The dialogue must sound "real," and good dialogue is very different from the way people actually speak in conversation. In real life people ramble, grunt, break off in mid-sentence, and never get around to finishing the thought.

Confession dialogue is an "edited" version of real conversation. In real life, people often say the same thing in three ways, thinking they are making three new points, when they are simply repeating one. Repetition in conversation is not easily caught or even noticed by the ear, but in written dialogue the eye will almost always catch it. So if your characters have something to say, let them say it *once*—and then get on with the next thought. This moves the story ahead and keeps the dialogue brisk and lively.

In narrative, it may take pages to delineate clearly what the narrator and other characters are like; dialogue, on the other hand, can often accomplish this same task in a very short space.

"What do you say we go out on Saturday night?" Jake drawled. He smiled down at me and his eyes swept over me like a caress. I swallowed hard. Butterflies batted in my stomach.

"I-I don't know," I stammered. A hot flush crept up my cheeks.

"Sure you do," Jake said, assuredly, and smoothed a wisp of hair away from my face. "You want to go out with me as much as I want you to. Admit it!"

Jake sounds cocky and sure of himself. The narrator? Shy, and inexperienced.

In real life, good manners are often ignored. People interrupt one another all the time. Confession characters do it, too—and it quickens the tempo of the story, as in the following:

"Sure I love you, sweetheart," Royce said smoothly as he turned away from me and dried his face with the fluffy towel. "Whatever made you think that I didn't—"

"Because of the way you act!" I broke in. My voice shook with anger and fright. "You-you used to be so gentle and caring. You acted like I was the only girl in the world. And now you act like—"

"Like what?" Royce prompted innocently as I fumbled for words. His eyes were mocking as they met mine in the steamy bathroom mirror. I squeezed my eyes shut and pushed the words out.

"Like a male hooker! You're always on the . . . make!"

Dashes are useful in writing dialogue. They give the effect of forward movement and urgency. A few stuttered words can lend credibility to a nervous, upset, or deceitful character. The elliptical, broken, or unfinished sentence, indicated by dots . . . is a good way to make dialogue read with the rhythm of a spoken sentence. People hesitate, pause, and use silences for emphasis. In an interrupted thought or phrase, this kind of break provides the pause needed for special effect.

When polishing a story, keep in mind the final word length you are aiming for. The average confession stories accepted range from about 2,000 to 5,500 words. Many magazines limit stories to 6,000 words, but some confessions publishers buy longer stories. A few markets use—and pay more for—stories of novelette length. This is a difficult length to write because you must keep the story fast-paced and dramatic to the end. Because quality novelette confessions are difficult for most writers to handle successfully, the competition tends to be less intense, and good novelettes find a ready market.

Sometimes beginning writers purposely pad and lengthen stories in the hope of earning a few extra dollars if the story sells. This isn't a good policy; editors can spot padding immediately. If the choice comes between a padded story and a compact one, the shorter, tighter story will be purchased.

Polishing is one of the keys for producing a salable story. Experienced professional confession writers can often write a finished draft the first time through and sell the story. But few do, since "one-draft" stories that make it into print often have rough spots that the writers wish, too late, they had the opportunity to polish and correct.

The beginning confession writer will probably need two or possibly three drafts to polish the manuscript sufficiently. But there is such a thing as too much reworking that can cause the story to sound too "pat" and lifeless. There is also the danger of becoming so familiar with the story that you can no longer be objective enough to recognize what is good or bad, or if the story is boring.

If the story bores you as you work on the revision, then it will probably bore the editor and readers, too. Start cutting out the needless details that serve no purpose and slow the story's pace. You will know the story is a good one if you can read through the draft, revision, retyping and proofreading without becoming bored or feeling that the story drags here or there.

An important point to remember: if your story can't hold your attention as you work on it, don't expect it to catch and hold the editor's attention either, and without that, your hard work will have been a wasted effort.

XII

NONFICTION IN CONFESSION MAGAZINES

A FEW confession magazines publish only fiction. But the
majority of the confession magazines *also* publish nonfiction articles to round out the magazine and to enlighten
as well as entertain their readers.
If you are interested in researching and writing nonfiction articles for the confession publications, you will
find many editors receptive to them. Editors look for
subjects of general interest and relevance, handled appropriately for the confession readership. In general, they
want articles on sex, or service features on decorating,
crafts, personal care, how-to pieces, fashion, hobbies,
beauty, cooking, health and other similar topics. A writer
with something to say, who can write with flair, select a
catchy topic, and do accurate reporting, can make regular
sales of nonfiction to the confession magazines.
The articles that many confession editors buy are not
far removed from the pieces regular women's magazines
use. Often the topics covered will be identical; the difference between the two is mainly a matter of handling,
style, and slant. The wholesome confession group regu-

larly publishes a number of informational and how-to articles on various general subjects. The racier confession magazines seem to use fewer articles, and the topics almost invariably deal with sex in some way.

Because the average confession reader is not as worldly as those who regularly read the women's slick magazines, confession articles are not as sophisticated; they are slanted more directly to the average confession reader's comprehension and interest level.

The factual confession article must be written in a style to attract—and hold—the confession reader's attention to the end. The writer can achieve this by creating articles containing several components: a good lead paragraph; sample case histories; provocative—but accurate—information; and a personal, down-to-earth writing style.

The lead paragraph serves as the introduction to the article. It is as important to the nonfiction article as the narrative hook is to a work of fiction. The lead should capture the reader's interest and offer clues to what will follow in the body of the article, and should define the slant and focus of the article as well.

Subjects that will guide and benefit readers are very salable. Although the narrators in many *confession stories* don't have the forethought to use contraceptives before they have affairs, *articles* on contraception appear with regularity in the varied confession magazines, so that the reader (unlike the story heroine) is aware of what methods of contraception are available to avoid unwanted pregnancy.

Just as the confession stories are often written to prove a point, so are many of the confession-magazine articles. The following is the lead paragraph for an article I wrote, entitled "Contraception: a Comprehensive Guide for Modern Women" (in *Foxy Confessions*). It stressed in the first two paragraphs why such information is important to the socially and sexually responsible woman:

Unprotected sexual intercourse that results in an unplanned pregnancy can be very costly emotionally and economically. An abortion is a financial and emotional drain. And the responsibility of rearing a child for an estimated twenty years runs into the thousands and thousands of dollars, with immeasurable emotional support expended.

Either of these would be a stiff price to pay for a moment of carelessness when modern, reliable, low-cost, safe contraceptives are readily available.

The thrust of this article was prevention. I gave case histories relating personal experiences of real women who used the various birth control methods. Through direct quotations, the women shared with the confession reader their fears and feelings; discussed side effects; and compared the safety of one method against the reliability of another. By reading the experiences of others, a woman reader would be better able to decide on a contraceptive method suited to *her* lifestyle. Armed with this knowledge she could avoid the mistakes of the confession heroines she reads about in the fiction stories.

In "Is Your Husband Cheating?" a nonfiction article, published by *Real Story*, the lead is handled in yet another way. Because confession readers are "people-oriented," the author begins her article with a person—a case history—named Barbara.

Barbara is getting married. Barbara is very average both in looks and figure. The man she's marrying is an executive in the company where she works. He makes an excellent salary and is quite handsome.

That's not all. When Barbara came to work for the company, he was married—to a very attractive blonde. How did "average" Barbara become—not only "the other woman," but an "other woman" who broke up a marriage and got the man?

Reader interest is quickly achieved by sketching in the details of Barbara's situation. Then, before the reader's interest can wane, Barbara, the case history, identified by her first name only, speaks:

"It was easy," Barbara said. "I really didn't have to do much. If you want the truth, his wife gave him away! Oh, maybe she loved him. But even so, she made it easy for me."

After this short quote, the article goes on in narrative style to explain to confession readers the ways in which wives make it easy for a husband to be stolen by the "other woman." Advice is given on how wives can look for trouble spots in the marriage—and remove them—before the husband is tempted to stray to the "other woman" who is waiting for her chance.

Suggestions include having the wife learn to be more understanding and less critical, or try to run a serene household that is a haven for her husband to come to after a hard day. The article then offers ideas on new beauty treatments, flattering hair-dos, and a diet-and-exercise program to improve the wife's appearance.

Following this advice comes solid logic. The wife who may be faced with a cheating husband is advised to remain calm to avoid further alienating her husband by having tantrums and hysterics. She is urged further to point out to him the difficulties that will arise if they separate and are divorced. The wife is told not to play the role of the martyr, and to develop a life of her own, and is given other suggestions that might be helpful for saving a rocky marriage, or finding the strength needed to face and cope with the situation, if the marriage proves unsalvageable.

Nonfiction articles of this type can be written by laymen. Most people, when asked their opinions on sex or sexual experiences, will confide in a writer if they know anonymity is guaranteed. And, if you promise them anonymity, be sure to preserve it. Give details that flesh out the case history and give it a ring of truth, but do not do so by revealing so much that you endanger the confidentiality or invade the privacy of your informant.

Many articles can be written by a layman with clever ideas and access to persons willing to be interviewed. The suggestions given in the preceding example were all based on common sense. Here are some ideas that could be researched by a writer on her own, or used in conjunction with the information gathered from friends: "How to Find a Boyfriend"; "How to Turn Your Husband On—Without Turning Him Off"; "Twenty Ways to Make Your Man Feel Loved."

A sampling of confession magazines shows the diversity of nonfiction they are buying and publishing. "Easybake, Fabulous Bread!" and "Instant Needlecraft," in *True Confessions*, "Unusual Gifts for All Occasions," in *Soul Confessions,* "Do You Set a Good Example for Your Children?" in *Real Story*, "Sauces and Dips," in *Daring Romances*, "Child Abuse" and "Do Singles Have More Fun?" appearing in *Hip*—all illustrate the broad spectrum of topics suitable and salable to the confessions today.

Most confession publishers prefer nonfiction articles that are quite short. Some want only filler length, ranging from 300-1,000 words. Others specify article lengths up to 2,000 words. Rarely will an article over that word limit be accepted.

The pay rate for nonfiction is generally in scale with what is paid for fiction, although some confession magazines pay a bit more for the shorter nonfiction, and a few pay a flat rate for articles regardless of length.

Good ideas for successful nonfiction articles come from asking your friends for topics of articles that they couldn't resist reading, or want to know more about, or would find personally helpful to them in private relationships. Then, research, and write. But remember to keep the article provocative, helpful, educational, accurate, and short!

XIII

FACTUAL CONFESSIONS
FOR GENERAL MAGAZINES

THE TRUE or factual personal-experience article is one of the most salable forms of writing, and is closely related to the type of fiction bought by confession magazines.

Many of the women's slick magazines publish such articles. They could be described as "confession stories," but, editors of such publications as *Cosmopolitan, McCall's, Ms., Redbook, Ladies' Home Journal,* and *Good Housekeeping,* to name a few, prefer to call these features "personal-experience articles" or "first-person narratives."

The range of topics and subjects is very broad. Published articles have dealt with such personal experiences as being a compulsive gambler, being the victim of a sexual con game, getting arrested for shoplifting, becoming addicted to prescription drugs, and marrying a homosexual.

Many titles of these published pieces *sound* as if they also could be found in the fictional confession magazines. There is a sharp difference: Confessions published in the fictional magazines are not true; those published in the women's magazines are.

"They're true," stated the editor of one of the biggest women's magazines in the United States. "But they're not souped up and romanticized . . ." as are fictional confessions.

In the article, "I Was a Battered Wife," featured in "My Problem and How I Solved It" in *Good Housekeeping*, the problem is told immediately.

> The woman was admitted to the emergency room at 11:20 P.M. The left side of her face was puffed and purple. One eye was swollen closed. Blood was flowing from her left ear, and X-rays showed that she had two broken ribs.
>
> When the doctor questioned her about her injuries the woman answered, "I fell down the stairs."
>
> How do I know so much about this incident? *I* was that woman . . .

And the anonymous woman goes on to describe her problem, in detail, and how she reached her decision to make a new life, alone with her children.

Sometimes the personal-experience confession also includes the narrator's reasons behind an intimate decision.

"I Was Sterilized" is a true account by a young woman which was published in *Cosmopolitan*, so that readers who might agree with the author's viewpoint can gain courage and insight from her story, and become better able to follow their own convictions.

> This year I celebrated the fifth anniversary of my tubal ligation, and because I haven't become pregnant since the operation, my gynecologist has deemed me "cured"—i.e., I'm sterile and will never have to worry about pregnancy again.
>
> Other people have called me (among other things) "sick" . . .

After this brief introduction, the author of this personal-experience article outlines why, and how, she came to make what was, for her, a sound, sane judgment. Some first-person narratives are written with the intent of creating sympathy in readers by revealing reasons for a seemingly unexplainable action. "I Gave Up My Children," published in *Ladies' Home Journal*, was a true experience written by a woman who gave away her children from an unhappy first marriage. She and her husband were too immature at the time to make the marriage work, and she gave up her children because she felt it would be best for them. She frankly shared her background, the reasons for her decision, her fears, and her hopes for the children, which guided her in making this choice.

In *Redbook*, an article entitled, "City Mouse, Country Mouse," dealt with a simple theme, the true conflict that arose when a young woman from the city married a young man from the country. Each assumed the other would gladly make the change in life style. Soon after they were married, they began jokingly bickering about city versus country. Shortly the good-natured bickering turned first into heated arguments, then into serious fights. When their marriage grew rocky, the couple took stock of the situation, realized that marriage meant mature giving, and reached a compromise that they could both live with.

The writing of these factual confessions parallels the fictional confession stories more closely than some editors of slick women's magazines would like to admit.

In nonfiction confession pieces, as in fictional confessions, you narrate your story in first-person viewpoint. You should explain the conflict, frankly and intimately, and tell how it affected your life. You should tell when and how you came to know that the problem had to be solved, and how you anguished to find a workable, acceptable solution. You should share the actions that you took to free yourself of your problem, or, if your problem is one which could not be rectified, to gain the personal maturity and insight needed to live with the situation.

In true nonfiction confessions, you present the problem quickly, as in a fictional confession. While in the fictional confessions the problem should be described on the first page or the second, in the factual nonfiction confession article, the problem should be spelled out in the *first paragraph (or two)*.

Ideas for nonfiction confession stories that interest editors most have wide appeal to their readerships, which are generally made up of wives, mothers, homemakers, and single women, in a world where roles are rapidly changing. Editors search for problems their readers might face.

You need not write about scandalous or earthshaking personal experiences. In the course of your life you may have made mistakes you later regretted. These experiences, everyday problems, and situations (yours and other people's) are the raw material for factual confessions. Write about them in a factual but interesting manner, with sincerity, emotional impact, and helpful solutions.

Your articles may deal with disciplining children, learning to use credit cards without going into debt, winning over a hostile mother-in-law, or simply learning to say "no" to protect your time so that others don't take advantage of you because you hate to turn down requests for help.

In the factual confession piece sex rarely will be the only source of conflict, although it may be mentioned as a contributing factor to a problem that runs much deeper. Situations such as child abuse, obesity, alcoholism, abortion, living together before marriage, and other timely family and social topics, are excellent themes if you have had such a personal experience, can write of it in a style that is lively and readable, and handle the material with thought and good taste.

After you write your personal-experience narrative, you may wish to begin by submitting it to the big-name slick magazines. However, many articles that make excellent points aren't accepted by these publishers because competition is very keen. The volume of submissions is heavy, in part because these magazines sometimes run announcements encouraging readers, who are not professional writers, to submit their true-life articles, and the payment rates offered by women's slicks are high.

Still, you can often find a market for your personal-experience confessions in the smaller women's magazines, or even in the religious publications. To determine which type of magazine will be the most likely for your manuscript, you must analyze the topic, style, treatment, and vocabulary of your article, as well as the slant of the article. Obviously, you would not submit an article about undergoing an abortion to a Roman Catholic publication; such factors must be considered when searching for markets.

The structure of the factual confession article used by both the women's magazines and religious publications is similar. In some cases, the topics may be identical, but the specific slant will be what tailors the story for one publication or another.

The style of the personal-experience piece used in the women's magazines is personal, serious, low-key. The events are described in narrative, "told," rather than "shown" through heated dialogue and physical action, as they would be in a fictional confession story.

Choice of vocabulary is not as limited as it is in the confession field, because the women who read the slick magazines usually have a high-school or college education. If the unusual or the direct and frank word is the perfect one to describe what you wish to convey, you are free to use it without the risk that the word might not be recognized and understood by the average slick magazine readers.

Problems resulting from unusual sexual experiences, modern life styles, or social conflicts may be used as topics for personal confessions in the slick magazines. Their readers are in a higher-income bracket than the confession-magazine reader, are more liberal and liberated, and not as easily shocked, even by risqué topics.

The religious publications are frequently read by less sophisticated, more conservative, grass-roots Americans. But unlike what one might expect, the personal-experience confessions in religious magazines are not bland, dull, or predictable. On the contrary, they are often lively, captivating, thought-provoking, and emotional. The religious confessions are written in a more confessional, spoken tone than the sophisticated women's magazines.

Guideposts, Faith at Work, Christian Home, Decision, Moody Monthly and scores of other religious publications use this type of confession piece regularly. While the religious doctrines of these magazines may differ, a confession article found in one could easily fit into an issue of another, because the formulas, treatment, and subject matter are nearly identical.

In writing the personal-experience narrative for the religious field, you should make the lead paragraph set the mood of the piece, illustrating your situation and frame of mind, and revealing a sense of urgency as you introduce the problem.

Follow this "mood scene" by the "problem" scene in which the conflict develops. In the true-experience piece, as in the fictional confession story, the situation grows worse, because of personal faults and shortcomings, until there appears to be no way out of your situation. In the fictional confession, however, the heroine finds a unique personal solution from within herself, while in the factual religious confession, you would treat your spiritual problems by way of traditional methods, revealing how faith and adherence to religious doctrines lead to your acceptable solution. The solution to your problem might come through faith, or prayer, or from a concerned person who opens your eyes so you "see" a solution. It should be stressed that you gained renewed faith and strength, as well as insight to deal with the problem, and spiritual growth.

In my story entitled, "The True Gift Of Christmas," which was published by *Faith at Work*, I set the mood in the opening scene:

" 'Tis the season to be jolly . . ."
The Christmas carol playing on the radio mocked me. *I* was anything but jolly!
For me the season had been a series of disappointments, frightening medical problems, and the news that my parents would be unable to come for our long-planned Christmas visit.

As Christmas neared, the trees outside were stark, the ground was barren and covered with brown grass. Instead of fluffy white snow, there were clods of frozen mud. It wasn't Christmas outside.

Even though the bushy pine tree was decorated, with packages in pretty paper under its sweeping boughs, the usual candles and arrangements were in place, and greeting cards arrived with regularity, it wasn't Christmas inside, either.

Two nights before Christmas, my husband came home and informed me we were having company for Christmas Eve after all. When he told me who our guests would be, for a moment I wasn't sure I'd heard him right. Awful memories flooded over me.

I followed this introduction with a quick flashback scene that sketched in the cause behind a friendship broken several years before. I gave reasons for my apprehension and hesitation about resuming the relationship. Then came the "growth" scene:

I saw changes in myself. I had become stronger in my identity. I no longer hid my feelings and suffered in silence. I knew that Christmas would be a time of healing for us. And a time of peace, joy, and friendship.

The guests arrive. Three cold years melt away in the warm glow of renewed friendship, and Christmas Eve became a happy reunion as well as a new beginning.

In this true confession article, the writing style set the mood and underscored the seriousness of the conflict in my life. The growth scene and ending bore out the theme of peace and forgiveness. Because the message was non-denominational, and the theme was universal, the story could have fit into almost any church-related magazine that publishes such articles.

Salable confession articles in the religious field deal with a vast array of topics, ranging from common situations such as being overweight because of personal weakness to infidelity, child abuse, uncontrollable temper, excessive drinking, selfishness, greed, and acts that caused heartbreak for everyone involved.

In the religious field, articles do not necessarily have to be based on your own experiences. You can write true accounts from the lives of friends, if they are willing to share their experiences with you, agree to allow you to market their stories, and give you signed permission to do so. In such instances, even though these are not your own experiences, you still write in the first-person viewpoint. Ask the person questions about her emotional reactions and thoughts when the event was taking place, and have her describe places and people, so you can write what she experienced, as if she were telling it herself.

These articles may be presented under a joint by-line, such as "Jane Doe with Mary Smith," or "by Jane Doe as told to Mary Smith." If your subject is a famous person, some magazines have you write the piece from this famous person's viewpoint. You will collect the check; the famous person will have the sole by-line.

Topics that are salable to the religious publications are often commonplace. What sets the acceptable manuscript apart is that it is written in an enticing manner that can make even an average problem seem unique and interesting.

In an article in *Guideposts* called "Of Elves and Rainbows," the teen-age narrator, who works for an elderly woman after school, finds the old woman so disagreeable that she decides to quit her job to be free of the old lady's sharp tongue and demanding ways. She learns that offering kindness, understanding, and patience, instead of the rejection that would be produced by her resigning, causes the woman to respond with warmth.

"The Healing" (also published in *Guideposts*) is the moving account of a teen-age girl who is rejected by the exchange student who came to live with her family. The narrator is hurt when the visiting student asks to be moved to another home where the parents aren't so strict. The narrator realizes that she is lucky to have parents who care enough to say "no."

"The Right Direction," one of my true-experience confessions published by *Christian Home*, is my personal account of the years when I tried all the latest child-rearing tactics on my children—and failed. After confusion and chaos, I abandoned the "experts," applied my faith to our family situation, and found success and new serenity in our household.

Personal experiences like these, that give spiritual solutions to everyday problems and situations and offer lessons in faith and understanding that can benefit others, appear in issue after issue of the religious publications.

In the religious magazines and the women's publications (unlike the fictional confessions) the writer will have a by-line, which is, of course, valuable. Occasionally, though, facts in a personal-experience article may be too painful for the narrator to share with others without anonymity. Most religious publications realize the sensitive nature of these factual confessions and will print such stories under a pen name, or with the notation "name withheld by request" to avoid possible embarrassment if the writer's true identity is revealed.

The writer should make clear at the time the manuscript is submitted if she wishes to have her name withheld to protect her identity. The manuscript may be submitted under a pen name, but if so, you should give the editor your real name, and you may also indicate your reason (personal or professional) for not using it.

XIV

TITLES TO TEMPT THE READER

To MAKE a good impression in the confession field—
use a suggestive title!

Confession titles are usually quite long, and are in the form of a declarative sentence. The title hints broadly at what "sin" or action the narrator has to confess.

Before sex became acceptable fare for the confession stories, titles were often misleading, simply "come-ons" for readers. They promised wild sex but did not deliver, as in such titles as "Daddy Made a Pass At Me Every Day of My Life." Sound incestuous? The story might have been about a young girl who grows to mature womanhood with her doting Dad making a "pass" by her apartment every day on his way to work to make sure she was all right.

It was simple to come up with provocative titles before stories and articles with explicit sex appeared in the magazines. Now that sex is generally accepted, and in the majority of cases, *required,* you can (and must) deliver what you promise in the title. It is not always easy, however, to come up with an appropriate title that does not give away the climax of the fictional story. For example, when I wrote a confession story dealing with a woman who is lured into working as a sex surrogate at a swingers' club, I first titled it, "I Was a Sex Surrogate." Her job as a surrogate takes place late in the story—near the climax—so I decided this working title ruined the "element of surprise" that I had worked to create. Since the narrator meets her contacts at a swingers' club, I decided that "We Played Mixed Doubles at the Swinging Singles" was more effective. The surprise ending was not spoiled.

In another story, a couple who lived out their weird fantasies in a bizarre sex game didn't always play their games in the privacy of their own home. They got into trouble because they broke society's "rules." The title? "We Got Beat At Our Own Sex Game."

For the tender story of a young married woman who suffers a false pregnancy, the title, "I'm Pregnant with a Baby I'll Never Hold in My Arms," suggests illness or death of mother or child, instead of a false pregnancy. The unsuspected fact there there *is* no baby is kept from the reader until the truth is revealed in the climax scene.

Today, confession titles for *fiction* are lurid, and sometimes a trifle misleading to keep the readers from guessing the outcome of the story. But, titles for the *"factual,"* personal-experience confessions used by the women's magazines tend to be accurate, and honest, with no attempt to be clever or to camouflage an ending.

Usually the titles of factual confessions state simply, in declarative sentences similar to those used in the fictional confessions, what is to be confessed in the article. "I Gave Up My Baby," "I Had an Abortion," "I Abused My Children," "I Was a Battered Wife," "I Had to Choose Between My Career and My Marriage," and "My Ex-Husband Is Getting Married. Should I Let Our Children Go to His Wedding?" are typical of the non-fiction confession.

Confession titles in the religious publications are similar to titles used for short stories in the slick magazines. They tend to be short—a phrase rather than a complete declarative sentence—and usually they relate to the theme of the story or article, or to the event in the story that links the problem to the solution.

"Mama's Life Insurance" was the perfect title for a story in *Guideposts* in which a woman recalls how her mother's faith and belief sustained her throughout life, with "her dividend of hope" cleverly connecting the title to the theme ("insurance"/"dividend").

"One Summer Night" was the title of a story about a child whose spiritual awakening took place on a camping trip, and was later shared in *Guideposts*.

"The True Gift Of Christmas," used in *Faith at Work*, was the perfect title for a personal-experience story stressing spiritual rather than material presents.

Sometimes trying to create a winning title seems to be a losing proposition. The only title that seems to come to mind is unsuitable. If this happens, postpone titling your manuscript for a little while. You don't have to come up with a title until you put your manuscript in the mailbox! Often, as you write, revise, and do the final typing and proofreading, the perfect title will be suggested by a phrase or word or sentence in the story or article itself.

XV

THE MARKET—AND HOW TO REACH IT

To GET AHEAD in confession writing, you must treat it as a business. To be accepted, you must submit what you write, not keep it in your desk drawer.

When I first began submitting confessions, if a story came back rejected, I didn't bother sending it out again—I put it in a drawer, and wrote a new story. I assumed if one editor did not want the story, another confession editor wouldn't, either. One day out of desperation, I cleaned the file drawer and sent out over twenty manuscripts. Two weeks later, much to my surprise, I sold my first confession story—*the second time it was submitted.* Now, many of my stories sell on the initial submission, but others have sold only after as many as fifteen submissions.

The magazines that are markets for fictional and factual confessions, their addresses, requirements, preferred word lengths, payment rates, and other vital information, can be found in the writers magazines or in the market section of *The Writer's Handbook* (published by The Writer, Inc.).

Additional markets can be located by browsing at newsstands. Jot down the names and addresses you have not seen before. This information is usually located on the masthead page.

It is a good idea to buy and read several issues of a publication to become familiar with its special style, characteristics, emphasis, tone, and range of material before you submit your work to it.

Even magazines that do not appear in any market listings may be receptive to the work of free-lance writers. Query the editor if you are in doubt, and request writer's guidelines.

Some confession magazines are published by the same firm, or "group," and these markets state that they consider a single submission as being offered to *all* the confession magazines published by that company. Occasionally a good story *will* be passed from one editor to another. This, however, happens infrequently. Professional confession writers submit each story to an individual editor, by name, within the same confession-magazine publishing "group." Their experience bears out the fact that a story read and rejected by an editor one month may a month later be submitted to, and purchased by, another editor with the same company.

Editors of confession magazines seem to have no special preferences regarding the form of a manuscript as long as it is typed neatly, with dark, readable ink, double-spaced, and has the writer's name on all pages, which, of course, are numbered consecutively. The approximate number of words in the manuscript should appear in the upper right-hand corner of the title page. Always keep a carbon or other copy of your manuscript.

The manuscript should be mailed flat in an envelope large enough to hold it and the folded self-addressed, stamped envelope. A short manuscript of only a few pages may be mailed in a number-ten business envelope with a business-size return envelope and sufficient postage.

As a rule only one story should ever be submitted in an envelope, because to submit two stories in one envelope can appear to give the editor a choice. Stories should be packed and mailed individually, even if you intend to submit two stories to an editor on one date. Of course, the same manuscript should not be submitted simultaneously to more than one publication. An editor assumes that your story is being offered to her exclusively.

A cover letter can be a useless waste of time, or it can be an invaluable aid, depending on what you have to say. As a rule, it is not necessary to write a cover letter stating that you have enclosed a story for the editor to consider and you hope she likes it. Obviously, she can see the story in the envelope, and she can assume that you hope she will like it enough to publish it in her magazine or you wouldn't have submitted it.

A cover letter is appropriate, however, if you have something specific to tell the editor: Perhaps you are submitting a story on a subject about which you have considerable expertise, or are writing about a little-known medical phenomenon. In your cover letter, impress upon the editor the factual nature of the piece by informing her of your credentials or reference materials.

A confession writer I know who was temporarily out of the field began submitting confessions again and wrote to the editors she had worked with informing them that she was back in the field and would be submitting regularly. This is another example of a useful cover letter.

The manuscript may be mailed either first class, or, more inexpensively, by Special Fourth-Class Manuscript

Rate. The average 6,000-word confession (20 pages) will cost only a little more to mail first class, and the service is faster. Special Fourth-Class Manuscript Rate mail is charged by the pound, rather than the ounce. A heavy, book-length manuscript can be mailed inexpensively at fourth-class rates, but the envelope must read, "fourth class." Fourth-class manuscripts will not be forwarded or returned to the sender if undeliverable.

Before mailing your manuscript, record on a card the story or article title; wordage; and a word or two about the theme. Write down the name and address of the editor and the magazine to which you have submitted it, and the date you mailed it. If it is later rejected, write down the date returned, then send it to the next editor on your list, again with notations on the card. Keep these cards in a small filing box. If the story sells, file the notecard with the carbon copy of your script, and the issue of the magazine (or tearsheets) with the published version.

If, according to your records, an editor has held a story an unusually long time (over three months) without responding, write to the editor and inquire courteously about the manuscript. Usually editors reject promptly the material they do not wish to use, and hold longer the works they are seriously considering. Some editors send out acceptance slips, but others do not, and the writer learns that the story has been purchased only when the check arrives. Editors are likely to accept stories and hold them without notifying the writer of the acceptance when dealing with experienced confession writers. These authors will assume that a story is sold if it is not returned within a certain time.

Do not hesitate to write a letter inquiring about the status of your manuscript. Write a follow-up letter, too, if necessary.

"Don't be afraid to write to me about a submission," one confession editor stated. "Often a letter may cause me to make a yes-or-no decision that I've been putting off making."

One of the most worthwhile things that a confession writer can do is to make an "editors' chart." List the editors and the names of all the confession magazines they buy material for. When you submit a confession, write the title and the date you sent it out under the appropriate editor's column. When you finish another confession story, mail it to an editor on the chart to whom you have not submitted a manuscript for that month. Send the story or article out to her and make a note of it under her name. Follow this procedure as you complete new stories. Try to submit one story per month to any magazine under the editor's direction.

If a story is rejected, simply cross it out under the first editor's name, submit it to another editor—one to whom you have not submitted your "limit" of stories for the month—and note this in the appropriate place on your chart.

With an editors' chart you can tell at a glance where a story is, where it has been, for how long, and, also, whether it's time to send another submission to a particular editor. (It is a good rule-of-thumb not to submit more stories per month than an editor has magazines under her editorship. If she edits one magazine, submit one story. Two stories may be submitted if she edits two titles.) This prevents you from accidentally oversubmitting by bombarding one editor with so many stories she must make choices. Only submit more than your limit if the editor requests that you do so.

A "theme chart" is done in the same manner as the "editors' chart": Write on the chart the theme—"sex change," "gay husband," "runaway teen," or whatever—for *accepted* confession stories. This will give you a clue to the stories of yours that a particular editor has bought, and it will ensure that you don't send a story or article on a similar theme to the same editor.

If you then write a story dealing with the same topic, consult your theme chart for an editor who has not purchased a confession story from you on that theme—and send it out to her. She will naturally be more receptive than the editor who already bought a story from you on that particular theme. (Of course, this only applies to *your* work—editors may already have bought a story on the same theme by a different writer, but your viewpoint of that topic may be so different that the stories do not conflict.)

Form rejection slips are the norm with many publishers now, in all fields. In the past, some confession publishers sent detailed criticism with every story they returned. With increasing office expenses and salaries, however, publishers can no longer afford to provide such criticism.

Editors in the confession field are more likely to offer help and advice to writers (for both stories and non-fiction articles) than editors of the slick magazines. This makes rejection slips from confession editors easier to take than turn-downs in other fields.

Personal rejection notes from confession editors are frequent, and when compiled and reviewed, may constitute a mini-course in writing. When a story comes close to being publishable, many confession editors will say so, and may go on to tell the writer exactly why the story wasn't purchased.

Sometimes a manuscript will come back from an editor with a detailed request for revision and the invitation to resubmit. In this case, begin writing immediately! Try to make the story fit the editor's wishes. She knows what she wants. It's up to you to be professional enough to give it to her. Rewrite the piece to her specifications, and, when resubmitting, write a brief cover letter to remind her that she asked to have the piece back for consideration when changes were made.

A writer who shows promise, determination, and a desire to find a place in publishing is sure to get encouragement, and maybe, after the writer has gained a reputation with an editor, assignments.

One confession editor likes working with reliable writers she has come to trust over the course of years. She realizes that occasionally writers can become "dry" of ideas. To alleviate this, she gives her preferred writers "assignments." These assignments are simple. She sends the writer a story title, and asks for a confession story which fits the title. She says: "This ensures that I will always have a suitable cover story, keeps my stories from conflicting with those used by other editors of sister publications, and allows the confession writer to look for a regular income, even in months when her ideas may seem stale." This editor will also look at a list of prospective titles from her preferred writers, and assign them stories to write on their titles.

A writer who will work hard, shows dependability, and is cooperative, is sure to find encouragement from a busy editor who values these qualities. At first, the encouragement may be minor, perhaps, but that is infinitely better than none. And there is a very real chance that if you work hard you can develop a friendly, professional, and mutually rewarding relationship with the editors you write for.

Religious-magazine editors are more likely to offer personal attention than confession editors, to *every* writer, because many times their submission loads are not as heavy. If a personal-experience confession is submitted to a religious magazine, and is good—but not quite on target—the editor may point the writer in the correct direction by suggesting ways to strengthen the article, or supply names of other possible markets. Most letters of rejection have a personal comment which softens the blow.

Frequently a fictional confession story is not purchased the first time or second time out. Maybe not even the fifth or sixth. What then? A perfectly salable story may be rejected because the subject is ahead of its time. Once I wrote what I knew to be a very good story regarding a sex-change operation. I sent it out twelve times. Finally one editor I sold to regularly wrote to say that I treated the topic as if sex changes were common. I still believed in the story; so I decided to bide my time, and I put the story into my files. Two years later when I sent it out, it was accepted immediately. The theme was no longer ahead of its time.

What should you do when faced with rejection? Read between the lines. Revise if requested to do so. Keep your determination up. Continue writing new stories. And above all: *try, try again!*

The confession field pays moderately well. Some magazines pay on acceptance—which means you get your check immediately. Others pay on publication—which means you don't get paid until your story appears in print. Even with pay-on-publication magazines, your accepted story is used and paid for within six months in almost every case.

Most confession magazines pay according to the length of the story, but a few pay a flat rate. The average payment is three to five cents per word, with some publishers setting a maximum of $150.00, while other publishers pay for the total word count regardless of length. A few publishers pay up to ten cents per word, which adds up to a respectable sum for a story.

The pay rates for the leading men's magazines, such as *Playboy, Oui* and *Penthouse,* should you sell them a male-narrated "confession" story, are very high. Payment rates for stories at other men's magazines are comparable to the flat fee, or three-to-five cents a word, paid by the publishers of female confession magazines.

All rights are purchased in the fictional confession field, and many confession publishers have writers sign statements to the effect that if there are any allegations, suits, or legal problems resulting from the story, the writer will be liable for costs. In the religious and general magazines, however, only first rights (the right of the magazine to publish the manuscript only once) are sold as a general rule.

The market for confessions and personal-experience material is wide open. Editors of many magazines are ready and eager to buy your confession stories, factual or fictional. Whether you write for money, to satisfy a need to create, for personal satisfaction, or to offer a solution to a problem, the material is there—deep within you. Write it—and success can be yours.

journey for food had taken too long. Their mates had finally given up and left, the eggs had been stolen by skuas, and most of the stones had been spirited away by other penguins. All that was left was a slight hollow in the rocks and a pitiful few stones that nobody else wanted. But the incoming birds sat there anyway. Occasionally one would stand and stretch its body and neck until it was comically elongated and then snapped back like a rubber band into the normal penguin shape. Then it would flap its flippers madly. This curious ritual passed in waves throughout the colony, as contagious as a yawn.

From where I sat, I could see a lone penguin heading off for food. It looked very thin. Perhaps it was one of the males that had just been relieved. If so, he hadn't wasted much time getting out of there. I watched as he skipped down the slope and hopped over on to the sea ice. He looked like one of the seven dwarfs, on his way to work. Chest thrust out, flippers held out rigidly for balance, he trotted busily along, rocking from side to side, the embodiment of industry and effort. Hi ho, hi ho.

Yesterday evening, over camp dinner, I'd reminded David of Apsley Cherry-Garrard's comment that no creature on Earth had a more miserable existence than an emperor penguin. I'd said that all Antarctic penguins seemed to have a tough life, and I wouldn't like to be reincarnated as any of them.

'It's definitely you against the world if you're an Adélie,' David had replied. 'There's a lot of things conspiring to extinguish your life force. You've got the ice, the ocean, big waves. You're trying to negotiate your way back to your colony, and land on a beach that's being pummelled by ice chunks that weigh tonnes, and there are leopard seals hanging around wanting to eat you. Even back at the colony you still have to worry about stone thieves and skuas, and when, or whether, your mate will come back to relieve you. But I dunno. They seem to smile a lot. They're probably happy.'

leader, Bill Wilson, repeatedly asked the other two if they wanted to return and each time they said no. Later he stopped asking and merely apologised, again and again, for the horrors he had led them into.

Still they trudged on, across the white emptiness of Windless Bight where the snow was so cold that it was like pulling over sand. The men could no longer drag their sledges in tandem. Instead, they had to relay them. Fumble and fasten your harness; heave through the cold and darkness for one mile; unfasten yourself; trudge back; hook up to the second sledge; heave, trudge, unhook, repeat. And all by the light of a naked candle, in temperatures that would freeze your soul.

Next came Terror Point, where the sea ice crams into the island creating mountainous pressure ridges over which they hauled their sledges, one at a time, up, over, down the other side, this one first and then back for the other. And then there were the crevasses. It was impossible in the darkness to see the snow bridges that draped them. All you could do was crash through, hope your harness would hold, climb out, crash through again, and hope and climb and crash and hope again. When they finally reached the emperor rookery, their bodies and minds were all but destroyed.

But at Birdie Bowers's insistence they built themselves a stone igloo. And then, aware that a storm was coming, they hastened down to the rookery and collected five eggs, cushioning them in their mittens. Poor Cherry-Garrard took two, but smashed them both. It wasn't just the darkness; he was also hopelessly short-sighted and the cold meant that he had no chance of wearing his glasses.

It was when they returned to their igloo, three remaining eggs in hand, that the storm struck. It shattered the canvas roof of their igloo. Rocks and snow rained down on them and the wind tore through like an express train. Beaten down by the force of the hurricane, they cowered in their sleeping bags, sucking on snow for water. But somehow, for the two long days that followed, they clung on to some shreds of their selves. They huddled together; they said 'please' and 'thank you'; they sang hymns, feebly, against the roar of the wind.

And then, when the storm finally died down, they staggered out of the igloo and went to look for their tent. I still can't believe they did that. In the half-light, in the aftermath of the most ferocious storm they had ever witnessed, they decided to look for their tent. It should have been impossible; there was almost no chance of finding it. But they went looking anyway. And perhaps the hymns had worked, because – miraculously – there it lay, intact, closed up like a furled umbrella, less than a kilometre away. Now they knew they would live.

Cherry-Garrard described Wilson and Bowers as 'gold, pure, shining, unalloyed. Words cannot express how good their companionship was.'[13] Both of them perished with Scott on the way back from the Pole, leaving Cherry-Garrard haunted by their deaths.

The eggs they collected are now housed by the Natural History Museum in its tiny outpost in the Hertfordshire town of Tring. One of the embryos is there too, sitting on a shelf in a jar of spirits, a forlorn white scrap with bulbous eyes, soft beak and tiny, perfectly formed wings. The remaining two embryos were passed from scientist to scientist, until 1934, when C. W. Parsons of the University of Glasgow finally concluded they had not 'greatly added to our knowledge of penguin embryology'.[14]

Cherry-Garrard was a romantic, especially about the process of discovery. 'Science is a big thing if you can travel a Winter Journey in her cause and not regret it,' he wrote.[15] And though the samples they collected turned out to be scientifically useless, he didn't regret it. Not one bit. With his two companions, he was

the first person in the world to see emperor penguins in the wintertime, eggs balanced on their feet to protect them from the sea ice, huddling together against the cold and wind and darkness.

'After indescribable effort and hardship we were witnessing a marvel of the natural world, and we were the first and only men who had ever done so,' he wrote. 'We were turning theories into facts with every observation we made.'[16] He, Wilson and Bowers were the first to share the penguins' world and the first almost to perish in it. And they did it all through sheer bloody-minded, insane, heroic effort.

The next morning, I walked back down on my own for another look at the Adélies. I passed Shackleton's hut, stumbling slightly on the stubbly volcanic rock streaked white with old guano. A skua down in a hollow began beating its wings and scolding me. When it saw it had my attention it took off, flapping in an unnecessarily showy way. Beyond it I could just see the egg on the ground that it was trying to distract me from.

I steered politely away and continued down to the colony, where I found a warm spot out of the wind. I was careful not to get too close to the penguins. The Antarctic Treaty forbids you from approaching any wildlife here – though it's OK if they come up to you. (To do the work that David and all the other researchers do here requires careful scientific justification and vast numbers of forms and permits. Even to visit here I had to be included on one of his permits, but after what he said I had no intention of violating the penguins' personal space, or, indeed, their sense of self.)

My vantage point was surprisingly restful. Most of the penguins were lying on nests, chattering vaguely to themselves. Occasionally, a bird trotted by for what I now recognised as a nest relief. Several were returning to empty nests. Thanks to the blocking sea ice the

'Even this year, when all their efforts are doomed by the iceberg?'

'You feel sorry for the parents who are doing their best to replace themselves. They don't know it, but I know that it's impossible. You can't just tell them, "You should just hang out now, relax, try again next year." It can be a little sad.'

Now I watched as the black spot grew smaller against the ice, taking the first steps of his thirty-kilometre round trip. There was something idiotically noble and, yes, almost human, about this endeavour, this appalling bloody-mindedness. There was no chance that there would be anything left to play for when he returned but he was doing it anyway. I remembered now what David said to me when I first arrived: 'Penguins have no self-doubt.' Trot trot trot, he went. Trot trot trot.

A large black eye was watching me steadily through the tight mesh of a fence. Its owner stood almost as high as my waist. He was pressed up against the wire, a few white feathers poking through. I was on the outside. He, however, was trapped. Leaning over the fence and looking down on him, I could see the smooth black top of his head, and the stripe of Velcro that had been glued on to his back. He continued to stare fixedly ahead.

My new acquaintance was an emperor penguin, the tallest and most regal of all Antarctica's birdlife. It was also, currently, an inmate of the 'penguin ranch', which was a set of brightly coloured huts out on the sea ice, a few hours' drive from McMurdo. I had come here in my favourite vehicle – the Mattrack with the bizarre triangular wheels that I'd also used to visit the seal camp – on a gorgeous sunny day, the temperature barely below freezing, the air completely still. The sign on the door behind me showed a Wild West cartoon of an emperor penguin, complete with cowboy hat, merrily riding a Weddell seal. Until now I had been in a buoyant mood, but I couldn't help feeling sorry for this magnificent bird. He looked like he was in prison.

The chief scientist of the operation, Paul Ponganis from Scripps Institute of Oceanography in San Diego, came out of the hut to greet me. Paul was another old Antarctic hand; he had been coming here about as long as David Ainley, and had a similar weather-beaten look, although his floppy white hair was tidier and more luxuriant, and he was much more at ease with people.

There are almost 100,000 pairs of emperors around the Ross Sea and about 350,000 around Antarctica, which is to say about 350,000 breeding pairs in the world. Like the Adélies, emperors are true Antarcticans; they never stray far from the continent's encircling ice. Paul sets up this emperor camp every year. He comes out on to the sea ice, catches a few non-breeding penguins and keeps them in a holding pen like the one in front of us. The fence ran unevenly round a large patch of ice containing perhaps a dozen birds, all standing more or less still in the bright sunlight.

I had seen many photographs of emperors, but they were even lovelier in the flesh. Their bellies were a soft creamy white. On each side of their heads was a white patch that shaded into gold. The side of their beaks bore a stripe of pink, which changed to a deep purplish blue at the tip. Their necks were impressively mobile. Some retracted them until they almost disappeared while others snaked their heads upwards or bent through what seem like impossible angles to preen their feathers or scratch their backs. They were sinuous and amazingly graceful. When one of the penguins balanced on one foot and his tail to scratch his head with the other foot, he still managed to look poised and polished.

Unlike the busybody Adélies, these birds had apparently decided that energy should not be wasted in stress or panic.

Their strategy was not to pack the entire breeding cycle into the few short months of the Antarctic summer, but to start early, brave the darkness and cold, turn their collective backs to the wind and incubate their eggs through the depths of the winter. That way, the chicks would become independent at the height of summer, when there was maximum food to be had. This is also why Cherry-Garrard and his friends had to make their winter journey; if they had waited till spring, the eggs would already have hatched.

In the centre of the pen a rough round hole, cut into the sea ice, was floating with pale green slush. A penguin emerged suddenly from inside the hole with a rush of wings and water. He landed on the ice with a thump, stood up and started to shiver, tapping his feet, quivering and shaking his head. 'That's Jerry – he shivers the most,' said Paul. 'The peripheries get cold when they dive – the wings can get to 32°F. And he's a good hunter so he'll have all this cold fish in his stomach. He has to warm everything up.'

As if in sympathy, the other birds started shaking their heads and stretching their wings out to the sun. But every movement was still somehow refined. If the Adélies were the over-caffeinated Jack Russell terriers of the penguin world, these creatures were more like Great Danes, measured and stately, using energy only when it was strictly called for.

I knew that the birds weren't exactly trapped; they were free to dive any time they liked. But the hole inside their pen was the only one around – Paul had checked carefully that there were no cracks in the ice for a radius of several kilometres – so they always had to come back to where they started. And seeing them confined on the surface like this was making me feel uncomfortable. Paul noticed me staring again at the first penguin I saw, the one pressing up against the wire. 'That's Zachary, my favourite,' he said. 'Whenever we're doing something with one of the other birds he comes over, checks us out, squawks at us, pecks at our bums.'

I was glad Zachary still had spirit. But something about the way he was pushing up against the wire made me want to bust him and all the other emperors out of the place. And yet, if I pulled down the fence, they would simply walk on to another patch of identical ice and do exactly what they were doing now. They were not humans. They were animals. I must not anthropomorphise them. Regardless of the presence of the fence, they were currently behaving just as nature intended.

I shook myself mentally and tried to pay attention. Paul was now telling me what he did with the penguins. Knowing that they had to come back here at the end of every dive meant he could attach sophisticated measuring devices to the birds, and recover the data when they returned. He glued on those Velcro strips with epoxy resin, then attached mini backpacks containing instruments that measured, for instance, the oxygen in their lungs and blood. 'As long as the backpack doesn't wobble, the birds don't mind,' Paul said. 'Unless you work with these birds you don't realise how strong they are. The backpack is nothing to them – it weighs less than two pounds.' But what about the Velcro strip? 'No problem. When they moult, they lose the Velcro and the glue, too.'

And the whole point of this effort was to follow these creatures underwater. Emperors are the most accomplished divers of all Antarctic birds – they can plunge to an amazing 1,500 feet below the surface and stay down for fifteen minutes, holding their breath all the way. To do this, they have developed some bizarre Antarctic adaptations. They slow down their heart rate and reduce their metabolism so dramatically that they end up diving in what to us would seem like a coma. They also have to eke out what little oxygen they have in their lungs, drip-feeding it to their muscles to make it last.

Paul's backpacks sought to measure all of this by recording the birds' oxygen levels at every stage of the dive. 'We can see how low the oxygen goes,' Paul said. And on the longer dives, his instruments showed that the penguins were returning on empty. By the time they judged the size of their hole, adjusted their swimming speed and shot back up into the air they had almost no oxygen left to speak of. 'They can function at the very far end, at levels so low that we would pass out.'[17]

In principle, Paul just wanted to understand how the birds achieve all this. But there could even be some kind of human application. Oxygen is powerful stuff. We breathe it to get enough energy from our muscles to be big and vigorous but, untamed, it can also tear our bodies' cells to shreds. In human heart attacks and strokes, oxygen gets temporarily shut off, but the real damage happens when the gas comes flooding back in unchecked. When these birds took their first breaths back in the air after a long dive, they had to be able to handle going instantaneously from zero to plenty. Maybe the penguins had some kind of special antioxidants. Maybe there was something we could borrow.

To the side of the hut was the entrance to the 'Observation tube', a cylinder sunk through the sea ice, which could give you a hint of the emperors' underwater world. From the surface it looked like a wide plastic chimney painted hospital green. Paul hefted off the wooden cover and I stepped gingerly in, feeling with my feet for the triangular hoops that served as a stepladder. For the first time I realised how thick the sea ice here was. I had accepted the idea that we could drive on it, build huts on it, land planes on it, but still it was shocking to climb down three feet, six feet, ten, fifteen and not have reached the water.

By the time I arrived at the bottom of the tube, where there were Perspex windows and a viewing platform, I was shivering in the dank coldness. A ghostly green light was filtering through the thick overhead ice, just enough to make out the many penguins in the water around me. I was astonished by the way they moved. On the surface they were sinuous and graceful and a little bit slow, so in the water I had half expected them to be like seals, writhing and balletic. But no. They were torpedoes. They were bullets. Whoosh! They ripped past me, leaving only a trace of tiny bubbles in their wake. Like shooting stars they were there, and then they were gone.

Dumont d'Urville, the main French base in Antarctica, is a haven for penguin researchers. Not only is it built around an Adélie colony, but it is also the only year-round station on the entire continent that has an emperor penguin colony within strolling distance. The movie *The March of the Penguins* was filmed there, and French scientists have been studying their imperial neighbours continuously since 1956.

The base lies more than 1,500 miles south of Hobart, at the very edge of the East Antarctic Ice Sheet, and the usual way to get there is by sea. Long-suffering French Antarcticans sail back and forth between Hobart and DDU, as the locals call it, on a notorious little ship. The *Astrolabe* is bright green and plucky and 200 feet long, with a rounded hull that helps prevent her from being crushed in the pack ice but does little or nothing for her stability as she lurches through the big seas of the roaring forties and the furious fifties. The journey south can take anything between five and ten days, while waves lash the windows all the way up to the bridge, the ship yaws and rolls and most people lie in their beds, groaning weakly and trying not to think of food.

Luckily for me, there was another way. The French had an agreement with the Italians to share the use of a Twin Otter plane each summer season. It usually flew between the Italian and French bases, but if I had not mistaken a crackly HF radio conversation, it would swing by McMurdo to pick me up and fly me and a couple of other passengers over to DDU.

The plane was piloted by a cheerful Canadian called Bob Heath, who looked like a dark-haired Santa Claus. He was bearded, and rotund, with a booming belly laugh and an irreverent line in pre-flight briefings. 'You have the usual choice between too hot and too cold. If you're too hot or too cold let us know. We won't change anything, but we'll look sympathetic.' (I learned later that he spoke both French and Italian fluently but with equally atrocious accents, and that everybody loved him.)

The temperature on board might not have been perfect (too hot, in this case, and we all ended up stripping off most of our compulsory cold-weather gear) but the flight itself was gorgeous. We passed over the sepia mountains and sweeping glaciers of the Dry Valleys before hitting the blank white slate of the East Antarctic Ice Sheet. The first sign that we were reaching the coast was a set of crevasses running in parallel lines as the ice sheet began to feel the sloping of the rock beneath. As the ground steepened, the ice became stippled and tinged with blue until it terminated abruptly in great white cliffs that reminded me, incongruously, of the chalk cliffs of Dover.

DDU itself was on an island, part of a small archipelago about a kilometre from the coast. It had jaunty bright buildings painted orange, red and blue, built apparently on stilts on the uneven rock, and connected with steel walkways. Perhaps it was because the island was half-covered with snow, or perhaps it was the rocks, which were paler than McMurdo's grimy volcanic base, but the base looked lovely – less of a mining town and more of a holiday camp.

After the formality of the American system, I was struck by

how little orientation I was given here and how few forms (none) I needed to fill in. I was just welcomed, shown to my room, which was bright and pleasant, though small, with two bunk beds, a desk and little else, and then led off for dinner in the main set of buildings.

They say that Antarctica magnifies people's personalities and perhaps it does the same for cultures. The immediate impression that I had on meeting French Antarcticans for the first time was their attitude to food. This was a small base, with perhaps sixty people in the summer and maybe twenty or thirty in the winter, but they had two chefs – one for the main meals and one to make fresh bread, pastries and delicate little cakes. At Mactown, alcohol was forbidden in the galley except on the most special of occasions. At DDU there were carafes of wine at the table every dinnertime.[18] What's more, we sat down, eight to a table, and had waiters serve us four courses – starter, main, cheese, dessert. Everyone on the base took turns at being waiter for the day. Why did they do this? Why not just have self-service? My hosts were bemused at the question. 'Because it's civilised' was the best that someone could manage.

While McMurdo was also like a large staging post, this base was much more of a destination. People didn't just come in order to bounce on out to field camps; they stayed here to do their science. And the reason was the overwhelming abundance of Antarctic life that crammed every corner of this small island. As well as the emperors, Weddell seals dotted the remaining sea ice, skuas and snow petrels flew overhead and Adélie penguins were everywhere underfoot.

DDU was built back in the days when there were no rules about staying away from penguins, and approaching them only sensitively, armed with stacks of permits. In the 1950s, before the Antarctic Treaty even existed, you could build a station wherever you liked, even smack in the middle of a huge Adélie colony.

They were everywhere, hooting, hollering and honking. Unlike at Cape Royds, there was also an unmistakable and pervasive smell. Throughout the base, the air was thick with the heady, ripe, fishy reek of guano, produced by the overactive metabolism of birds that were in a hurry.

It was appropriate in a way that the Adélies should be here. DDU was named after nineteenth-century French explorer Jules Dumont d'Urville, who discovered this part of the Antarctic coast in 1840. There was a bust of him outside the main building, square of jaw and of shoulder, with his captain's epaulettes, looking nobly out to sea. (Another French explorer's ship was called *Pourquoi Pas? – Why Not? –* which is as good a way as any to explain the motivation of many of the early heroic adventurers.) Jules's wife was called Adèle, which is why this part of Antarctica is called Adélie Land, and also where the Adélie penguins got their name.

Still it seemed odd to find the Adélies so tangled up with human habitations. Their nests peppered the rocks surrounding each of the buildings, they hopped over and under the steel walkways and used the human-made snow paths to trot down to the sea.

The next morning, on my way to visit the emperor colony, I was treated to an extreme version of this. In front of me, two French workers were sauntering down one of the snow paths, not moving quite quickly enough for an Adélie coming up behind. In a flash, this little creature, which barely reached their knees, marched up, extended its flipper, and gave a mighty *whack!* on one person's calf. He jumped to one side and yelped and the penguin trotted on past. Out of my way. Job done.

I was impressed. David Ainley had told me they did this, but I hadn't quite believed him. I would come back to the Adélies later – I had already made an appointment to talk to the researchers about them when I'd finished with the emperors.

But for now, I registered that one little whack had won over a corner of my heart. It wasn't the cuteness that was beginning to captivate me, but the bravado, their sheer pint-sized chutzpah.

The emperors were at the back of the island, the south side facing the mainland, where a drape of sea ice remained from the winter. My guide was Caroline Gilbert, a penguin researcher in her early thirties from the Hubert Curien Institute at the University of Strasbourg. She warned me to be careful as we left the rocky island and stepped out on to the sea ice. It was mainly thick enough to bear us, but where it abutted the rocks there could be dangerous cracks.

I already knew about this. Over breakfast that morning the station doctor, Didier Belléoud, had told me cheerfully that somebody fell in there every year. He had come down to spend his second winter here, and – as is traditional at the base – he would also be base commander on the principle that unless someone fell sick he would otherwise have the least to do. But already this year he had been called into dramatic action. Within two hours of arriving he had to perform an appendectomy on a mechanic. The summer doctor on station was the anaesthetist, and the two vets helped. (I tried to imagine how I would feel coming round from an operation to find two vets looking down at me, and decided that I didn't want to know.) The mechanic was apparently fine.

We had safely navigated this danger zone and were now on the sea ice proper, which felt just as solid as the land. Though we were not yet at the colony, we were already starting to see lone emperors sliding past. They were zipping along on their bellies, but still they did it with dignity. If an Adélie penguin were tobogganing like this it would be exuberant, but the emperors were businesslike in their approach. They paddled efficiently with their feet, right, left, right, left, picking up impressive speed, while their heads remained motionless and their flippers stayed neatly at their sides.

Now we had reached the colony, where several thousand birds, loosely gathered, were standing around near their chicks. Their cackling was loud but oddly muffled. The adults looked like slightly officious aldermen. They moved ponderously, their ample bellies spilling slightly over what would be their trousers, the gold at their throats like a mayoral chain. Their infants, a soft dove-grey colour with big owlish eyes, had the impertinence that comes from privilege. As Caroline disappeared off to survey her subjects, I sat on the snow a little way off the colony, and a bevy of chicks immediately came and crowded around me, staring with open, confident curiosity.

Caroline returned from her sweep of the birds and crouched down next to me. 'Lots of people prefer the Adélies,' she said. 'They're easier because they have their own nesting sites. Emperors are more anonymous. It's very difficult to recognise individuals and get involved in their behaviour. But I prefer emperors, because they're more peaceful.'

The chicks were in late adolescence. They were almost as tall as their parents and, already, most of them had started losing some of their downy coats and showing patches of their adult feathers. They would soon need to go off and forage for themselves, building up fat reserves to see them through the winter. But it would be in a few years' time, when they were old enough to breed, that the fat would really hit the fire. Emperor penguins, particularly the males, have one of the toughest winter experiences on Earth. Unlike real aldermen, their dangling bellies come from cold hard necessity.

The whole thing begins in April, just after the sea has hardened for the winter, when males and females reconvene at the colony – a patch of sea ice usually in the lee of some cliffs or other nearby landmark. They quickly meet, woo and mate.

Emperors are deeply loyal for the season, but like the Adélies they are serial monogamists. If last year's mate doesn't show up on time, they will quickly find someone else. They have to. Time is too short to tarry. Those that have paired will stand slightly out of the crowd, billing and cooing a little to make sure they are fully imprinted on each other.

A few weeks later, the female will lay a single egg, which drains much of her body's remaining reserves. In a delicate operation, she carefully shifts it on to her mate's feet. Even here, which is one of the most northerly colonies in Antarctica, temperatures can by now be as low as -4°F, and if an egg touches the ice for more than a few minutes, the chick inside will perish.

The female will now disappear; she will walk until she finds open water, and then feed herself furiously to make up for the weight she has lost. The male will be left holding the egg, for two months, sometimes more. He can't eat. He can only wait, and hope. The nights will grow darker and longer, the temperature colder, storms and winds will whip up into a frenzy. But he must shut down and carry on. He has a special silhouette, hunched and quiet. Only if he stands up and stretches can you see the flash of white that is the egg, before he settles down again, draping his stomach, keeping his infant warm.

Caroline's research was about what happens during that long dark winter after the females have left and before the eggs have hatched. She became fascinated by how the males can survive the cold, the hunger and the wind. So four years ago she chose five males that had successfully mated and would therefore be incubating eggs, caught and instrumented them before the females left, and then watched them throughout the winter.

The instruments were complicated. Working with the doctor in a specially adapted operating theatre, wearing blue hospital gowns, hair nets, sterile rubber gloves and using sterile green sheets, she surgically implanted a data logger to record the temperature just under the skin and the bird's core temperature.[19] On its back, she glued another logger measuring temperature and light levels. She painted a number on its white breast using a home-made preparation of a black waterproof liquid, and stuck a piece of coloured tape under the feathers on its back. That way she could use binoculars to see either the colour or the number, depending on whether the bird was facing inwards or out.[20]

Didn't the operation and the instruments bother the penguins? 'No. We followed them closely and they behaved completely naturally. They still had eggs, chicks, went out to sea. We really do care about not disturbing them. They need to live their life. If not we don't get good data.'

And then her professional detachment left her for a moment. 'I went almost mad with them,' she says. 'I had to know everything. They're so human-like you really get attached. If they're not marked you can't follow them, you don't recognise them. But for the marked males I watched everything. If you spend three hours every day watching, taking notes, by the end you need it. When the weather was too bad with snow and wind and I had to stay here it was frustrating. It's like a drug. I needed to see them. You get addicted, you want to know what they're doing, is the female back? Does he still have the egg? Is everything OK? In some ways they were my experiment. In some ways they were my friends.'

Unlike virtually all other seabirds, emperors are not at all territorial. They don't even have their own nest sites, unless you count their feet. Instead, charmingly, they actually huddle together to stay warm.[21]

And it works. Caroline's experiments show that temperatures within the huddle can be searing. In a lab, the magic numbers for an emperor penguin are between 14°F and 68°F. Above that range the penguins start to sweat. Below, they have to expend extra energy to lift their temperatures upwards. In between, they're happy.

But the sensors Caroline implanted showed that inside the huddle, the temperature of the penguins' skin often shot up above the magic 68°F mark and sometimes got as high as 98.6°F. They ought to have overheated, but they didn't. The core temperature stayed absolutely set at 96.8°F, the optimum value to incubate the eggs.

Caroline thinks that the birds selectively shut down their metabolism depending on how warm they get. From the outside the temperature is bitter, the winds biting. But inside the huddle, the birds are drowsy and warm. It's as if they're in a deep sleep, hibernating vertically, with an occasional shuffle to shift whose turn it is to take the outside slot, and turn their broad black backs against the wind and snow.[22]

Now the emperors' achievement sounded less like a heroic struggle against the odds, and more like a warm bath or a long lie-in. When I said this to Caroline, she shrugged. 'Emperors are Zen. They know how to be here in the winter. We can learn a lot from them.

'A plumber who wintered with me said that Adélies are like the summer people, frantic, all over the place, so much to do! Emperors are like winterers. They're quiet, calm and focused. The winterers here leave car, home, France, everything behind. To survive here in the winter you have to cooperate, just like the penguins.'

That afternoon I went back out on to the sea ice, this time on my own. Already the mood had changed; the sky was darkening and the wind was rising. Though the chicks came back up to me, they now had chunks of hard wet snow lodged in their downy fur. I tried to imagine how it would feel to spend a winter out here on the ice. That morning, lying in the pleasant sunshine, I had been half joking when I talked to Caroline about long lie-ins and warm baths. But now that every bit of my exposed skin was being whipped by the growing wind, I felt a proper respect for the emperors.

Their story was certainly a romantic one. Caroline had described the scene when the long-awaited females return from their foraging. Each will pause on the edge of the vast huddles of males, sing, stop, listen for an answer, and walk on. Three or four times she will sing, then – among the calls of thousands – she hears the answer she has been waiting for. She brightens, lifts her head. The male shuffles eagerly towards her, balancing the egg or perhaps even the chick. And the two birds hug. They really do. They press their chests up against each other and stroke each other's heads.

I saw now that this wasn't anthropomorphising the birds so much as putting affection in its proper place in nature. The emperors hug for more or less the same reason that we humans do. Evolution insists on that level of connection and commitment for all of us, as a necessary counter to the harshness of the world outside.

I also thought of what Caroline said at the end. 'To survive here in the winter you have to cooperate, just like the penguins.' That's how Apsley Cherry-Garrard and his two companions made it out of their appalling winter journey. They huddled together in their makeshift igloo. They said 'please' and 'thank you' and kept each other's hopes alive.

That evening the wind picked up even more. As we ate in the dining room we heard it tuning up outside and then launching into a full-blooded symphony. It started with a rumbling bass, then a throaty roar, with a high-pitched whistling and whining around the windows. As the intensity increased, the middle register came in and I could feel the building swaying slightly. Someone said that it had reached 100 knots.

After the dessert plates were cleared by today's band of waiters, everyone else gathered around the large TV screen for a showing of *Braveheart*, but I pulled on my parka and slipped outside. The blast of the wind in my face took my breath away. Imagine riding full tilt on a motorbike without a helmet. Imagine sticking your head out of the window of a speeding intercity train. I hung on to the railing helplessly for a moment until I could steady my feet against the onslaught. I pulled on my goggles and, bowing my head and shoulders, I dragged my way up the steel walkway and on to one of the paths that has a rope strung alongside – I now knew why.

The Adélies lay impassively on their nests. They were hunkered down, drawn into themselves so that they had become the shape and size of rugby balls; they were facing into the wind, their eyes closed, their feathers caked in snow. Unobserved by them, or indeed by anyone else, I dragged my way round to the lee of the hill that tops the island. This felt crazy. Already my shoulders were starting to ache.

Once in the wind shadow of the hill, I could stand more or less upright; there were still strong gusts but I was free of that relentless onslaught. I made my way carefully down to the water. The wind was coming from behind, from the continent. It was born up on the domes that marked the high points of the East Antarctic Ice Sheet. The still, cold air spilled down the sides of these domes, gathering momentum as it fell, Niagara-like, until it reached the coast with the force of a hurricane. From where I sat, wedged up against a rock at the water's edge, I could actually see the wind arriving around the sides of the hill. It sent the snow on the ground curling upwards like smoke, and skimmed across the surface of the water leaving stippled waves and spray in its wake.

I decided to try to climb up the hill, but soon I was on hands and knees, and then lying almost flat and inching upwards, while

the gusts threatened to pull me away from the rocks I was clinging to. I hadn't even reached the top when, raising my head
slightly, I felt the full force of the wind like a water cannon and I
was shaken. This wasn't fun any more. Spooked now, I stumbled
and tripped back down to the nearest walkway where I dragged
myself back to the dorm building. I was out for only two hours.
Habitations and help were always at hand. I couldn't begin to
imagine how the early explorers coped with those conditions
out on the ice, on their own.

The next morning the wind had abated just enough for me to
fight my way out to inspect the damage. I rounded the hill and
stared south in astonishment. Between us and the mainland there
was now nothing but clear blue water. The solid sea ice that I had
walked on the previous day had blown clean away, taking the
emperors and chicks with it.

The penguins wouldn't especially care. They would be used to
it. Now they would be off somewhere in the sea, huddled
together on the floating ice floes beloved of cartoonists. But even
though I'd been out last night in the wind's full fury, I still couldn't
believe that it could pick up an entire stretch of solid sea ice and
whisk it all away.

When Australian geologist Douglas Mawson hatched his plan to
explore the newly discovered Adélie Land, west of Cape Adare,
he had no idea that he was choosing one of the windiest spots on
the windiest continent on Earth. Perhaps he would have come
here anyway. He was, above all, a scientist. He had no interest in
stunts such as a dash to the geographic South Pole, a random
point in a featureless landscape that is the notional axis around
which the Earth spins but has otherwise little to recommend it.
Instead, as part of Shackleton's *Nimrod* expedition, Mawson had
travelled to the south magnetic pole, a much more scientifically
satisfying spot that marked the place where all the Earth's

magnetic field lines gather together – and could help explain the behaviour of compasses the world over.

Now Mawson wanted more. Adélie Land offered the dual prospect of exploring further the strange magnetic fields around the south geomagnetic pole, as well as performing geological studies that could connect this unknown terrain with previous explorations to the east.

Mawson would have been a valuable member of anyone's team. He was six feet three, physically strong, relentlessly determined and an intellectual powerhouse. And he had Antarctic form. Scott had already tried to persuade Mawson on to his latest expedition, even offering him a guaranteed place in the sledging team that would make the latest attempt on the Pole. Not a chance. Mawson had his own scientific agenda and he was sticking to it.

So on 8 January 1912, just a week before Scott's team would be trudging wearily to the geographic pole, Mawson's own Australasian Antarctic Expedition steamed into a bay just to the east of what is now Dumont d'Urville. Even while they were unloading their equipment and building their huts, Mawson and his men began to realise what they might be up against. The winds were extraordinary. The invisible air picked up materials and equipment weighing hundreds of pounds and flung them around like matchsticks, before shattering them on the rocks. Mawson and his expeditionary team learned the art of 'hurricane walking', leaning so far into the wind that it seemed they were perpetually on the point of crashing face first into the ground (and when, on occasion, the mischievous wind dropped for a moment, so did the hurricane walkers).

Describing the experience drove the pragmatic Mawson to poetic heights: 'The climate proved to be little more than one continuous blizzard the year round; a hurricane of wind roaring for weeks together, pausing for breath only at odd hours,' he wrote.[23] 'A plunge into the writhing storm-whirl stamps upon the senses an indelible and awful impression, seldom equalled in the whole gamut of natural experience. The world a void, grisly, fierce and appalling. We stumble and struggle through the Stygian gloom; the merciless blast – an incubus of vengeance – stabs, buffets and freezes; the stinging drift blinds and chokes.'[24]

One of Mawson's colleagues, a young lieutenant named Belgrave Ninnis, who had been passed on to Mawson from Shackleton, took a more whimsical approach to his description. 'It really looks as if there must have been a large surplus of bad weather left over after all the land had been formed at the Creation, a surplus that appears to have been dumped down in this small area of Antarctica.'[25]

Come the end of the winter, having been largely trapped in their hut by the force of the endless storms, the men were restless and ready for work. Three parties set out with dog teams in different directions, all still battling the ongoing gale. Ninnis joined Mawson and another man – Xavier Mertz – on what was likely to be the toughest leg, a long sledging journey to the far east.

The men had been sledging east for more than a month and all seemed well, when the first disaster came not from the wind, but the ice. Ninnis was travelling behind the other two men, jogging along beside his sledge. Mawson heard a faint whine and assumed one of the dogs had received an encouraging flick of Ninnis's whip. But when he turned, there was no sign of Ninnis, dogs or sledge, just a gaping hole in the snow. Mertz and Mawson raced to the edge of the hole. Peering into the darkness they could see one wounded dog and a few items of equipment on a shelf 150 feet down, far beyond their longest rope. Of Ninnis and the rest of the dogs there was no sign. They shouted for hours but they were powerless to help.

Beyond the horror at the sudden loss of their companion

came the realisation that they themselves were now in terrible trouble. Assuming that the first sledge would be the more vulnerable to crevasses, they had packed almost everything of value on the second one; most of the food, the tent, the spare clothes, the six best dogs, and all of the dog food had now vanished, with Ninnis, into the ice sheet. The only way home would be with makeshift gear, feeding the dogs to each other and to themselves. 'Mawson and I have to hold together, and with the few remaining things, to do our best to find the way back to the Winter Quarters,' Mertz wrote in his diary. In his, Mawson wrote: 'May God help us.'[26]

Within days they were boiling dog paws to make them palatable, hungrily devouring every bit of the scrawny animals left behind. The livers were especially tasty, but also deadly. Neither man knew that dog livers contain poisonous amounts of vitamin A. Indeed, nobody at the time knew that vitamin A, or any of the other vitamins, even existed. But they did notice that they were unaccountably weakening. The skin began sloughing off their feet and hands. Pale blood trickled from their nostrils and fingernails. Mertz eventually died in Mawson's arms, and, after two days sitting helplessly beside the body, Mawson buried him and struck out again, alone.

Shortly afterwards, the snow gave way beneath him. 'So this is the end,' he thought with weary resignation as he fell. But the sledge above him jammed in the hole that he had broken through and he came up short, dangling in his harness at the end of 14 ft of rope. Without stopping to think he began the climb back out. A tremendous struggle brought him to a knot in the rope, then to another. He reached the overhanging snow lid, was on the point of heaving himself out, when the snow gave way and he crashed back down.

Now he was dangling again in the faint blue light of the crevasse, turning slowly as the rope twisted this way and that. He had nothing left. His only two regrets were that he had not eaten all the remaining food when he could, to have felt satiated for one last time in his life; and that he had no pill in his pocket with which to achieve a painless death. Instead the end was to be slow and miserable. Or, he could just slip out of his harness and fall into the darkness below. His hand moved to the straps.

What would you have done? What would I?

It was at this point that Mawson remembered the lines from Robert Service's poem 'The Quitter':

> *Just have one more try – it's dead easy to die*
> *It's the keeping-on-living that's hard.*

And he chose pain, and life. He took his hand from the harness buckle and put it instead on the rope. *Heave.* Then another hand. *Heave.* Somehow he managed to haul himself out a second time. He lay on the snow for several hours, unable to move. Then, endowed by nature with the belligerent drive for survival that marks out all true Antarcticans, both human and animal, he roused himself, prepared some food, and constructed a rope ladder for all the subsequent times that he would crash into crevasses between here and home.

When Mawson finally reached the edge of the plateau he was already nine days late for his rendezvous with companions, and ship, back at Winter Quarters. The danger from crevasses was all but over, but now he had to contend again with the Adélie Land winds that came roaring down on him from the ice sheet. Twice he was stuck in his makeshift tent for two days, while the clock ticked and the prospect of rescue receded. 'The tent is closing in by weight of snow and is about coffin size now,' he wrote. 'It makes me shudder.'[27]

At last he reached Aladdin's Cave, a magical place of scintillating ice crystals that the men had used for storage, less than six

miles from the hut. There, Mawson gorged on oranges and pine-
apples while the blizzard roared about him day and night, trapping
him for a week of agonised impatience before there was just
enough of a lull for him to slip and slide down the ice to Winter
Quarters. But the hurricanes of Adélie Land had played their
final cruel trick of timing on this great survivor. Staring out to
sea he could just make out a black speck on the horizon. He was
too late. The ship had gone.

Five people had volunteered to stay behind, not to rescue him
– he was presumed dead – but to seek out his corpse in the
spring. Desperately they sent a radio message begging the ship to
return. But the brief lull in the weather was over and the winds
returned in furious form. It was no longer safe to attempt a
landing. The ship steamed back to Hobart, and Mawson was left
trapped on the continent for another winter, with the darkness
and the blizzards, and a handful of reluctant colleagues, one of
whom went quietly mad.

Thierry Raclot was a tall, imposing figure with a shock of tight
black curls that fell frequently across his face – from where he
brushed them back impatiently. I had seen him around the base,
climbing up among the Adélie nests or watching and taking
notes, and once with a little Adélie squirming in his arms. He
took a no-nonsense view of his birds, which suited me fine,
although I also noticed that the generally fearless Adélies skipped
smartly out of the way if you crossed them anywhere near
Thierry's lab.

Thierry and I were braving the wind to check on his Adélies.
There were nests everywhere, with parents stolidly incubating
their eggs. The lucky ones were those where the females had
already come back and given the males a break to go off and
hunt for food after their long fast. 'It's that first nest relief that's
the critical one,' said Thierry. 'After that, when the chicks are

hatched and the short foraging trips start this part of the work is done.'

He and his research group were trying to probe what happened if the female was late. There could be many reasons for this. She might be exhausted from laying those two large eggs; it might be taking her a long time to find enough good food to replenish her reserves; there could also be accidents out there, or killer whales, or leopard seals.

But for whatever reason, the males left behind needed to decide when to give up the ghost. If they stayed on the eggs too long, they would starve to death. If they left too early, they would lose their unborn chicks. Thierry wanted to know what triggered that critical point when the urge to feed overwhelmed the urge to breed. He suspected it might be a stress hormone called corticosterone. But the only way to find out was to catch the abandoned males in the act of leaving. And that was harder than it sounds.

This year, they had marked fifty pairs with the same black waterproof stuff that Caroline painted on to her emperors. They noted the laying date, the number of eggs, they checked on the males each day, saw who left, caught them in the act, measured their weight, the size of their flippers, beak, chest and the amount of corticosterone in their blood.

'It can be quite difficult. You try to catch them on the rocks because on snow they can move very fast – even faster than you. Some try to escape and you have to run after them. It's much better if they stand and face you and try to fight. If the weather's good you can use a crook around the neck but in this wind you can forget it.'

The male leaves when his weight has dropped in half, about eight pounds. Of the marked group, Thierry had managed to catch five males in the act of abandoning. Nineteen had been successfully relieved by their females and most of the rest had sneaked off. 'It's a long hard process. We would like to have a few more birds for our data but – luckily for the penguins and unluckily for our study – it's hard to get data at this late stage of fasting. You have to monitor a lot of birds to get the data from just a few of them.'

High up on the bank, in the middle of a crowded set of nests, a penguin was lying flat on his eggs. I could just make out the top part of a smudgy black number on his chest. 'That's number eighteen,' said Thierry. 'He's the last of the males. He's fasted for forty-five days and it looks as though the female isn't coming back. But the main problem is to be there to catch him when he leaves. He doesn't tell you 'I'll be leaving in an hour'. I check him throughout the day. Today the weather's too bad to be out there for long, but on a good day I can be watching for three or four hours at a stretch.'

We had both had enough of the wind now, and Thierry took me to see the other half of his experiment. Next to his lab there was a holding pen, where a handful of Adélies stood or lay. Their breasts were marked with numbers that were now turning brown. They had coloured bands on their flippers and two small instruments, half the size of a cigarette packet, glued to either side of their backs.

Thierry told me that much of what they already knew about the signal to abandon nest came from these experiments on captive birds. In early December, they chose a few males that hadn't managed to breed, captured them and brought them here. Every day they weighed them and took blood samples, which revealed what was happening internally. First the birds used up their carbohydrates, very quickly, within a few days. Then they started on the body lipids – the fat store. Finally, when the lipids reached a dangerously low level, about 20 per cent of the starting amount, the birds started to burn their proteins. Now they were like marathon runners, hitting the wall, literally digesting their own muscles. And that was when the warning bells started to go off inside.

You could tell because that was also the point when the birds started to move. The instruments on their backs functioned as a sort of pedometer. At first the birds stayed more or less motionless, just as they would on the nest. But when they were ready to go they started hopping restlessly from foot to foot, moving around the pen. That was when Thierry released them. Usually there were four to six captive birds in here at a time, and every time he released one he caught another. This season he already had gone through about fifteen birds.[28]

Amazingly, the birds seemed to know exactly when the lipid levels got low, when they had started digesting their muscles. How could they be so in tune with the internal subtleties of their metabolisms? And was there anything we could learn about sensing – and manipulating – our fat-burning phases?

Thierry and his group hit on corticosterone as a possible signal since it seemed to encourage other seabirds to start foraging. To test this, they had been giving some of these captive birds different levels of the hormone. So far it looked promising. The birds that received the highest hormonal dose started in on their proteins sooner than they needed to, and also started moving around. And the level of another hormone, prolactin – which encourages parental care – abruptly fell. Now he wanted to know if corticosterone levels rose naturally when the birds hit the wall. All he needed was to catch a few more birds in the act.

On my way back to the dorm I passed number eighteen's nest. He was still there, the brown smudgy number clear on his grubby chest. He was still starving, still hoping that his mate would come. His hormones hadn't kicked in yet. He knew his life was not yet in danger. But the turning point was closer than I realised. Later that evening in the communal bathroom I bumped into Thierry brushing his teeth. 'We missed him,' he said sadly. 'Number eighteen has gone.'[29]

· · ·

It was still only midsummer, but I could sense that evolution had already chosen this year's winners and losers in the Antarctic breeding game. The emperor chicks were somewhere else, sinking, or swimming, on their own merits. The last of the unrelieved Adélie males had given up and gone, while the successful parents were beginning to hatch their young and stuff them full of food to prime their overactive mitochondrial hothouses.

But there was one more species of true Antarctican that still had breeding sites and nesting strategies left to play for: snow petrels. Like the Adélies, snow petrels never stray far from the ice. They come here in summer to breed and raise their young, and then join the Adélies in their winter quarters, hanging around at the edge of the pack ice, feeding on fish and krill and waiting for the summer to return.

Olivier Chastel is a specialist in Antarctic seabirds. A biologist from the French National Centre for Scientific Research in Villiers-en-Bois, he has studied many different species in the south: albatrosses, skuas, petrels and penguins. I had arranged to meet him in his office, and he told me that of all the birds he had studied, snow petrels were his favourites. 'You know, they're pure white, they have this romantic name.'

Yes, they were romantic, these angels of the Antarctic world. I'd seen them wheeling overhead against a brooding purple sky. Early travellers thought they were the souls of dead sailors. They were heart-stoppingly beautiful. I said this to Olivier and he smiled. 'I'll show you now if you like. But you'd better not look at them too closely. Because when you've seen them fighting you'll have a different image.'

First, we stopped at a skua nest to check on the eggs. 'I like skuas, too,' Olivier said. 'They're tough. They're not afraid of you. As soon as you put a ring on one of these birds, it has a personality. Some birds are shy, some are nasty, some are clever, some stupid. One skua specialises in taking off people's hats and dropping them in the sea. A friend lost a lens cap from his camera. They test everything to see if it's edible.'

On the bare rock there was one unhatched egg and one bemused-looking ball of fluff. The egg was lying in a pool of meltwater, which put it in imminent danger of freezing. Oliver climbed over and did his best to drain the water while the two parents screamed madly and dive-bombed him, their wicked beaks shining with menace. Automatically, he put one hand up in the air above his head as he crouched.

'This pair is one of the easier ones,' he said over his shoulder. 'With the others I have to carry a stick and hold it high in the air. Then they don't attack.'

'Why?'

'I don't know, but it works.'

'What makes them so aggressive?'

'We don't know that either. You might think they had high levels of testosterone, but in fact it's pretty low. Probably because testosterone is expensive. It suppresses your immune system and down here you can't afford to get sick.'

He backed off and the mother settled on the nest, rolling the egg carefully back into the puddle of water. Olivier shrugged fatalistically and we moved on.

Now we were walking up the rocky hillside, skidding on penguin guano and slushy snow, carefully stepping over the conduits that hid the network of cables keeping the station alive. 'Snow petrels have the same problem with meltwater,' Olivier said. 'There's fierce competition for the best nesting sites – the ones that are sheltered from snow or drain water well. The birds live forty years or more, so it's tough for young new breeders.'

Researchers had been banding both chicks and adults here since 1963. It was impossible to tell how old the adults were when they were first banded, but when they settled into a nest site you could then watch them for the rest of their lives. 'They are very faithful to the nest each year. If a bird is missing for two years it's probably dead. They don't breed elsewhere. If you destroy a breeding site, they won't breed for the rest of their lives.'

The colony was a regular bank of rocks, just like all the others, except that many of the crannies and hollows held birds. They were a little smaller than doves; their beaks, feet and eyes were black and the rest of them was snow-white.

Olivier told me that, like Thierry with the Adélies, he wanted to understand what inner hormonal signals drove the snow petrels. They, too, shared parental duties, and if their mate was late they had to make exactly the same decisions as the emperors and the Adélies. This summer, he was studying the stress hormone corticosterone to see if it played the same role here, too.

'Many other birds have a totally different strategy. Robins, say, or blackbirds, only live for a couple of years, and they lay four, five, even six eggs at a time. But all the birds here are so long-lived that their strategy is to favour their own survival over that of their chicks. A snow petrel can go five, six years without breeding. They only lay one egg and won't re-lay if they lose it. Even if no chicks survive for one year, the population can still be stable because the parents don't take risks. Their priority is their own survival – there will be many more chances to breed.

'We think corticosterone is the key. But it might depend on age, too. Young breeders are very prudent. But if the older ones have only one or two seasons left in them, they might take a few more risks.'[30]

He told me that the science was surprisingly easy to do here. Since good nest sites were so hard to come by, and possession was most of the law, snow petrels incubating eggs were reluctant to leave their nests for any reason. That made them easy to catch. They were so attached to the nest site, they wouldn't even try to fly away.

They would, however, fight. Young birds challenged the owners all the time for good sites. As we walked through the colony one such youth decided to try its luck. It launched itself at the nearest nest possessor with a fierce flurry of beak and wings. Now the two of them were shrieking, stabbing brutally with their beaks and scratching with their claws, grappling and rolling over each other like cage fighters egged on by a crowd.

Olivier was right. In spite of their angelic appearance, they were more vicious than the skuas. But it was about to get even worse. The owner of the nest threw back its delicate white head and *splat!* A glob of bright orange goo emerged from its beak, arched through the air and landed squarely on its opponent's back. *Splat!* There went another one, this time barely missing the recipient's eye. The poor creature was vanquished. It yielded hastily and our hero returned to its nest with something like a swagger.

These graceful birds *spit*? Olivier grinned at my shocked expression. 'It's an effective weapon for them,' he said. 'They use oil from their food to make the spit and it's bad for their feathers.' We both watched as the unfortunate recipient of those lurid orange gobs rushed off to roll on the snow and try to get clean. 'Some birds can be lovely,' Olivier remarked. 'When you lift them to check their leg ring they will gently preen your hand. Others see you and spit immediately. And the spit stinks – which is why we're the smelliest people on base.'

He said this cheerfully, as though it was a badge of honour. 'I've kept the jacket from one winter I spent here. It still smells fourteen years later. When I'm in a bad mood at home I get it out and smell it and remember.'

Olivier was still investigating which hormones drove the snow petrels to fight, and which made them yield for the year. And he told me that emperors too could be victims of raging hormones.

'Failed breeders can kidnap chicks. There can be up to five or six adults fighting over a chick and quite often the chick will die. Or they can adopt a chick for a few days and then kick it off. We think this might be because of another hormone behind parental care – prolactin. When the female emperor returns after two months, she has no idea if the incubation has been successful. So she has to have lots of prolactin to keep the urge alive. Then the male goes off foraging for a month and has to be motivated to return.'

Emperors also have an inbuilt hormonal trigger for when to quit. They will always abandon their eggs or chicks rather than risk their own lives, and of the owl-eyed chicks that crowded confidently around me yesterday, fewer than one in five will make it to adulthood. 'Some emperors are more than forty years old. Like snow petrels they'll have many more opportunities to breed. It's better to fail one year but stay alive.'

It was better, in Shackleton's words, to be a live donkey than a dead lion.

That evening after dinner there was another movie showing, but I slipped out again and walked down to the sea. I diverted past one of Olivier's snow petrel colonies. They were beautiful still, and their spitting didn't make them less so. It just gave them bite.

Down by the sea there was the usual procession of Adélies, trotting down the snow paths, queuing to jump into the quiet waters and stock up on fish to feed their hatchlings. I watched them for more than an hour; the leaps looked dramatic but made almost no sound, and the whole scene was deeply peaceful. They knew what they were doing, these little beasts. No wonder they had no self-doubt. Like the Antarctic heroes of old they would battle against extraordinary odds, survive appalling conditions and push themselves to the limits. But like the emperors and the snow petrels, too, they had also inherited another important lesson from their forebears, and it was the same lesson that Shackleton had to swallow just a hundred miles from the Pole. To survive down here, you also have to know when to quit.

Eventually, my muscles stiffening, I got up and started to walk home. But I had the feeling that someone was watching me. I turned abruptly. One of the Adélies was about six feet behind me, staring up at me, motionless, unblinking. I turned again, walked a few hundred feet and then quickly looked back. The penguin had matched me step for step. It was standing there, perfectly still, six feet behind me, looking up with that same measured stare. We repeated this game once, twice, three times. It was playing statues with me. Each time I turned it was motionless. Each time I walked, it walked with me.

We were almost back at the dorm now, and it had followed me all the way. I remembered David Ainley saying that Adélies treat you as if you were an overgrown penguin, and how I thought at the time that he seemed to see himself the same way. I looked down again at this little creature and it looked unflinchingly back at me. I don't know who was anthropomorphising whom, but – though I stepped inside the dormitory and closed the door firmly – I knew that I had succumbed. Penguins have melted stonier hearts than mine. I never stood a chance.

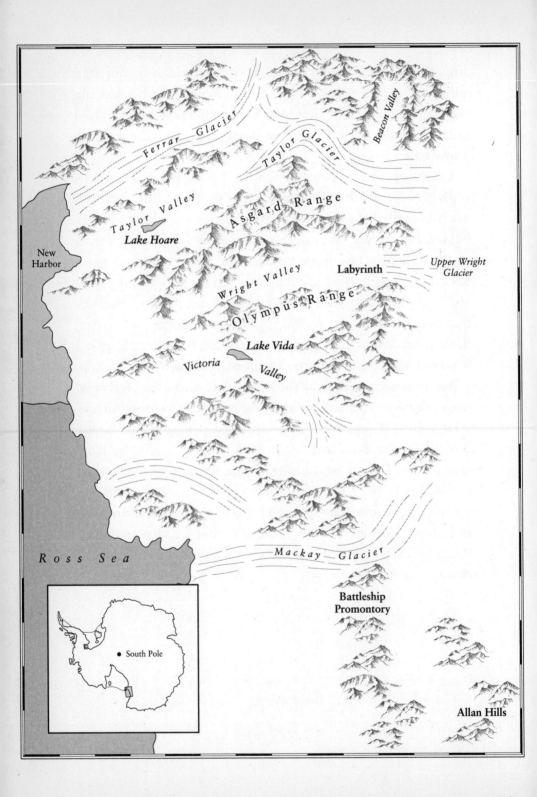

3

MARS ON EARTH

The McMurdo Dry Valleys are the closest thing we have on Earth to the planet Mars. A set of bare rocky valleys running in parallel from the edge of the ice sheet down to the sea, they are 'dry' not just through lack of water, but through lack of ice. They are also all but monochrome. The jagged mountain ranges that separate the valleys are run through like a layer cake with alternate slabs of chocolate brown dolerite and pale sandstone. This is an unearthly place, intimidating and harsh in the bright light of noon. But at night in the summer, when the sun never sets but merely hovers close to the horizon and casts its long low shadows, the peaks seem to soften, the dolerite rock grows richer and the oatmeal sandstone takes on a golden glow.

It's not just the colours that look their best at night-time. Those long shadows also pick out the features that tell the history of this extraordinary place. There are weird raised beaches, jutting out halfway up the mountain sides, which mark ancient high stands of water; rock ripples and gigantic potholes that were once carved out by a waterfall the size of Niagara; and bulbous glaciers and frost-cracked soils that show how cold and dry this land has now become.

Fifty-five million years ago, Antarctica was warm, wet and brimming with life. The surface shifted and shuddered, driven by grinding tectonic forces in the crust beneath. As the crust tore, this part of the ancient world lurched upwards. And with the rising land, the rivers on its surface now had something to get their teeth into. They cut down into the raised rocks, carving out this set of parallel valleys as they surged from the interior to the sea.

Meanwhile, tectonic happenings on the other side of the soon-to-be continent were beginning to make themselves felt. After millions of years of gradually separating itself from the rest of the world's land masses, Antarctica had only one remaining point of contact: the long thin arm of the Antarctic Peninsula was still clinging on to the southern tip of South America.

And then, some thirty-five million years ago, it slipped its hold. Seas surged between the two former partners, and currents began to swirl around the new continent, building up into a vortex that cut it off from the warmth and comfort of the outside world.

The opening of Drake Passage had slammed Antarctica's freezer door shut. First its trees disappeared, then its tundra faded to dust. To the south, up on the Antarctic plateau, a mighty ice sheet advanced towards the coast. It would have swamped the valleys but a saw-toothed range of mountains, thrown up along their southern edge by those earlier tectonic convulsions, stopped the ice sheet in its tracks. Instead, the valley floors stayed bare, growing steadily colder and drier. A few small glaciers built up from snow banks on the mountains, and spilled down on to the valley floors. Cold air poured down from the plateau in the form of mighty winds that scoured and shaped the rocks, carving holes in them that whistle eerily. No rain has fallen in the interior of the Dry Valleys for millions of years, and there has been precious little snow. This is the coldest, driest, barest patch of rock on Earth.

That alone would be enough to excite many scientists. To understand our home planet, people always want to go to the extremes. But the Dry Valleys have something more alien to offer. For the history of this region mirrors the early history of Mars, one of our nearest, and most intriguing, extra-terrestrial neighbours. Like the Dry Valleys, Mars once had liquid water on the surface, and was possibly also warm. Its surface is still cut through with channels where water once ran, basins that were once giant lakes, and beaches that once marked out ancient seashores. Now, though, its average temperature is -67°F and it is one of the driest places in the Solar System. That's what's really special about the McMurdo Dry Valleys. At some point in its life, Mars may have passed through the same stage that they are experiencing today.[1] This is Mars on Earth.

And just as on Mars, there are no visible signs of life. True, you sometimes see the twisted, mummified body of a seal, its teeth bared in a rictus grin where the skin around the mouth has shrunk back. Nobody knows how old these mummies are, nor why the seals they once were took that wrong turning from the coast and perished up here for lack of food and water. But apart from them, the land is bare and apparently lifeless. When Scott first observed the valleys in December 1903, he wrote this: 'It is worthy to record ... that we have seen no living thing, not even a moss or a lichen; all that we did find, far inland amongst the moraine heaps, was the skeleton of a Weddell seal, and how that came there is beyond guessing. It is certainly a valley of the dead.'

His description was accurate, but his conclusion was dead wrong. The Dry Valleys are home to plenty of life, though it's not as we usually know it. That's because, though dry, the valleys are not entirely devoid of water. A few days each year the temperature there creeps above freezing, just long enough to melt a little ice from the glaciers that spill down into the valleys, and to make trickling streams that flow into long thin lakes on the valley floors. The lakes are, all of them, covered with a thick layer of ice; but they don't freeze solid thanks to this small annual injection of liquid water, and warmth.

Where there's water there is – usually – life. And this bleak landscape is already telling us extraordinary things about the possibility of life on Mars.

The valleys are just a short helicopter ride from McMurdo, and their unofficial capital is Lake Hoare in Taylor Valley. There has been a camp of sorts there since the 1970s, but the modern version, built in 1993, has three laboratory huts – one for radiation work, a general chemistry lab complete with fume hood for anything noxious, and an instrumentation lab bristling with electronics. Though residents sleep in tents, they eat and hang out in a further communal hut that is warm, spacious and jaunty with fairy lights. The camp manager, Rae Spain, fitted much of it out herself a few seasons ago when she worked here as a carpenter.

Rae was warm and welcoming, with a long blonde plait and a friendly smile. She was the archetypal camp mom. She had been coming to the ice since 1979, from the very earliest days that women fought their way on to the continent and into the programme. At first she intended to come just that one time, for the adventure. But she couldn't get Antarctica out of her head. 'It haunts you,' she says.

Though it was technically a camp rather than a fully fledged base, the living and working quarters were unusually comfortable. Meals there were spectacular. After a hard day in the field you might come home to hand-rolled sushi, sesame chicken, miso soup or pork vindaloo, or a tasty barbecue with rosemary potatoes, carrot cake and freshly baked cookies. Then you could check your email (internet available 24/7), make a phone call anywhere in the world, or e-order something that would arrive by helicopter just a few weeks later. Camp residents might drink their water out of old jam jars, but this still felt more like the gimmick in a trendy pub than a disagreeable necessity. This was about as cushy as it got.

It was also a literary camp. I noticed Margaret Atwood novels on the shelves, and Rae told me she travels into Canada from her native Washington State to pick up books for the base. Next to the books were board games and piles of knitting yarns for the times when the weather closed in and there are no chores left to do. As with most parts of Antarctica, patience is a virtue here.

Rae had worked at all three of the main US stations – McMurdo, Palmer, out on the Peninsula, and the South Pole – but she was happiest here. It was even good, she said, on a bad day. Once someone had crashed an all-terrain vehicle into the edge of the lake, where the ice was thin and the water very close to the surface. The vehicle was wrecked and was going to have to be sling-loaded home on the base of a helicopter. Sling loads are always tricky. The helo doesn't actually land. You have to stand beneath it like the Statue of Liberty, holding the hook from the chains high in your outstretched hand, balancing yourself against the downdraft and the noise, trying not to think about the massive hunk of metal hovering just above your head as the helo pilot inches down to reach you.

On this occasion, she got word that the helo was on its way so grabbed eighty pounds of chains and webbing and struggled onto the lake, crashing into melt pools until she was wet and frozen. She arrived at the vehicle to find that it was in pieces and needed to be reassembled so had to send the helo away. And then she trudged back to the camp, dragging the chains miserably behind her, only to discover that the U-barrel had been over-filled with urine, and she had to try to siphon some off the top.

But going outside, looking at the view, taking a few deep Antarctic breaths, she realised that even the worst day here was better than the best day back in Mactown. 'After all, where else would I get a job as varied as this? Doing helo ops, building schedules, monitoring the generator and the solar energy systems, cooking food ... burning shit.'

For yes, even that came under her purview. Rae lays out the Dry Valley rules to every new arrival, including those of the scatological variety, and the environmental regulations are strict. Solid matter goes into 'rocket' toilets that are burned in rotation. Pee goes first into a bottle and is then poured into large U-barrels. (One of the Antarctic rules repeated most often to newbies was this: Never *ever* drink from a bottle marked 'P'.)

If you're caught short out in the field you carry an empty pee bottle with you, and then bring the full one back to camp. Anything solid goes into plastic bags that you also carry with you. It's best to avoid needing them, if you can. I've heard some useful tips about pee bottles. In the endless thermodynamic battle to keep warm in a cold place, one researcher told me that it's always best to use a pee bottle during the night if you can. Any pee in your bladder costs you energy to keep it at body temperature. When the pee is in its bottle, on the other hand, you can even keep it with you in your sleeping bag, as a mini-hot-water bottle. The science makes sense but I admit I didn't try it.

You were also strictly forbidden to move rocks or stones, or to take any souvenirs. In this, as in all the Dry Valley environmental rules, there was no tolerance. Rae was a formidable exponent of the regulations. Though she was mild in appearance, I didn't need to hear the stories about sling-loading to know she was made of steel when necessary. In the early days she saw off her fair share of foremen who didn't think women should be on the ice, and tried to send her home. I would not like to be caught by her with an illicit souvenir in my pocket.

I had come here mainly to see biologist Peter Doran from the University of Illinois in Chicago, who had promised to take me out on to the lake.[2] This turned out to be a wide expanse almost filling the valley floor and running nearly all the way up to the steep sides of the Canada glacier. Around the edge was a 'moat' of clear, dark, glassy ice, but as I stepped gingerly over this I found myself on a frozen surface that looked nothing like I had imagined. I'd assumed it would be flat and white, but this was a tortured terrain of ice towers, pinnacles and hollows, streaked with patches of dark brown soil.

Some of the towers were almost at eye level; if I crouched down, I could peer into miniature ice caves with filigree walls, and what seemed to be an earthen floor. But I knew that beneath the soil was more ice, ten or twelve feet of it, capping the liquid lake beneath. In fact, the ice was so thick that there was no chance of accidentally breaking through into the lake, but we could still crash through a sliver of ice masking a pool of frigid surface meltwater, or break an ankle in a crack. Peter was taking no chances. 'This is where it gets dicey. Follow my footsteps.' He placed his feet carefully on the ice and I matched him meticulously, step for step.

As we walked, Peter told me that the dirt came in with the winter storms, and that the glacier up ahead plugged the end of the valley, and acted as a windstop, forcing the wind to drop its load of soil on to the ice. Where the soil landed, it formed an insulating layer, protecting some parts of the ice while the rest evaporated away into the dry air. Hence the towers and sculptures. Confounded by the unearthly landscape I asked Peter how he would describe it. He grinned, and said: 'Mars-like'.

Peter had been studying Antarctic lakes for most of his career. He was tall and slim and precise. When you first met him he seemed flat, his voice dry and mechanical, his language scientific. But when he smiled, you could see the other side of his personality, the part that brought him down here. He had never been one to sit patiently in a lab looking through a microscope, always preferring the bigger picture, what he called the 'flashy stuff'. He was a bit flashy himself. Peter came here because he read a paper about these strange frozen lakes that could be analogues for Mars. He was fascinated by places that don't belong on Earth, and if you could add a pinch or two of adventure, so much the better.

It wasn't enough for him to study the lakes from the outside. His first dive in an Antarctic lake came in the early 1980s, on an expedition to the Bunger Hills Oasis, near the Russian station of Mirny, on the other side of the continent from here. In fact it was the first time anyone had plunged into this particular lake. No one knew what to expect. Finding himself close to the bottom of the gloomy water, he sank into the soft mud, up to his waist. He had no idea whether he'd sink farther, or if he'd get safely out. As he told me about it, his eyes shone. 'It was wild. It's true discovery. I think that's one of the things that attracts people to Antarctica. A lot of science has become routine, but here you're genuinely exploring.'

He had now done dozens of Antarctic dives, but it was still far from routine. Out here in the middle of Lake Hoare, he showed me the dive hole we'd come to see: a neat circle melted through the ice, now filled with dark green water.

The first challenge in a dive was getting into the lake proper; the ice here was sixteen feet thick, making the entrance more of a tunnel than a hole. Though the water looked forbidding, he told me that it wasn't as cold as you'd think. You could be down there for an hour and a half and be perfectly warm. You were wearing a dry suit, thick rubber gloves, a full-face mask with communications to the surface through a safety tether. When you made it to the lake itself you were free to wander, but you were also relying on the tether to see you safely home. Though some light did diffuse down through the ice, there was no beam coming through the hole to guide you back. There have been times when divers have lost their tethers. 'That's the scariest story I've ever heard,' Peter said. 'It would be like being buried alive. Or lost in space. Diving in the Dry Valley lakes is the closest thing to a space walk I'll ever do.'

Unlike the myriad sea creatures back in McMurdo, the life here took the form of giant mats that look as though they're woven of some sludgy seamless material. In fact, they were made from microscopic cyanobacteria, held together by a sticky mucus. One of the strangest aspects of this primitive life was that, though the mats formed on the sediment at the bottom of the lake, some 30 m below us, they also generated bubbles that lifted them up and made them float around like mocking ghosts. One mat, which Peter and his colleagues dubbed 'the ghoul', bore holes eerily reminiscent of a skull's eye sockets and nose. Another, a shroud-like cylinder nearly two metres high, looked like a dead body rearing up from the depths. 'I turned round and saw that lurking in the darkness. It makes you start at first, and then you realise there can't be anything down there, there's nothing moving, it's all microbial. You make yourself swim through this stuff, but it's bizarre, it's really bizarre.'

And if he's right, similar creatures might once have floated in the freezing lakes of Mars, before they finally dried up and blew into dust. Walking back over the crunchy lake surface, we saw scraps of these mats, like soggy yellow strips of chicken skin, embedded in the dirt and ice. I picked one up and rubbed until it disintegrated in my hands. As pseudo-Martians go, this wasn't exactly glamorous, but it did prove that life could survive even in these harsh conditions. The annual average temperature here was zero and in the winter it could drop to 40°F below.

And yet, even today in the height of summer, when the temperature was a drop below freezing, there was enough direct sunlight to melt a little of the glacier beside the lake, sending a thin trickle of water to penetrate through the cracks in the ice. Peter and his colleagues have calculated that this trickle, running for just a few days a year, fuels the lake with enough heat to keep it liquid.

So that was one answer that research here has provided to the Martian question – you don't have to have temperatures above freezing to maintain liquid water on the planet's surface. The Dry Valleys show that cold is not necessarily dead.

Peter was also fascinated by another of the Dry Valley lakes: Lake Vida. This had an ice lid sixty feet thick, so thick that for decades scientists thought it was frozen solid. But when Peter took radar instruments to map the bottom he saw a strange reflection about fifty feet down, in a pocket about one mile long and a half-mile wide. It couldn't be water. Down there the temperature should be around 10°F, and water would definitely freeze. But it could, perhaps, be brine. If so, it would be about as salty as water can get without turning to pure salt. That would be hard for anything living to take. But the lesson from the Dry Valleys was that life has a knack of finding a way.

One reason Peter cared was that these would be some of the most hostile conditions on Earth. 'What are the extremes of life on this planet?' he said. 'How far can you push life before it doesn't become life any more? Maybe life on Earth started like this. Maybe it will finish like this. Maybe this is the end.'

He has now been to Vida three times, to drill into the brine layer and beyond. Below fifty feet the drill hole quickly filled with salty slush but even though they went to one hundred feet, which ought to be the lake floor, they didn't find water. However, they did find unmistakable signs of a perfectly viable microbial world, living quite happily in the salty darkness.

And that could be the most intriguing aspect of Lake Vida: these creatures lurking within the ice could be a mirror of the very last Martians to survive. This, after all, would be the very final pool of anything resembling liquid water before a Martian lake finally froze solid.

'This would be the last vestige of something living on Mars billions of years ago,' Peter said. 'The last stand for life on Mars may have been a swim in a frozen lake.'

Mars might not even have needed a lake. In the soils here, researchers have found minuscule round worms called nematodes, and abundant bacteria. And anywhere with the slightest hint of moisture, they have also found tardigrades, or 'water bears', the toughest animals on Earth. These grow up to a millimetre long, making the adults just barely visible to the naked eye. They are stubby and cute with four pairs of fat little legs, a vole-like snout, and the complexion of a gummy bear. You can (and in fact many researchers have) freeze them to within a whisker of absolute zero, boil them, dry them out or zap them with radiation and they simply shut down and wait for the ordeal to be over. For them, the Dry Valleys are a breeze. When any particular habitat becomes too dry for comfort, they replace the water in their bodies with a specialised form of sugar, adopt a shape like a microscopic beer barrel, and sit it out. They can do this, apparently, for decades, probably more.

Up on the glacier, Andrew Fountain from Portland State University in Oregon had found more hiding places for life. He was a big bearded bear of a man, and when I said that I was afraid of slipping on the glassy ice, even with crampons strapped to my bunny boots, he barked out a laugh. 'Don't worry. You're a human fly now!' Andrew's main interest in the glaciers was figuring out how they were different from ones in warmer climates, and how they fed the lakes to keep them liquid. He had placed bamboo poles to measure how much snow accumulates, and gauges to measure the water trickling down the streams at the base. In one place, he had installed a closed-circuit security camera. 'To make sure nobody steals the glacier?' 'Yup,' said Andrew. 'We're hoping we might see an alien landing.' (In truth the camera was there to watch for lumps of ice calving off the face.)

But there was also something else that he wanted to show me, another way that the creatures of the Dry Valleys cling to life, and to see it we'd have to climb. The sides of the glacier were steep – a feature, Andrew told me, of the cold ice, which flowed more sluggishly than ice in warmer regions. He showed me how to use my ice axe to hew out rough steps and together, clamped reassuringly on to the surface by our spiked crampons, we made our way up on to the main body of ice.

Up aloft the wind was biting; it picked up snow from the surface and flung it in our faces. We pulled up our scarves and in a muffled voice Andrew explained what he was looking for. To survive, life needed liquid water, and up here where the ice was at -4°F there was precious little of that. But in the few places where dirt and debris streaked the white ice, there was a chance. Where white ice reflects sunlight, dark soil soaks it up and can get hot enough to melt down into the ice. More snow and ice puts a lid on this deepening canister; sunlight still filters through the lid, keeping some liquid water in play, ready for any bacteria that are caught up in the soil when it blows up on to the glacier.

It sounded far-fetched, but Andrew started casting around until he spotted a slightly darker patch on the ice surface. He held out his hand for my ice axe and started jabbing at the ice with the axe head. Chips flew up into the air to mingle with the blowing snow and then, suddenly and shockingly, liquid water welled up in the hole. 'Woo hoo!' he crowed. This was a big patch. Water began to appear in a wider area, then Andrew found smaller circles, broke them open, and water frothed out, filled with the bubbles that showed that microbes had found a way to grow, and breathe, and live. We were surrounded by champagne bottles of life, entombed aquaria that had been completely hidden in the ice. I noticed that the wind had dropped and there were hints of evening sun through the cloud. Andrew leaned on the ice axe and grinned. 'There's debris like this on the polar ice cap of Mars,' he said. 'You can see it on satellites, spiralling out from the centre. This could be another way to find life on Mars.'

We made our way back down the glacier and paused at the base. The sun had now fully broken through the clouds and we stared down the valley at the debris-strewn lake and snow-streaked mountains. I asked Andrew why he came here, but the question was almost rhetorical. He replied quietly. 'It's "memory burn",' he said. 'You're back home and you smell something, the cleaning fluid they use in the dorms or kerosene, helo fuel, or you hear a Hercules taking off at Oregon airport and bang, you're back here. You close your eyes and you see this view, and you miss it. And you have to come back.'

Battleship Promontory, on the far side of the Dry Valleys, was a broad scoop of steep sandstone cliffs, a couple of hours' helicopter ride from McMurdo. About halfway up lay a wide ledge, several hundred metres deep, pocked with turrets and spires of sandstone and dark dolorite pebbles. From the air, I could see human footprints on patches of snow leading, ant-like, to a handful of brightly coloured tents. As the helo set down, Chris McKay climbed out of the biggest tent to meet me.

Chris McKay works at the NASA Ames Research Center in California and he's a veteran of the ice. He's been coming down here since 1980. He's a giant, standing nearly six feet six tall in his stockinged feet, so that I wondered how he could fold himself into one of these small tents. He spoke slowly and carefully and peppered his conversation with literary allusions. One minute he was referring to *The Iliad*, and the next he was quoting Lewis Carroll. (Talking about how strange the visible absence of life seemed when he first came down, he quoted 'The Walrus and the Carpenter': 'No birds were flying overhead – There were no birds to fly'. To Carroll, that was supposed to be nonsense, but to Chris here in the Dry Valleys it was an everyday reality.)

He told me that, unlike many other Antarctic veterans, he has never felt at home here. The lack of obvious life was always in his face, making it clear that he was somewhere alien. And yet, he knows more than most people about the myriad ways that creatures can eke out a living in this land that is utterly hostile to life.

Straight away he offered to show me around. He disappeared inside the main tent and re-emerged with a geological hammer. 'I can't walk around without a hammer in my hand,' he said. 'It would be like reading a book without holding a pen.'

From the air the cliffs looked golden, but close up the rocks were either grey or coated with a rust-like desert varnish where the iron in the dolorite had been weathered by wind and snow. But in places the rocks were pitted and mottled. 'You see that?' said Chris. 'It's almost like a disease.' This was the first sign that life had found an extraordinary new way to survive in the Dry Valleys. Chris picked up a lump of pitted sandstone and gently chipped off the outermost scale. Through the pale rock I could see a hint of green. Then he turned the rock over and smartly rapped it with his hammer, knocking off the corner. Running in a thread just below the surface was a bright emerald stripe, like a jewel. This stripe was made up of thousands of cyanobacteria, that were living, breathing and growing just as they do in drainpipes, ponds and puddles the world over. But these ones were different. They were doing all this *inside a rock*.

As I was turning the emerald stripe over in my hands, Chris told me how they manage it. They stay frozen all winter. Summer comes, the rock warms above freezing and the creatures inside wake up. They are close enough to the surface, and the sandstone rock is just translucent enough, that they feel the first touches of sunlight. Snow melts in the sun and trickles inside to give a drop or two of water. And then it's a race to profit from all of this as quickly as possible, to make what Chris called a 'mini rainforest' inside the rock. They have only a few hours a day for a few weeks of the year when the sun is warm enough to break through. And then the sunlight fades, and the bacteria sink back into sleep.

It might sound hard for them, said Chris, but this isn't such a bad life. 'They're getting water, they're getting light, they're getting a warm enough temperature. The conditions here are either perfect for sleeping or perfect for growing. There's no confusion. It's a great job if you can get it. You sleep for eleven months then you work hard for one month of every year. And the great thing is you don't age in that eleven months of sleeping because you're frozen solid. So you can live a really long time.'

Why do they do it? In most parts of the Dry Valleys where you find them, the reason would be water or, rather, the lack of it. If they tried living on the surface of the rocks, these bacteria would dry out quickly in the wind. But here, the story was a little different. By a quirk of geography, Battleship Promontory was unusually warm and therefore unusually wet. The cliffs acted as a mirror magnifying and focusing the sun's rays. 'At 1 p.m. the sun will be full on here, and here,' Chris said, pointing to the cliffs ahead and a patch of dolorite in front of us. 'And then it's a cooker.'

We walked farther down to a cleft in the sandstone, a minia-ture suntrap, where ice was gleaming wetly and the rocks were dark with damp stains. He took another rock and broke it open. Sure enough, there was the emerald streak of life hiding inside. But then he pointed to the rock surfaces and I saw that the black stains were not just dampness but something clinging to the surface. Something that was alive.

'What do you reckon?' Chris asked me. 'Why do *these guys* [he pointed at the green streak] live underground when *these guys* [the black surface stain] are happy on the surface?' He looked at me expectantly and I shrugged, waiting for the punch-line. There was obviously no problem in this little patch with dryness, so I couldn't see why anyone would need to live inside a rock here. But the trouble, it seemed, was with the intensity of sunlight. 'They're both cyanobacteria,' Chris said. 'The reason these ones are black instead of green is that they're excreting a pigment that absorbs UV light. Basically, they're putting on sunscreen.'

So these black surface blobs were sunbathing bacteria. I peered at them, intrigued. That explained how they coped with the intense summer light here, and this, said Chris, was the only place in the world where you could find them.

Now that we were in a hollow and the wind had dropped, the sun was baking. My parka began to seem ridiculous, even though the air temperature was technically far below freezing. I felt sleepy, and had a sudden urge to lie down and bask on one of the rocky surfaces. I knew what the cyanobacteria saw in this place. It wasn't even that hard to live here. Thanks to the weird combination of geometry and height, life really was a beach.

And yet, Chris had found his rock dwellers throughout the

Dry Valleys. And similar rocks may also have provided one of the final refuges for life on Mars.

Just beyond Battleship Promontory lies another part of Antarctica's living Martian metaphor: a place where space itself comes to Earth. This is an area known as the Allan Hills for the few isolated mountains that poke their necks up through the ice. Apart from these, the surface up here on the edge of the vast East Antarctic Ice Sheet is mainly featureless. A helicopter pilot told me that in his first season he was detailed to take some researchers up into the Allan Hills and asked for a map. His boss took a blank sheet of paper, put a pencil dot in the middle and handed it to him.

But remote or not, this is one of the best places on Earth to find rocks from space. An astonishing amount of extra-terrestrial debris falls on the Earth every year. Some is in the form of dust that blazes brightly through the sky as a shooting star but burns itself up in the process. Once in a while there is also a really massive space rock, an asteroid, which collides with the Earth with devastating consequences. That's what did for the dinosaurs, and we humans could meet the same fate if we encountered a similarly unlucky strike. The really big hits like these carry so much energy that there's little or nothing left of them afterwards, just a mighty crater and a planet of dazed or dying creatures. In between these two extremes are moderately sized rocks, large enough that something survives the burning through the atmosphere, and small enough that they land relatively gently, and remain on the surface as an alien rock. It is these remnant rocks that we call meteorites.

Almost all meteorites come originally from the asteroid belt, a ring of potato-shaped rocks that marks a failed planet, between Mars and Jupiter. Jupiter formed so quickly and became so large that its gravity disturbed all the building blocks in its vicinity, and prevented them from forming a planet of their own. The asteroid belt is builders' rubble, left over from the creation of the Solar System. Rocks from there tell us about the birth of our planets, our Sun, and even about what came before.

But that's not the whole story. A very few, very rare meteorites come from more exotic locations. Antarctica has gathered more than its fair share of these precious alien visitors, along with their extraordinary insights about us, and our place in the world.

Ralph Harvey, a long-time meteorite hunter from Case Western Reserve University in Cleveland, Ohio, runs a programme called ANSMET (which stand for the Antarctic Search for Meteorites).[3] The programme is a strange beast, unique among all the science that takes place on the continent. It's funded by a combination of NASA, the NSF and the Smithsonian, and the field party always consists of volunteers. Though they are usually experts in meteorites, they themselves have nothing to gain. Anything they find must be bagged, logged and handed over to the authorities. They can then put in a proposal to study any of the meteorites they find, but will be treated like any other researcher: no special privileges, no queue jumping. And certainly no private collecting of samples.

Ralph tells his volunteers this every year before they even make it out on to the ice: 'It embarrasses me to say this, but there are no meteorite souvenirs for you guys. Don't look for personal satisfaction in terms of the rocks you've found or the rocks on your shelf. What I want you to take home is the ability to tell great tales. If you want a souvenir, buy a T-shirt.' He calls the programme 'extreme altruism.'

And yet every year he gets hundreds of applicants. Ralph handpicks the teams himself and, though he considers every application that he receives in writing (test number one: can you write a letter, using a pen, on a piece of paper?), it's probably not worth bothering unless you also know someone who can recommend you. Character matters more than anything in this particular game, and Ralph requires personal or good second-hand knowledge of everyone he chooses.

He's not interested in adventurous types. It's more important to have the ability to be still, to read books calmly in a tent for days while the wind is up, to be respectful and give other people their space. Machismo is also out. When you're feeling miserable you need to say so. 'If you're cold, tired, hungry or thirsty enough that you're skipping over meteorites, the whole system breaks down,' he said. 'I'd rather call the day short than miss something and if one person is feeling ineffective there will be others at least on the verge. Everyone has times that they feel weak, and we all have to agree to admit this and accept it.'

Still, being on an ANSMET team is not for the faint-hearted. If you're selected you'll find yourself on some windy part of the plateau for weeks on end, out on a skidoo from early morning on every possible working day. Days off come when the weather says so, not when you're tired, or fed up, or it's the 'weekend'.

The worst days are the ones where the wind is just low enough that you can work, but still high enough to hurt. It pokes its fingers into any tiny gap it can find, between your gloves and your parka, or where your neck gaiter has slipped slightly. Your goggles fog up constantly. Your big red hood is up, your vision restricted to one small oval framed in fur. You're wearing 14 kg of clothing, manhandling a hefty snow machine, struggling with the pain of 'skidoo thumb' from constantly holding down the throttle. You're bumping over sastrugi – ridges of wind-hardened snow – and if you hit one the wrong way you can find yourself unceremoniously dumped off the back of the skidoo. The automatic cut-off will trigger so you don't then have to chase the machine, cartoon-fashion, but it's still mortifying if anyone sees.

And, of course, it's always windier and nastier when you're not finding meteorites. But then, when you do find one, the wind feels a little lighter and the air warmer and the sun brighter. 'Each one you find, there's a switch in your brain that says "that's a rock from space",' Ralph told me. 'If someone new finds it, it's like giving a child a present, but everyone has a first meteorite every day. It's like mini birthday parties all day long.'

Searches are highly systematic. You go out in a posse of five or six skidoos, sweeping back and forth like Olympic lane swimmers, perhaps one hundred feet apart. You always start into the wind. It might sound masochistic, but the first pass is usually just reconnaissance and this way you have the wind at your back for the return, when you're looking more carefully. You'll probably have to wear your full-face mask and heavy gloves for the upwind part, and downgrade to goggles and light gloves for going downwind. But no one ever does passes with a crosswind – or whichever way you were heading you'd be miserable.

If you see a meteorite, your heart might skip, even if it's your tenth or twentieth of the day. You'll jump off your skidoo, wave your hands, shout, do whatever it takes to get everyone's attention. (If someone else is shouting you stop, throw an ice axe overboard to mark exactly where you'd got to, then head over to check it out.) Then you get out the Collection Kit, a black and white daypack. In the front pocket is a plastic bag of aluminium strips bearing numbers, and a chunky metal counter, a hand-me-down from the Apollo missions. You pull out a metal strip at random – the number will be the meteorite's name until it can be properly curated. You punch that same number into the counter, hold it just above the rock and take a photo.

The next step is to collect the specimen. From the main pocket, you take a sterile plastic bag. You might use a pair of sterile tongs to pick the meteorite up. More likely you'll scoop it into the bag without touching it, brushing it with your parka or letting your nose drip on to it. You should always make an effort not to contaminate your rock from space, though everyone knows that accidents sometimes happen. Ralph has probably already put you at your ease about this. 'I ran over one last year,' he sometimes says. 'Someone was waving and saying "I found one". I looked over there and then felt a crunch. Ouch. I found one, too.'

You fold the top of the bag over several times, slip the aluminium number into the top of the bag and roll it over a few more times for luck. Now you use tape from the side pocket to seal the bag tightly. (Don't forget to fold the end of the tape over so it's easy to find next time, or you'll be awarded the 'white badge of shame', a length of tape stuck to your parka for the rest of the day.)

Now's the fun part, the chance to look at the meteorite in detail and see what you've got. You might get your hand lens out to have a closer look. You note down its size, its description, if there seems anything unusual about it. These field notes will dictate what order the meteorites are opened in, when they have gone from a frozen boat to a frozen truck to the lab in Houston. A helpful clue for the curators is how many exclamation marks you add. Use of capital letters is also a clue. One meteorite hunter once wrote: 'ABUSE ME FIRST!!!!!! Very, very, very sexy' in the field notes for a rock he had found. It did indeed turn out to be a special one, though that's another story.

But even if you've found a meteorite that turns out to change the world of science, you're not supposed to claim the credit. It's just the luck of the draw – anyone could have found it. And for morale purposes within the group you have to stick to your lane.

If you see something enticing on someone else's patch, there's strictly no poaching.

When you have finished bagging and inspecting your find, the meteorite goes into the pack and everyone returns to their posts and starts up again. Days can be long, and the constant concentration wears you down. But you still have to save some energy for the chores back at the camp. Before bed you'll need to dry your gloves and socks, fuel up and cover your skidoo ready for morning, fill up an ice bucket for water, and pull food from the frozen stores for dinner. Unlike many camps, ANSMET doesn't take a cook or a communal tent. You'll be sharing a pyramidal Scott tent with one other person, and you'll cook together over a primus stove, wedged between your two sleeping areas, bathed in a cheerful orange glow as the twenty-four-hour daylight filters through the canvas. Space in the tents is tight. By the end of the trip you'll be more blasé about bodily functions than you've ever been before, and you'll have got to know your tent mate *very* well.

The ability to relax is also a key part of the camp requirements. When the weather closes in you have to be able to let go of your frustrations, listen to music, read trashy novels, drink the camp drink – cocoa with a splash of Amaretto – and be as unproductive as you can. Email access is banned because it sucks up too much energy. For the six weeks or so the volunteers are out on the ice, this job will take every ounce of concentration they have.

In the thirty-plus years since it began, ANSMET people have found more than 20,000 meteorites. Add these to the ones found over the same period by people in Japanese and European programmes and the Antarctic total is more than 50,000. Even though many of these are probably fragments of the same rocks, that's more meteorites in a few decades than have been found in the rest of the world in two centuries.

One reason, of course, is that in Antarctica there are no trees, plants, roads or soil to obscure the view. On the ice, everything stands out. And the meteorites that land there can stay deep-frozen and unchanged for hundreds of thousands, even millions, of years (unlike, say, in the warm wet environment of London, where they would disintegrate in just a few decades).

But there's another reason that Antarctica is such a treasure trove for meteorites. The ice doesn't just collect them – it carefully concentrates them and presents them conveniently to the world. All this was figured out back in the 1980s by the founder of ANSMET, Bill Cassidy, a meteorite scientist from the University of Pittsburgh in Pennsylvania. Even in the early days of the programme Bill realised that Antarctica was special when it came to meteorites. There were places where you could pick them up by the bucketload. And all of these had exposed blue ice at the surface.

That's strange in itself. Though most of the continent is made of ice, up on the plateau it's usually buried under tens or hundreds of metres of snow. Unless you dig very deep, you'll rarely touch the blue stuff.

But scattered around the continent there are a few surface ice fields, pale blue against the white. They usually form when there's an obstruction beneath, a buried mountain range, say, or just an isolated hidden peak. As the ice flows out from the centre of the continent it hits the obstruction and rears up; strong surface winds then scrape off layer upon layer of snow until the ice itself emerges into the sunlight.

Bill Cassidy noticed that this was where the meteorites were, and he thought he knew why. The flow of the ice was like an in-built winnowing mechanism, concentrating the meteorites in just a few places. Over thousands of years meteorites fall randomly, are buried by snow and squashed together deep below the surface. Next, ice from different regions unites as it flows to the outer edges of the ice sheet, concentrating the meteorites further. Around most of the continent, snow, ice and meteorites eventually tumble into the sea. But in certain places the ice runs against a mountain range, and is forced to the surface in those blue patches, carrying its load of meteorites with it.[4]

If the mountain is fully buried, the only rocks you'll find on the surface must have come from space. But in some cases the tip of the mountain range pokes through the surface, scattering terrestrial rocks to confuse the picture. In that case, part of the training involves getting your eye in – learning to spot the rocks that are different from the crowd.

Ralph took over from Bill and has been running the ANSMET programme since 1996. But the first meteorite hunter that I met on the ice, John Schutt, goes back even farther. He has been working continuously for ANSMET since 1981 and – though he'd never admit it – he's probably the most experienced meteorite hunter on Earth.[5]

It was almost the end of the season when we met.[6] I'd been eager to join the meteorite posse on a hunt but they were long gone by the time I reached the ice. But John was still around tidying up a few things, and he took pity on me. He had to go and pick up a few bits of equipment from the Allan Hills Main Icefield. Did I want to tag along?

There was nothing standard issue about John Schutt. His shaggy brown beard was streaked with white, and strands of hair had escaped his ponytail and were jutting disreputably from beneath a faded baseball cap. His wind pants, enlivened with a crazy patchwork of red, orange and grey where the fabric had repeatedly frayed, proclaimed him as one of the oldest hands on the continent.

Our expedition wasn't, strictly speaking, a meteorite hunt. The Main Icefield had been picked over dozens of times so the chances of finding anything that someone had missed seemed remote. Worse, this was one of the sites with terrestrial rocks to confuse the eye. The ice butted up against the visible tip of a mountain and the field was already scattered with a disheartening array of earthly rocks, pebbles and stones. Muttering to myself about needles and haystacks, I climbed out of the helicopter to join John, who had leapt out while the rotors were still turning. Clearly his blood was up. 'There are meteorites around here,' he declared. 'I can smell them!'

The helicopter pilot, Barry James, was as curious as I was to see a real meteorite, and I waited for him to shut down and climb out of his seat. From up ahead John beckoned us over. 'Here, look at these,' he said and thrust out his hands containing two small pebbles. We studied them obediently. One was pale with very fine crystals, the other darker, packed with large crystals. 'The meteorites we're looking for won't look anything like these,' he said, and tossed them over his shoulder.

We all started casting around among the stones. Suddenly John dropped full length on to the ice, lifting his glasses to peer intently at a small rock. Barry and I held our breath. 'Nope,' said John. 'That's a leavitrite,' and he stood up and dusted himself off. 'Leave it right there?' Barry hazarded. 'You got it,' John replied briskly, and set off again.

John's clowning had lifted my mood and my optimism was soaring. It began to seem almost inevitable that we were going to find a meteorite, in spite of the odds. Our best chance was to find the most common kind of meteorite, an 'ordinary chondrite'. It would have medium-sized crystals, in between those we'd just seen in the terrestrial stones. But it would also contain tiny spheres called chondrules. No one knows what these are, but they come from the very earliest days of the Solar System, before the Sun or planets had even formed. They probably started out as patches of space dust that were flash-melted by a sudden burst of energy and then cooled into a rain of solid droplets.

Plenty of things could have supplied the energy. My favourite theory is that it came from an exploding star – a supernova. I like this because that same explosion may also have been the kick needed to make a random cloud of dust and gas start whirling and coalescing into our Sun, and planets. There are no chondrules left in terrestrial rocks. Anything here on Earth has been cooked, melted and fried by billions of years of grinding tectonic plates and volcanic outbursts and the chondrules are long gone. But most asteroids are too small to have all this activity, so chips off these particular blocks still bear the fingerprint of the stuff that gave birth to our worlds.

The biggest clue to a meteorite, though, would be its fusion crust, the molten outside layer formed as it tore through the atmosphere in a blaze of heat and light. Fusion crusts are usually very dark brown and uniform, somewhere between glossy and matt, as though someone had painted a layer of dark chocolate on the outside. At its simplest, the rocks around us were mainly pale, and we were looking for something dark.

But time was running out. We only had sixty minutes assigned ground time and if we didn't radio in to Mactown soon to confirm that we were lifting off, we would trigger an automatic Search and Rescue Mission. And then, when it was almost too late, when Barry and I were still peering rather hopelessly at rocks with John a tiny multi-coloured figure in the distance, we suddenly saw him beckoning. 'Come here,' his voice floated over the ice. 'I've found one!' We ran to meet him, skidding and sliding on the glassy blue surface. 'There it is,' he beamed, gesturing at a small brown stone, 'the oldest rock you'll ever see.'

About an inch or so in diameter, John's find was an ordinary chondrite, typical in every way. One end had been sheared off, revealing medium-sized crystals and a few small chondrules. The unbroken side was smooth and rounded, like a pebble in a stream. And, yes, there was the dark chocolate coating, too. It was textbook. We took turns lying flat on the ice, having our picture taken beside a genuine rock from space.

Being there at the find really is a thrill. But in meteorite terms ours was still 'ordinary'. Researchers now have thousands of these chondrites to prod and grind and test. They make up the vast body of meteorite finds the world over.

Rarer are the achondrites, the ones without little solidified blobs of pre-planetary putty. These must have come from bigger bodies, asteroids large enough to get some internal heat going. Some asteroids are large enough to begin to separate out into an internal iron core and lighter crust, which is why we can find meteorites on Earth made entirely of iron, or with other strange compositions. The truth is, everyone secretly wants to find the special ones, the achondrites. Because although most of these come, like the ordinary chondrites, from the asteroid belt, a handful come from somewhere else entirely.

18 January 1982, Allan Hills Main Icefield

If it weren't so close to the end of the season, John Schutt might have delayed the trip. The sky was already grey by breakfast time and it was getting greyer. John wasn't worried about a snow-storm. This was the high desert where snow almost never fell. But if the clouds descended low enough, they could lose all the shadows. That's OK on the blue ice patches, but in between, where everything was white, no shadows meant no surface defi-nition. And that meant the wind-sculpted sastrugi became all but invisible, making it perilously easy to overturn a skidoo. Worse, in these days before satellites could pinpoint you wherever you went, if you couldn't pick out your own tracks in the snow you might never get home.

But there was a new arrival in camp, Ian Whillans, who had come in from Mactown just two days before. Ian wasn't an expert on meteorites, but he knew a lot about ice and he wanted to check out the meteorite sites for himself. While the rest of the team stuck around camp, John had offered to take Ian out to the Middle Western Icefield a few kilometres away.

Anyway, John knew the terrain better than most. As the two of them fired up their skidoos and roared out of camp, he kept a watchful eye on the descending clouds as well as on the ice around him. Nobody knew if there were meteorites to find but up here where there were no earthly outcrops to distract you, anything dark had to have come from space. So they'd look around, take a few pictures, and maybe – if they were lucky – find a few rocks.

When they reached the ice field, the two companions spread out. Almost immediately, off in the distance, John saw Ian stop and wave his arms. Beginner's luck. Ian had clearly found his first ever meteorite. But when John went over to check it out he was baffled by what he saw. Though he'd seen a few hundred meteorites by then, he'd never seen anything like this. The rock, which was about the size of a golf ball, had a weird fusion crust that seemed to be some kind of frothy green glass. Part of it had sheared off and inside were chunky angular fragments of a white mineral called feldspar, making a sharp contrast with the dull grey background.

John opened his collection kit and pulled out an aluminium strip. He punched the number – 1422 – into the counter and held it over the meteorite while Ian took what is now one of the programme's most famous pictures. Then he carefully bagged it and wrote this in his notebook:

#1422 – Strange meteorite. Thin, tan-green fusion crust, ~50%, with possible ablation features. Interior is dark grey with

numerous white to grey brecchia (?) fragments. Somewhat equi-dimensional at ~3 cm.[7]

In retrospect, everyone involved said they should have known immediately where this new meteorite had come from. To a trained eye, John's description had all the right clues. But though there was mild interest back in camp at this strange specimen, it went into the pot with all the rest and was promptly forgotten.

Even when the meteorite finally reached Houston several months later, it wasn't the first one to be processed. Perhaps John should have put a few more exclamation marks in his description. Knowing what he knows now, he would also probably not have stinted on the capital letters. But back then, the curators didn't turn to meteorite #1422 until they had already processed four others. So it became ALH81005, the fifth to be processed from the Allan Hills region, from finds made in the season beginning in 1981.

But when the researchers at NASA's Johnson Space Center (JSC) took a closer look at the meteorite, they began to understand the significance of this physically small but scientifically giant find. And the bevy of researchers who clamoured for tiny fragments to test confirmed these suspicions. Those white chunks that John had so faithfully recorded turned out to be anorthite, the chalky mineral that makes up most of the lunar highlands. ALH81005 hadn't come from the asteroid belt or anywhere near. It had come from our very own Moon.[8]

This was nearly fifteen years after the Apollo programme had brought back abundant quantities of Moon rocks. Any geologists worth their salt knew that large parts of the lunar surface were made up of fragmented white anorthite in a pale grey background. Why did none of the experts who had already seen the sample manage to identify it?

The main reason for this collective snow blindness is that it simply shouldn't have been possible. According to the wisdom of the day, meteorites could only come from asteroids. The energy needed to break off a piece of another planet and blast it into the sky should have pulverised the rock. And even if a fragment did survive long enough to escape its home planet's gravity, it would be just one small speck in the infinite blackness of space. Small chance that it should fall on to the Earth, and infinitesimal chance that anyone should find it. But that reckoned without the concentrating power of the Antarctic ice. Just as we had gone to the Moon, so the Moon had now come to us. And if chunks of the Moon could be chipped off and survive long enough to arrive on the surface of the Earth, perhaps pieces of other planets could come to us, too.

The first to appear was the Chassignite, a four-pound lump of extra-terrestrial rock that landed in Chassigny, France, at 8 a.m. on 3 October 1815, just months after the Battle of Waterloo. It was followed on 25 August 1865, at 9 a.m., by another peculiar meteorite that fell near Shergotty in India. Like the Chassignite, this one was hefty, weighing in at ten pounds. Also, like the Chassignite it looked different from the normal run of meteorites. It had no chondrules. Its crystals were more like those from earthly rocks that had melted in the heart of volcanoes. It also turned out to be disturbingly young. Meteorites from the asteroid belt all date back to the first days of the Solar System, and they are uniformly 4.5 billion years old. This new meteorite, dubbed a Shergottite, measured its age in the mere hundreds of millions of years.

And at 9 a.m. on 28 June 1911, a shower of at least forty stones fell near the village of El Nakhla El Baharia, twenty-five miles east of Alexandria in Egypt. One of the stones reportedly killed an unlucky dog. By the late twentieth century, it was clear that this 'Nakhlite' bore striking similarities to the Shergottite. It was born in lava, and, though older than the Shergottites, by meteorite standards it was still extremely young.

These three meteorites collectively gave birth to a new category of alien stones, affectionately known as SNCs (pronounced 'snicks') for Shergottite, Nakhlite and Chassignite. Over the years, more SNCs showed up and by 1980 nine had been found, including three in Antarctica, but nobody knew what they were. They existed on the fringe of meteorite research, in an undefined category of their own. And yet, certain researchers had begun to murmur about the SNCs. If they were volcanic, and they were young, they had to have come from a body big enough to have internal heat and violent eruptions. And that meant a planet. An alien planet.

But nobody spoke too loudly because this, of course, was impossible. Or so it seemed until sample ALH81005 hit the big time. If a meteorite could come to us from the Moon, what were the chances – whisper it – of rocks also coming to us from Mars? In 1983 something happened to turn the whispers into a roar.

EET79001 was clearly a SNC. The ANSMET posse had found it near a scattering of Earth rocks called Elephant Moraine in 1979, and the rock was peculiar enough that the curators at Johnson Space Center had unwrapped it first. It weighed a hefty eighteen pounds and, like the other SNCs, was made from cooled solidified lava. But when researchers sawed through, they found some odd dark blobs that stood out starkly against the pale grey background. Whatever had smashed this rock off its first home had also compressed it with a shock wave of energy. As the rock relaxed, parts of it had melted, creating these glassy blobs along tiny fracture lines. And while they were still liquid, the blobs had dissolved a little of the atmosphere around them. Tiny bubbles, trapped inside these dark receptacles, might yield a vital clue about where the rock had been born.

Encouraged by the new lunar finding, in 1983 researchers re-melted, collected, measured, and held their collective breath. And the results as these minuscule whiffs of gas were released from their glassy prison were unequivocal. They looked nothing like the composition of our own earthly atmosphere, but exactly like the elements that remote satellites and robot space missions had already measured on Mars.[9] The SNCs were definitely Martian.[10]

Though the world had, by this time, sent several space missions to our nearest planetary neighbour, and there were many more to come, a sample return was (and still is) a very distant prospect. We can measure the planet remotely, but it will be a long time before we can bring a piece of it back. But the Antarctic ice had shown us something that we would otherwise scarcely have believed. Earthbound people, many of them, had already held a piece of the Red Planet in their hands.

This was exciting news indeed, and yet all the SNCs hailed from relatively recently in Mars' history, from the days when the planet itself was in late middle age, cold and drear and almost certainly lifeless. That's not particularly surprising. Mars bears an impressive belt of volcanoes including Olympus Mons, the largest in the Solar System, which is three times the height of Mount Everest and stretches for more than 600 km. Much of the Martian surface has been repeatedly swamped with outpourings from these melting mountains, leaving older surfaces deeply buried. Small wonder, then, that the SNCs were all so young, and that none of them reached back to the wet Noachian Epoch, when water was apparently abundant on the Martian surface, and the planet might even have supported life.[11]

But imagine this, for a moment. If an asteroid happened to hit one of the rare remaining older surfaces; if its strike were glancing enough that it didn't pulverise the surface, but forceful enough that it ejected a chunk of rock with an escape velocity of

12,000 mph; if that chunk, flung out into space, wandered aimlessly for a million years or two before feeling the gravitational tug of a nearby planet; if it tore through the atmosphere of that planet in a blaze of glory and landed on one of the planet's frozen ice caps; if the chunk was buried in snow, squeezed, shoved and harried until it re-emerged, blinking, into the strangely blue daylight; and if, tens of thousands of years later a few local bipeds happened upon it, might it contain signs of alien life? If so, it would surely become one of the most exciting pieces of real estate in the entire Solar System.

27 December 1984, Allan Hills

It had already been a great day. The ANSMET team had been searching the far western ice field, back and forth, in the bright sunshine. After lunch, with a good haul already in the bag, they rewarded themselves with a jaunt. Along the top of the nearby escarpment was a fairyland of ice towers and wind scoops and giant sastrugi. There were huge wind-sculpted pinnacles up to 10 m high and crevasses filled with hard snow, pounded and packed in by the winds. When the light was just right, the pinnacles could shine as if they were on fire. It was a magical place for a little rest and relaxation.

The team swooped along the crest of the escarpment for a while, catching the glimmer and mood, before it was time to head back down, get back to work, do a few more passes before the end of the day. On the way down they hit patches of bare ice among the pinnacles. Instinctively the six of them spread out on their skidoos, eyes suddenly peeled. And there, on a gentle slope, lying on a small patch of ice, was a chocolate-brown squarish chunk of rock, about the size of a grapefruit. It was an achondrite, with no little round chondrules to mark it out as part of the Solar System's early builder's rubble. It had been born from melted rock, in a volcano. Maybe it was just a trick of the light, but it had a greenish tinge. The team photographed it, bagged it and threw it in the backpack.

Back at the Johnson Space Center, this was the first meteorite that year to be opened, earning it the sobriquet ALH84001. At first and even second glance it looked like a visitor from the asteroid belt. For one thing it was at least four billion years old – very much older than the SNCs. The curators decided that it had come from an asteroid called Vesta – which was interesting, though not Earth-shattering. Suitably identified and labelled, it was safely filed away.

Seven years later, while fiddling around with a sample of this same meteorite, a researcher named David Mittlefehldt from the JSC saw something that puzzled him. Though it was supposed to have come from Vesta, ALH84001 contained a few minerals that were more like the ones found in some of the SNCs. Could it actually have come from Mars? If so, that would be really exciting. This would be the first Martian meteorite from that early, old, wet period, when there was the best chance that there had been Martian life.

There was one way to find out. The element oxygen comes in several flavours, called isotopes, with slightly different weights, and their ratio in a rock works as a sort of fingerprint, showing exactly where the rock came from. David requested an analysis and the results came back with astonishing news. ALH84001 had the classic characteristic fingerprint of the Red Planet.

On the much closer inspection that it now received, ALH84001 turned out to have a very interesting history. It had been formed several miles below the Martian surface in the planet's earliest days. As the crust of Mars bucked and heaved, our rock worked its way upwards. About four billion years ago, it received its first big shock, when parts of it shattered as something hit the surface above its head, very hard. But the smack wasn't quite enough to dislodge the rock and it stayed put. It may, though, have felt trickles of early Martian water passing through its fractured veins.

Nothing much happened for the next few billion years until something else hit the Martian surface even harder, and the rock that was to become ALH84001 was flung out into space. It roamed the Solar System for seventeen million years and then finally, 13,000 years ago, it fell on to the Antarctic ice and lay there, unnoticed and unsung.

This awakened the interest of a colleague of David Mittlefehldt's – another David, but this time called McKay. The most interesting stage from David McKay's point of view was the early part. He decided to see whether ALH84001 had really been in touch with Martian water, and if so whether there had been anything alive in the water. First, he found orangey-red carbonates in the rock. That was promising. Carbonates form out of water, often with something living involved in the process. Next, he found something even more intriguing: certain organic chemicals that form when living things indulge in chemistry. And then came the most intriguing finding of all. When David and his team sliced off a piece of the meteorite and put it into their most powerful microscope, they saw something astonishing. Within the matrix of the rock were tiny worm-like shapes that looked like bacteria. They weren't alive, that was for sure. But they might once have been.

Quickly, David's team prepared a scientific paper,[12] but before they could publish, the news started leaking out. On 6 August 1996, NASA head Dan Goldin issued a statement announcing a press conference the following day:

NASA has made a startling discovery that points to the possibility that a primitive form of microscopic life may have existed on Mars more than three billion years ago ... I want everyone to understand that we are not talking about little green men. These are extremely small, single-cell structures that somewhat resemble

*bacteria on Earth . . . The NASA scientists and researchers who
made this discovery will be available at a news conference tomorrow
to discuss their findings.*

The world went wild. Headlines around the planet broke
the news. President Bill Clinton himself stepped out on to the
South Lawn of the White House at 1:15 p.m. on 7 August
1996 to address the jostling crowd of journalists. He spoke of
how NASA's announcement had vindicated the US scientific
and space programmes and how he intended to pursue the
study of Mars more aggressively than ever. And then, he said
this:

*Today, rock 84001 speaks to us across all those billions of years and
millions of miles. It speaks of the possibility of life. If this discovery
is confirmed, it will surely be one of the most stunning insights into
our universe that science has ever uncovered. Its implications are as
far-reaching and awe-inspiring as can be imagined. Even as it
promises answers to some of our oldest questions, it poses still others
even more fundamental. We will continue to listen closely to what
it has to say as we continue the search for answers and for knowledge that is as old as humanity itself but essential to our people's
future.*[13]

More than a decade later, debate is still raging. But although
most scientists remain sceptical about the claims for Martian life in
the rock, nobody has yet managed to prove beyond all doubt that
ALH84001 has no traces of life. At first it seemed as though the
carbonates must have formed at temperatures that were far too
high to allow the existence of life, but, no, they could also have
formed at comfortably low temperatures. The wiggles that looked
like worms were too small to be bacteria, except that we have now
found similarly small 'nanobacteria' on Earth. The organic chemi-

cals could easily be formed by perfectly normal chemistry that has nothing to do with life. But they are also a natural by-product of life itself. ALH84001 is far from conclusive. But it is still the most intriguing evidence to date that life might have existed elsewhere in space, that we humans may not be alone.

And if this proves to be right, there is a fascinating corollary. The earliest days of the Solar System were like a celestial billiards game with half-formed planetoids slamming into each other. Most scientists agree that life could not begin on Earth until this early bombardment had calmed down, and the rocks had stopped melting and the atmosphere had stopped boiling away. However, the evidence suggests that life started on Earth *immediately* after the bombardment ended. Which begs the question: how did life get its toehold on Earth the very moment that conditions were right?

Perhaps the answer lies elsewhere in the Solar System. Mars is much smaller than the Earth, and its weaker gravitational pull would have attracted fewer incoming missiles. For it, the bombardment would have finished earlier, and thus life could have arisen earlier. And if life did appear on Mars in its earliest days and if (as we now know to be true) meteorites can be chipped off Mars and carried to Earth, could some of those rocks from space have brought Martian life along with them? If so, life might have evolved just once in the Solar System – on the planet Mars – and then come belatedly to Earth on the wings of an incoming rock or two. If that is true, and thanks to all that we have learned from Antarctica, we might all of us be Martians.

Mars, Mars, Mars: you hear about it everywhere in the Dry Valleys. But the most Mars-like of all is a remote valley tucked up against the edge of the ice sheet, almost level with the Allan Hills. It is hard to reach, almost hidden by the bright white ice that all but surrounds it.

Beacon Valley is an elongated horseshoe, protected by a semi-circle of mountains, its flat northern edge disappearing seamlessly into the interlocking system of valleys and glaciers that stretches all the way down to the sea. It lies in the upland region of the Dry Valleys, the coldest, driest, most desolate part. And it is not just the closest place to Mars that humans have ever seen. It is also a valley where time stands still.

From above, Beacon Valley's floor looks like the scaly skin of a crocodile, or perhaps the cracked mud from a dried-out river bed. While the other Dry Valleys are smooth, this one is shot through with many-sided shapes that look too regular to have formed by chance. They are called 'contraction-crack polygons' and they show up in small patches in many cold, bleak parts of the world. But here they stretch for miles, the defining character-istic of an otherwise bare valley floor.

Through my helicopter window the polygons looked so small and tidy that it was a shock to land and find that they were metres wide; so wide, in fact, that at eye level you could no longer make out the patterns. They seemed instead like random jumbles of rocks, set in shifting gravel and silt, with no discerni-ble purpose but to turn your ankles and bar your way. The pilot had been in radio contact with my hosts and told me they were expecting me. 'They're over there somewhere,' he said with a grin and a jerk of his thumb.

As I watched him take off, I was feeling a bit bleak myself. The helicopter pad was just a small square in the middle of a polygon, with some of the biggest stones removed to make it flat. In the centre was an 'x' formed of yellow sandstones that stood out against the grey; the edges were marked with red tent bags weighted down with more stones. Just beyond were three pyram-idal Scott tents, two yellow, one white, a few smaller dome tents and a large, brightly striped Endurance model that was probably where they cooked. There was no sign of anyone in camp. I was

tempted for a moment just to stay there and wait for the end of
the day, but I resolutely dumped my sleeping gear and stumbled
off in search of the field party.

I'd come to meet a double act of scientists, a partnership that
Peter Doran described to me as a 'match made in heaven'. The
leader of this expedition was Dave Marchant from Boston
University.[14] Dave was an expert on geomorphology – the shape
and structure of ice-formed landscapes – and he knew this
particular landscape as well as anyone alive. With him would be
Jim Head, from Brown University in Rhode Island, who was a
world expert on Mars. According to both of them, Beacon Valley
was the most Martian of the Dry Valleys, the closest you could
get to the Red Planet without leaving Earth.[15]

To be sure, the rocks I was stumbling over reminded me of the
famous pictures from NASA's missions to Mars. There were
boulders everywhere, with polished sides like gemstones, and
slightly rounded edges where they had been shaped by the wind.
The winds must be strong here. Some of the more exposed ones
had a scooped-out hollow in the gravel in front of them, and a
long drawn-out gravel tail behind. Many of the rocks were pitted
with holes that had been scoured by a combination of wind, salt
and sand. I watched, fascinated, as a stray flake of snow landed on
one of these pits and bounced from one side to the next before
it finally settled and melted.

The polishing by the wind had varnished these boulders,
giving them a rust colour that looked even redder through my
sunglasses. I sat for a moment with my back against a boulder and
imagined that I was on Mars. The gravity was too strong, but I
tried to let go of that. I pictured a pink sky, alien moons, Earth as
a distant neighbour. The first overwhelming impression was one
of loneliness. I shook myself and stood up. Maybe I overdid it.
But now, a feeling of responsibility had kicked in. If I were really
on Mars, then anything I touched had never been touched

before. I started jumping from rock to rock like a child avoiding the cracks, so that I didn't leave any footprints on the soft gravel. On this ridged landscape, I could see nobody else in the entire valley. It was foolish, but I suddenly needed to climb up on to one of the highest ridges of the nearest polygon and peer out ahead until I caught sight of a handful of red coats in the distance and felt a rush of relief.

As I stumbled over the polygon rocks towards them I heard a mighty thwack. A figure in a red parka and jaunty green hat had slammed a sledgehammer against a small square of aluminium on the ground in front of him. The plate rose into the air with a silver flash like a leaping salmon and from where I was standing I heard two distinct 'tings' as the sound reached me first through the ground and then through the air. Two other figures were operating monitoring equipment and a handful more were looking on. The man with the hammer turned out to be Dave Marchant. When he saw me, he put the hammer on the ground. 'OK, men!' he barked in a mock-military tone though there were clearly women in his team. 'Five minutes. Smoke if you've got 'em. Check your socks. If you've got a buddy make sure he's OK.' His students were clearly used to this. They grinned, stood down from the equipment and started pulling chocolate bars out of their backpacks.

Dave was an odd combination of the light-hearted and intense. He was in his forties, his face deeply tanned and crinkled with laughter lines. His eyes were strikingly blue. He worked so hard and relentlessly that his students called him, to his face, 'Cyborg'. But he required little persuasion to tear open his parka and fleece and show off the T-shirt he often wore underneath, bearing a picture of his infant son with the same striking blue eyes.

While the rest of the crew took their break, Dave climbed with me over the boulders, pointing out his favourite features of this, his favourite valley. The main thing he wanted to show me was how it defied the normal rules. The one constant on earthly landscapes is usually change. Our home planet is restless and the continual assault of wind and weather, water and ice, is what shapes its surface.

But not here. Dave calls this landscape 'paralysed'. There has been no running water in Beacon Valley for fourteen million years. Most of the snow on the ground has blown in from elsewhere rather than fallen from the clouds. The wind may scoop and pit the boulders but it doesn't move them. 'You see that rockfall over there?' He was pointing to a large skirt of rocks and boulders that had tumbled down from the mountain across the way. The rocks lay neatly where they had fallen, just as you'd expect from a fresh young landslide. If it had happened long ago, they should have been shuffled and shifted, confusing that neatly sloping pattern. 'It looks recent, doesn't it?' said Dave. 'Well, we've dated it and it's a million years old!'

He was delighted by my look of confusion, and walked over to where a small rock was sitting on the gravel. 'Think about it,' he said. 'My family is religious, I went to church, heard about the time of Jesus two thousand years ago. Think of everything that has happened to the world since then, and through all that time this rock has just been sitting here. If I'd walked here a million years ago it would have looked like this. Ten million years ago, before humans ever walked anywhere, this is how this valley looked. It's a window back in time.'

The tectonic forces that cause the rest of the world to buckle and warp have been subdued here for an extraordinary stretch of time. 'You're looking at the most stable landscape on Earth,' said Dave. 'Nothing even comes close. The Grand Canyon was carved in its entirety; the alps in New Zealand have risen to their great heights and all the while nothing happened here.'

I was awed by the sense that time was standing still there. And not just in the past but in the future, too. Though other parts of

Antarctica might now be feeling the heat, Beacon Valley was insulated from almost everything. Only a big tectonic change – a clashing of continents that altered ocean circulations – would be likely to have an effect here. And that isn't likely since the rest of the world's continents are now all moving away. 'We know what the future's going to hold in Beacon Valley,' said Dave, 'and it's more of the same.'

And that's what makes Beacon Valley Mars-like. Today, the Red Planet is old, cold and dry. Nothing moves; nothing changes. Just like here.

As we walked, our bunny boots made striated oval footprints on the silt, like the ones Neil Armstrong left on the Moon. I told Dave about imagining myself on Mars, and then hopping from rock to rock on the way here so that I didn't leave any violating human trace. He laughed. 'This landscape isn't just old, it's also stable,' he said. 'So if you change something it wants to go back.' He pointed to my space-man footprint. 'The tread will be gone after one storm. The outline after a summer. And after a year, there will be no sign that it was ever there.'

Back at the site, I met the other half of the scientific match. Jim Head appeared graver, with a soft, courteous Virginia accent. He was maybe twenty years older than Dave, and his white hair and beard, and the staff-like pole he was carrying, made him look like Gandalf, the wizard from *The Lord of the Rings*. Though he was the elder and more experienced of the two scientists, he was the guest here, and marked this, slightly self-mockingly, by calling Dave 'sir'.

Jim's first job, just out of graduate school, was to advise the Apollo programme where to land on the Moon. (He said he had answered an advertisement that read: 'Our job is to think our way to the Moon and back. Call this number.') He had to choose somewhere that was interesting geologically to make the science of the mission worthwhile. But if the soil had been too soft in the Sea of Tranquillity, the Eagle could have sunk irrevocably into the lunar dust. If the ground had been sloping, the craft could have rolled. Buzz Aldrin and Neil Armstrong would have been tossed and tumbled inside their craft and their journey might have ended there. When the world watched on 20 July 1969, Jim's daughters asked: 'Where's Dad?' Dad, it turned out, was in a side room at the Apollo Control Center, watching and listening as the pictures rolled in. His choice of landing spot worked perfectly.[16]

Since then he has been obsessed with planets. He talks about them with an easy familiarity, as though they are old friends. 'On the Moon you could move along pretty fast. On Apollo 17 Jack [Schmitt] really got the lunar gait down. He practised a lot of different ways but the best one was hopping. There are some very funny pictures.' What about Mars? 'You probably wouldn't hop on Mars,' he says. 'The Moon's surface is much more forgiving, like a soft soil. On Mars you could launch yourself more than you wanted to and come crashing down. Trudging is the way to go there, pretty much the way we do it here.'

I asked him what his favourite planet was. 'The Earth,' he said immediately. 'But after that, Mars.'

And that was why he was here, in this most Martian of places. Though he had trained astronauts for manned missions and robots for flights to Venus, Saturn and Mars, he had never walked on the planets he studied, or touched them, or tasted them. His job was to use his imagination. What should the astronauts collect? And later, what would the landers and rovers see? What should they pick up, or turn over, or test? How can you picture a landscape when all you had to go on was the rigid view of a robot camera?

He started telling me about the Vallis Marinaris canyon system up on the Martian region of Tharsis. The canyon itself is vast, a single feature stretching the equivalent of the distance from

Boston to Los Angeles. And yet, the resemblance to here is still uncanny. Beacon Valley is almost a montage of parts of Vallis Marinaris: the wind, the quiet, the ancient surface, the steep cliffs, the polygons and rocks that look just like those seen through the camera of the Viking lander.

There is also the way the ice here tiptoes over the land without leaving a footprint. In most other icy parts of the world, glaciers are wet. They scrape along on a thin film of water, gouging out valleys and scratching the rocks as they pass. That's what you get in the Alps, and the other places that have informed glaciologists and geologists for generations. But here, glaciers behave differently. They are old and cold and slow, and their bases are stuck to the ground. Instead of sliding, they flow sluggishly like treacle. They leave few scrape marks on the surface, but the piles of rocks they leave behind – formed as rocks fall from the cliffs on to their surfaces – look exactly like the ones on Mars.[17]

When Dave first told Jim about Beacon Valley he was gobsmacked. 'It was an epiphany for me. It was like, shht, that's how it works on Mars, too!' (He actually said 'shht'. That's how he pronounced it. Jim might mimic swear words but I can't imagine him actually using one.)

Now Jim was excited as he started reeling off the many ways that Beacon Valley reminded him of Mars. There was the lack of liquid water; the low erosion rates; the incredibly cold climate. Here in the upland zone of the Dry Valleys, he said, it was a hyper-dry cold polar desert. 'And that's what Mars is pretty much everywhere.'

So though Jim was helping Dave investigate the scientific details of Beacon Valley's surface, he was also on a training exercise for his imagination. 'When you're here you can walk around. You can look. You don't have to wait for the wind data to come in, you can feel the wind. You see the way the light falls. You can immerse yourself in the landscape.'

In his office in Brown University one of his students had painted a sign in calligraphy to hang on his wall. It bore one word: Daydream. 'You know,' he said, 'in case I forget.'

That evening, I discovered that Dave and Jim ran the most whimsical camp I had yet encountered. They used animal sounds for the wake-up call – a different one for each day. Tomorrow, Saturday, would be 'Eee-awww' which turned out to sound like a donkey with a bad hangover. Sunday would be the cawing of a crow and Monday, ambitious, this – 'a mockingbird imitation of a jay'. They named their thermos flasks according to a theme. This year, the theme was 'obscure people'. Jim's was named after Joe Engle, who was the astronaut kicked off the Apollo programme at the last minute to make way for Harrison 'Jack' Schmitt, 'the only true geologist who's ever been to space'.

Toilet facilities were unusual, too. There were the normal pee bottles of the Dry Valleys, to be poured, when full, into a U-barrel. But for the rest, there was an arrangement little short of a throne. To use it you 'declared' in front of everyone, so there was no danger of subsequent embarrassment through the lack of lock, or indeed of door. A short stroll then took you to a sit-down box on the edge of the camp, set in the natural shelter of a small wall of boulders. To the right were age-old chocolate-coloured cliffs. In the distance, the folds and sweeps of the Taylor Glacier. Barring the few souls in the camp behind you the nearest human was hundreds, perhaps thousands, of kilometres away. This was a smallest room with the biggest, most majestic view.

Though people slept in individual tents, the main activity centred around the cook tent, which contained two cots that doubled as couches, and two stoves on either side of the door. Hanging from the ceiling, among the defrosting dinner, plates, drying socks, gloves and hats, a cock-eyed Santa Claus and his spindly legged Rudolph, were two miniature speakers, precariously attached with duct tape beside an iPod cable. I'd brought fresh fruit and bread to try to win these guys over, but maybe fresh music would be a better idea. It was 8 p.m. now, and most of us were already in the tent, waiting for Dave to join us. Hesitantly I offered my iPod. 'Are you looking for some new tunes?' I asked. Conversation stopped. Someone said: 'You don't ... by any chance ... have any Tom Jones do you?' Seven pairs of expectant eyes turned to me.

As it happened, the answer was yes. I'd made my collection as eclectic as I could and now it looked as though it would pay off. Everyone was bizarrely excited. 'Shh! Don't say anything. Quick! Before he comes!' Within a few minutes the first few bars of 'It's Not Unusual' came belting out of speakers cranked up to top volume. Outside there was a roar. Dave ripped open the door and lurched into the tent, his eyes shining. Everyone was laughing and shouting at once. Eventually I discovered that Dave long ago declared this to be the official camp song; but someone took the CD last season and they'd been missing it like crazy. Tom Jones has no idea, I thought to myself. This was about as unusual as it got.

That night, I wondered why so many men and women in Antarctica felt the need for whimsy like this. In some cases it might be like whistling in the dark: you had to show bravado in the face of a hostile environment. But Dave and Jim and the team didn't seem remotely afraid of this place. They clearly loved it. In the end I decided that it was partly because they worked so incredibly hard here, from early morning till late at night; the laughter was for release. But I also sensed that it came out of exuberance at doing their science in a place that clearly made them feel alive.

The next morning brought clear weather and a good working day. As we hiked over to a new site, Dave explained what he was investigating this season. It was all about ice. Beacon Valley was ringed around with smaller valleys like catchers' mitts, which trapped the snow blowing down from the plateau and turned it into ice until it formed glaciers.

Rocks tumbling down from the steep sides of the valley coated the glaciers with a thick dark surface, and this protected the ice at least for a while. But as the glaciers moved sluggishly towards Beacon Valley the prurient fingers of the wind succeeded in poking through gaps in the rocks, sand and silt and whipping away whiffs of ice vapour. By the time it reached the centre of Beacon Valley, far away from the sources, the ice should all have vanished.

But it hadn't. One day, when he was digging around in the rocks, Dave's shovel clanged against something that was unmistakably ice, where no ice had the right to be. Yesterday's experiment with the sledgehammer was intended to send seismic waves down through the ice to the rock beneath, to measure how thick it was. Today, he meant to drill into the ice and pull up some samples.

As we hiked, I started to think about the heroic explorers of old. Like most of the people that I'd met down here, the team had read about those early Antarctic exploits. But very few from the heroic age made it this far into the uplands. Beacon Valley was barely touched till the helicopters could make it in – and even now very few people had stood here. I wondered if that made these scientists feel like explorers themselves. Dave considered the question. 'For me it's the science,' he said finally. 'It's not about standing where no one else has stood. It's about finding things. Thinking where no one else has thought.' He stopped suddenly, his face alight. 'Oh, wow! Let me show you something *really* interesting! I didn't know we had already crossed over into the yellow brick road.'

He started scrabbling at the pale golden rock that had appeared beneath our feet, half hidden by chocolate-coloured boulders. 'Look at him, he's like a leprechaun,' Jim said, adding with a heavy Irish brogue: 'Pot o' gold.'

'Precioussss ...' hissed Dave, piling slabs of the yellow rock into his arms. 'Master says I can have it.' He was leaping and bounding from side to side, making us all laugh, before he stood up and started placing the samples into a bag. And then he looked at me with a wide grin. 'You know how we were talking about discoveries. Well, you just walked on one.'

This pale yellow rock was once volcanic ash; though it didn't look like any ash that I'd seen before, that was because it had been around for a while. But the important thing was that if you had ash you could get a geological age. When a volcano erupts, the cloud of debris that it throws into the air contains minerals that act as tiny cages trapping radioactive elements inside. The cage is so small that nothing can get in or out. All the radioactive elements can do is gradually decay, tick, tick, tick, at a precise rate just like a clock. If you find these tiny cages and measure the ratio of what is left inside, you know how long ago the eruption happened.

That mattered because this particular layer of ash lay on top of Dave's buried ice, meaning the ice must have formed before. And when he measured those ticking clocks, they told him that his buried ice was at least eight million years old.[18]

Ice! The most vulnerable solid on Earth. The material that melts as soon as you look at it. It's almost inconceivable that such stuff could survive intact on Earth for so fantastically long. At first nobody would believe it, and Dave has had to make his case again and again, with multiple ashes and detailed models, to win over his scientist peers. But now, most were convinced that the ice buried in Beacon Valley was by far the oldest on Earth. And by drilling into it, Dave hoped to get samples, actual bubbles, of the ancient air trapped inside.

So far, Dave hadn't managed to get a clean clear signal of ancient air from his ice cores. There was evidence that cracks in the ice had mixed up the bubbles from different times and muddied the picture. But he was convinced that if he succeeded he would find the clearest window yet into the Earth's distant climate history.

Jim was just as excited about the prospects for ice on Mars. 'I think it's very likely that there's still ice on Mars, buried under the same kind of rocks that we have here and it could be tens or even hundreds of millions of years old. Imagine that! We could go there, and drill into it, and get a pristine climate record of the whole history of Mars!'

And so I stayed and watched for the next few days, as the team hefted their drilling apparatus to site after site, faces falling as the cores cracked or the rocks shattered, and shining with delight when a clean ice core went into its bag ready to be analysed. And I sang along with them to Tom Jones and Meatloaf. And I did my best to listen to the silence of the valley, when everyone else was asleep.

On my last day there, as we were walking back to camp, the wind had dropped. Though the temperature was 21°F it felt surprisingly pleasant – the sun was warm on our backs and there were no clouds.

Dave looked at me quizzically. 'What do you think?' he said. 'Are we crazy to spend six weeks out here? Can you imagine doing it?' Yes, I could. I could imagine staying here much, much longer than that. I found myself envying him the serenity of this valley that time forgot. 'I'm tired of rushing around,' I said. 'I'd like to stay here long enough to get bored, and then go beyond the boredom and see what's really there.' He seemed to understand. 'It's when you've been here for a while, when you really get in the zone, like a runner with a second wind, when the weather's good and you've had a good day doing good science, you can just stop and listen and ask "what are you telling me?"'

Ask who? The landscape? I wondered if he was being whimsical again but I could see from his face that he was in earnest. 'It does talk to you,' he said. 'Antarctica has this way of clearing your mind. Part of it is that there's no distractions. They keep saying to me "why not just do day trips" but I say, "no, you have to be here, to be immersed in it. You have to feel the landscape – to start to feel like Antarctica. That's when you can hear what it's telling you."'

As we arrived back in camp we all heard the distant 'whup whup' of a helo breaking the silence of the valley. My ride would soon be here. I raced to my tent to pick up my gear. Soon I was back in the air, flying over the scaly polygons and out over the glacier. Behind and below me, the oldest landscape in the world was still telling its story to anyone who stayed around long enough to hear.

2

THE HIGH PLATEAU

Turning Point

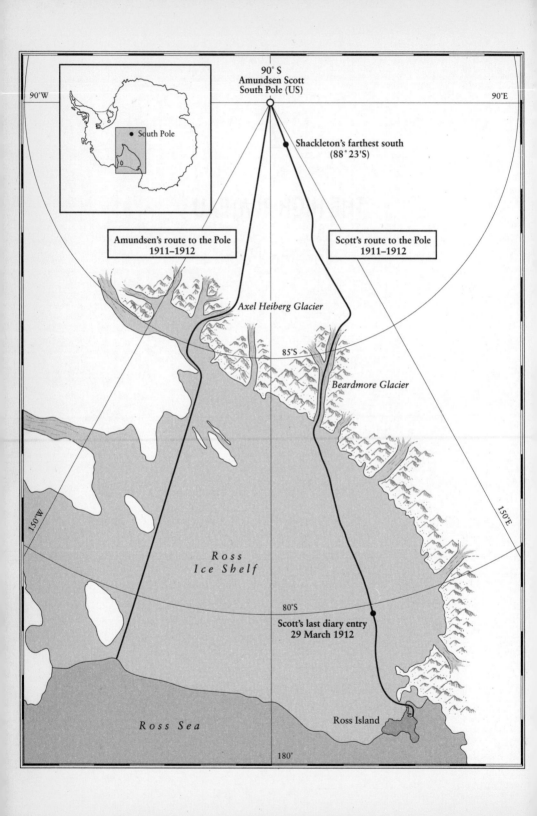

90° S
Amundsen Scott
South Pole (US)

90°W

90°E

South Pole

Shackleton's farthest south
(88°23'S)

Amundsen's route to the Pole
1911–1912

Scott's route to the Pole
1911–1912

Axel Heiberg Glacier

85°S

Beardmore Glacier

150°W

150°E

Ross
Ice Shelf

80°S

Scott's last diary entry
29 March 1912

Ross Sea

Ross Island

180°

4

THE SOUTH POLE

You can describe the South Pole in many different ways. It is an imaginary dot in a vast field of white; the farthest south anyone can go; one of only two places on Earth where all the lines of longitude meet, where if you make one full turn your feet pass through every time zone, but where the Earth itself does not spin, and the ground beneath you is still. Unlike the North Pole, it is also the site of a surprising amount of human activity: dormitories, offices, trucks, pool tables, shower blocks, saunas and science.

There are two physical markers to tell you that you're standing at the South Pole. One is ceremonial, a red and white striped barber's pole topped with a mirrored globe and surrounded by the flags of the first twelve countries to sign the Antarctic Treaty. This is where the dignitaries go to have their picture taken, and where you can lean in and see your face, weirdly distorted in the globe's mirror, with ice and sky and buildings stretched out behind.

Not far away is the 'real' Pole, marked by an understated steel rod and topped with a small brass cap. A new cap is lovingly designed and machined each year by a resident technician whiling away the long dark winter, and the marker is relocated in an official ceremony every New Year's Day. The geographic pole itself doesn't move but the ice slides over it, about thirty feet per year, and, without this annual shift, the marker would drift inexorably away from the true pole.

Alongside this, an American flag flutters over a white panel declaring that this is the 'GEOGRAPHIC SOUTH POLE', with a red cross at the centre of a map of Antarctica in case you were in any doubt. The panel also bears quotes that reveal the very different fates of the two teams that first reached the Pole. On the left, dated 14 December 1911, is Roald Amundsen's laconic: 'So we arrived and were able to plant our flag at the Geographic South Pole'. On the right, dated 17 January 1912, is Captain Robert F. Scott's testament to the misery of coming second in a race in which there were only two entrants: 'The Pole. Yes, but under very different circumstances from those expected.'

The Anglo-Saxon literature traditionally describes Amundsen's crew as efficient in a way that implies dull. They did, however, have their own trials along the way. Amundsen was acutely aware of the danger that he could be forestalled by Scott, and decided to start out on his journey very early in the spring. Too early, as it turned out. The weather was too cold, the dogs suffered terribly, and in the end the teams had to dash for home. One of Amundsen's crew complained so loudly, bitterly and publicly after this episode that Amundsen gave him formal written orders relieving him and two of his colleagues from the polar party and sending them instead on a make-work exploration to the east. This was harsh, but probably smart. A polar journey is hard enough without dissent in the ranks.

However, in the end, the dogs worked beautifully, the weather cooperated, the snow held firm, and Amundsen and his men made it to the Pole with food and time to spare. His diffident description of his achievement has probably helped it to be dismissed as almost unsportingly easy. But one of his companions, Olav Bjaaland, wrote of the fears that had beset them. 'We reached the South Pole at 2:30 today, tired and hungry, thank God we have enough food for the return journey.' And then, charmingly, he addressed his mother and entire family: 'Yes, if you only knew *Mother* and Saamund and Torne and Svein and Helga and Hans, that now I'm sitting here at the South Pole and writing, you'd celebrate for me.'[1]

The journey was certainly not easy for the British team. Thirty-four days after Amundsen had reached his goal, on the eve of their arrival at the Pole, Scott and his four companions spotted a black Norwegian marker flag next to the unmistakable traces of skis and sledge runners and dog prints. 'The Norwegians have forestalled us and are first at the Pole,' Scott wrote in his diary. 'It is a terrible disappointment, and I am very sorry for my loyal companions . . . Tomorrow we must march on to the Pole and then hasten home with all the speed we can compass. All the day-dreams must go; it will be a wearisome return.'[2]

They continued to make their own measurements of the height of the sun at noon, calculating for themselves where the Pole should be. But Amundsen's tracks led to the same place, to the pyramid tent that he had left, with a Norwegian flag and a letter to King Haakon of Norway, enclosed in a note to Scott himself:

> *Dear Captain Scott,*
>
> *As you probably are the first to reach this area after us, I will ask you to kindly forward this letter to King Haakon VII. If you can use any of the articles left in the tent please do not hesitate to do so. The sledge left outside may be of use to you.*
>
> *With kind regards I wish you a safe return.*
>
> *Yours truly,*
>
> *Roald Amundsen.*

The temperature at the Pole was -20°F, a hard wind was blowing and the sun obscured by a gloomy fug of ice smog. 'Great God! This is an awful place,' Scott famously declared, 'and terrible enough for us to have laboured to it without the reward of priority.' Of course, for him and his companions the worst was still to come.

My first visit to the Pole was in 1999. Unless you are an adventurer determined to retrace heroic steps on skis, the journey in the modern age is by Hercules aircraft. The flight is noisy and uncomfortable, window-free, squeezed into webbing seats, wedged up against crates of cargo. But it only lasts three and a half hours, and if you are lucky and the crew knows it's your first time, you might be invited up on the flight deck to see the view, drink hot chocolate and bandy words over a headset with the pilots from the American Air National Guard.

The beginning of the flight takes you over the Ross Ice Shelf, the great floating Ice Barrier of the heroic age. Then, as you reach the Transantarctic Mountains that mark the edge of the plateau, you see the first stirrings of the mighty glaciers that spill down from the ice sheet into the shelf below. These were the gigantic staircases used by early explorers to climb up from the low-lying ice shelf on to the plateau. You follow the path of the one chosen by Shackleton and then Scott, the Beardmore Glacier, which is one of the largest in the world. (Amundsen found his own farther east, which he named the Axel Heiberg Glacier after a Norwegian patron of polar expeditions.)

The scale of the Beardmore is unimaginable. From above it looks like a thousand-lane superhighway, stippled and folded with crevasses and great sweeping flow lines. And guiding it on either side, like gargantuan kerbstones, the brown tops of the Queen Alexandra and Commonwealth Mountains are just visible above the flowing ice.

And then – when the tips of the mountains are finally swamped and the ice sheet takes over – there is ... nothing. Not a thing. Now you're flying over the East Antarctic Ice Sheet, which is by far the largest body of ice in the world. In places it is four kilometres thick, and it extends over more than ten million square kilometres. It contains so much ice that, if it completely melted, it would raise global sea level by more than 200 feet. Picture the entire Pacific Ocean, stretching round a third of the globe from China to California; then add in the Atlantic, the Indian Ocean, the Southern Seas and the Arctic. And then imagine every square centimetre of our watery world rising by more than the height of the Statue of Liberty. That's how much ice lies beneath you as you fly.

And yet, it just looks flat, greyish, and, frankly, rather dull. On my visit in 1999, with first-timer flight-deck privileges, I craned my neck to peer out of a small side window, trying to imagine trudging over the plateau for day after day, week after week, leaning against your harness, gasping for breath in the thin air, squinting into the sun, bracing yourself against wind and cold. But instead, there on the jump seat, drowsy with warmth and hot chocolate, my imagination failed me and I fell asleep.

I woke to a nudge from the navigator. 'South Pole's in sight,' she said. Hastily I sat up and saw a bright white smear against the flint. Gradually tiny buildings came into view and then our descent became noticeable, the co-pilot counting the height in feet as the instruments wound their way downward. 'Rainbow at two o'clock,' he said suddenly over the headsets and everybody turned to the starboard window where a blotchy smudge of rainbow hung in the sky. 'Rainbow at ten o'clock,' the pilot replied and we turned to see its twin, staring at us through the port window.

Then the skis hit the runway and I had to unlock my harness and scramble back down the rickety ladder to grab my parka and gloves and kitbags and prepare to climb on to the ice. Out of the aircraft, dazzling sunlight combined with the roar from the propellers just a few metres away. I was vaguely aware that someone was standing between me and the props. Her job, it later turned out, was to stop befuddled newbies like me from blundering into their blades. Dryness and coldness joined forces, as the mucus inside my nostrils abruptly froze and the first gasp of air rasped my throat.

And then I looked up. The 'rainbows' we had seen in the cockpit were two bright round splodges of light called sun dogs, one either side of the sun, joined together by a golden ring of light. The cause of this atmospheric phenomenon was dancing all around me: the air was full of tiny shards of ice crystals, diamond dust, which were refracting the sunlight, and glimmering and sparkling with the effort.

I remembered then that this was Scott Day, 17 January, exactly eighty-seven years after he had reached the Pole in misery and dismay. The contrast was shaming. I was warmly clothed, rested and fed, and as if to labour the point the continent had put on this glorious light show. It was as if I had fallen down a strange white rabbit hole into wonderland.[3]

That first trip was short – just two days. But the second visit, five years later, looked set to be more measured. The US National Science Foundation, which runs Amundsen–Scott South Pole Station, had granted me two boons: this time I had been permitted to come in early November, right at the start of the summer season, when the station had only just reopened; and I would be allowed to stay for nearly four weeks. I could afford to slow my pace, soak up the atmosphere and try to catch the echoes of the winter just gone.

Antarctica is a continent of extremes and winter is the most extreme way to experience it. In the heroic age there was no choice; in order to be there in the summer when the sun was briefly present and you could sledge and race and seek out new territories, you had to spend at least one and more often two winters dug in against the black night, squeezed in uncomfortable proximity with a band of increasingly irritating comrades in a small smoky hut, while the elements outside rattled your teeth and froze your heart.

In 1915 one early explorer, stuck on a ship that was making its slow and weary way through the pack ice, wrote this prescient entry in his diary:

> I do so wish sometimes that I could just pop home for an hour or two as easily in the flesh as in the spirit. No doubt the explorers of 2015, if there is anything left to explore, will . . . carry their pocket wireless telephones . . . and . . . of course there will be an aerial daily excursion to both poles then.[4]

He wasn't so very far off. In the summers these days there is a plane from McMurdo to the Pole most days; you can come here just for part of the season, when the sun has returned, when the temperatures are cold but bearable and a steady stream of planes is bringing in resupplies and options.

But if you are really hard-core, if you are ready to see the continent at its harshest, and get a taste of the isolation that the early explorers experienced, you need to spend a winter here. In winters, there are no planes and no chances to pop back home. Even today, it is easier to leave the International Space Station in an emergency than it is to leave the South Pole after the last plane has gone, after the continent has dropped its dark curtain and you are frozen into the silence. I have never spent a winter in Antarctica, and probably never will. But I am still gripped by the idea of it, a fascination that was only quickened by the many winterers that I met there.

'The winter is a totally different animal from the summer. It's like comparing apples and . . . pick-up trucks.' Larry Rickard was a carpenter from New Jersey, who I ran into in the galley the day after my arrival. He was eating 'midrats' – midnight rations – which were supposed to be just for night workers but which anyone could join if, like me, they were hungry and couldn't sleep, and asked the cook nicely. It was 5 November, the US had just re-elected George W. Bush, and the galley staff had served up a themed menu of 'pork barrel roast, mashed hopes potatoes, big business gravy and squashed dreams'. On the wall was a red bell labelled 'whining alarm' with a sign underneath saying 'no sympathy for the picky'. One side of the galley had nothing but huge picture windows framing the ceremonial pole and its flags just a few metres away, and, although it was midnight, the summer sun was streaming in.

Larry had already spent two winters on the ice, one at Mactown and one at Pole, and he was about to embark on his third. He was wiry and full of coiled energy. He had tight black curls and words tumbled out of him almost more quickly than he could frame them. If he were a cartoon character, he'd be a fast-talking, wise-cracking black Labrador.

It was Larry who told me that the slang for people at the South Pole was 'Polies', and that they got special clothing – hefty Carhartt overalls and extra thick green parkas, which were a badge of honour as you passed through McMurdo and turned your nose up at the red parka brigade. But he also had his poetic moments, as when he struggled to explain what the winter here was truly like. 'If I were to describe it with just one word, it would be: surrender. It's not giving up, it's giving in. Relinquishing all power to do something else, realising that whatever happens you just can't leave. It's very powerful. That's what makes it addictive to me.'

He knew the base inside out and, since the following day was his day off, he offered to show me round. First stop was the new station. This was being built as a replacement for the previous one, which had been constructed in the 1970s and was now both too small for the current scale of science, and too susceptible to drifting snow. I was already staying in a berthing wing of the new building, and the galley was also now in operation. But we explored the new medical facility (labelled, by tradition, 'Club Med') containing a dentist's chair and operating room and other stark reminders that in the winters here you were medically on your own. We poked our heads around the doors that would eventually lead to science labs, gymnasiums, weight rooms, and more berths, but were now just sites of hammerings and sawings and scrapings.

A huge silver cylinder housing a spiral staircase provided both the passage between floors and one of the main exits to the outside world. Everyone on station called it the beer can because that's what it looked like. The rest of the station was designed in wings like capital letter Es lying on their sides. Most of these were yet to be constructed, though the steel structures were in place for some. And the exterior of the building was still an incongruous yellow, though it would eventually be a cool steel-grey. The doors were the massive insulated kind that you find in industrial freezers. But in this case, the freezer was on the outside.

As we stepped out, there was the familiar dazzling sun-snow combination, the same gasp at the intensity of the cold. Temperatures were hovering around -58°F. Thanks to its thick mantle of ice, the South Pole lies 9,350 feet above sea level, and the coldness of the air gives it an effective altitude more like 11,500 feet. From the moment you step off the plane everyone you meet warns you to take it easy, drink plenty of water, avoid caffeine and alcohol, not to move too fast or carry too much until you're acclimatised. For most of the first few days you walk sluggishly, as if in a dream, gasping if you try to take the stairs too quickly. You have a persistent nagging headache and an unpleasant tingling in your feet from the side effects of diamox, the pill pressed on all visitors to the Pole to ward off altitude sickness. And then, suddenly, your head clears and your breath returns and insanely cold temperatures begin to seem normal. Dashing between buildings at -58°F, you might neglect to put gloves or hat on. Acclimatisation, it turns out, is as much about attitude as altitude.

(You can, however, take this too far. Though the sun may be shining and you may feel like you're inured to the cold, there are certain things you just shouldn't do. Larry told me how late one summer he was sitting in the computer lab when one of his colleagues came in. Both sat silently for a while, then they caught each other's eye and Larry said: 'How're you doing?' 'Thon't puth a penthil in your mouth when you're out-thide,' came the reply. It turned out that the graphite in the pencil had frozen to his tongue.)

The famous South Pole Dome lay just a short walk away from the new station. It was a geodesic Buckminster Fuller segmented dome that had been built here in the 1970s by the US Navy. It must have seemed like a good idea – make something that was strong enough to withstand the weight of blowing snow that would land on it, and round enough to deflect the ferocious winter winds. Oh, and that was also utterly gorgeous, a shining seventies image of a moon base, just as the stark new station reflects modern images of how we might live in space. But the shape turned out to be far from ideal. It seemed to attract drifting snow rather than repel it. Every year, huge amounts of fuel and time went into shifting the drift that had accumulated around it in the winter. And even so, where the entryway was once on the surface, it now lay down a steep incline of snow, dubbed 'heart attack hill' by those who struggled to climb back out. (Though little fresh snow falls at the Pole, plenty is carried in by the winds, gradually burying anything that humans have brought in. When I arrived in 1999, the ceremonial pole was chin-high, but now, five years later it barely came up to my knees. The new station was on stilts that could be jacked up to keep it ahead of the drifting, but eventually it, too, would succumb.)

And yet, there was something glorious about the Dome. It wasn't heated, but simply provided shelter for the more prosaic container-like buildings inside. So the roof was encrusted with enchanting stalactites of ice, and the networks of steel arches housing the gym, fuel bladders and storage facilities were crystal caves of wonder. The buildings, though blocky, were cosy and idiosyncratic, decorated over the years with odd mementos from around the world. On the door of the bar, a sign filched from somewhere in Australia declared that this was 'the last pub for 250 kilometres' and someone had scratched on an extra '1' to make the distance a more accurate 1,250 km. Although this past winter was the first in which the new station was officially occupied, Larry and many of his comrades chose to stay here instead. It might be less comfortable, but it had more soul.

Behind the Dome, Larry took me round a few half-cylindrical sheds to the bizarre sight of a Russian biplane pegged into the snow with guy ropes. Apparently, this Antonov-3 landed at the Pole on 8 January 2002. Since the leader of the expedition was Artur N. Chilingarov, Deputy Chairman of the Russian State Duma, the plane was accorded an official welcome and the right to be refuelled. (Official NSF policy is to give no support whatsoever to 'private expeditions, US or foreign, in Antarctica'. In practice, this means that all private teams have to bring all their own life support with them, though they do at least get to visit the station store where they can mark their passports with a South Pole stamp and buy T-shirts that say things like: 'Ski South

Pole, 2 inches of powder, 2 miles of base', or, my personal favour-ite: 'South Pole Station: Not all who wander are lost'.)

However, when the occupants spilled out of the plane, the visitors turned out to include a group of tourists who had hitched a ride. That might not have been a particular problem except that, when the tours had been completed, T-shirts bought, photos taken and the team reloaded on the plane . . . the engine wouldn't start. The government delegation was eventually flown back to New Zealand via McMurdo on a US Hercules, and presented with an $80,000 bill for their stay at the Pole, the fuel that was uselessly pumped into the biplane, and the plane ticket back to civilisation.[5]

The number of private visitors who make it to the Pole is steadily increasing, and the NSF's policy not to share resources is more and more rigorously enforced. This seems unusually uncooperative for a base in the dead centre of the most coopera-tive continent on Earth. But the National Science Foundation has no control over the preparedness, or otherwise, of the adven-turers who come here. On 17 December 1997 six people – two Norwegians, an Austrian and three Americans – attempted a sky dive from a Twin Otter plane over the Pole. Three – the two Norwegians and one American – were skilled and well prepared and their jump passed without trouble. The three remaining people made many mistakes, which culminated in the worst one of all: they failed to open their parachutes in time. It was NSF staff who had to go out there with the body bags and pull their frozen corpses from the ice. (The station was shocked, of course. But with the black humour that seems to be an integral part of polar personalities, somebody later commemorated the event by half burying two boots upside down so they were sticking up in the snow.)

If someone takes pity on certain visitors and sneaks them in, they can get some highly unofficial privileges – though it is still likely to come at a price. On my first trip I found myself sitting in the galley next to four Frenchmen who had skied unsupported from the coast to the Pole, a gruelling journey of more than 900 miles. Between mouthfuls they told me cheerfully how they had also skied to the North Pole and climbed Everest and achieved a host of other feats of endurance that left me dizzy. I felt honoured to meet them, but when they had finished their meal they 'paid' for it by heading off into the kitchen and helping with the washing-up. And then they left the station buildings and went back to their freezing tents.

It seems harsh, but then all resources are scarce here. My initial orientation warned me that water was precious at the Pole because it had to be melted using fuel flown in from the coast. Showers should be no more than two minutes and were permitted only twice a week. If you noticed that somebody consistently ran over their allotted time, when you passed them in the corridor you growled 'shower thief!' And good behaviour, or winning a tournament or a fancy-dress party, could gain you the right to a five-minute shower, officially inscribed on a certificate by the base manager.

Of course, they could simply have installed two-minute cut-offs for the showers but there was an ethos of trust here that I supposed was necessary when you squeezed a small number of people into a remote place and expected them to get along. There was also, perhaps necessarily, a general goofiness in the air here that belied the official solemnity. On the way back to the station as we passed the ceremonial pole, Larry suddenly stopped, took the camera hanging around my neck, thrust it into my gloved hands and said: 'Take a picture!' Then he sped over to the pole, and sprung into a handstand while I obediently snapped. He ran back, laughing at my puzzlement, pressed the review button and turned the camera upside down. There on the screen was a figure, clad in a green down parka and bunny boots, apparently clinging to the mirrored globe as he dangled precariously downwards from the pole at the bottom of the world.

South Pole winter, February–March

The last plane leaves around the middle of February. In a way, the timing is arbitrary. The temperatures are high enough that you could still fly later than that if you wanted to. The sun is still shining, and from one day to the next the conditions are more or less the same. But the choice is made by the logistics guys, the date is set in everyone's calendar, and it's a momentous one. When you wake up that morning, you know that there is still a chance to get on the last available plane out of town. And later, after it has gone, you know that you are now effectively trapped until October.

Your first reaction is probably relief that the rush is finally over. The last few days of the summer season are always the most frantic. People are scrambling to finish their summer tasks. The ones who are leaving are talking vacation plans; the galley is full of ideas about how to spend your summer salary in tropical travel spots. You have to close your ears to this kind of thing. You can't let it get to you. But it's hard when the energy levels rise, as the last plane gets closer. When they finally leave, it's like the quiet that hangs in the air after a family reunion, when everyone has gone home and you can digest it all in peace.

But if this is your first time, you'll probably also be feeling jittery. In the twenty-first century there are few places left on Earth where you can be genuinely stranded. And yet here you are, in the middle of a thick mantle of ice sliding over a bare continent of rock. And whatever happens they're not coming to get you. They're just not.

When this jolt of panic subsides (as it usually does) you'll be left, if you're lucky, with another kind of relief, the sense that you have little to worry about beyond your own work, and that of the people immediately around you. In Larry's memorable phrase it's not about giving up, but about giving in. (This is also the time when you can guarantee that you can't be packed off home. If you had a twinge of backache or a slight toothache in the past week or two, you'll probably have stayed well away from the doctor just in case. Now that it's too late to be repatriated, chances are there's a queue already forming outside Club Med.)

By long-standing tradition, the first act of the new winter crew is to gather around the TV for an official screening of the two versions of *The Thing*. Both are horror stories set in remote polar stations. The older one, set in the Arctic, looks foolish to modern eyes. Its monster is a unimpressively wooden kind of Frankenstein, and a woman wearing a powder-blue parka with a fetching furry trim keeps popping up to smile and offer all the men coffee. John Carpenter's later version is much more frightening. This one is set in an Antarctic station in the winter. For those who don't know it, I won't spoil the story but an alien presence becomes increasingly disturbing, and the claustrophobia is extreme. Perfect viewing, in sum, for a team of people who are about to be isolated in a remote Antarctic station for nine long months.

The next few days will be for taking stock. Now that the population has gone down from two hundred to just a few dozen, there's space to breathe. Nobody's working nights any more – everybody is on the same daytime shift. You might be nailing down everything that could be blown away by the winter storms, or taking down the flags that marked the runway and putting up new flag lines, one marker every three metres, between the main station and all the outer buildings. These might look redundant while the sun is still shining, but when the darkness comes, and the raging blizzards, these flags and the ropes looped between them might just save your life.

And each day, the circling sun dips almost imperceptibly closer to the horizon. The two Poles are the only places on Earth that experience a single day per year. Both places have exactly six months of daylight and six months of darkness, the transitions marked by a single sunrise and a long drawn-out sunset lasting three weeks or more. The first sign of the coming sunset is the lengthening shadows. Each day those thrown by buildings, storage piles, skidoos will stretch a little, until they seem to reach almost to the horizon. Your own shadow will seem impossibly long and as you walk two vast legs will mimic every step you take with a gigantic stride.

Now while there is still some daylight and the weather isn't yet too cold, you might grab the chance to sneak into Old Pole, the Station That Nobody Mentions. This was built back in 1956 under the supervision of former Boy Scout Paul Siple, and marked the first human presence at the Pole since Scott and his men had trudged disconsolately away nearly half a century earlier. (Paul Siple was wholesome enough in his appetites to make Baden-Powell cringe. At the end of an earlier Antarctic expedition, when finally back in New Zealand, he wrote how 'I hurried to a field where I flung myself on the ground and lay daydreaming in the soft warm breezes until my body cried out for a glass of milk and some fruit.'[6])

Originally Old Pole was on the surface, but the ice has since taken it, as it will one day take everything else. Most people know that it lies roughly over there, buried some-where under that large patch of ice; but in the summer few people dare risk going in — I certainly didn't — for fear of being summarily sent home. Entering it is strictly forbidden, officially for safety reasons though there are some who mutter that officialdom would prefer everyone to forget it exists. But in the winter, what can they do? Sack you? Visits certainly take place and photos are later passed round the station like contraband, showing images that are misted with frosted breath hanging in the air. Though some of the rooms are still intact, others are dramatically contorted, their steel joists twisted and buckled by the awesome power of the ice.

By now the sun will be touching the horizon, and the first colours will appear in the sky. Don't expect deep spectacular reds; there is no dust in the air to scatter the setting sunlight, only crystals of ice that give colours that are paler and more subtle – pinks and mauves rather than crimson. On the side of the horizon opposite the Sun, you'll see a purple haze like a visor, as the Earth casts its own shadow on to the air. And as the Sun dips deeper, you will have a better chance than most to see the famous green flash. In principle this can happen anywhere in the world at the end of a sunset. Light travels more quickly in the thin upper air than in the low dense air, so it tends to bend a little round the curved Earth. And since green light curves more than red, a flash of green is often still visible when the sun has disappeared over the horizon. In the tropics this might last a second. In the stretched-out saga of a polar sunset, a green stripe comes and goes over the course of a day or even two.

Next come long days of a ghostly grey twilight. Half the sky darkens to deep blue, royal blue and then black, specked with stars, while the other half is still infused with leftover light from a sun that is only just over the horizon. As the sky turns, or rather you turn beneath it, the dark half moves, too, picking out different constellations like an inverse searchlight. And then you notice that the rest of the sky has also grown darker, and then there's no light at all. This is the true winter, the crown jewel of an Antarctic stay. And it is now that the Dark Sector, home of the station's telescopes, comes into its own.

•   •   •

Tony Stark and I didn't get off to the best of starts. Someone had already pointed him out to me so I knew he was a veteran astronomer from Harvard University, there at the Pole to work on one of the telescopes. One evening in the galley I went over to speak to him, but before I could introduce myself he made it obvious that he already knew what I was there for, and didn't particularly approve. 'I hope you're going to do a good job,' was his opening line, 'because you're taking the space of someone who could be critical to the scientific enterprise.' ('Charming to meet you, too,' I thought, but luckily didn't say.)

Tony's attitude wasn't that uncommon among the scientists on the US Antarctic Program. Though many see the poetic and mysterious side of the continent where they work, others are at best irritated by the drama and the difficulties. Yes, yes, it's an extreme place and all that, but we're doing science, and that's all that matters. If you're here to help us do our science, that's fine. If you're not, then get out of the way.

This seems particularly disingenuous at the Pole. There are some excellent scientific reasons for being here, especially to do astronomy. The cold, dry air and steady winter darkness provide a stability and clarity that make this one of the cleanest windows on Earth for peering out through the atmosphere into space. But it's not perfect. Though the Pole lies at the geographic centre of the continent, it's also on a slight slope. The winds on the continent are born on local high points and then spill down the sides till they reach the coasts with a furious flourish. And on the way, they pass by here, stirring up the air and muddying the view.

But if you recall that the science in Antarctica also serves as a political placeholder, the reason for this location makes more sense. Before the Antarctic Treaty came into effect back in 1961, eleven nations had staked claims on various parts of the continent. Though these claims are now officially on hold, they have never been wiped from the record. And, significantly, they are all great wedges of land that meet at ... the South Pole. The US has never staked a claim of its own, but it has built this station right at the touching point of all the other claims, an unofficial geo-political finger poking into everyone else's pies.

Still, science was something that the South Pole was very good at, and Tony was one of its ablest practitioners. When he relented enough to take me back to his lab, in the Dark Sector, the stories he told me of their discoveries make me very happy that I bit my tongue when we first met.

The Dark Sector, where the telescopes lived, was about a kilo-metre and a half away from the main station, but it seemed farther. Temperatures had still barely lifted above -58°F and the wind drew tears that instantly froze into globs of ice, gumming my eyelashes together, rendering me all but blind. As I rubbed at my eyes, I noticed belatedly that everyone else was wearing goggles. I thought they were only necessary if you were riding on a skidoo. I knew better now.

The Dark Sector was separated from the main station to avoid any light and radio wave pollution when the darkness finally fell. There was one main building called the Martin A. Pom-erantz Observatory (MAPO)[7] and various smaller ones, some with towers and visible telescopes like classic radar dishes point-ing up into the sky. Inside were offices, computers and banks and banks of electronics with spaghetti tangles of wires. And a gi-gantic poster of a mad-looking Jack Nicholson in *The Shining*. 'Heeeeeeere's Johnny!' *The Shining* used to be one of the movies that the winterers watched on the day the last planes left, but lately they had been saving it for midwinter.

Tony's telescope was called AST/RO. The letters stood for 'Antarctic Submillimetre Telescope and Remote Observatory'; the slash was to distinguish it from all the other telescopes whose owners have devised acronyms to be able to call them ASTRO. And as we sat in the main astronomical building in the Dark

Sector, warming our hands with mugs of hot tea, he explained what AST/RO was looking for.

The Galaxy in which we live, the Milky Way, is fairly typical, large and flat, shaped like a child's drawing of a flying saucer with a bulge in the middle surrounded by a disk of spiral arms. Our home planet and the others in our Solar System inhabit a provincial spot in the outer part of one of these arms, some 30,000 light years from the bulge at the Galactic Centre. Though it sounds like a measure of time, a light year is actually the distance light can travel in a year, which is a shade less than ten trillion kilometres. Light moves so quickly it took humans until relatively recently to discover that it moves at all. Our own Sun is about eight light minutes away, the next nearest star about 4.2 light years. Thirty thousand light years seems almost unimaginably distant, but by the scale of the Universe, which was the scale Tony Stark lives and breathes, it's still not that far. 'I feel very at home in the Galaxy,' he told me when casually tossing out these figures. 'I think of it as if it were some kind of nearby real estate. I'm not overawed by it any more.'

The problem when it comes to studying the centre of our Galaxy is not the distance, but the many intervening clouds blocking our view. The stars in the night sky are all relatively close by. It seems as if there are many of them, but there are a million times more packed into the Galactic Centre. We can't see these because clouds of molecules like hydrogen, carbon monoxide, nitrogen and methane soak up all the light they emit, and cloak them from our view. 'There are twenty-some magnitudes of visual extinction in the Galactic Centre,' Tony said. 'Not only can you not see it, but you can't see it twenty times over.'

So if we stuck with visible light, the sort of light that our weak human eyes can detect, the main activity of the Galaxy would be for ever out of view. But AST/RO's eyes went beyond this. It could detect light coming in with longer wavelengths than the typical colours of the rainbow. In its preferred range of so-called 'submillimetre' (or far infrared) wavelengths, molecular clouds shone brightly, and the Galactic Centre was an open book.

The trick for seeing with radio eyes is to have as little water vapour as possible between you and outer space. That's why the South Pole is so very good at it. For every 10°F below freezing, the amount of water vapour in the air drops by half. When the temperatures here got cold enough, in the deep midwinter, AST/RO could pick out the many molecular clouds that dot the night sky. But more than that, looking through this pristine Antarctic window it could see right into the heart of our Galaxy, to the bulging centre of commerce, activity and drama.

And when it looked, AST/RO saw something that impressed even the phlegmatic Tony Stark. Spinning around the centre of our Galaxy was a molecular cloud to dwarf all others. It was nearly a thousand light years across, and contained two million times as much material as our Sun. Like a storage ring it was soaking up dust and molecules dragged in from the rest of the Galaxy. And it was getting denser all the time. AST/RO showed that this massive ring was right on the edge of stability. It was so dense that after just one more tweak, in another few hundred thousand years at most (which in galactic terms was the merest twitch), it could tip over the edge. Then, as if you had dropped a mighty slug of vinegar into a giant galactic sauce, it would curdle and coagulate into blobs of gas that would fall in on themselves in a spectacular celestial light show. It would become a massive centre of star formation. At present there were only a handful of new stars created in the Galaxy each year. When this kicked off there could be thousands. They would be every colour and size, supermassive blue ones that blaze brightly but burn out quickly; more measured, smaller orange and red ones. As some were still barely switching on, others would be reaching the ends of their short lives and exploding dramatically, before new ones eventually reformed again from the material that was flung out.[8]

That's not all. Astronomers believe that at the true centre of the Galaxy, the point that everything else was rotating round, lies a supermassive black hole, some four million times heavier than the Sun. At the moment this is quiescent. Rather than performing the usual black hole habit of sucking in all the material around it, it is starved of nearby fuel and hence effectively switched off. But if the star formation kicked off, new material would fall into the black hole's vicinity, activating it into a voracious monster. As dust and gas were dragged inwards, an accreting ring around it could shine like a thousand Suns, and giant jets of recycled stuff could burst out of its north and south poles and shoot out in magnetic maelstroms above and beyond the rim of the Milky Way and into intergalactic space. All of this would be hidden from us even if it were happening now, blocked by all the clouds in between. 'But if you had radio eyes it would be fireworks.'[9]

This was very dramatic, of course. But there was another more intimate reason why we should care about molecular clouds and bursts of newly formed stars. Tony called it the 'ecology of the Galaxy'. As molecular clouds collapse into stars, some of the stars live much longer than others. But all in the end will die, either in massive explosions – supernovas – or in a gradual loss of form as the outermost parts are gently blown outwards in a streaming wind. And the material thrown out in this way goes on to make new molecular clouds, and ultimately new stars and planets.

So our Galaxy is one massive exercise in recycling, mingling and reforming. But there's more. From what we now understand about the lives of stars, we can tell where the material in our own Solar System came from. And that shows something extraordinary. Not only are we all made of stardust, but we are made of the dust from *different* stars. All the material around you – this book, your clothes, the tea bag that Tony Stark had just taken out of his mug – is made up of atoms that have been processed and recycled through a succession of stars. So has every atom in your body. And some of your atoms have been through a different set of stars than others.

'So I have atoms next to each other in my body that have come from different stars, from different parts of the Galaxy?'

'Yes.'

'That is really spooky.'

'That's what star formation does.'

Tony said all this in a matter-of-fact way. Perhaps he had grown used to it, the way he has grown used to the scale of the Galaxy. But I couldn't. Even now, every time I think of this, it still blows my mind.

Tony no longer spends winters at the Pole, but there are plenty of others who do. Unlike Larry and the other construction workers (whom he described as 'indoor cats'), the astronomy technicians have no choice but to leave the comforts of the station and make the daily trek to the Dark Sector where the telescopes await their attention.

German technician Robert Schwarz, a self-styled 'telescope nanny', was about to embark on his fourth winter. His hair was close-cropped, and he was inclined to be terse. (Typical conversation: 'What's it like here in the winter?' 'Cold, and dark.') He had last year off, but had come back to the Pole to work on one of the biggest imaginable questions: the origin of the Universe.

Robert's telescope would be picking up the faint afterglow of the Big Bang itself. For the first few hundred thousand years after the Big Bang the entire Universe glowed hotter than the Sun. A roiling plasma of negatively charged electrons and positively charged ions circled around each other, eager to join forces and become neutralised, and yet constantly breaking apart as soon as they united, because of the searing heat. And all was bathed in a brilliant blaze of light.

Eventually, as the Universe stretched and cooled, the electrons and ions fell into each other's arms to become the atoms that make up the stars, the planets, and us.[10] And the light streaked out across the Universe, bearing the slightest, almost imperceptible traces of erstwhile lumps in the cosmic maelstrom, here the light a little denser, there a little more insubstantial. This faint glow is still out there, its elongated wavelengths now too far from the visible rainbow for human eyes to see. But with the right telescope, in the right place, you can see through the dirty window of the Earth's humid air and pick out, if you look hard enough, those traces of primordial structure. And if you do, you can calculate nothing less than the mass of the entire Universe.

Astronomers call the afterglow of the Big Bang the 'Cosmic Microwave Background' (CMB). 'Background' because it exists in every direction in the sky; it is the canvas on which all the stars and galaxies are painted. 'Microwave' because the light that was once visible has now been stretched into roughly the same patch of the spectrum as the microwaves that power your oven, though it is feeble enough not to burn us all to a crisp. And 'Cosmic' because, well, that's what it is.

As for AST/RO, Robert and the other CMB researchers need air that is as devoid as possible of water. But unlike AST/RO they need to look away from the main body of the Galaxy — what the starburst people see as nascent star nurseries, the microwave background people dismiss as 'galactic smog'. Instead, the CMB researchers angle their telescopes to look up and out of the flat plane of the Galaxy, where there are no spurs or arms or patches of molecular clouds to spoil the view. And then, thanks to the thin dry air at the Pole, the CMB researchers find themselves looking through one of the cleanest patches of sky in the world.

It's not perfect. To get the best results you need to look at the largest possible area – ideally the whole sky. As the Earth spins on its axis, a telescope at the equator sweeps through a huge area of sky every twenty-four hours, whereas the South Pole rotates constantly beneath the same relatively small patch. But with the long, cold, steady winters you can bore into that patch very deeply.

Back in 1998 a South Pole telescope called VIPER, the brainchild of University of Pittsburgh researcher Jeff Peterson, performed measurements on the Microwave Background and picked up those almost imperceptible traces of ancient clumping. Added in with data from a telescope in the arid Atacama Desert in northern Chile, and a couple of balloon flights that set off from McMurdo and made long, slow circles around the Pole, the researchers came up with a number for the mass of the Universe. The answer was:

100 000 000 000 000 000 000 000 000 000 000 000 000 000 000 000 000 000 tonnes.

Give or take a few pounds.[11]

Now the astronomers wanted to go deeper, to find out what the Microwave Background could tell us about the structure of the Universe, the strange invisible 'dark energy' that it seems to be filled with, how it truly began, and how it is likely to end. Next winter, Robert would be working on a new CMB instrument, and plans were already under way to build a whopping 10-m telescope here, the South Pole Telescope, that would have nothing but the Microwave Background in its sights.

Robert's friend and fellow telescope nanny Steffen Richter, who was also German, would be on a much weirder kind of telescope called AMANDA, which stood for Antarctic Muon and Neutrino Detector Array.[12] Unlike the other telescopes, which all looked like oversized TV satellite dishes, AMANDA was completely invisible. It was made up of strings of detectors that were buried hundreds of metres down in the ice. Any day now, construction was going to begin on a much bigger device called Ice Cube because it would stretch over a full cubic kilometre of ice, with AMANDA making up one small corner of this behemoth.[13]

Both these telescopes were for studying spectacular astronomical occurrences: exploding stars, colliding black holes, gamma-ray bursts and the rest of the Universe's biggest and most cosmic bangs. These all generate debris in the form of particles. But to do astronomy, you need to know exactly where they came from. And as they travel through space, most are hopelessly wayward. Cosmic rays are charged, so can be dragged about by any stray magnetic field. Free-flying neutrons fall apart within minutes.[14] The only particles whose subsequent path through the Universe is straight and true are tiny, chargeless, faceless creatures called neutrinos.

However, the same thing that makes them come to us so directly also makes them very hard to detect. Neutrinos don't stop for anybody or anything. A magnetic field can't turn them, gravity doesn't bother them and they zip through solid objects without a backward glance. Trillions of neutrinos pass through your body every second. They are doing it now, and have been ever since you were born, but in your entire lifetime the chances are that only one of these will stop to wipe its feet.

Still, if you look for long enough, over a wide enough area, you can sometimes catch a neutrino in the act. Once in a very rare while a cosmic neutrino will crash into something – an atom of air, say, or of ice – and spit out another particle called a muon, which announces its presence with a tiny burst of blue light. Measuring this light will tell you exactly what direction the neutrino was coming from and how much energy it had. And that in turn will give a hefty clue about where and how it was created.

The problem is that cosmic neutrinos aren't the only things that create muons. In fact, the sky is filled with the wrong kind of muons. For every tiny burst of blue light from a genuine inter-galactic messenger, there are a billion flashes from common- or-garden cosmic rays. Picking out that one in a billion is all but impossible.

What's really clever about both AMANDA and Ice Cube is that they were designed not to look up, but to look down. The idea is to use the Earth's rocky body as a sort of gigantic sieve. Of all the useless muons generated in the far-off northern skies, only one in a million will make it through the centre of the Earth to this, the southern side. But all the neutrinos will slip through unscathed. Now the odds are more favourable. Using Earth as a filter means that you generate one special neutrino-derived muon for every thousand dud ones. And those are the kinds of numbers that astronomers can handle.

The strings of detectors that make up Ice Cube would be sunk down more than a kilometre and a half, to reach the depths where the dark ice was at its purest and most transparent. It would cost $270 million, so much, in fact, that it required its own line in the Congressional budget (though the researchers point out on their website that, if you count in the ice as well, this amounts to a mere twenty-five cents per tonne).

When it is fully operating, Ice Cube should pick up several hundred cosmic neutrinos a year, which should be enough to do some exciting physics. In a way, neutrinos are the latest in a long line of new ways of seeing the Universe. Prehistoric humans started off by looking at the visible light that shone from the stars; since then we have invented ways to pick up X-rays, gamma rays, radio, microwaves and now neutrinos; and each new way of looking told us more about the sky above us. The more literary of Ice Cube's proponents are fond of quoting from Marcel Proust: 'The real voyage of discovery consists not in seeking new landscapes, but in having new eyes.'

Unlike Tony Stark, I sensed that both Robert and Steffen cared about the landscape and the experience of the Pole at least as much as the science itself. In the end both of them told me certain stories about their experiences, but they were also guarded. They didn't particularly want to share. During all our conversations, the message came through loud and very clear. They would readily tell me about the cold of an Antarctic winter, but not about its heart.[15]

South Pole winter, March–May

When the darkness has finally fallen, and the temperatures are too cold for skidoos, the only way to get to the Dark Sector is to trudge. The walk takes twenty minutes, maybe half an hour, in pitch black, as winds rise to 20, 30 or 40 knots and the temperature falls to mind-numbing depths. The telescope nannies will make this return trek at least once a day, sometimes twice. And that's just fine with them. 'Some years ago they talked about making a tunnel to the Dark Sector,' Steffen says. 'No way. We like to commute.'[16]

The snow crunches under your feet. Construction workers often just wear normal work boots to dash between buildings; then the snow sticks to the soles and quickly accumulates into a dense ice layer, turning the boots into towering tap shoes. But for the journey out to the Dark Sector you need bunny boots, which slough off the snow, and have a trapped layer of insulating air to keep out the cold in all but the worst conditions.

As the temperature slips down towards -76°F you start to hear your breath freezing. The sound is like blowing softly through into a piece of paper held up to your face, and making it reverberate. Hhhhhwwwwwooooohhh. And your breath hangs in the air as a frozen cloud of ice blocking your view. If you're working outside you have to blow to one side, and then work for a little while, and then blow to one side, and then work again.

And all the time you are watching out for the signs of frost nip, the milder cousin of frostbite. Frost nip is basically a burn, but it's impressive how much it hurts. First your skin goes white and numb and then, when the blood rushes back in, you feel as if someone has hit your hand hard with a hammer, or as if an elephant has crushed your toes.

If you ignore the frost nip long enough it will become frostbite, the stuff that blackens your skin and takes first your fingers and toes and then entire limbs. When you finally make it to the Dark Sector buildings, people will inspect your face and hands for white patches. You're supposed to look out for each other. Frost nip is not something to take lightly. 'At home in the mountains you might get a bit numb,' says Steffen, 'but you won't start losing body parts.'

If anything, the darkness is easier to deal with than the cold. When dark stops defining night-time and becomes omnipresent it can almost be comforting. People call it enveloping, like a benign blanket. And if you're an astronomer, chances are you're going to be excited to see the night sky, the Southern Cross almost stationary overhead, and the other constellations seeming bigger and brighter than they do farther north. Whatever you do, don't get into the habit of using a headlamp. They just give you tunnel vision, blinding you to anything that's not in your immediate field of view. Instead, let your eyes adjust. The starlight is enough to help you feel your way; you get to recognise the landmarks, the dim outlines of the buildings, the shapes of the snow-drifts that redefine the landscape after every big storm. And when the moon is full, it lights up the snow like quicksilver. It's almost dazzling. You could read a newspaper outside.

If you're lucky on your daily commute you will see the other great reward for braving the darkness and cold: Antarctica's glorious light show. Just as in the far north, the south polar skies are periodically filled with the dancing colours of the southern lights, the *aurora australis*. Auroras can come and go at whim, but after a while you start to get a feel for it, like farmers looking at the sky and saying how the weather will be. Perhaps there will be a slight streak of green, a patch that will deepen and then grow. Then another patch on the horizon, like a green search-light. And then shivering curtains of light can fill the sky, or looping spirals, or flickering flames of green and purple, and candy-apple red. It feels as if they should be accompa-nied by dramatic sounds, the bangs of fireworks or the roar of rockets. But these are utterly silent, almost solemn in their dancing. And yet they can be comforting in their own way; as if in this remote and frozen wilderness there's something else out there that is alive.

Inside MAPO and the other Dark Sector buildings the biggest problem, stupid as it sounds, is cooling. To enable the telescope dishes to sweep their eyes around the sky with pinpoint accuracy requires banks and banks of electronics racks, their rears sporting a mad tangle of multi-coloured spaghetti wires. These pump out massive amounts of heat, which the dry air of the polar plateau is very poor at soaking up.

The next thing you have to worry about is sparking static. Thin, dry, cold air is also a very poor conductor of electricity and as you shuffle along the carpeted floors you will be building up static charge that leaps from your fingers in a shocking blue arc, like a bolt from Harry Potter's wand, as soon as you touch anything metallic. This is a perennial problem throughout the station, and some parts are particularly prone to it. The metal doorknob on the library in the Dome was a particularly sore spot. It got me every time.

But here in MAPO you'll get more than just a jolt. The sparks are strong enough to break delicate electronic equipment. They can wipe out a laptop with one touch. You need to get into the habit of discharging yourself constantly by touching anything metal that you see. This can quickly become so ingrained that you find yourself doing it back home, obsessively touching anything metal that you pass, while your friends cast odd glances behind your back.

It's easy to forget the dramas behind the star-bursting, cosmic-scale science when you settle into your daily telescope routines. The first thing to do is probably to download data and check that everything is working. Usually something will have broken and need to be fixed. If you're lucky, whatever's broken will be inside. But you'll still have to pull your gear back on and head outside, to brush blown snow off the detectors and check that everything is intact.

For that, the hardest part is keeping your hands warm, especially if you are working on some delicate task for which clumsy mittens are hopeless. Robert calls himself a 'soldering iron and wrench physicist' and for the sort of mechanical fixes he needs to do on equipment and cables he wears three layers of thin gloves; but even so after less than a minute his hands start feeling painfully cold. And below -67°F soldering irons don't get hot enough, and cables become rigid and brittle, and can snap beneath your hands. Something that indoors would take a few minutes to mend can end up taking hours.

But still, you mustn't stay out too long, and above all never lose sight of the flag line. Nick Tothill was telescope nanny for AST/RO last winter and he has no patience with complacency: 'We are here on sufferance. Sure we can heat things, we can create our little environments and we can make stuff work, but ... you don't even need stupidity or carelessness to die here. You can just be unlucky and it can still kill you. It's a really hostile environment. Most of the time we do a good job of ignoring that. Scott would have made it back if he'd just had a bit more luck.

'I'd be uncomfortable thinking that somehow I had matched myself against the power of Antarctica and emerged victorious. It's more like I came down here for a year, and Antarctica never quite got round to swatting me like a bug, because it could. There were about three times over the winter when I got turned around out there in the dark; I made it back but it's not that difficult to imagine how I could have missed my way entirely and died of exposure. One time I got turned around 180 degrees and ended up at the station when I thought I was heading towards the Dark Sector. It took me about three hours to go back outside again because, while I was sitting there telling people about it and laughing, part of me was thinking: "it wouldn't have been that difficult for me to be dead right now". You can't fight Antarctica, you can only hope that it doesn't try to kill you.'

In all the fifty-plus years that people have spent winters at the Pole, nobody has yet died of the cold; but one person's death in the winter there has cast a pall over all subsequent crews. Rodney Marks was an Australian astronomer, working out in the Dark Sector with the other telescope nannies in the winter of 2000. He was taken ill very suddenly; nobody knew why. The doctor put out a call for the trauma team; they tried to resuscitate him but he just ... died. Was it food poisoning? Some strange illness? The doctor had to take samples for an eventual autopsy. Rodney's body lay out under one of the frozen arches on a banana sled, until the carpenters made him a coffin and some of the guys buried him in the snow near the Pole, and planted an Australian flag to mark the spot.[17]

This much is easy to glean from the official reports that came out afterwards. The cause of death is also a matter of record: he had died from methanol poisoning. Rodney used methanol all the time in his lab. But he was smart enough to know that methanol was poisonous, he had plenty of access to normal alcohol if he wanted it and he wasn't behaving remotely like someone who had tried to commit suicide. The death remains a mystery. His parents have given up hope of finding out what happened. The only thing that's really clear is that it had a profound effect on the winterers that year. Nick Tothill, who wasn't present, advised me not to probe any deeper about Rodney. 'Nobody will talk to you about it,' he said.

However foolish it might be to imagine that you are pitting yourself against the continent, it seems at first as if machismo is a fundamental part of what draws people, especially support workers, south. You don't have to be on the ice long to discover that there is a strict pecking order according to how much 'ice time' you have put in. It's not just a question of how many months, or how many seasons. It also matters exactly where you did your ice time. Palmer Station, off on the balmy Antarctic Peninsula, is considered to be a holiday camp. McMurdo is better, but the Pole is best, and winters at the Pole are best of all.

In his book *Big Dead Place*, Nicholas Johnson has this to say about the implicit hierarchy among support workers in the US Antarctic Program: 'Though Polies probably do have the most lucrative bragging rights, swaggering one-upmanship is common at every level of The Program. If you've only done one summer, you are a fingee [which stands for 'fucking new guy/girl']. If you do multiple summers you haven't done a winter. When you do a winter ... then you haven't done multiple winters. If you've done multiple winters, you haven't been to Pole. If you've done a summer at Pole, you haven't done a winter at Pole. If you've done a winter at Pole, you haven't done multiple winters at Pole. And, finally, once you've done multiple winters at Pole, you are afraid to leave Antarctica because you'll have to pay for food and look both ways when crossing the street.'[18]

By these criteria it was evident from the moment I touched down at the Pole who was the real king of the ice. Forget the current station leader, the biggest baddest man in town was one Jake Speed. I'd had him pointed out to me with a nudge as he crossed the galley surrounded, usually, by a gaggle of acolytes. Other people stepped respectfully aside to let him pass. He was tall and strong looking, in his mid-thirties but with a boyish face, a neat brown Jesus beard and long pony tail. He had spent five winters at the South Pole. And not just that, he had done his five winters *in a row*[19]. Ten months at the Pole, a hasty couple of months back in the north, and then back again for another long dark stint. Five times over, without ever taking a single one off. Jake Speed was The Man. And to prove it, I noticed with irritation, he chose to wear battered old Carhartts, which he no doubt stored each year to retrieve the following winter. 'Your clothes are new and shiny', this seemed to say, 'because you are not an old hand here. But I am a rugged and experienced Antarctic explorer. Look and see how old my gear is. And weep.'

I'd have to talk to him, I knew. But I kept putting it off.

Eventually, a previous station leader, Bill Henrickson, caught me on my way somewhere and pulled me aside. 'Talk to Jake,' he urged. 'He'll play the clown, but if you can get him to open up to you, I think you'll find something important. He's a very deep thinker.' I thought of the pretentious Carhartts and had my doubts. But that evening I went up to where he was sitting on a bar stool and politely asked if I could interview him. To my surprise (and, it later turned out, to his), he agreed. I was about to discover that in my initial hasty judgements of him I couldn't have got him more wrong.

I met Jake later that night in his shack, an insulated cabin a short walk from the Dome. It was full of bits of half-mended equipment, nuts, bolts and cables. A notice board was crammed with postcards from far-off places and scraps of paper bearing legends that I couldn't quite read; the only one that stood out enough to catch my eye as I sat down said this: 'All you've gotta do is . . . be excellent to your fellow man.' Jake poured us each a whisky and lit a cigarette. He was nervous. We both were.

We started with the easy stuff. Jake Speed wasn't his real name – he was born Joseph Gibbons, but acquired this nickname along the way. He grew up near Taho in California in a vaguely hippy family, and as soon as he was old enough to leave home he found spectacular ways to exhibit an almost pathological restlessness. After six years of roaming the world with the US Merchant Marine, he then walked the entire length of Australia; he walked across China; travelled from Panama up to the north of Canada, all under his own steam. By the time he reached the Pole he had travelled to thirty countries, and it was years since he had spent more than six weeks in any one spot.

And yet, when he stepped on to the ice, he was thunderstruck: 'I fell in love as soon as I got off the fucking plane,' he said. 'I came down through the entrance to the Dome, I was looking at the arches and all the crystals there and some snow cat was driving by and I thought oh my God this is it! This is so, so cool. It's dynamic, it's beautiful, it's frontier, it's all the things that really turn me on.'

OK, I got that. It was a striking place and from the little I knew about Jake I could see why it would appeal. But why then spend so many winters here? For someone this restless, why would he choose to spend one winter trapped at the Pole, let alone five? 'Wintering is just really enticing,' he replied. 'It's a relief to be in a place where you don't have any other options. There are very few times in anybody's life when they are really that locked into a situation that they can't get out of. A lot of people haven't taken a good hard look at themselves before, and there in the middle of winter, that's what they're faced with. There is no place to go here. You have to deal. You do deal.'

So perhaps if you had been running from one place to another all your adult life, the attraction of this place was that you had to stop. For those months when the planes weren't flying, you had no choice, and maybe that helped you find peace. But it also meant you were forced to put the rest of your life on hold, with no chance to change your mind. Most people couldn't do that. 'It's hard to carve ten months out of your life to spend a winter here,' I suggested, carefully. He paused. 'That's an interesting perspective but it's not one that I share,' he said. 'I'm not carving ten months out of my life to be here during the winter, I'm carving out two months to be away every year when they kick me out.'

That was plain perverse. After wandering the planet for years, he had chosen for his home one of the few places on Earth where he wasn't allowed to stay. Everyone has to leave for at least two months every summer; if you don't, they're afraid that you will go crazy. I didn't say a word, but my face obviously showed what I was thinking. Jake burst out laughing, acknowledging an unspoken hit. 'Yes, I know,' he said. 'It's ironic that after travelling so hard for so long I've found the one place where I want to stay, and they won't let me.'

The first two winters, he worked as a general Mr Fix-It, but since then he had been operating the heavy machinery – the big macho snow cats – moving snow, fuelling the outer buildings, doing water runs, bringing in food for the galley or raw materials for construction. He quickly discovered that even in the full darkness it was easier to operate without lights. You learned to spot something on the horizon that was darker than the rest, something that you would want to avoid. And once in a while you could motor up to the flag line and buzz the scientists, pretending not to see them and making them jump.

The cats can operate all the way to -80°F. Down to -85°F they can do station-critical things like gathering snow for the water melter. But if it had been below this for days, Jake would sit glued to his monitor, here in the shack, watching for the moment the temperature rose. 'It doesn't matter if it's noon or three in the morning, as soon as it hits -80°F I'm out of the door. Because it hasn't started blowing yet. I could have a window of twelve hours, three days, or two hours before it warms up enough that it starts blowing like hell.'

The other main hazard, he said, was the sugar snow. These are crystals that have been blown around so much by the storms that they have lost all their delicate limbs and are just lumpish squares. For snow crystals to stick together, they need to have barbs. Sugar snow doesn't cohere. It's more like quicksand. If you drive a cat into a patch of sugar snow, it's like going down in an elevator shaft; you could drop more than three feet before you get some kind of traction. Sugar snow is almost impossible to see on the surface, but when you're backing out you can tell the difference in the texture. You can apparently taste the difference, too.

Jake, it turned out, was an inveterate snow taster. He started telling me about the taste of the different crystals in the archways of the Dome. They were quite musty in places, where the growing icicle had taken on board gases from the power plant, or from loading trucks, keeping an inadvertent record of everything that happened in the air around them.

But his favourite thing to do, on his time off, in that freezing, lifeless darkness, was to go outside and watch sastrugi grow. These are great, sculpted waves of snow, which make the plateau look like a frozen ocean. In summer, they are delicate, as if rippled by an invisible breeze. But with the powerful winds of winter they can grow into behemoths. And Jake would watch them do it.

'It starts with just a few grains, the way the wind crosses and hatches, and those minuscule crystals hook on to each other and form this goliath, four feet high and twenty feet long. And it's constantly changing throughout the season. You can lay down out there, under a full moon or a really good aurora show and you can watch it fucking happen. It's alive. Anybody who comes here for the winter and says it's boring, dead, there's nothing going on, is a stupid fool with their eyes closed. There is so much happening, you just have to be aware of it.'

He leaned back and lit another cigarette.

'You don't talk like someone pitching himself against elements,' I said.

'I don't think you'd make it through a winter if you did,' he replied. 'I love watching those guys who come in with that swagger, and you know they'll be sucking their thumb and asking for momma by July.' And then he grinned. 'There's nothing wrong with sucking your thumb and asking for momma, that's normal. Everyone should do that. It's the macho attitude that's the problem.

'This place has a lot of patience. Think about it. A glacier sculpts mountains. And when that's happening, where are you? You're nothing, you're tiny. You're insignificant. So if you walk in here with that attitude of "I'm going to kick this place's ass", you're wrong.'

We had been talking for nearly two hours now. I changed the disc on my recorder and Jake poured us each another slug of whisky.

'You must have been here for the medevac,' I said. In 2001 the Polies achieved the first, and only, medical evacuation ever done from there in the dark. Jake brightened. 'That's probably one of the highlights of my entire life,' he said. 'It was one of the most challenging things I've ever done.'

It was at the beginning of April that the station doctor, Ron Shemenski, reported a problem. He had been feeling more and more ill and was now in agony. For the doctor to be getting sick was especially bad news. The two people on station you really can't afford to lose are the doctor and the power plant mechanic. If a scientist or carpenter gets sick, the job goes on hold; if the cook gets sick everyone can get by on macaroni cheese. But the power plant mechanic and the doctor together equal the life-support system of the whole station.

But then it became clear that the problem was even worse than that. What the doctor had was seriously life-threatening. He had passed a gallstone and suspected that he had pancreatitis. Though he didn't want to leave, the physicians back in the US told him he had to get out of there or he probably wouldn't make it through the winter.

Though the Hercules flights to the Pole were long over and the sun had already set, there was still a chance of rescue if everyone acted fast. This was a job for the cowboys, the Twin Otter planes that could slip into places on bumpier air strips and colder temperatures than the Hercs could dream of. But there was almost no time left. Twin Otters could only make small hops.

They would have to fly from their home base in Canada down to the bottom of South America, and then hop over Drake Passage to land at the only available airstrip on the Peninsula, at the British Rothera research station, while one of them remained on standby and the other continued on to the Pole. And Rothera's airstrip would be accessible for only a few more weeks.

The Otters scrambled, and Jake and his colleagues at the Pole began their preparations. They took down the flag line that crossed the skiway, and they started trying to make a decent runway for the Otter to touch down on. It was so dark, and the steam and smoke were so thick that Jake couldn't see the front of the snow cat's blade. The temperature was south of -90°F, and there was almost no friction on the snow. They wanted to make a strip like marble, but it was more like wet cement. The pilots of the Twin Otter were risking their lives coming in here; everything depended on a safe landing. By the time the plane came in and made a faultless touchdown on the snow, without even doing a practice fly by, Jake had been working thirty hours straight.

'It was brutal, but we took care of it. We took care of our own. That felt pretty good. And then we were talking to a couple of people in Rothera on the satellite phone. They sent some T-shirts down and we sent some T-shirts back. It ties you together. We knew that there was another brotherhood, another clan, ten hours' flight away, who we would never see, we would never meet, but they just helped save one of our guys. It ties this frozen continent together. I get a tingle even now when I think about it. I don't even know who those guys are.'

Now he had tears in his eyes. There is something truly striking about that warmth in Antarctica, which transcends the boundaries in the outside world. Here, it seems that what matters most is that you are Antarctican.

And, then, Jake took me by surprise.

'I was there in 2000 when we lost Rodney Marks,' he said.

I held my breath. Rodney Marks: the only person ever to die at the Pole in winter; the one whose unexplained death had cast a silent shadow over every winter since, and yet who remained out of conversational bounds. 'Nobody will talk to you about it,' Nick Tothill said. But now Jake Speed, of all people, was doing just that. 'He was an incredible guy,' Jake was saying. 'Talk about a renaissance man. He taught us all astronomy courses that year. But he also had a purple Mohawk haircut when he was going through customs in New Zealand. When they were suspicious of him and asked "What do you do?" he replied, "I'm a scientist." He loved pushing their buttons.'

I waited for one beat. Two. And then Jake said: 'I was in there when he died in my hands.'

That was my opening. And three weeks ago when I first arrived on station, I would probably have taken it. I would have gone straight in there, asking him: what does it feel like to have one of your colleagues die in your arms? What was the atmosphere on station? Were people scared? Were you scared? Did you think you might be next? And yet, sitting there in Jake's cabin, I didn't dare. The pain in his eyes as he spoke about Rodney was almost indecent to witness.

'I wasn't going to mention it,' I said.

'That's OK,' he replied. He stubbed out his cigarette. 'Everything's intense here. Obviously the weather and the climate, but I don't think that's the most intense thing. It's the people, the interactions that you have with them, that's what hooked me. In winter here you've got a small tight-knit group, a very small tribe. You're all in it together, there's no titles, there's no job description, there's no HR, there's no bullshit.

'Even though your professions may be profoundly different, you can maintain this wholesome, unique, excellent friendship. Nowhere else are you going to meet a carpenter, a high-energy astrophysicist, a cook and an administrator, who will be having dinner together on a nightly basis. I've never seen something so dynamic in the outside world as I have this place in the winter. It's out of control.'

By this point, I'd almost forgotten about Jake's Carhartt overalls, but I noticed again how battered they were. Bill Henrickson had been right; Jake was indeed a deep thinker, and he was also one of the least macho people I had ever met. So why on earth did he insist on reusing his clothing every year? Just to show off what an old hand he was?

'What's the story about the Carhartts?'

'Well, um, you put them on, you wear them.'

'Yes, but what happens to everyone else is that they get their clothes issued new each season . . .'

'These were brand new at the beginning of this season.'

'That can't be true!'

'It is.'

'Jesus Christ!'

'Well, think about what happens to a fibre at a hundred below, it shatters. I'm not winding you up. Look at these bunny boots, they're shattered, they're gone. Everything takes a beating.'

And then, looking ruefully down: 'I guess they are pretty wasted.'

South Pole winter, June–August

Now that you are several months into your winter, you will probably be used to the permanent darkness and the intense cold. You may also have got used to the idea that you are stuck here no matter what happens. And that focuses everyone's attention on taking very good care of the place that's keeping you alive.

Fire is taken seriously here, very seriously, especially in

the winter. If you're in the fire team, the moment the alarm sounds you will leap up, swear and run for the comms room. If your gear is handy, you will have pulled it on before anyone else in the room has registered that there's a bell ringing. They call it 'Fire Alarm Tourette's'. I saw it happen once, in summer, in the galley. Bell, jump, swear, gear, run . . . all in the time it took me to lift my fork to my mouth.

As part of the fire team, you will already have done your training at the Rocky Mountains Fire Academy in Denver, in the US. It's an organisation that caters for professionals, so they can be quite snooty about training a bunch of amateurs. They don't understand the power that fire has down here. But they do give you a decent grounding in how to use the bunker gear – fireproof jackets, pants, a hood, breathing apparatus, so that every scrap of skin is covered and you could survive temperatures up to 2,200°F. They will have sent you through a burning building to see what it feels like. You get hot under the gear, but not unbearably so, and you begin to feel confident that it will keep you safe.

If you're still uncomfortable about marching into the flames, you might be assigned as a first responder, just to go and assess the situation. Nobody will ever go into a blaze, even down here, unless there's somebody's life to be saved or the chance to save a building that's crucial to survival. Mind you, in the winter most buildings are pretty crucial. If the power plant goes, or the water melter, or the human habitation, that puts everyone's lives at risk.

In the depths of winter it could still be possible to summon a Twin Otter or two, as happened for the 2001 medevac. But it takes at least two weeks for them to fly down from Canada to Rothera, assuming the runway at

Rothera is accessible, say another week or two at Rothera, waiting for the right weather conditions at the Pole, and even then fuel and size limitations mean that an Otter can only take out two or three people at most. That's no way to evacuate an entire base. Depending on the conditions, you might be able to get a Hercules to fly over and do an airdrop of food and fuel. But if a fire took out the base, most of you would have absolutely nowhere to go.

The new station has a sprinkler system, which is a big improvement on the Dome; but that would still only help slow a fire down. There is also a sort of inner sanctum sealed from the rest of the building by extra-heavy insulated fire doors, equipped with an emergency generator, beds, a kitchen and ... a laundry. (When I asked why it needed a laundry, I was met with a surprised look and the response: 'Even if the station has burned down, you'd still need to wash your clothes.') If the whole station went, there would always be the possibility of bedding everyone down in the outer-lying science buildings in the Dark Sector or the clean air sector. There are emergency rations stored out in the frozen berms – bags of food where you just add hot water and stir. As long as you can maintain power for heating and water, you'd survive the months before the Hercs could come and get you. But it wouldn't be pretty.

By now, if you don't have to go outside, you probably won't. Unless you have some purpose out there, even just a few minutes at -90°F and a blowing wind isn't much fun any more. There is, however, one magic temperature that you might still be waiting for. If the temperature hits -100°F you will immediately hear an announcement on the station loudspeakers: 'The temperature is now minus one hundred degrees Fahrenheit'. This is your cue to go racing for the sauna. Somebody will probably have started firing it up already. It usually only goes up to a maximum of 180°F so you will probably have to put the thermostat in some water to get it to creep up to the important (and sweltering) figure of 200°F.

You will sit there, naked, until you can hardly bear it. Then, and this is the important part, you will leave the sauna, pull on some bunny boots and a face mask — but strictly no other clothes — and run out into the snow. If you are really hard core, you will run, naked, all the way to the Pole and back. This is not recommended for the faint-hearted. In fact, it's not recommended for anyone. But if you do it, you will have experienced an instantaneous temperature change of 300°F and become a member of the legendary — and highly exclusive — '300 Club'.[20]

A less insane way to celebrate your presence on the ice takes place on 21 June, the Midwinter Festival. Cooks begin planning the menus for the feast weeks in advance. Everybody dresses up. Across the continent, all wintering bases exchange specially designed greetings, usually in the form of photos of the winterers with some additional message inscribed over them.

It is around now that relationships with the outside world may start to break down. The headquarters for the US support staff is in Denver and winterers often complain that they have little or no understanding of what life is like down here. 'People in Denver are in a completely different world,' says Jake. 'Few of them have wintered and they have nothing to base any of their demands or requests on. You can be standing there on the phone saying "OK, so, you want me to go out and count all of the cargo chains. They are under seven feet of ice and it's a hundred below and . . . you want me to count 'em? We're not going to use them until a month after you get here, so maybe we should count them when it's sunny and warm and there are all kinds of new people here who aren't frozen."' When he really wants to throw someone from Denver off balance, he simply asks them: 'can you feel your fingers?'

In 1997 the cook decided to roast some turkeys for the midwinter feast. There were twenty-eight people on station and twenty-two frozen turkeys. The request went out for permission to use some of them. Permission was denied. Word came from Denver that the turkeys had to be saved for station opening. For station opening! When new flights could bring in turkeys galore, and freshies that the wintering Polies could only dream of! 'Midwinter is a big deal here,' says Robert. 'We get Midwinter greetings from the White House. But we weren't allowed to cook our turkeys. It went all the way up to the National Science Foundation. Finally they said OK but it was too late, because the turkeys would have taken too long to thaw.'

To be successful, any winter station manager has to be an excellent mediator. He or she has to maintain the respect of the wintering crew while also keeping sensible relations with the outside world. And though the resentments from the winterers are easy to understand, the people in the north can sometimes also be in the right.

When the midwinter celebration is over and there is nothing more to look forward to but long months of darkness and cold, life turns in on itself, and the station becomes even more of a pressure cooker. 'It's like a colony here,' Larry says. 'When it's dark out all the time and you're in one building you get the impression that you're in some Stanley Kubrick movie heading out towards Jupiter 9. Nothing goes unnoticed. If you do something more than twice it's a habit.' NASA has spotted this phenomenon and there have been many attempts to do biological and psychological studies on wintering Polies, to see how a genuine Moon base might play out, or one on Mars.[21]

One thing researchers have learned is that as the winter progresses you will start to lack T3, a hormone produced in the thyroid that winterers seem to divert from the brain to the muscles. There is also evidence that your core body temperature will drop by a degree or two, even if you don't go outside. Perhaps it's the lack of sunlight, or disrupted sleep patterns, or the cold. Perhaps it's a psychological effect associated with being thrown together in a small group, and unable to leave. But the symptoms seem to be real.

Psychologists call this phenomenon 'winter-over syndrome'. Polies call it 'going toast'. Everybody becomes at least slightly toasty in the depth of the winter. The first sign is that you stop paying attention to the way you look or the way you smell. People get a thousand-mile stare. While talking to you, they will trail off in mid-sentence, without noticing. And if you're toast enough, you might not notice either. You might walk into a room repeatedly, each time forgetting why you have come. You might step out of the shower wondering if you are on your way in or out. You might sit in the galley quietly crying over your plate, then leave it untouched and wander out again.

'We all know we go toast,' says Jake Speed, 'and it's true you can't remember one thing from the next, what day of the week. I think the people who struggle the most are the ones who try to hang on to those normal constructs that are part of our day-to-day society. Look around you – you're not in Kansas any more. If you try to turn it into Kansas you will not survive. Just relax, go with the groove. You wanted this winter experience, and when that last plane took off you were happy. Well, this is what it really is. So just hang in there.'

Jake knows better than most how to do a successful winter. He says that good winterers will have a positive approach; they'll stem poison; they'll have a sort of peaceful resonance. Bad winterers can't handle themselves, and so can't handle other people. They'll either cocoon themselves in their rooms or come out and start stirring things up.

Polies call the bad version of the syndrome 'burnt toast'. 'That's when people get really bitchy, and want to pick fights,' says Jake. 'It gets to the point where you can be in the galley and someone could be on the other side of the room and just their presence is so unsettling that you can't stand it. People begin to figure out – OK, he goes to dinner at 5:30 so I'll go at 6:15. It's not even necessarily conscious. It just begins to work its way out.

'Mid-July to mid-August is mean month. It's OK to go up to someone then and say, "I fucking hate you" for no reason, no instigation. Instead of saying "good morning" you just tell them right what you think. All inhibitions are gone, and all the filters are off. You don't even know you're doing it.'

This is also when territorial troubles can start to play out, when it really starts to matter if someone is sitting in your chair. Last winter, Larry, Jake and a friend named Jed Miller made a joke out of the mad territoriality at the station. They put a tablecloth, made out of a bed sheet, on their favourite table in the galley. In July they started drawing on it, dividing it into imagined terrains with little mountains and landscapes. Larry's was called 'Larryland'. Jed's was Jedanasia. Jake's territory was the smallest. They called it the 'United Front of Jake Insurgence'.

'He was the rebel that we were constantly trying to quell,'

says Larry. 'If you look at him, he's like the rebel of the station; I mean, have you seen the state of his Carhartts?' Jake was constantly moving his plate into Jed's territory. Jed hated this. Napkins would fly. Food would fly. 'We had a beautiful centrepiece as well, a lit-up Christmas tree about eight inches high, when we turned it on it would glow red. That was our thing. Our table was our world.'

But that was also about the time when the galley broke out into what became known as the 'light wars'. 'One guy, Chuck, would come into the galley and flick on five or six extra lights at a time,' says Larry. 'Some people who miss the sun like having bright lights but to others it was like vampires having garlic thrown in their faces. There would be hollering and screaming. It almost turned into a fist-fight.

'Chuck enjoyed doing it every day, and finally one day he was outnumbered. The people who hated the extra lights would alternate at turning them back off. Chuck turned them on, someone went out of the galley all the way down to the end of the hallway, came back down the corridor, came in another entrance and turned the lights off again. And then they'd go round the whole thing again. Lights on. Walk down the hallway, back to another entrance, lights off again. There was yelling, fists, insults, sneers. Eventually everyone had to sit down and talk about it; station emails were sent; management got involved. We ended up with alternating days with the lights higher or lower. It's almost embarrassing to think of it outside winter.'

'Everyone's allowed a couple of toasty psychotic episodes,' says Jake. 'As the first glimmers of light come over the horizon, the good ones start to make up. "I'm sorry I called you an asshole …" The bad ones just keep going.'

The stories of the bad ones, the ones who couldn't

hack it, are legion and legendary. One year, the AST/RO guy tried to ski the 800 miles back to McMurdo in the dark with just a few chocolate bars in his pocket. He made it about ten miles before someone noticed he was missing and brought him gently back. There are other, perhaps apocryphal tales: the man whose friends shaved his head when he was drunk – and it took him three days to notice; the winterer who took a more novel approach to escaping to McMurdo by solemnly packing his bags, bidding everyone farewell and then trying to walk there on a treadmill.

Polar madness isn't limited to the South Pole. In the 1950s an Australian was locked away for most of the winter after he had threatened people with a knife. In the 1960s a Soviet scientist killed a colleague with an axe because he was cheating at chess. In 1996, the cook at McMurdo had to be isolated after he attacked someone with the claw end of a hammer. In 1983 the doctor at Argentina's Almirante Brown Station on the Peninsula hated the winter so much that his bags were packed and ready for days before the relief ship steamed in. When the incoming crew broke the news that there was no replacement available so he would have to spend another winter there, the doctor promptly burned the place down.

The various different programmes have tried many ways to guard against the crazies. The best way, most winterers say, is to look for people with mixed motivations. If your work is your life, and something breaks down while you're there, you could go crazy. If you're only there for the romance and adventure, and discover how little time you can spend in the Great Outdoors during the winter, you could go crazy. Paradoxically, it also seems to help if you're not the sort of person who needs to resolve issues right here and now. One study of French winterers showed that the ones who performed best were neither extroverts nor assertive. Everyone goes a little toasty and you're better off letting most of it slide.

'You've got to be able to take everything,' Jake says. 'The toasty psychotic episodes, the gossip – this place is the biggest gossip mill of all time – and let it all just roll out. It doesn't matter that you can't tie your shoes any more; it doesn't matter that so and so said something about you; it doesn't matter that somebody tried to stick a spoon into someone else's ear at dinner. You've got to let it roll off your back. If you allow these things to matter too much in the winter, you'll become consumed by them. And then I can't help you.'

The National Science Foundation puts every potential winterer through a psychological test known in Antarctic argot as Psych Eval. The results are never published, leaving some wags to suggest that the people who come out as unbalanced are the ones eventually chosen.

The satirical website *Big Dead Place* has a more cynical take on the procedure: 'Nearly every paper worth its salt written on the selection of winter-over personnel at isolated polar bases has come to this conclusion: psychological profiling is not an accurate method of determining who will or will not successfully integrate themselves into a polar community. Questionable introverts have flourished because of their tolerance of personal idiosyncrasies, and shoe-in extroverts have been shunned at bases for their relentless neediness.

'Psychological profiling can help weed out the claustrophobic, the hypochondriac, and the manic-depressant, but when July rolls around ... one begins to wonder whether there is as much to fear at the winter base from the overt psychotic as there is from the covert neurotic, that is, the "normal" member of society. Though apparently both of these types have no trouble passing the Psych Eval, the psychotic at least provides the community with a few laughs and occasionally a little excitement to spruce up the daily grind.'[22]

Other programmes such as the British one ignore the lure of psychological testing and rely on personal interviews, which seem to work at least as well. But it's also striking how many of the people brought into the American programme already know someone down here – and the same applies to the French, British and Italian[23] programmes, too. It's not so much nepotism as the power of personal recommendation in weeding out the unstable and unsuitable. If space agencies really want to send a small number of humans out into a space colony, when choosing who to send they should probably begin by trusting their own instincts.

Even in a good winter, there can be times when you regret the choice you've made. There are stories of people getting 'Dear John' or 'Dear Joan' divorce letters by email while they are incarcerated down here and can't do a thing about it. In 2003, Robert Schwarz's brother was sick and all he could do was send emails and make calls. 'It's a time when you want more than anything to be with your family.' In one of Larry's winters, he learned that his best friend had died. 'One of my worst fears was realised,' he says. 'It challenges your idea of surrendering and giving in and not worrying. That's the only time I've ever wished that I wasn't here. You work past it, and you realise how tight the community is. But that's when you also realise that nothing waits for you. You feel as if everything is on hold while you're here, but life outside is passing you by.'

•   •   •

The only remaining scientific block that I hadn't yet visited was the Clean Air Sector, where researchers studied the atmosphere.[24] But now I had the perfect opportunity. During the South Pole summer, every Friday was 'slushies' night. This consisted of a general invitation from the guys at the Atmospheric Research Observatory (ARO) to come over and drink cocktails that were cooled into slushies using a scoop of the cleanest snow on Earth. It was my chance both to find out about their science and to sample some of the legendary mixes.

ARO was only about half a kilometre from the main station but it was enough of a hike that I tried to beg a skidoo ride. No chance. Skidoos were strictly banned to protect the cleanliness of the air. The only way to get there was on foot.

The building was big, blue and blockish, set up on criss-crossing stilts over two floors, with snow-covered metal staircases running up the outside. The windows were large and oval, like elongated portholes looking over the frozen ocean. Most of them faced outwards, away from the station and the views were to die for: a glorious white emptiness of sculpted snow and shadows, delicately shaded in pastel colours by the softly slanting sunlight.

ARO looked oddly isolated against a backdrop of bare white plateau that stretched in an arc more than a third of the way around the Pole. To keep the air here as clean as possible, this entire arc upwind of here had been designated strictly no-construction. The prevailing winds blew true; for more than 90 per cent of the time they arrived directly from that empty stretch of ice. This meant that the air sucked into the sensors on the roof of this building was the purest on Earth. It was the background into which all of our human, industrial, polluting wastes were elsewhere being poured.

Squeezed in among all that astronomy, ARO was one of the few South Pole projects that had no interest in outer space.

Instead, it was using the way the Pole stripped away outside influences to find out what we could learn about home. It was one of five global observatories run by America's National Oceanic and Atmospheric Administration to measure long-term changes in the air. This was the extreme end-member of the group, the base level against which all the others could be judged. It has also been responsible for some of the longest continuous records in the world; scientists had been measuring the air here since 1957. Long records aren't necessarily sexy. They don't tend to throw up exciting new surprises or eureka moments. But they are good at showing up the sorts of slow but inexorable changes that really matter to our climate, the ones that we wouldn't notice if we were only looking week to week or year to year.

And probably the most important record here was the one for carbon dioxide. This exists perfectly naturally in the atmosphere but we have also been adding to it ever since the Industrial Revolution, by burning first coal, then oil and natural gas. And the CO_2 that comes out of your car's exhaust pipe or a power station chimney eventually finds its way here. CO_2 is a survivor. It doesn't fall out of the air easily like soot or dust, but can stay up there for a hundred years or more, spreading to the farthest corners of the globe. The graph of ARO measurements placed prominently in the entrance hall showed that, over the past few decades, carbon dioxide had been rising upwards like a rearing cobra, waiting to strike.

ARO was built to replace the old Clean Air Facility, and had been around for only seven years. But already it had all the warm homely touches that the new station currently lacked. There were artificial flowers everywhere. One of the windows held a vase with plastic sunflowers; a fake poinsettia tied with a tartan ribbon was precariously balanced over one of the desks; and a plastic spider plant appeared to be growing out of the bathroom sink. A lopsided sign outside the bathroom read 'Ladies' Powder Room'. (Apparently this came originally from Old Pole, the first South Pole station – not that ladies were allowed to visit there until the 1970s.) Another sign hanging from the ceiling of the tech shop suggested that this was the 'Mental Ward'. Beside the small wooden table that functioned as a coffee station was a metal trolley crammed with bottles of whisky and gin, Grand Marnier and rum as well as more brightly coloured and dubious looking liqueurs. There was also a blender, though here the ice came ready slushed.

Beside the bar were bottles of soap solution and large improvised bubble wires. Blowing bubbles? In Antarctica? One of the slushies team quickly offered to show me how. Outside, the temperature was now around -40°F, which turned out to be perfect. You had to blow quickly or the liquid froze on the wire. But when you succeeded in making giant bubbles, you watched in wonder as they frosted over and shattered in the air, leaving frozen fragments to fly around your head. The pieces looked like plastic but if you tried to catch one, it broke up into fine wafers in your glove.

Back inside, my companion handed me some small sample bottles and bundled me on to the roof. Up aloft there was a stiff breeze, which made the cold almost unbearable – even for just a few minutes. But I drew my parka hood close, and followed my companion's instructions for collecting the perfect South Pole souvenirs. I held out my genii sample bottles to the wind and captured, and sealed in, magical whiffs of the cleanest air on Earth.

Downstairs, the party was now motoring. Someone had brought in a bucket full of snow and the room was full of Polies, with cocktails already in hand. I had decided not to be daring. Larry Rickard warned me days ago about the power, and pain, of high-altitude slushies hangovers. But after a couple of gin and tonics it began to seem churlish not to join in. My favourite was the concoction mixed for me by an ex-marine (and also ex-bartender), which contained Kahlua, Baileys and vodka – and of course perfectly pristine snow. It tasted delicious, like chocolate milk. The pain the next day was everything that Larry had warned me about. But it was still worth it.

Just as ARO was studying home rather than away, there was one other experiment at the Pole that was looking inwards, to the core of the Earth. I had heard about it, but hadn't much hope of getting out there. It was called SPRESSO, which stood for 'South Pole Remote Earth Science and Seismological Observatory', and it was concerned with measuring earthquakes. Not nearby ones. There were no earthquakes at the South Pole. Instead, like ARO, this experiment was all about focusing on what was left when the messiness of the outside world had been left behind. And just as ARO had to be placed where the air was cleanest, SPRESSO needed to be in the quietest zone on Earth.

In principle, the South Pole was already a good spot for this. Elsewhere in the world, cars, trains, rattling cables or something as slight as the rustling of leaves could be enough to swamp the most delicate seismic instruments. But even here there were problems. The quiet sector was initially sandwiched between the dark and clean sectors, but half a kilometre from the station was too close. The researchers could hear the distant rumbling of the snow cats so clearly that they knew when the heavy equipment operators went to lunch. So they had to move their instruments out of town. After three years of construction and drilling, SPRESSO's delicate seismometers were now buried deep in the snow, some five miles away.

That far from the station, SPRESSO might as well have been on the Moon. There was no way anyone was going to let me go out there on my own, and little chance that anyone could spare the time and the vehicle to take me there. But then I hit lucky. It just so happened that two SPRESSO researchers, Kent Anderson and Steve Roberts, were coming through town. I grabbed them in the galley the day they arrived. Yes, they were planning an expedition out to SPRESSO. And, yes, I could come, too.

Kent was a stocky man, square of body and round of face with a tidy beard and jovial appearance. Steve was quieter and taller, sandy-haired and clean-shaven. Our expedition would be in the Sloth, a rumbling, grumbling yellow lump that ran on tank-like caterpillar tracks and had 'US Navy, For Official Use Only' stencilled on the side. As its name implied it was known more for solidity than speed.

We were equipped, Steve told me, with full survival gear: orange bags packed with spare clothing, survival bags, emergency food and stove, two radios and an iridium satellite phone. In the outside world, packing all that for an eight-kilometre trip would seem absurd. Here, where the weather could turn on a sixpence, he assured me that it was essential.

As we jarred and jolted our way over the snow, Kent told me about SPRESSO. It was, he said, part of a global network, jointly funded by the United States Geological Survey and the NSF, through a university consortium called IRIS (Incorporated Research Institutions for Seismology).[25] Appropriately for a station at the end of the world, and just like ARO, this was the extreme end-member of the network, by far the quietest seismic station on Earth.

The quietness mattered because, with no outside distractions, you could pick up the subtlest possible signals from the other side of the world. An earthquake doesn't just shake the nearby ground. It sends seismic waves down into the bowels of the Earth where they pass through the hot rocks of the planet's interior, squeezing and compressing them or nudging them from side to side. And when these waves, much diminished in strength and stature, make it out the other side, they bear traces of the rocks they have passed through. By measuring the relative speeds of waves that have come from different places and passed through different parts of the planet, SPRESSO could act as a sort of inward telescope, constructing an image of the Earth's mantle of rock, its liquid outer core made of almost pure iron, and the hot hard solid sphere of iron that lies at the centre of the Earth.

The South Pole was especially good for this not just because it was so quiet. Its unique positioning on the Earth's axis of rotation also meant it could hear events with a clarity that other stations couldn't reach. That's because in most places the Earth's own rotation can get in the way. 'If you think of the Earth as a bell and you hit it with a big earthquake, it'll vibrate and the way it vibrates tells you something about the structure of the interior of the earth,' Kent said. 'Anywhere where the Earth is spinning, the vibration of the ringing bell also changes. Here at the axis of rotation is the only place where you can hear the true ringing of the bell.'

SPRESSO was also uniquely placed to find out about the very centre of the Earth. Most stations pick up only the waves that have taken glancing paths through the Earth's interior. Here, you could detect ones that had passed through its heart. And SPRESSO was on hand to make sure nobody was cheating on the Nuclear Test Ban Treaty. Nuclear bombs also set off seismic waves. If they are far enough away, they will be faint. But sensitive SPRESSO would pick them up in a heartbeat. 'If someone tried something in the middle of nowhere, in the southern seas, we would probably hear it.'

When we finally reached the SPRESSO site, the only surface sign of its presence was a set of brightly coloured flags, red, yellow, orange and green, fluttering on an apparently empty plateau. Some, Kent told me, marked the corners of the buried building, some the three boreholes where the seismic instruments lay and some, well, 'just don't walk there,' he said.

As we came closer I realised there was a vent pipe, comically poking up out of the snow like a periscope from a submarine. There were also two hatches covered first with snow and then, when we had brushed that aside, with wood. One led to a few near-surface instruments, the other to a yellow stepladder that took us down to the surprisingly warm and cosy hut that serviced the seismic instruments.

Inside, as he stripped off his parka and gloves, Kent told me that they'd have preferred to put the site farther from the main station – twelve miles or more. But that was going to be too complicated, and expensive, to service. So the compromise was to put the instruments closer in but deeper down in the snow. It took three seasons to set up the hut and drill the holes and now the seismic instruments were irrevocably buried under a thousand feet of ice.

'The chamber round the instruments is at about -51°F,' Kent said, 'but the instruments themselves are wrapped in heat tape, so they're more like +25°. And if one tape fails, they're already wound with a back-up.'

'What happens if both heat tapes fail?'

'Then we've lost the instrument, so let's not think about that.'

Eight thousand miles from here, on the other side of the world, a piece of the Earth's crust might be straining. The Earth's tectonic plates that hold our continents and oceans are constantly shifting, pushing and grinding against each other, striving for dominance. Sometimes, something has to give. Perhaps up in the Aleutian Islands off the coast of Alaska a section of crust might suddenly rise or fall. Tsunami warnings will chatter out from instruments around the Pacific. Sirens will sound, and sensible coast dwellers will head for high ground if they can. But the heaving crust won't just set off a mighty wave of water. It will also send other waves, seismic waves, downwards into the inner Earth.

Seismic waves travel by squeezing and stretching whatever material they are going through, just as sound waves squeeze and stretch the air on their way to your ears. They will pass easily through rock. Though some will stay close to the surface, others will skim the liquid outer core of the Earth or sweep through its solid centre before emerging here, to be picked up by SPRESSO's listening ear. These waves will be full of fascinating information about the rocks they have passed through. They can tell us about the subtleties of the parts of our planet that drillers will never, ever reach. They can help us understand how the iron core of the Earth feeds our planet's magnetic field and why sometimes in the ancient past it suddenly switched, making north become south, and south become north. Or what sets off vast plumes of hot rock that start at the boundary between core and overlying mantle and slowly make their way to the surface. (These events are mercifully rare in Earth's history – when these gigantic mantle plumes reach the surface, they can cause the kind of epic volcanism that can flood half a continent with molten rock.)

The seismic waves from our Aleutian quake would be rich with such information, just waiting to be read. The detectors waiting 900 feet below ground would feel the first stirrings. And they would send their message up to the instruments here, which would wink and beep to register the shock, providing us with a unique window into the world far beneath our feet.

We watched, but for now nothing happened. All was quiet on this quietest of southern fronts. Kent and Steve decided to climb out and test out a new communications system, burying an antenna in the snow and going out on to the plateau. I waited around for them, taking in the view.

Out here, with nothing but wasteland in all directions, I felt for the first time as if I were truly on the Moon. On the horizon there was a single soft white wedge of cloud; the rest of the sky

was a clear cerulean blue. The sastrugi stretched out in that familiar pattern of frozen white wave tops. Some looked like porpoising
dolphins, caught in mid-leap; some were stippled as if a giant
hand had blotted paint; some looked like writhing coils and
some just smooth drifts of sugary snow. For all of them the side
shaded from the sun had a dull bloom, the colour of pewter, and
the hollows were in deep blue shadow. Cutting through it all was
the stark white scar of the Sloth's tracks. It was a beautiful, guileless scene. My eyelashes and hair had quickly frosted, and inside
my gloves my fingers were already numb. But I still found it hard
to believe that this place could ever be cruel.

When Kent re-emerged from the sub-glacial chamber, I asked
him what he thought of the place. Was he just in it for the science,
or did he find something special about the landscape? Definitely,
he said, the landscape was a big part of it.

'People find beauty in different things. I live in the desert in
New Mexico. Coming out here, which is the world's largest
desert, there is absolutely no life, nothing green to look at. Maybe
I'm a strange person for cherishing it, but it puts into perspective
what's important to me.' He was earnest, struggling to explain
something that clearly mattered to him.

'I study seismology, I look at the power of the Earth; when an
earthquake goes off, just a little tremble on the surface can wipe
out whole swathes of civilisation. And Antarctica is so big, it kind
of scales everything. I mean this is a fairly big operation at the
South Pole but compared to the vast nothingness around us,
we're hardly anything here. We're so insignificant compared to
what the Earth can do.'

I heard this sort of thing a lot on the ice. 'It makes you feel
small,' people kept saying to me. And they didn't mean small in a
bad way. It wasn't about feeling humiliated. They seemed to find
something reassuring about being in the presence of something
that was unquestionably bigger and stronger than they could

ever be. It didn't matter how much money you had, how big a superpower you were, what technology you had devised. Sometimes it might look beautiful, sometimes guileless, but down here, if Antarctica said no, then that was final.

'Believing you are important as a human being brings with it a certain responsibility,' a French doctor told me at Dumont d'Urville. 'You're important so you have things to prove. Here you have nothing to prove because you can only submit. It's almost a relief. You are relieved of your image of being important.

'It's different from choosing not to prove things – that implies you can't get better, it's pretentious. The value here is that the choice itself is taken away. And if you take away false choices you can ask yourself the true questions: what's important for me? What direction should I take? Who are the people I miss and why? Who misses me?'

South Pole winter, September–October

Ever since midwinter the sun has been creeping up on the dark side of the horizon. And now, with September, comes the return of twilight. The stars fade and so – largely – do the auroras. By the end of the first week, you can take down the blackout sheets that keep the artificial lights inside the station from leaking out. The solstice, around the third week, brings the first signs of sunlight and the beginning of the long slow polar sunrise.

Perhaps you'll be one of the people who's excited by this, who plays 'Here Comes the Sun' incessantly over every available loudspeaker. Perhaps, like the rest, you'll be feeling sadness at this loss of the comfort blanket of darkness and the beginning of the end. But as the sun slowly rises and the time of the long shadows returns, don't be fooled into thinking that the light has also

brought warmth. The temperature will still be south of
-75°F and those first feeble rays do little more than stir
up the winds. 'That fucks you up,' says Jake. 'You associ-
ate dark with cold and light with warm. It's light out but
it ain't warm. Everyone's tired, you want it over with.
The ones who haven't cracked yet, that's when they
crack.'

And there will now be stacks of work for everyone,
making the station ready for opening. There's heating the
summer housing for the people coming in, taking down the
flags that helped you feel your way in the darkness, marking
and grooming the skiways for planes to land, and preparing
the fuel lines ready to recharge the station for another year.

Still, just as with the coming of the sun, the station will
probably be split between those who can't wait to get out
of here and those who dread the coming invasion. For with
the station opening comes the promise, and the threat, of
the world beyond the ice. 'Travel plans. "I can't wait to see
my girlfriend" plans. I can't even listen to those conversations,' says Jake. 'Everyone is checking out. It's not over yet
but they're already done. I think they're missing out on a
major part of the winter. I'm in a different place. I'm putting
all my energy back in. Storing it. All the patience is paying
off at that moment. It's blossoming. It's the first spring
flower starting to stretch itself towards the sunlight.'

If you're lucky, and you're also one of the people dreading
the invasion, the weather might conspire to hold it off for a
few more precious days, as happened in 1997. 'That year, it
was a very late opening,' says Robert. 'The weather at the
beginning of November was awful. The first plane was trying
to come in for twelve days. Every day we were in comms,
getting reports, "the weather is still too bad". We were cele-
brating. One day they flew over, three passes, but still they

couldn't land. We were getting emails from McMurdo saying, "It must be terrible for you". Not at all, we had a big party, twenty-eight people and food for a hundred!'

But in the end they will come. You will be kicked out of your room, bewildered by the new people running down the corridors. Someone will hang a parka on your peg. Someone else will sit on your chair. They will be fresh from the world outside, amused by your pale faces and toasty stares. As well as running AST/RO, Nick Tothill was last year's winter science leader. He began his final report leading up to the Opening with a quote from *The Epic of Gilgamesh*:

> *I shall break the doors of hell and smash the bolts,*
> *And the dead shall eat with the living . . .*

But at least the living bring treats along with them – magazines and newspapers, physical mail, and freshies. The hydroponic greenhouse will have been supplying you with some green stuff over the winter, the odd bit of lettuce and the very occasional tomato. But now there will be fruit and veg by the planeload. 'When the first strawberries arrived, Cookie slipped me one while I was waiting in the queue,' says Nick. 'I took a bite. I can't describe the sensation. I stood stock still for five seconds. Perhaps in three weeks I'll be back to being as spoiled as everyone else, but right now every bite of fruit is so very good.'

You may feel more exposed that you ever have, but perhaps also more balanced. 'So many of your crutches get knocked out from under you,' says Nick. 'Down here, you have to learn to trust yourself. Stuff that you may have been struggling with for years just kind of goes. An

Antarctic winter scours your personality down to the bedrock.'

And whatever happens when you return to civilisation, don't expect the experience to fade quickly. 'I don't think this place ever leaves your body,' says Larry. 'You can't ever fully get away from it. Five years later you can look at a calendar in February and think "station's closing". Ten years later, on 21 June, you'll think "it's midwinter". It never leaves you. Why? I don't know. Coming down here isn't hard, it's going back that's hard. You've got to pay for things. Try walking into a supermarket after winter. It's probably one of the most daunting experiences you have. You're used to "this is what's for dinner" and then suddenly you're faced with that kind of choice.

'You get back and the world is different. Things have changed, of course they have. Watching the sun rise and set in a twenty-four-hour period. Not treating everybody like your best friend, as you would here. Getting used to the idea that you're not living on top of everyone any more. Sitting in your room, listening to your clock tick and thinking: what do I do now?'

So, however toasty you might now be going, however eager to click your ruby slippers and get yourself back to Kansas, there's another piece of Antarctic slang that you should probably now be made aware of. According to Polies, the phrase 'I'm never coming back here again' translates into Antarctican as 'See you next year'.

It was Jake Speed's penultimate day at the Pole and he had offered to drive me round in a skidoo, showing me some of his favourite places. We visited an igloo that the winterers built, swooped around the berms where much of the station's supplies were stored and where Jake had spent a large part of the past five years.

And then we ended up just outside the station, on the empty plateau, to watch a sastruga grow.

In the winters, great windstorms sculpt these sastrugi into magnificent forms that can be ten feet high. Today we had to make do with a stiff, trickling breeze that sent the snow curling and writhing over the surface like parallel threads of smoke. Jake pulled out a lighter and stuck it upright into the snow to make a suitable obstruction. He lay down with his face close to it and I followed suit. And, sure enough, grain by grain, the snow began to build into a miniature hill on the windward side of the lighter, leaving a growing trail in the lee.

We both lay there for a while in silence. Then I asked Jake the question that had been bothering me for days. I'd noticed that Robert and Steffen, the two telescope nannies – and, now I thought about it, other people who had spent winters at the Pole – were all happy enough to talk to me about mechanical details, but guarded when I tried to dig deeper. So why did Jake agree to speak to me?

He smiled. 'It's hard to break in,' he said. 'You caught me in a strange place. Normally I wouldn't have talked to you. I'm pretty protective of all this. But I've just done what no one else has done and I felt like it was important for me to share.'

So why are the others so much more guarded? 'Obviously the weather and the climate are intense, but the most intense thing about this place is the people, the interactions that you have with them. I know that Robert gets up every morning, then takes his right eye with his left index finger, rubs it three times and then brushes his teeth. I know that guy like a wife.'

'Does it feel like a betrayal to talk about it?'

He considered this for a moment. 'I know a guy who did one winter and did it poorly and then he ran out and started shooting his mouth off about it. Number one, I thought he was an asshole when he was here. Number two, now he was making himself look even more of a clown. Number three, he was romanticising this place way out of proportion, giving away all of our intimate details without our consent. This is home for us, this is where we live, this is where we breathe, this is what we do. There's a lot of things we do in the wintertime that we won't tell people about because it is ours.

'You feel that once you become more intimate with this place, it would be dishonourable to give away all those little treats and cherished moments and insights and knowledge and experience to somebody ... it's very heartfelt. It's like getting involved in a relationship.'

So it wasn't just machismo; nor were the winterers some kind of Masonic order where only the initiated were allowed to see the inner sanctum. Jake talked about Antarctica as if it was a person, a lover. To him, and perhaps to most of the people who have been really touched by the experience, the hidden stories of Antarctica's winters were like whispered secrets across a cold white pillow. The only way to hear them was to be there. And it occurred to me then that a lover's secrets are so intoxicating not just for what they tell you about your lover, but for what they tell you about yourself.

I had been at the Pole for barely four weeks, in the bright white summer with a station continually crowded with new arrivals; and yet when I heard the moaning sound that meant the plane was coming to take me home, I felt a sadness that lingered for most of the journey back. There were only two of us on the flight to Mactown, so I wheedled my way on to the flight deck and spent the ride staring out of the window at the great white plateau and daydreaming about the final days of Scott and his men.

After they left the Pole, they followed their own tracks home, sometimes gaining enough wind to sail on their sledges, but mostly doing the Antarctic man-hauling trudge. At first all seemed well; they were reaching each of their caches of food and fuel just before their supplies ran out. But the temperature began to plummet and their skis stuck fast on the frozen snow, as if they were pulling on sand. As the way grew harder so the men grew weaker.

We were flying down the Beardmore Glacier now, where Edgar Evans succumbed to a hand injury that refused to heal, and then head injuries from a series of falls, then the depredations of frostbite. He died somewhere near the bottom of the giant ice staircase. Now we were above the floating Ross Ice Shelf, the great Barrier, where the ailing Captain Oates – who knew he was holding the rest of his companions back – stepped out into a snowstorm. Scott, his loyal lieutenant Wilson and the indefatigable Birdie Bowers continued onwards, but it must have been somewhere around here where the three men made their final camp.

They were less than a day's march from a depot of fuel and food, but a blizzard kept them trapped in their tent until they were too weak to move. On 29 March 1912, Scott wrote in his diary: 'It seems a pity but I do not think I can write any more.' And then later, in one famous anguished scrawl: 'For God's sake, look after our people!'

Poor Apsley Cherry-Garrard had been sent out with the dogs from Cape Evans, to reprovision the depot. He did so merrily, unaware that his companions were close to death just eleven miles away. He didn't look for them. He had been told not to. At that stage nobody imagined the polar party might be in danger and he had been warned not to put the dogs at risk. Still he was haunted all his life by the thought of what might have been.

The next spring, when the men from Cape Evans found the bodies, they turned the tent into a tomb. Long buried by successive snowfalls, it has travelled along with the ice, heading inexorably towards the coast. Nobody knows exactly where the corpses are now. But one day they will reach the edge of the great Barrier. When the ice around them calves off into an iceberg, they will go, too, and they will finally find rest, and decay, when the berg melts and they drift gently to the bottom of the sea.

Amundsen, of course, returned home to Norway, and glory. But though he was feted the world over, he was never really content with his triumph. He made voyage after voyage to his first love, the far north, almost daring the elements to take him. Eventually he disappeared in 1928 while flying on a rescue mission over the North Pole, as if that was the only fitting end for a true polar hero.

When an expedition goes fatally wrong, it is easy enough to find fault with the explorers' decisions or with their methods. Do so if you dare. But, first, remember the words of Charles Dickens, chiding those of us who would criticise too readily: 'Heaven forbid that we, sheltered and fed, and considering this question at our own warm hearth, should audaciously set limits to any extremity of desperate distress! It is in reverence for the brave and enterprising, in admiration for the great spirits who can endure even unto the end, in love for their names, and in tenderness for their memory, that we think of the specks, once ardent men, "scattered about in different directions" on the waste of ice and snow.'[26]

Scott may have made mistakes, but his luck was also against him. One atmospheric scientist, exasperated by all the carping she heard about Scott, decided to calculate some of the odds around the two approaches.[27]

Interestingly, although Scott's two huts still stand, there is no trace of Amundsen's camp. The place he chose to spend the winter has since broken off into a giant iceberg and floated out to sea. There was a one in twenty chance this would happen while Amundsen was there. He took the risk, played the odds and won. There was also, as it happens, only a one in twenty chance that the weather would be cold enough during Scott's return from the Pole to slow him and his colleagues down until they ran out of food and fuel. Scott was also playing the odds, but he turned out to be the unlucky one.[28]

And yet, these dramatic tales and the language that goes with them do help to burnish the image of the ice as hostile and alien, inimical to those warm-blooded creatures foolish enough to try to penetrate it. The changes at Amundsen–Scott South Pole Station seem similarly designed to perpetuate the myth. The Dome is now gone and the new space-age station finished, cladded with its iron-grey coat. Today the thirty-foot South Pole Telescope has begun probing deeper into the afterglow of the Big Bang. The last string has been frozen in for Ice Cube and the South Pole's neutrino eyes have opened.

These changes lend further weight to the notion of the South Pole as distant and alien. But there is another scientific side to the Pole, one that's looking inwards rather than out. Think of ARO, testing our own world's air, and SPRESSO's seismic ear, pressed close to the ground to hear the slightest ringing of the quiet Earth.

Larry Rickard's last words to me, when he came to see me off at the plane, echoed this from the personal side. 'I've listened to people talking about what's the meaning and the feel and the heart and the soul of this place,' he said. 'But you can't. It's like trying to find the meaning of life. To me, this place, it just is. But I'll tell you one thing. When you come here you're not finding something in a desert, you're seeing a mirror. Antarctica tends to knock you down to what you really are.'

Jake Speed clearly understood this. He lay on the snow in the dark, cold winter, watching sastrugi grow grain by grain: but he also said that it is all about the people. And I remember now how Jake described this place that he knew better than anyone else alive. He didn't use words like 'hostile' or 'unforgiving' or even 'indifferent'.

He called it 'patient'.

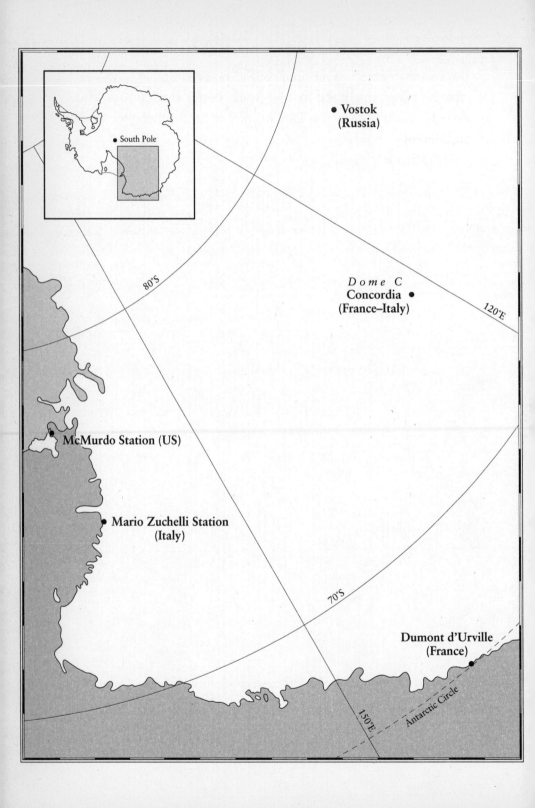

5

CONCORDIA

It is 800,000 years before the first humans set foot on Antarctica, and snow is falling. Not the exquisitely intricate flakes that you find near the coast; the snowflakes here in the interior are more like tiny misshapen lumps. Most of their delicate fingers have been sucked away by the dry air, and the rest break off as the crystals tumble and roll on the surface, harried this way and that by the wind, until they finally settle into a hollow and are buried by more flakes from above.

Dim light filters through as snow piles upon snow. Someone walking on the surface now might hear a muffled popping sound, like bubble wrap bursting, as pressure from their footsteps causes the snow crystals to join together and break apart. But there is nobody to do the walking. *Homo sapiens sapiens*, the human race itself, has not yet evolved.

Still, the snow changes subtly where it lies. The warmth of the summer sun is just enough to meld its crystals into a distinctive crusted layer, which will mark out this year's snowfall from the one below, like the growth ring on a tree. And then winter comes and then summer, and another year's snow has fallen, and another. The layer gets buried, and the weight of snow overhead presses it into a new form called 'firn'. It becomes rigid, with the texture of polystyrene, threaded with crannies and tunnels through which the air passes freely from above.

Years pass. Now there is no more daylight. The burden overhead grows heavier, until finally it squeezes so hard that the crannies and tunnels collapse, slamming shut the exits, and trapping tiny bubbles of ancient atmosphere. The firn layer has now officially become ice and its cargo will turn out to be a precious one.

In far-off Africa, the ancestors of modern humans are making their way out into the world, outcompeting the Neanderthals for the world's resources. They are surviving ice ages, making tools and fire, growing crops, building cities and burning them down. And all the while our layer descends in the silent darkness towards the bedrock as a mountain of ice builds from above.

And now the humans are building roads and cars and factories. They are learning to burn fossil fuels – coal and oil and natural gas. And they are belatedly learning that their activities are changing the atmosphere, and perhaps also the climate that they depend on for their life.

The only way to find out for sure is to measure what came before. But it's too late for that. The air around them is already pumped full of pollutants, and the information these humans need to understand their world is now long gone. Except, that is, in those deep dark pockets of ice, where ancient air still lingers. Perhaps scientists can find these places, beneath the continent's great domes where the ice is thickest and oldest. Perhaps they can drill down into this ice, capture its unpolluted air and read the many layers of its long, cold climate history.

Dome C is one of a handful of points on the East Antarctic Ice Sheet even higher and drier than the South Pole. The summit stands more than 10,000 feet above sea level; the ice sheet is almost as thick as it gets, and the layers of ice at its base are among the oldest on Earth.

From the air I was half expecting it to look obviously pointed, like an ice mountain. But in fact its summit was so broad and its slopes so distant and gentle that it seemed just as flat and white as every other part of the vast Antarctic interior.

And when we landed, the sunlight on snow was just as blinding as at the Pole, the shock of taking my first breath in a temperature of -40°F was the same – as the air flash-froze the mucus in my nose and scoured the back of my throat. But there were some differences. At the Pole, it was always windy but here I could feel no wind at all. That was a benefit of being in a place where the great Antarctic winds were born. The air from these domes might spill down to the coast with great ferocity, but here it was surprisingly still.

Dome C lies about 600 miles south of the French coastal base of Dumont d'Urville, about the same distance from the Italian coastal base of Mario Zuchelli Station at Terra Nova Bay, and nearly 1,300 miles from the South Pole. Its name came originally from an unimaginative application of letters of the alphabet to the various high points that geographers discovered, and it has been variously dubbed Dome Charlie and Dome Circe. But these days the C is more likely to be associated with 'Concordia', because that is the name of the new station being built here, jointly, by France and Italy. The previous base had temporary buildings that could be occupied only in the summer. This one would now be available in the winter, too.

I was intrigued to see the only station on the ice that was run by two completely different countries. True, the French and Italians share a certain romance in their language and culture, and a similar obsession with food, but a co-owned base seemed odd even for Antarctica – the most collaborative of continents.

Their influence was immediately obvious. I remembered arriving at the South Pole and receiving stern injunctions from the Americans on preventing altitude sickness. Drink plenty of water, they had said. Avoid caffeine. Avoid alcohol. Here, our Twin Otter was greeted by a Frenchman bearing a tray of glasses filled with champagne; and at the first building we reached an Italian offered us dense, rich espressos.

The clichés extended to my hosts' clothing. As usual on the ice, the nations were neatly colour-coded, with the French wearing blue cold-weather gear and the Italians red. But although my American gear was also red, my parka felt suddenly ungainly. The Italian parkas were svelte and sleek. Some people were wearing one-piece suits, nipped in at the waist, with darts and tucks and strategically placed black patches. They looked like Formula One racing drivers. The Americans may have the only ATM on the continent, the French may pay most attention to food, but it was immediately evident that the Italians wore the most stylish clothes.

The base was much smaller than the Pole, more like Dumont d'Urville in scale, with about fifty people here in the summertime. From the outside the buildings looked like shipping containers welded together. The first room, the one with the espressos, was lined with wood, like a chalet. As I lingered there, Rita Bartolomei, the station secretary, came to show me where to go. She was Italian, open, cheerful and very beautiful, with an air of utter dependability. As we walked down the dormitory corridor to a small room with two bunks, and a square window through which the sunlight was pouring, she told me I was lucky. Most of the workers here slept outside in long cylindrical tents heated with stoves. If you left your clothes on the floor at night there, in the morning they would be frozen. In fact, most of the other buildings here were tents, and the locals referred to this as a 'summer camp' rather than a station.

All the notices on the walls were in English, which turned out to be the official language of the camp though few people here were native speakers. I supposed it was better to choose an international language than to have squabbles between resident French and Italians about whose should prevail. But I thought it must make for a certain amount of confusion.

I dumped my bags and hurried back out into the bright light. I'd been trying to get to Dome C for a long time now to see a project called EPICA (European Project for Ice Coring in Antarctica), a massive European-wide effort to drill down into the ice sheet and capture its climate record.[1]

EPICA was the scientific part of what drew me to the ice. Years ago, before I even imagined setting foot on Antarctica, let alone falling in love with it, I worked on the journal *Nature*, handling scientific papers about topics to do with earth, air, water and climate. I enjoyed finding the secrets that were hidden in our planet's mud and sediments and rocks and fossilised trees, how layer by layer the past wrote itself into the present, if you knew how to read the hieroglyphs. Find an old enough tree, pull out a core from its bulk like an absurdly elongated wine cork, and you can measure how thick or thin the rings are, and divine which were the good years and which the bad. Drill down into the mud beneath lakes, and – if you have a good enough microscope – you can measure the grains of pollen that fell in from the air, layer by ancient layer, and see which plants flourished when. The rocks themselves bear subtle signals written into the details of their chemistry; if you crush them and pass them through your high-tech machines you can catch lingering clues about the climate of the past.

But all of these methods of looking back in time have one thing in common: they need a vast amount of interpretation. The science is as sound as we can manage but it's still several steps removed from truly touching and tasting the Earth's real history.

And then I read about ice cores. Ice doesn't just keep a record of dust, volcanic ashes and the other subtle changes in atmospheric chemistry that together give us our weather. It has an extra property that belongs to no other history book on Earth. Living as it does on a perpetual knife edge between solid and liquid, strong and weak, ice is sensitive enough to capture tiny pockets of air, and strong enough to keep them. I read that scientists in Antarctica were drilling down into the ice cap and pulling up cores containing air that was older than the human race itself. Not interpretations of air, or subtle chemical signals where the air used to be, but genuine bubbles of the real thing.

I had already seen many scientific papers describing what that ancient air contains. I had talked to dozens of scientists about the results; I had visited the giant freezers back in Europe where the cores were held, watched while researchers sawed them and melted them and passed them through their machines. But I had never seen the drilling in action. This wasn't just a scientific expedition for me. It was a pilgrimage.

The drill tent was a short, blinding walk away from the main summer camp buildings. It wasn't hard to find. The arched roof was two storeys high and the white walls stretched to more than sixty-five feet long. Inside, the first thing that hit me was the heady smell of the drilling fluid. I could see a barrel near the door containing Forane 141b, a chemical now banned for its ozone-destroying properties and which drillers had to get special permission to use. It smelled dizzying, psychedelic, and I wondered how they could stand it. (I later found out. Within an hour or two, I was so inured to it that I no longer noticed it either.)

The fluid wasn't there as a lubricant – it was to keep the hole open. The ice was so plastic, so strong and so determined to revert to its original form that beyond a kilometre or so of depth the mere time it took to bring the drill up after one run and send it down for the next would be enough for the hole to start closing. This heady fluid was the perfect density to resist the shoving and squeezing of the ice sheet.

The floor of the tent was wooden, and the scene was dominated by a vertical steel drill tower that reached almost to the ceiling. A hefty cable fed by a winch was threaded through the tower and disappeared into the ground. On the far wall, three posters decorated with hand-drawn penguins marked the dates in past years when the drillers reached 1,000 m, 2,000 m and 3,000 m below the surface. This season they had only a few hundred metres left to drill and they were very close to the end.

One person – an Italian, judging by his outfit – was standing by the tower watching the disappearing cable. Several other people were inside a small hut with glass walls, crowded round a bank of computers. I recognised one of them, the chief driller, Laurent Augustin. I'd met Laurent before, when I went to interview him in Grenoble. He was compact of build, friendly but introspective, and I knew that some found him aloof. He wrote poetic descriptions of the landscape; he went for long solitary walks and he meditated; he was vegetarian, didn't drink alcohol and had banned smoking from any of his workplaces, to the great chagrin of many of the French workers; he was also one of the world's most experienced ice drillers, had spent decades both here and in Greenland, and understood better than most the strange, temporary intensity of life on the ice.

When I entered the hut Laurent greeted me with a smile and made room for me around the computer. But the atmosphere was tense and he told me that the drilling was getting steadily harder. Close to the surface the ice was at -65°F but, surprisingly, the deeper you went the warmer it got until, near the bedrock, the gentle heat emanating upwards from the Earth's interior was enough to warm the ice almost to its melting point. That was a double problem for the drillers. Soft ice was harder to cut, so barrel after barrel had returned to the surface empty. And worse, as the cutter's teeth bit, the ice around it could melt then refreeze, potentially jamming the drill down the hole for ever.

To try to get around this, Laurent was borrowing an idea from his Greenland days. For these last few runs, he was now attaching a long transparent sausage-like length of plastic to the barrel, filled with a mixture of alcohol and water. There was a spare one on the shelf beside me. It looked bizarrely low-tech, like the sort of party balloons that you twist into doggy shapes to amuse children. When the drill started rotating, a tiny screw would rip into the plastic, allowing alcohol to flood the hole right next to the drill head. This should keep any melted ice from refreezing long enough for the drill to get in and out without sticking. Or at least that was the idea. The team called this contraption a 'cognac bomb'.

The drill head had just reached the ice and Saverio, who was at the controls, was about to start cutting. Coloured lines on the computer screen reared up as the various activities went into distant action. The drill was now rotating, the cognac bomb must have burst and spilled its contents around the cutting head. But something seemed to be wrong. The current was soaring in the cutting motor. Saverio hastily switched off the blades and instructed the winch to pull on the cable. Now everyone's eyes turned to a small white box, whose red LEDs showed a number that was steadily rising. It said 5,000, then 10,000, then 15,000. Heeeaaave.

As the tension on the cable rose, so did the tension in our small hut until, at 17,463, the cable suddenly rattled into upward action and there was a collective sigh of relief. There might be no core, but at least the drill was free. Everyone stood down from the computer and Laurent told me that we now had nearly an hour to wait until the drill – moving at a human walking pace – would reach the surface. I was astonished by this statistic. It was easy to believe that the ice extended more than two miles below my feet, but the idea that it would take me nearly an hour of walking vertically downwards to reach the bedrock made it seem both farther away and more real.

This run was likely to be a bust, but the team wanted to bring up the drill to see if there were any clues about why it nearly stuck. This was more important than it sounded, because six years ago, when the drill really did jam, the game was almost lost.

Dôme C, 20/12/1998.
Diary of Laurent Augustin

It's Sunday, 13h. I take the controls after the Saturday evening break and send the drill down for the first pass of the week. 700m, 780m, 784m. I stop the descent 2 metres above the bottom of the hole and start to approach slowly. Everything is normal: motor current, suspension, temperature, inclination, the values are all normal. The knife slowly starts cutting the ice. The motor current rises.

It is rising far too much.

'What's happening? The current is more than 3 Amps.' I'm forced to stop the progress of the drill – if not it's going to jam in the bottom. Immediately the motor current returns to normal.

'Ouf!'

I wait a few minutes for the whole thing to stabilise. All is perfect again.

'But what happened? Perhaps an accumulation of chippings at the bottom of the hole during the Saturday evening break?'

I start the drilling again, even more carefully. The teeth have barely touched the ice at the bottom of the hole when the current rises again to abnormal levels. I stop drilling for the second time. All returns to normal.

'Why? What's going wrong?'

I check the computer screen very carefully. There is absolutely nothing to indicate that something abnormal is happening 786 metres under my feet.

'Ok, I'll try one last time. If it doesn't work, too bad, I'll bring it back up to the surface. It would be one pass wasted, but better to play safe.'

For the third time the motor current rises to abnormal values. I stop the cutting and start to bring the drill back up.

The cable goes under tension, I hear the winch straining, 1.9 tonnes, 2 tonnes, 2.3 tonnes of tension. The winch has given its maximum pulling value. In front of my eyes, the cable has stopped moving. The drill isn't coming. I try putting some slack on the cable in the hole, once, twice, three times, ten times, nothing doing. The drill isn't rising.

'Merde.'

This is serious. The news spreads quickly in the camp. 'The drill is stuck!' All the drillers are now around me. The cable is at its maximum tension: 2.9 tonnes. Nothing is moving.

We need to find a solution quickly: the whole season of work is in play. Glycol. We need glycol – antifreeze – which could dissolve the ice chips around the drill that are undoubtedly making it stick. We call the Italian base at Terra Nova Bay where the Twin Otter is just about to leave for Concordia, loaded and ready to take off with four astrophysicists on board.

Our four colleagues are summarily disembarked and replaced by the barrels of precious liquid. Five hours later 800 litres of pure glycol arrive at Concordia. We tip 500 litres of glycol into the hole. After the first try nothing happens. After the second try, 12 hours later, the tension on the cable drops very rapidly. Hope

returns to the team. Spirits rise. The drill also rises but only by
2 metres before it stops again. Huge disappointment.

We try to help the drill by shaking the cable back and forth,
sending waves down its entire length. All these attempts are in
vain. The only hope is to wait for the glycol to do its slow job and
dissolve the chippings. That could take weeks or even months.

Most of the scientific team is now redundant and returns
home. A small team of drillers and a few scientists will wait
until the end of the season, just in case the drill frees itself. If not,
we will have to come back next season. All scenarios are possible.
The drill is free and we can carry on. The drill is still stuck and
we have to start again with a new hole at the surface. In any case
we will need more money. Assuming the European Community
continues to have confidence in us!

That drill never moved again. It lay there still, nearly 3,000 feet
under the ice, not far from where we were standing now. Laurent
and his depleted team spent the last disconsolate weeks of the
season trying hopelessly to free it. Two seasons of effort and hundreds of thousands of euros poured into a deep dark hole. And
then they had to beg the money and time to bring a new rig in
and start again from scratch. Luckily the European Community
did continue to have confidence in the team, and the project.
Everyone knew that this kind of work was hard. But still, you
could tell that Laurent's pride was sorely wounded. It wouldn't
happen again, not on his watch.

The new drill was now about to re-emerge. The two Italians –
Sergio and Saverio – headed out into the cold outer tent and
started lifting up a line of trapdoors. Beneath these, they had dug
a long narrow trough in the snow perpendicular to the drill. The
part next to the hole was perhaps six feet deep, but as it moved
outwards the trench grew shallower until it reached the surface
about thirteen feet away.

At first this puzzled me, but as the drill's head finally poked up from the hole I understood the logic. With the various barrels, the motors, drivers and all the paraphernalia, the drill was more than thirty-two feet tall. If they had had to bring it up to its full height at the surface the tent would have had to be twice as high, and the procedure would be ten times more unwieldy. Instead they simply levered it until it was lying on its side. The top part swung down behind the rig, the bottom part swept up through the trough in the snow and the two men quickly replaced the trapdoors and pulled in wooden frames for the drill to rest on horizontally.

We all approached the bottom part of the drill, the business end where the cutters were and where the ice core was supposed to be. It was dripping clear fluid from its jaws, but as everyone already suspected there was no core. Above the core barrel, though, was another chamber where ice chippings were guided by spiral channels, and this one was almost full. That was the problem right there.

Laurent decided to do a cleaning run, not to cut any core but to remove the interfering chippings. He saw me looking wistfully at the machines: 'Do you want to do this run?' I slid quickly into the driver's seat before he could change his mind.

He showed me the controls. There was a huge red emergency stop button ('feel free to press this at any time'); a knob to control the cable winch speed; a switch to trigger the cutters and turn them back off. I practised twiddling the knobs and watching the computer screen. Then through the windows I saw a nod from Sergio outside and started the winch slowly, watching the numbers and coloured lines rolling past on the screen. Outside, the drill swayed a little from side to side before Sergio grabbed it and steered it safely into the hole. Technically, since I was driving it was my job to make sure he closed a small trapdoor afterwards so nothing could fall in and wreck the drill. But he had done this many times before and I kept my attention on the cable speed, which I was now allowed to ratchet up.

Over the next hour, the drill continued its progress downwards, though at one point Laurent chided me gently for letting it go too fast. The whole system was much more skittish than I expected, like a nervous horse. Small tweaks had big effects, and that was before you started factoring in the places the team had already encountered where the ice was brittle, or soft, or just plain ornery. As instructed, I carefully stopped the cable when we were sixty-five feet above the ice, then restarted, inching slowly down to nine feet. Now I could start the cutters, dislodging the chips so they could be safely steered up to the chip barrel.

I flicked the switch, and then asked Laurent the question that had been bothering me. This whole thing was becoming difficult and potentially dangerous. So why didn't he just stop, with more than 10,000 feet of ice safely recovered? He didn't want to, he said, nobody wanted to. There was still more ice to be drilled. The deeper they went the older it was, and the more likely it could tell us an important new part of the Earth's climate story.

And so they kept on trying whatever they could think of. One cognac bomb. Two cognac bombs. Alcohol that was more diluted. Alcohol that was more concentrated. Pure alcohol. ('Perhaps we should try real cognac,' Saverio said, as Laurent recounted this litany.) They had even tried grease, though Laurent was a bit reluctant – and he drew the line at any other lubricants. It was important, he said, not to mess up the hole by throwing in any old junk. And it was also important to keep cleaning it of the ice chippings and alcohol that had started to clog up the bottom. (Though it might seem shocking to be pouring all these chemicals into the pristine ice, everything up here on the plateau would eventually slide down to the sea and break off as icebergs. Antarctica had its own internal cleaning mechanism. It was only a matter of time.)

The drill continued, chewing the chips and spitting them out and up. I had to watch the current. If it rose, I'd have started cutting ice instead of chippings and must immediately stop. And there it went. I flicked the switches to stop both cable and motor. 'Sorry,' Laurent said, 'you're not cutting any core on this run.'

I know, I know. And yet, for some reason, I was reluctant to stop. Perhaps I was also beginning to understand a little of why these guys were prepared to come to this place to spend days and nights in this freezing tent, fiddling with tiny screws in ungloved hands, heaving this massive steel barrel (with a core inside, the lower, detachable part of the drill weighed as much as a hefty human), enduring frozen fingers and aching backs and legs, and then staring hopelessly into yet another empty barrel, before re-prepping the drill and starting all over again. Just like the meteorites, it was a kind of treasure hunt. There was ice down there and I wanted to get it.

I said nothing, but Laurent had clearly noticed. 'Be careful,' he said, 'it's a drug.'

It also took an inordinate amount of patience. We had to wait another hour for 'my' run to re-emerge. (And I was proud to note that the barrel was suitably crammed with chippings.) Then the drillers prepared a couple of cognac bombs and set the drill up for a real run.

As it descended I wandered off in search of food. When I returned, everyone was crowded round the computer in the small hut. It seemed they had been cutting, or at least they thought they had. Now was the moment to stop the blades from spinning, and heave on the cable. This should activate the 'core dogs', teeth that shot out and helped snap the ice cleanly across so that the core segment could be brought back up to the surface. I watched the figures with a newly knowledgeable eye, as the tension on the cable mounted then abruptly fell and the drill started rising. Looking good. And then, nearly an hour later, the head of the drill appeared in the hole, and the team moved into action, lifting up the trapdoors in the floor of the tent, lying the drill on its side and levering it up and out of the trough. This time, too, it was dripping with clear fluid, but as the end swung up into view it gleamed with a cargo that was rather more precious than diamonds.

There was an ice core.

We couldn't remove it yet, though. First the core barrel had to be detached from the rest, have cords tied around it at either end and then be heaved up and over to a temperature-controlled oil bath where it would sit until its own temperature had steadied. Laurent told me that the ice was near freezing point at the bed but had travelled up through ice, and drilling fluid, that grew colder and colder until it reached -65°F. For the ice, that would have been a tremendous shock. It needed to be gently warmed to a temperature closer to the one it was used to before it could be removed and studied.

And, then, the team opened the lid of the bath, heaved up the barrel and used a wooden pole to push the core out on to a waiting holder on the bench. It was gorgeous: a perfect transparent cylinder, about a metre long, cut through with large crystal boundaries that were clearly visible as if through a window. It had never before been seen by human eyes. It was the oldest part of the oldest continuous ice core on Earth. I put my face close to it, careful not to touch, holding my breath.

Laurent, standing behind me, contemplated it with satisfaction. 'Don't ask me why this one worked while the others didn't,' he said. And then he turned to prepare for another run.

Now the ice was playing ball. Over the next day the team brought up another core and then another. They were getting perilously close to the bedrock. Dorthe Dahl-Jensen, a professor at the University of Copenhagen, was the current chief scientist for the drilling and she was starting to worry. At some point above bedrock the ice tipped over the edge from solid to liquid. There was at least a pool of water, which might be part of a whole system of under-ice rivers and lakes. They couldn't afford to contaminate it with drill fluid, just in case. Perhaps it represented a whole new ecosystem. Perhaps there was something that they shouldn't contaminate.

Laurent wanted to keep going; Dorthe wanted to stop. And then the decision was taken out of both of their hands. There had been no warning. But on 21 December news spread through the camp faster than fire. The drill was stuck!

It was the same old story, a horrible echo of that day back in 1998. A perfectly normal run ended with a lurch in the motor current and however hard it pulled the cable couldn't help. Maximum tension. No effect. At least this time there was glycol ready to hand. Laurent sent solid chips of it rattling down the hole, clanging against the cable and then sinking slowly down in the fluid. All there was to do was wait.

The hours passed, slowly, with the cable still pulling at maximum strength. One, two, three ... after four hours, the tension on the cable spontaneously dropped. Gingerly, Laurent took the controls and raised the tension again. And, miraculously, the drill rose.

That was it, the end of the drilling season and the end of an extraordinary project. Nobody was going to risk another run. Emails went out and congratulations started flooding in from around the world.

'We have finished with the drilling after having trapped and freed the drill at a depth of 3270.2m,' Laurent wrote in his diary. 'There is still 6m of ice left, which we will not touch for political and ecological reasons. We prefer to leave the impression that we have not polluted the base below the ice where water is present. Even if that could seem a very minimal impact, the image is too strong for us not to pay attention. The ego of the driller has taken a blow, but intellectually it's very satisfying.'

That evening there was a party, European-style, in the EPICA workshop. Using the biggest knife from the kitchen, one that looked more like a machete, Laurent briskly lopped the top off a magnum of champagne. The cork, wire retainer, bottle top and all flew into the air, leaving a surprisingly neat diagonal slice in the green glass neck. There was a general roar of approval from the assembled crowd of Concordians who then started passing round plastic cups that were frothing over with bubbles. When I received mine, I understood why they were still frothing. As well as champagne, each cup also contained chippings of 800,000-year-old ice. I detected a definite whiff of drilling fluid in the mix, but said nothing. Instead I wandered over to where Laurent was standing.

'How do you feel?'

'Like someone has cut the strings to my shoulders.'

Now the drilling was done, everyone was more relaxed, and this first celebration heralded the beginning of party season at Dome C. Christmas was upon us. Here, as in most parts of the continent, intensely hard work was the norm. Scientists, who were often here for only part of the season, could end up working round the clock to get everything done; the people who were here on contract for the entire season to maintain or build the station still worked ten-hour days six days a week, and on Sundays they were often out in snow dozers, levelling ground or preparing for new projects. But now there would be dancing and feasts and the entire crew would get a day and a half off.

The food would be spectacular. Frenchman Jean-Louis Duraffourg was the head chef, sharing his duties with a Swiss-Italian, who was responsible for the pasta. All the French called Jean-Louis the *Reine-Mère* (the Queen Mother), for his fussy, slightly camp persona. He was round of figure, with white hair and moustache and a bustling manner. Appreciate his food and he was your friend for life. He would beckon you into the kitchen to give you privileged access to first tastings of the delicacies that he was considering serving for the next feast. He was an Antarctic artiste. He had even devised a special recipe for making baguettes rise properly in the thin, high-altitude air. He wouldn't, however, divulge this no matter how much you begged. Jean-Louis had been coming here a long time, and his Christmas and New Year feasts were legendary.

Before the seven-course spectacular, there was to be a reception across the way in the free-time tent. I was wearing what passed for party chic in Antarctica: jeans, hiking boots, a black thermal top, but I also had an ice-blue furry gilet that my friends had bought me before I left, and I had dared to apply a little lipstick.

Now, though, I was feeling unexpectedly shy. This was my first taste on the ice of the wide gender imbalance that has been true of Antarctica for most of its human history. Though the American bases that I'd already visited were more or less 60:40 men to women, here we were six women and forty-four men.

Rita had already chatted to me cheerfully about this. When she first came here four seasons ago there were only two women, and the following year she was here on her own. 'You become everybody's sister,' she says. 'Or like a doll. People are very careful with you. And they're also proprietorial. You're not allowed to have one or two friends. If you speak with just one person, it only takes a few minutes before other men start to surround you. Some women deal with it by becoming surrogate men. Others make themselves invisible.' That year, she didn't touch her makeup. 'If you're alone, you don't want to be noticed so much – you don't want to draw attention.'

I write about science; it wasn't as if I was unused to being in groups of men with very few women. But there were still aspects of the environment that I found intimidating. I think I was supposed to. In the wooden room – the designated hangout of the Italian contract workers, which was also the first sight of the station for most visitors – there hung a girly calendar. And not a misty 'tasteful' one either. In this calendar the girls weren't just naked, they were tied up. There was a daily ceremony in which the boys chose which image to turn to, with general roars of appreciation. Apparently there used to be three calendars, but one year a (male) American scientist cleverly brought some maps of Italy and suggested they could talk about home instead. That was enough to displace two of the calendars, but about the last they were adamant.

Thanks to the concerted efforts of Patrice Godon, the head of logistics at the French polar institute, IPEV[2], whom I met in DDU, the French side was more enlightened. At his command the traditional 'wall of knickers' had just been removed from the macho outpost, Cap Prud'homme, which was on the mainland just across from DDU. (Before Patrice's intervention, every woman passing through Cap Prud'homme was supposed to leave a pair of knickers to be displayed, with their name, on the wall. Men working there brought in knickers from their wives. To put on the wall. I wasn't offended by this, so much as baffled.)

There were also a few more women in the French programme. Patrice had made it his business to hire women engineers and technicians. Two were here at the station – Marianne Dufour, a contractor who was spending the summer working on the construction, and diminutive Claire le Calvez, who was a full-time employee at IPEV. Claire would not just be the only woman in the first wintering crew here, but would also be head technician. She was candid about her relative lack of experience, which was perhaps one reason that she was universally respected. She was also the first woman to drive the gruelling two-week tractor train that brings heavy goods up here from the coast, more than 600 miles away. I couldn't imagine her ever complaining about anything. She was good-humoured, tolerant and self-possessed and I sensed that she would have a good winter.

But even so, on my tour of the new, French-designed station I noticed that the brand new women's bathrooms were half the size of the men's. When I asked why, I was told that there would obviously never be as many women as men here. When I said that the American bases used to have a similar imbalance but they are now more than a third women, I received the unanswerable reply: 'Women are more powerful in America.' At least the new women's bathrooms had the same facilities as the men's. When Rita first came, she had to clean her teeth, and pee, in the shower.

It might have been for all these reasons, or for some other reason entirely, but in spite of my enthusiasm for visiting strangers throughout the continent, I was suddenly reluctant to join the party. One of the ice-core scientists, a young woman named Inger Seierstad from the University of Copenhagen, found me lurking in a corridor, hooked her arm in mine and said: 'We'll go together.' And we walked into the tent to a great cry of 'the blondes!' in three different languages.

But then all was suddenly well. Although most of the men were in their thirties or forties, here on the ice they were like schoolboys. They were harmless. We were packed in, shoulder to shoulder, as every person on the station was called up to the front, to receive a wrapped gift from Camillo Calvaresi, the station leader, and a kiss on the cheek from Rita. The gifts were all the same – a mug with the Italian Antarctic logo. I was touched that, although I had only been there for a few days, there was also one for me. The mood was exuberant. And then there was Jean-Louis's magnificent seven-course feast, followed by dancing back in the free-time tent until what would be dawn in any part of the world where the sun was more reasonable about setting.

What a turnaround. This hadn't just been a fun evening in spite of my anxieties; it was a Christmas entirely without tension. There were no past, painful histories with these people that you had to tiptoe around, because you had no history with them at all. And yet, there was no awkwardness or sense that you were an outsider because everybody was in the same situation. I love my family and I love my friends. But at Dome C, among strangers, most of whom didn't speak my language, there was no pressure to enjoy myself or to prove myself (or to prove that I was enjoying myself). Just an instant network of like-minded people full of acceptance and warmth.

And the party had now broken the ice. In the days that followed, I watched movies with the Italians and played cards till late with the French. On Sunday we spent two hours outside, wrapped up like mummies in -30°F, playing pétanque with coloured balls on the white snow. Many of the men were reluctant to speak about their own experiences on the ice, but unlike at the Pole it didn't feel like being shut out. 'Page blanche', one Frenchman said to me, every time we met, 'blank page', which was all he wanted me to write about him. An Italian talked about life here as being like plugging in an electric cord when you arrived, and unplugging it when you left. And another Frenchman spoke romantically about how to be here was to experience 'life between parentheses'. I especially liked this way of putting it. Like a phrase in parentheses, life down here didn't change the meaning of life on the outside, but perhaps it somehow changed the flavour.

And then, Antarctica delivered a wonderful Christmas present, something I'd been wanting for years and never experienced. A bunch of us had been playing cards in the free-time tent, and as we emerged, blinking, into the late-night daylight the scene took us by surprise. Instead of the usual midnight sun, bright blue sky and long shadows, the world had turned a numinous shade of pale. Somebody whispered: 'It's a whiteout.'

I ran to the main building, where I'd hung my cold-weather gear. Though the temperature was -40°F, there was so little wind here that jeans and a jacket were usually enough for the quick jaunt between the camp's buildings. But to go out on to the plateau I would need wind pants, parka, gloves, hat, the whole Antarctic works. Inside I hastily told the guys in the comms room that I was going out for a walk. At first I thought they might forbid me to leave, but then one of them handed me a radio. 'If you have any trouble, call.' God bless Concordia. I'd been smothered and banned and protected everywhere I'd gone in Antarctica, in many cases probably for my own good, but here they understood that some-times you just wanted to be out there, alone.

I'd heard all about whiteouts from old Antarctic hands. There were two kinds. One was the sort you'd imagine, the raging bliz-zard where fat flakes of snow swirled around you. Blizzards were often unexpectedly warm compared to what went before. They were also suffocating, and disorientating.

When we were doing our initial field training back at McMurdo, the mountaineers there tried to prepare us rookies for what might come by putting white buckets on our heads. (We later discovered that these were painted on the outside with grotesque faces for the amusement of the many onlookers.) Our task was to line up along a rope, sweep outwards and try to find a colleague who had fallen in the 'blizzard' and was in danger of freezing to death. The buckets were to block our eyes, distort our voices and confuse our ears. It worked. When I watched the next batch of recruits try the same task, they stumbled and floundered, the apparently straight rope twisting into knots, as their colleague lay inches away, but undiscovered.

But I had been longing for the other kind of whiteout, the one that had apparently descended now without warning. In this variant, you could see anything in front of you quite clearly, but without any definition. Thick cloud somewhere high above us was scattering sunlight so completely that all shadows were gone. The white snow underfoot and the white sky above were indistinguishable, empty of any kind of texture or shade. Dome C had become a void.

I tested this as I walked away from the camp and into the emptiness. I could hear my feet crunching into the snow, but there were no apparent footprints. I knelt and put my face close up against the snow. Still nothing. I touched the surface. My gloved fingers could trace the hollows that my feet had left. But all I could see was white.

I hurried now, wanting to get as far as I could from the camp before the spell broke. Ten minutes of walking, twenty minutes, and when I turned there was no more sign of the bright orange tents and buildings. There was nothing.

I nudged the bulge of the radio for reassurance; I'd been careful to put it inside my many layers of fleece, wind-bib and parka, to keep the battery alive. And then I knelt on the snow.

It wasn't like sensory deprivation, or like being inside a cloud where your view was physically blocked. All my senses were functioning. I felt cold. I knew that I could see for hundreds of metres in front of me. The fur of my parka hood was clearly framing my view. Yet when I looked up, down and all around me, the real outside that I was seeing was . . . a blank. Nothing had ever been so empty. A white sheet of paper has the weft and weave dimly in view. A white-walled room has corners and shades. There are always shadows. Except here.

I had wondered about this experience ever since I first heard of it. What would it be like to sit still and alone in a living, breathing void? Would I feel frightened? Lonely? Bored? The answer was none of the above. The jabbering voice in my head was momentarily stilled. I felt a deep delicious peace. I wanted to bathe in it.

Or maybe it's not really about peace. There was nothing passive about this feeling. The world had shrunk, as if Antarctica had allowed itself to go from being intimidating to being intimate. And it had given me a deep sense of comfort that was almost overwhelming. This was the opposite of loneliness. It was also the opposite of being smothered. I felt utterly relaxed.

But then, as I was trying to cling on to this feeling, I caught sight of a tiny black shape on the horizon behind me. It was one of the drums that marked the edge of the runway. The cloud above must be lifting. The big, open, impersonal emptiness of Antarctica was back.

As I trudged back to the camp, now following my footsteps easily in the snow, I tried to understand why this touched me so completely. I had loved the welcome that I'd experienced in all Antarctic camps, and especially here. But I was more used to thinking of this as 'us against it'; the harsher the environment outside, the more we humans stuck together. I'd seen photos of Scott tents framed against a bleak white landscape, with a warm glowing light inside to lead you home. Or heard about Vostok Station, which was officially the coldest place on Earth. One winter they recorded temperatures there that were cold enough for steel to shatter; cold enough that you could cut diesel fuel with a chain saw.[3] But many people told me that it was one of the warmest, most human of all the bases on the ice.

And yet, the warmth of my human welcome here felt pale beside the depth of comfort that I had experienced just now, out on my own, on the 'hostile' plateau, in temperatures that should have frozen my bones. The emptiness had descended on me, and I didn't feel abandoned. I felt cradled.

·   ·   ·

Work was winding down now in the drill tent. The cleaning runs were all but done, and the drillers were packing up their equipment ready for the journey home. But I found Dorthe and Inger in the core-processing trench, working on the few remaining ice cores that had to be logged and bagged, and sent out into the world. Although the 'trench' was buried in snow, it was more like a large underground workshop, kept permanently at -22°F to protect the cores inside.

The fragility of the ice was evident in more than the temperature. When I closed the great freezer door through which I had just entered, I noticed a warning on the back, written in wobbly black marker pen. 'SLOWLY!' it said. 'DO NOT SLAM!' and there was a cartoon drawing of an ice core shattering.

The room didn't quite echo – but it seemed empty with its white, refrigerator-like walls and just two muffled figures inside. At the height of the project there were fifteen scientists, working in a bustling production line, measuring the lengths of the cores, sawing pieces off them, making the first quick measurements of the climate records they held. The walls were marked, here and there, with graffiti. Much was of the 'I was here' variety, in various languages, but since they were written by ice-core scientists many also said something like 'measuring the oldest ice on the planet'. Some showed evidence of impressive graphic skills. In one corner I found a manacle, ball and chain, drawn so convincingly I thought from a distance that it was real. Next to it, someone had marked out the number of days in lines, prison-style, that they were working there. And near the floor in the corner opposite was a skull and bones that seemed to be disappearing into the ground.

But there were also cheery reminders of home, a hand-made subway sign for the Bronx, a poster marking how 'Emiliano, Fabrice, Gianni, Mart, Matthias and Mirko' together held the

WORLD RECORD for ice-core processing, at thirty-five cores a day. The place seemed full of ghosts.

Dorthe showed me where the cores came in to be logged, where – in past seasons when ice cores were flooding in from the drill tent – the researchers would measure the lengths of the different segments, fitting broken pieces together like puzzles. I saw a piece of ice lying there, presumably from the past week or so. It was a beautiful pure cylinder, maybe half a metre long.

'Wow, what a great core!'

'You say that, but when I saw it I wanted to weep,' Dorthe said. She showed me the streaks near the surface. They were subtle but clear when you knew what to look for, all aligned in the same direction like animal hairs.

'That happened when it went into the oil bath,' she said. 'It started to melt. And now we can't use this to extract air – it's too dangerous.'

'Dangerous?'

'Some air could have escaped. We can't trust the answer we'd get.'

It was not enough, then, to battle the conditions, risk the drill, go through brittle ice layers that were always ready to shatter, and get all the way down to the soft stuff with your cognac bombs and your instincts for how far to go. When the cores came up above ground they were always in danger of melting.

And although the scientists on site would do a little bit of analysis, the complicated stuff – and that meant in particular the precious air trapped inside these cores – could only be analysed in far-off Europe. Cores or pieces of cores had to be transported safely to the UK, Switzerland, France, Denmark and all the other countries participating in this European mega-project. Any one loss was everyone's loss. There was only one piece of core for each slice of time so if one piece melted, the whole record suffered.

Scientists call it 'not breaking the cold chain'. The cores went out from here in a Twin Otter to be taken to the coast and put on ships with special freezers (and back-up generators). These would transport the cores to European ports where they would be loaded on to freezer lorries for the last stage of their journey. The story went that French lorry drivers picking up the cores at Marseilles were not allowed to stop for lunch on their five-hour drive to Laurent's lab in Grenoble in case there was a melting accident. In some places the cores were then stored in massive commercial food freezers. There was one near Grenoble, called *Le Fontanil*, where the ground floor held sides of meat, cheeses and frozen raspberries, and the upstairs, fanned intermittently to increase the wind chill, was a treasure house of ice cores from the world's coldest places. You could impress on contractors as much as you liked how precious these odd scientific samples were, but if they also had several million euros' worth of food on the same site they would make sure the electricity supply was properly backed up.

And there was an extra safety system. Inger showed me how every core that arrived in the trench had a piece cut off its entire length to be left here in the Antarctic snow as insurance against loss in the outside world. She took a cylinder of ice and pushed it carefully up against a horizontal saw. As blade hit ice the noise was suddenly deafening and there was a spray of white ice dust. Inger carefully lifted off the top segment which was placed in a clear plastic bag marked with a thick black arrow pointing to the TOP. The ice all looked more or less the same. It was crucial to mark which way up each segment should be, and to write on each sample the depth that it came from, and there was a system of numbers for this, indecipherable to the uninitiated.

'How deep was this ice?' I asked. Inger did a quick calculation.

'About 10,000 feet.'

'So how old would that be?'

'About 800,000 years.'

'You're telling me that this fell as snow 800,000 years ago?'

'Yes.' Then she added softly: 'It's a privilege to stand and look at it.'

I caught her mood, or maybe she was catching mine. Because, as I looked at this piece of ice and tried to picture the world of its birth, I felt a shiver. That ancient Earth was utterly alien to me.

The ice was completely clear, with a luminous translucence. There were no signs of melting, which was good, but nor were there any bubbles. At the extreme depth that this ice was pulled from, the pressures were so high that the air dissolved into the ice and formed a kind of ice-air crystal mix called clathrates.

'The air has dissolved,' I said to Dorthe. 'Doesn't that affect the gas?'

'No,' she said. She told me that it wasn't just the depth. Sometimes you got bubbles even at those depths, depending on how much snow was falling. And when you melted the ice and sucked out the air from the same depth, clathrates gave the same value as bubbles. She looked over my shoulder at the ice. 'It's a miracle that the air stays in there. But it does.'

Dorthe picked up a piece of metal and shaved the top of the remaining ice to clean it. Then she took a two-pronged instrument like a bent tuning fork and scraped it along the ice while Inger watched numbers on a monitor. 'Normally we'd do this much more carefully, millimetre by millimetre, but this is just to get a rough idea.' They were measuring the electrical resistance of the ice. The more dust there was in the ice, the harder it was for the electricity to flow, and more dust also tends to mean colder, drier conditions. In this case the resistance was quite high. 'It's fairly dusty, so it was probably an ice age.'

Now Dorthe took a thin slice that she had carved out of the ice and showed me how they put it under polarisers to measure the crystal size. I'd seen this before. Normally, in younger cores, the ice jumped into a psychedelic jigsaw puzzle of colours marking out the different crystals. But here there were just two shades of pink, with a boundary running down the middle.

The crystals here must be enormous. Closer to the surface, they would each be just a few millimetres long or less. But as they descended they embarked on a tug of war for ice, in which the larger winners grew and the smaller losers vanished. After this much time, the winning crystals had grown into great glassy structures several inches long.

That was all the analysis the two scientists would do here. Their main task was to finish off bagging up the cores ready for their journey to Europe. I watched them doing this for a while, but I soon started to get cold. Although it was a few degrees warmer in there than outside, standing still, away from the Sun, brought the chills. 'Come back any time,' Inger said as I left in search of hot chocolate. 'We like the company.'

There is always something faintly sad about the end of a long project. This was the end of an era at Dome C. For nearly a decade, the camp had existed mainly to support the drilling of this momentous ice core, the one that would go back farther in time than has ever been done before, and that would surely tell us vital things about the way our planet has changed.

Now it would take on a new identity. The joint Italian-French construction crew had almost finished the new winter station. It stood about half a kilometre away from the summer camp, two elegant circular buildings, attached together by a corridor. Each building stood on six massive steel legs that could be jacked up, so that the station would be able to step gracefully above the accumulated snow. The legs could be lifted individually, and the connecting corridor could slide up and down where it met the two buildings to enable them to be raised one at a time. All the outer panels had now been assembled and the construction crew were busily fitting out the interior. When they had finished, there would be workspaces and leisure rooms, eighteen bedrooms with elegant oak furnishings, bathrooms and a fully fitted surgery. I was especially enchanted by the fire escape from the top floor, which consisted of a gigantic stocking. In case of emergency, the stocking would be unfurled and lowered from the window like Rapunzel's hair, and the occupants would slide down the inside using their elbows as brakes.

The construction crew was racing to be ready; in six weeks all had to be in place for the first ever wintering crew to move in. This was a big deal. There were only two other winter stations on the plateau: the South Pole and Russia's Vostok. Both had been built back in 1957–8, during the International Geophysical Year, which was a massive continent-wide scientific effort that more or less began the age of big science on Antarctica. The new station being built at Dome C would be only the third year-round base in the interior, and the first new one for fifty years.

The thirteen new winterers, a mix of French and Italians, would experience conditions among the most extreme on Earth. Nobody knew how cold it would get, but it was higher here than the South Pole so temperatures might fall as low as -110°F.[4] They would also be the first humans ever to see darkness here, and to witness the night sky.

That was one of the biggest reasons for staying beyond the summer. Though there would be a couple of glaciologists and meteorologists in the winter crew, the highest scientific hopes for Dome C lay in its astronomical promise. The lack of wind meant that the telescopes should be able to see stars more clearly than at the Pole. Already automatic devices were perpetually probing the sky for any disturbances that could cloud a telescope's view. (One particularly annoying device came housed in a bulbous green hut, which everyone called the 'kiwi fruit' though it looked more like an unripe pumpkin. It spent its entire time sending out sound signals – sodar – to probe the air, in an eternal sequence of chirrups somewhere between a spooky sci-fi theme and an electronic bird. Luckily it was out of direct earshot of both the new station and the summer camp, but every time you passed you found yourself waiting for the change in sequence, then being irritated by it.[5])

The University of Nice had also set up several telescopes, to be manned through the winter by astronomer Karim Agabi. In keeping with the elegant architecture here, the platforms holding the instruments were carefully designed with sweeping curves of wood. Karim told me that the architect had initially planned to create a single arch, like the ones girdling the bottom stage of the Eiffel Tower. However, he persuaded the firms providing materials to hand over two for the price of one, and now two golden arches stand side by side. It was unfortunate that this immediately called to mind the McDonald's logo, but the structure was undeniably beautiful.

Karim and other researchers from the University of Nice had been testing the site for the past five summers using telescopes painted in a colour that the catalogue describes as 'Antarctic white', and even in daylight the conditions here were fantastic. If the winter results backed up what they had already seen in summertime, astronomy would soon take over from ice coring as Dome C's main raison d'être.[6]

But in truth this was far from the end for the EPICA cores. Many of them were already being analysed back in Europe, and they were adding to an extraordinary body of knowledge that has come to us from deep in Antarctic ice.

We already know from records written into rocks, mud and trees that temperatures have varied a lot in the past. In fact, the recent relative stability that we've had on Earth over the past 10,000 years (which just happens to be when humans were developing their civilisations) is unusual compared to the lurches in climate that have taken place, perfectly naturally, over most of our world's history. Earth is a restless planet, and change is part of its nature. We humans have been lucky to be spared the effects of that restlessness, so far.

The ice itself also contains a record of past temperature if you know how to read it. Ice comes from snow, which comes in turn from water sucked up from the sea, carried through the air, frozen and then deposited back on the ground. So solid ice is just a rigid network of the molecules that make up water, each containing one oxygen atom and two hydrogen atoms. Researchers can read past temperatures in these molecules because both oxygen and hydrogen come in different flavours, called isotopes, some of which are heavier than others. The heaviest molecules are hardest to lift from the sea up into the sky, and so rarely have the chance to become rain (and then snow) unless temperatures are high and there is enough energy to do the lifting. When it's colder, primarily lighter molecules make it up to the lofty heights that can then freeze and fall again.

So if you measure the ratio of light and heavy molecules in the ice, you get a measure of how warm or cold it was at the time it was sucked out of the sea. Couple this with information about the air trapped inside that same snow and you can draw some important conclusions about why exactly our climate is so highly strung.

Another ice core, already drilled by the Russians just a few hundred kilometres from here at Vostok Station, covers about half the timescale of EPICA.[7] Over the 400,000 years that the Vostok core sampled, the temperature rose and fell four times, in great glaciological cycles. Our most recent ice age is the most famous, but in fact the Earth has experienced a whole series of them – perhaps as many as twenty-five – and Vostok captured the four latest times that our planet has frozen, thawed and frozen again.

And as the temperatures rose and fell, so too did the greenhouse gases. Higher temperatures meant higher CO_2 and methane. Whenever temperatures were lower, CO_2 and methane were lower.[8]

In a way this shouldn't be a surprise. Both CO_2 and methane are chemically built to trap heat. If you put more greenhouse gases like these into the air, basic science says that they will catch more of the warmth radiating out of the Earth and fling it back groundwards like expert fielders in a ballgame. That's how greenhouse gases work.

And, in fact, it's a good thing that they do. Our planet is a little too far from the Sun for us to be truly comfortable. By rights the whole place should be frozen in space, a giant planetary snowball. But the soupçon of greenhouse gases that we have long had in our air is enough to avert this catastrophe. It doesn't take much. CO_2 is like chilli powder – if you want heat, a pinch is all you need.

Still, the results from the Vostok core were striking enough to cause a stir when they were published back in 1997, because the evidence was so clear and unequivocal. Looking into Antarctica's crystal ball of ice shows the effects of CO_2 more clearly than any attempt at complex extrapolation.

True, the temperature tended to go first, and the CO_2 to follow. But that doesn't mean that the CO_2 was an effect rather than a cause. Scientists have long believed that what first triggers the planet to cycle in and out of ice ages are slight wobbles in the orbit of the Earth around the Sun, which affect how much sunlight arrives in the northern hemisphere in summertime on a timescale of 100,000 years or so.

However, this change in itself isn't large enough to explain the ice age – it's just the trigger. When the world starts cooling a little, other feedbacks quickly kick in. Colder oceans start to soak up more CO_2 from the atmosphere, and freezing marshes and mires stop putting out so much methane. This cools the planet still more, which means more greenhouse gases disappear from the air, which means yet more cooling. The orbital wobbles start the process, but it's the greenhouse gases that provide the oomph. After that first trigger, the ice core showed how temperature and greenhouse gases marched in exact lockstep.

And there was something else. Though CO_2 and methane rose and fell perfectly naturally in this way, the Vostok record showed that neither had ever, in 400,000 years, begun to imagine the levels that we have reached today. By pulling coal, oil and gas out of the ground and burning them to make our energy, we have filled our atmosphere with that chilli powder, which is now starting to burn.

If we knew this so clearly, why bother going back further in time with all the EPICA effort? The Vostok record was spectacular but it captured snow falling in only one place. And what if there was something special about those four ice ages that doesn't apply any more? In particular, Vostok stopped tantalisingly short of the ice age that took place between 425,000 and 395,000 years ago. That's important because various intricate wobbles in the Earth's orbit around the Sun have a big effect on our climate, and this was the last time that the orbit was exactly the same as it is today. It's a sort of mirror of today's conditions. Scientists have long worried that the four latest ice ages have all had relatively short warm gaps in between, of six thousand years or less. It's already more than 10,000 years since the last ice age, so does that mean another one is on the way? With EPICA, the scientists wanted not only to test the Vostok results at a different site, but to go farther back, to a time when the whole climate regime might have been more similar to today's.

The EPICA record turned out to hold at least four more ice ages, including that intriguing fifth oldest ice age that was the orbital mirror of the modern world.[9] One thing researchers have found is that the warm gap that followed it lasted 28,000 years, so we probably shouldn't be expecting another ice age any time soon – even without considering the extra amounts of CO_2 chilli powder that we have already put into our air.[10]

Moreover, just before the mirror ice age, something about the climate pattern changed; the temperatures weren't nearly so low during these ice ages, or so high in between. And the EPICA record also reveals something more surprising. Even when our climate was in some other phase, some different way of balancing the many subtle influences that make up the wind and weather and warmth we experience, temperature and greenhouse gases still marched in lockstep. Higher temperature always went with higher CO_2. Lower temperature went with lower CO_2.

The other part of the Vostok story also holds true in the EPICA core. All the way back to the ancient ice beneath my feet, to the snow that fell nearly a million years ago, the story was still the same. Carbon dioxide has risen and fallen with the seasons, with the ice ages, with the different climate patterns. But in all that time it has never been within striking distance of the amount we have today. Through the entire EPICA record, the highest value of CO_2 was about 290 parts for every million parts of air. Now we are at nearly 400 and rising.[11]

The EPICA investigations are still going on and more cores are being drilled elsewhere on the continent. In 2009 the Chinese built a summer-only station called Kunlun at Dome A, where the ice is still higher, and older, than at Dome C, and they are planning both to drill ice cores and to set up astronomical research there.[12] Other researchers are looking at Antarctic sites with higher resolution, closer to the sea, farther from the sea, investigating all the subtleties of the story that Antarctica's ancient air can tell us.

But the most striking finding remains. In nearly a million years of repeated climate ups and downs, carbon dioxide is always highest when temperature is highest, and it has never been so high as it is today, thanks to our burning of fossil fuels.[13] The deepest voids of Dome C hold a warning that we would do very well to heed.

Antarctica doesn't just hold warnings of past change; it's also an agent for change. The evening after the Twin Otter arrived to take the drillers home there was an impromptu barbeque in the drilling workshop. Now that Laurent was no longer there, the construction workers moved in. It was late at night; we had been playing cards. People were smoking, and they were about to commit further sacrilege. Someone arrived with a steel brush and a bucket of snow and started vigorously scrubbing the top of the stove. Someone else brought strips of bacon, boxes of eggs and bread rolls filched from Jean-Louis's larder. Crack, splat, and the eggs were already starting to fry on the stove's sloping top. Now the bacon went on, and soon we were all tucking into an illicit midnight feast.

But then a few of the guys started to get giddy. Someone picked up my camera to try to take a picture of someone else. He in turn tried to grab the camera and it was now being passed over people's heads, and thrown from one person to the next. It was an expensive piece of equipment; I was using it to document my time here. I didn't have a back-up. 'Hey, give it back!' I said. And now I was the one they were keeping it from, a stupid game of piggy in the middle as if we were still ten years old.

At first I tried to reason with them, and then it was too late. I was enraged. The strength of my fury shocked me. I had never felt this angry before. I wanted to scream at these people who I'd been cheerfully playing cards with a few moments earlier. 'I need it for my work!' I said. 'Give me the fucking camera.' I stormed out of the tent, with no idea where I was going. When I returned, the camera was beside my empty chair. I picked it up without a word, and left.

The next morning at breakfast, Jean-Paul Fave beckoned me over. He was the designer of the new station, stick-thin, in his sixties, with a snow-white beard and known to everyone on the station as 'Papy' ('Granddad'). He patted the empty chair beside him and I slid into it. 'I hear that you were very angry last night,' he said. I nodded, shamefaced. 'They are just boys and they don't understand the work you are doing down here. I understand, but I am old. When I was their age I was just as foolish.' And then he smiled his gap-toothed smile. 'But you should also know that being down here affects people. You should not come here and expect to find people behaving normally. And that includes you!'

That shocking rider took me completely by surprise. Even me? But I was just an observer! And yet, what I'd experienced in all the bases I had visited, and especially here in Dome C, was the gratifying, enticing closeness that comes when – in a place that was famous for its hostility – you found such like-minded people who invited you in so readily. Everyone here was in the same situation. Nobody had their family with them, or their children, or their real lives.

And perhaps that was also one of the reasons why the ice exaggerated your emotions. You didn't just have a good day here; you had the best day of your life. You weren't just mildly irritated when someone was being an idiot; you were furious. The environment edged even the relatively well-balanced towards mania. I remembered how Jake Speed had told me at the Pole that the most successful winterers were the ones who let things slide, who were naturally the most laid back and tolerant people in the real world. This would not be a good place for someone who was highly strung, or at least not for any length of time.

The effect tended to wear off after a while, when you were back in civilisation. But I kept hearing warnings about the dangers of coming here too much and staying here too long. The Americans have a joke about the reasons that contract workers came down here: 'First, they come for the adventure. Then they come for the money. Then they come because they no longer fit in anywhere else.'

And, now that I thought of it, Laurent had issued the same warning before he left, when I asked him if he'd miss the place.

'No,' he said. 'I've spent enough time on the ice caps that I could stop now and I wouldn't miss it. I like it. I love it. I do it with enthusiasm, but I'm not attached. I see people here who are attached, hired, kind of lost, because they don't realise what's happened.'

'What has happened?'

'They get enough money to leave for six months, then they come back. They're out of the system somehow, and they don't realise it. Nobody warns them really. It takes time to find out for yourself. Even companions are given to you. Here you have instant parties and you don't have to worry whether people will come, because they're already here. I understand how people get lost when they have nothing back home.'

I remembered hearing something similar from a French doctor who had just spent his second winter at DDU. 'People I know who've done many winters, four, five and even one who spent eight, they start a new life every time. I don't want to be like them, to exist for only twenty people and at the end of the year, at the end of the adventure, that's all finished, and then you start again with another set. It's not sane.'

Perhaps over-winterers were like Persephone in Greek mythology, who became too involved on her first, forced, trip to the underworld[14], and was therefore doomed to return every year. Antarctica changes the things it touches. And if you enter this world of ice too completely you might be trapped into returning year after year, constantly seeking out the same blank slate, the same do-over, while life in the real world slides by.

Richard Brandt was an American snow researcher from the University of Washington in Seattle, though he usually worked from his smallholding in the Adirondacks. We came in on the same plane from McMurdo and Richard had been an ally here from the beginning, the only other native English speaker on the base. He was the one who saved me a place on the 'international table' at the various holiday feasts, as far as possible from the big Italian group. He warned me they would get rowdy and that food might fly. It did.

Later he taught me to do trick riding on a skidoo, jumping over a specially constructed hillock that was strategically out of view of the station. His skidoo had a toy penguin called Waddles on the front. Richard carried it everywhere with him, taking photographs of the little bird's latest adventures and posting them online for eager schoolchildren.[15] He was a thoroughly nice man. And now, he had offered to show me his own research, at a snow pit and tower about a half-mile beyond the new station.

It was another beautiful blue Dome C day, and Richard found me a pair of skis. It was, he said, the only way to travel. But I soon realised that he was probably born on skis. He was politely gliding along, keeping pace, not bothering to use his poles, while I was puffing and panting beside him.

To save breath I used an old runner's trick: if you want to be less winded than the person you're exercising with, ask them a short question that requires a long answer.

'What do you love about snow?' I said.

It worked, in a way. Richard didn't get any more breathless, but he did tell me about what happens when water freezes. He talked about how water is a tangled mess of molecules that romp around, catching each other's hands and releasing them again, squeezing together and recoiling. And then, when it freezes, all the dignity returns. The molecules line up formally, obeying careful rules for where to stand.

They also hold each other at arm's length, which is why ice is less dense than water, and why ice cubes float. Though we're so used to that we scarcely notice, it's actually incredibly rare; if you put a lump of most solid things in a pool of their own liquid they would sink. It's just as well for us that ice floats instead; if it didn't, rivers and oceans would freeze from the bottom up, and our planet's episodic ice ages might have wiped out all life on Earth.

And then he talked of how just a few simple rules about where the molecules had to fit when they froze could lead to such a glorious variety of crystal shapes.

'Is that why you love it, because snow is beautiful?'

'Yes, but it also transforms things. Where I live, on our small-holding, everywhere you look there are jobs to do. But when it snows the jobs all disappear. Snow turns the whole world into a playground.'

We arrived at the snow pit, which was two square holes side by side, each ten feet deep, separated by a thin wall of snow. We shed our skis and climbed in, and Richard reached up and dragged a cardboard 'lid' over the pit we were standing in. At first I didn't understand why, but when he pointed over to the thin wall of snow I gasped. Its snow layers were now backlit by the sunlight pouring through from the pit on the other side. You could clearly see the annual layers, where jutting crusty ledges marked the summers and soft snow underneath, the winters.

And the colours. There was a spectacular gradation in the light from an aqua white close to the top to pale blue, deep sky blue then violet. Richard took what looked like a broom handle lying on one side of the pit and pushed a hole into the wall, though not entirely through it. Now the bottom-most hole was an intense violet tunnel with lilac walls.

'Look at that,' Richard said. 'It's the purest colour you'll ever see in nature.'

He told me that snow appeared to be white because most of the sunlight hitting the surface was scattered by ice crystals, with no favouritism for any particular colour of the rainbow. But some rays made it past this first hurdle and succeeded in penetrating into the snow's interior. Now the frozen water molecules were ready to dance to the rainbow's tune. And here in the snow pit we were cleverly positioned to witness what happened next.

Water molecules are choosy. They like to vibrate, but will do so only in response to certain specific colours of light. Here, close to the top of the pit, they were picking out the red light, soaking it up and resonating like tuning forks. As the light travelled a little farther down, they were taking out the oranges, and purples. Blue was the survivor. Water simply doesn't resonate at this blue frequency, so it was the one colour ice couldn't stop. Look one metre, two metres, three metres down the wall, and blue was still going strong, evading any attempts to absorb it.

This is why the oceans are blue. As light penetrates below the surface all other colours are stripped away by the jangling water molecules. It's also why blue light gleams from crevasses and cracks in a glacier, and why even quite small blocks of ice still have that bluish tinge.

Richard and his team had been sampling the snow all around

here, prodding it with probes to different depths, and they had measured the exact frequency of this lovely blue. It was the end of the rainbow, the last colour that human eyes could see before the light tipped over into ultraviolet and everything went dark. It was as pure a colour as they come, one single wavelength of precisely 390 nanometres (about four ten-thousandths of a millimetre).[16]

I was enchanted both by the colour and by Richard's explanation. Just as the ice filters away all the other colours, so life here removed all your distractions — same food, same clothes, no children, no pets, no bills, no bank accounts. It felt good to relish that absence of minutiae and to focus on what seemed essential. And yet if this pure blue were the only colour on Earth it wouldn't be enough. Come here, the message seemed to be, stay here and learn what you can, but if you are wise you will take what you find home with you, and work out how to understand it in the messy, complicated but ultimately colourful world outside.

But that wasn't the whole story. We left the snow pit and walked to a hundred-foot tower that Rich built a couple of years ago with a French collaborator from the Glaciology Lab in Grenoble. It looked rudimentary, with simple aluminium struts, but there was a metal staircase running all the way to the top. We climbed carefully, not letting any exposed skin touch the metal. You could be fooled here. With so little wind, in the midday sunshine you could forget that it was -13°F and that skin would stick to frozen metal, and then rip.

At the top there was enough of a breeze to burn and I buried my face in parka and scarf. The view was magnificent. We could see the entire base, the new station, summer camp, rows of tents and heavy machines. And we could also see the flat white plateau, a frozen ocean stretching out to infinity. The top of the tower was bestrewn with instruments – anemometers whose tiny cups were spinning in the breeze to measure the wind speed, and cameras trained in all directions. But the ones that Richard had come to tend were looking both high and low at the sunlight. They were measuring how much energy was arriving from the Sun, how much was being soaked up by the snow surface and how much was bouncing back.

The reason was to get a background check, a ground truth. Satellites were spinning overhead measuring the radiation coming in from space, and the equivalent radiation being poured back out from the surface. Finding the balance between these two helps establish what our climate is actually doing. But after a while, the satellites can lose their focus; their measurements drift and they take their instrumental eyes off the ball. So researchers find certain special places, like this one, where they can measure the numbers on the ground and use them to drag the satellite readings back into line.

Dome C is particularly good for this because it's so flat. There is very little wind, which means the surface is smooth and the reading is similar regardless of the angle at which you look.[17] Perfect for Richard's purposes. He wasn't here to look for signs of change; he just wanted to be sure the satellites were telling the truth.

Here in the continent's interior, on the old, cold, dry and above all thick East Antarctic Ice Sheet, nothing much is changing or likely to change for a very long time. Whatever we do to the Earth, chances are that there will be ice on this part of the continent for thousands or tens of thousands of years.

But although this part of Antarctica is set in its ways, others are starting to stir. Over in the west the ice sheet is thinner and more nimble on its feet. Gigantic glaciers speed over the ground at what is for ice a dizzying pace. The ocean is already beginning to lap at certain parts of the coast, eating away at floating ice shelves, undermining them. And the satellites that Richard helped to calibrate are showing that the Antarctic Peninsula, that great finger of land that is embedded in the West Antarctic Ice Sheet and points accusingly up towards South America, is currently warming faster than anywhere else on Earth.

3

WEST ANTARCTICA

Home Truths

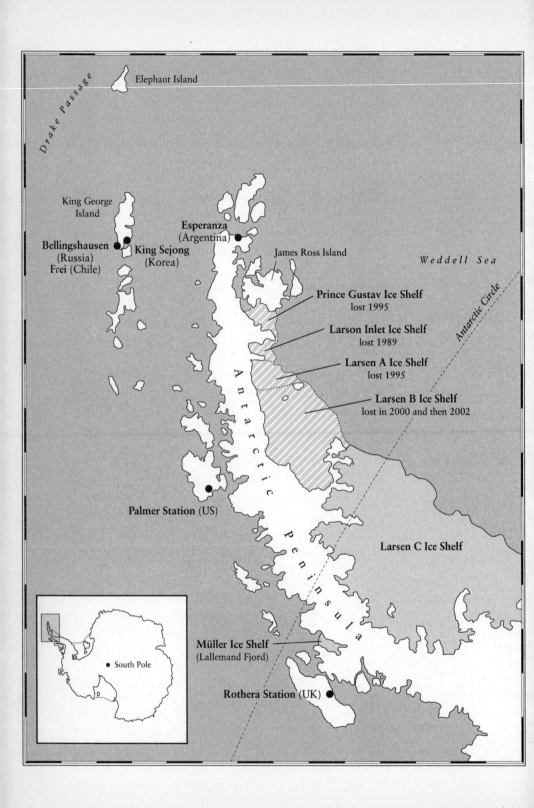

Elephant Island

Drake Passage

King George
Island

Bellingshausen
(Russia)
Frei (Chile)

King Sejong
(Korea)

Esperanza
(Argentina)

James Ross Island

Weddell Sea

Prince Gustav Ice Shelf
lost 1995

Larson Inlet Ice Shelf
lost 1989

Larsen A Ice Shelf
lost 1995

Larsen B Ice Shelf
lost in 2000 and then 2002

Antarctic Circle

A
n
t
a
r
c
t
i
c

P
e
n
i
n
s
u
l
a

Palmer Station (US)

Larsen C Ice Shelf

South Pole

Müller Ice Shelf
(Lallemand Fjord)

Rothera Station (UK)

6

A HUMAN TOUCH

The Antarctic Peninsula is the northernmost part of the continent. It's also the most conventionally beautiful place in Antarctica. Take the Alps, and cross them with the Grand Canyon. Stretch them both so that the mountains are higher, the cliffs sheerer, the glaciers wider and longer and bluer. Now put this glorious mix beside the sea, next to icebergs and penguins and seals and whales, and all within just two days' sail of civilisation.

There you will find bright blue days or silent grey ones, when the water is eerily still. You can sail down narrow channels, only passable for a few weeks of the year, where mountains and ice plunge steeply down to the sea on either side, and researchers in field camps on the banks call up the ship's radio for the sake of a little contact with the outside world, or signal their greetings with waves or cartwheels.

It's not surprising, then, that this is also the most visited part of Antarctica – the human face of an otherwise inhuman continent. More than 20,000 people come here every year, most of them by sea.[1] And the voyage may be gentle or riotous, depending on nature's whim.

If you make this journey south, you will probably start off at one of three ports: Punta Arenas in Chile, Ushuaia in Argentina, or Port Stanley in the Falkland Islands, just off the Argentinian coast. These are small, remote southerly towns, whose hotels have names like 'The End of the Earth'. But they aren't, or at least not quite. It's the ice-reinforced ships that sail south from here that will take you to the real end.

At first, as you enter the Atlantic and head south, the seas will probably be calm; you'll be shielded from excessive weather by the coast of South America on the starboard side. But after perhaps half a day's sailing you will emerge beyond its protective tip, and out into the wide-open seas of Drake Passage.

This is the gap that first opened around thirty-five million years ago, when South America released its geological handhold and drifted away, and the oceans were finally free to swirl unchecked around the entire continent of Antarctica. From west to east, with no land left to stop them, they built up a vortex of currents that isolated Antarctica from the warmth of the north and allowed it to fall into a deep freeze.

That same unbroken geography also renders this stretch of ocean the stormiest in the world. Winds and waves circle the globe here with no land to break their momentum, and the Pacific and Atlantic oceans can clash with such devastating fury that Drake Passage is notorious in shipping lore. Before the Panama Canal was built, rounding Cape Horn at the bottom of South America and braving these southern seas was the fastest way to get from the Atlantic to the Pacific and also the most dangerous; in the past four centuries of sailing more than a thousand ships have been wrecked here. It is rich with mysticism and romance. On the tip of Cape Horn, beside the tiny military base, is a monument bearing the silhouette of a wandering albatross and a poem by Chilean poet Sara Vial:

> I am the albatross that waits for you
> At the end of the Earth.
> I am the forgotten soul of dead sailors

Who crossed Cape Horn from all the seas of the world.
But they did not die in the furious waves.
Today they fly in my wings to eternity
In the last trough of the Antarctic winds.[2]

Before you cross this boundary and sail out into the passage, you'll need to tie down or pack away everything that can move. You'll also learn what to do if the ship's alarm sounds: how to find and drag on the unwieldy, suffocating rubber immersion suits; where to gather beside the sealed melon-shaped lifeboats that will be your last resort; how not to think about what it would be like to be squashed inside one of these with twenty other humans, while the ocean tossed you about like a football.

If the winds are bad, you will understand why so much of the ship's furniture is screwed to the floor, and why the tables have wooden rims. If it's not fastened down, the chair you are sitting on can fly through the air. Waves have been known to crash so high that they smack against the windows of the bridge, sixty feet up. The only way to move around the lurching ship is to cling with both hands on to doors and railings. You will not be going outside. You will probably not be going anywhere much, just lying weakly on your bunk, holding on to the wooden sides and wishing for it to be over.

There is not much you can do to escape a bad crossing, apart from avoid tempting the fates. Superstitious sailors, which is to say all sailors, will give you a list of things not to say or do. If the rim of a glass starts ringing, stop it immediately. Don't whistle while on board, or you'll 'whistle up' a storm. And – this one is nicely perverse – don't wish anyone 'good luck' as it will assuredly bring bad luck down on you all.

But if you are lucky, and the storms never come, you will experience instead one of the world's loveliest ways to travel. As the long lazy waves fetch up from the Pacific you will feel hour upon hour of rolling swell, rocking you like a cradle, like a lullaby. Once in a while a larger wave might come along, making the ship judder slightly as if she had hit a bump in a road, before resuming her gentle swaying. And if you look outside, chances are that you'll see the grey-white form of an albatross gliding serenely beside the ship.

If you have one of these crossings you will be infused with a sense of perpetual well-being, and sleep deeply and dreamlessly, however thin your mattress or narrow your bunk.[3]

At some point towards the end of the second day, you will begin to sense the impending ice. It might just be a chill creeping into the air. But if it's foggy, or dark, or both, you will know there is ice out there when the captain switches on searchlights, and trains them like cannon on a point a few metres in front of the ship.

The lights are for small chunks of ice that could still make a sizeable dent in the hull: bergy bits, or, worse still, growlers, which are almost completely submerged and are much harder to spot. They're not for icebergs. By the time you saw a berg with the spotlights, you would be far too late to avoid it, and you'd also be in big trouble. They can be huge, these bergs, the size of a ship, the size of an island.

Instead the crew must count on a radar screen whose arm sweeps periodically around revealing an array of glowing green blobs. It can be eerie up on the bridge, surrounded by mist, knowing there is ice out there and yet seeing nothing. The crew will be tense, and focused, their eyes flicking constantly between screens and lights. To be allowed to stay, it's best to keep quiet; and above all, don't get between the crew and their consoles.

And then, if the day breaks and the fog lifts, you will see your first iceberg. It might be small, and irregular — a chewed-off chunk that has melted and fragmented almost all the way to oblivion. Or it might be vast, high and square, as if a granite cliff had floated into the sea. These tabular icebergs are an Antarctic speciality; they break off from the huge floating shelves of ice that rim the continent.

This is all perfectly natural, and has been happening, to some extent, since the ice was born. However, as well as being the most human part of Antarctica, the Peninsula is also currently a place of change. There are many who suspect that this segment of Antarctica is behaving like a miner's canary, feeling and responding to the trouble that may soon come for us all. Researchers and tourists alike are now flocking here: the former to find out exactly what is happening, and what it means for the rest of the world; the latter to witness this extraordinary wilderness before it changes for good.

The first thing that strikes you when you reach the Peninsula is the overwhelming abundance of life. Compared to the rest of this remote and barren continent, the waters here are awash with living things. Chinstrap penguins in small, synchronised packs porpoise neatly past the ship's bow, making barely a splash as they cut through air then water then air. There are rockhopper penguins, with absurd golden feathers that sprout like fascinators from either side of their heads. And gentoos, which look like Adélies apart from the white strip that runs over their heads and ends in a white blob next to each ear, as if they were wearing iPod headphones.

Then there are the seals, of course, usually lolling motionless on passing icebergs, dark smears against the white: Weddells, and thuggish thickset leopard seals. Also crab eaters, slender and silver and bizarrely misnamed since they actually eat a smaller shrimp-like crustacean called krill.

You might also see humpback whales, and if the rest of the animals are jumpy that probably means that a pod of orcas will soon be cruising past, with their boastfully tall black dorsal fins, and beady mean-looking eyes. A more charming prospect is the minke whales, the second friendliest and most curious of all the whale species around here. They don't just spout in the distance like the humpbacks; they come and play right by the ship.

The friendliest of all the whales are the southern right whales, the golden retrievers of the cetacean world. They love human company, or, rather, they did, and this unfortunate tendency led them to be hunted nearly to extinction in the early part of the twentieth century. They are called 'right' whales because they were the 'right' ones to catch for oil and bones and profit. Though the population is recovering, you'd be lucky to spot one today.

The relative accessibility of the Peninsula and its surrounding islands coupled with the abundant whales and seals that the earliest explorers found in its water mean it has the longest record of exploitation on the continent. The human touch here is at its most evident, and also at its most unedifying.

In 1892 one American sealer, who had worked in Antarctica then for more than twenty years, told the US Congress:

> We killed everything, old and young, that we could get in gunshot of, excepting the black pups, whose skins were unmarketable, and most all of these died of starvation, having no means of sustenance ... The seals in all these localities have been destroyed entirely by this indiscriminate killing of old and young, male and female. If the seals in these regions had been protected and only a certain number of 'dogs' (young male seals unable to hold their positions on the beaches) allowed to be killed, these islands and coasts would be again populous with seal life. The seals would certainly not have decreased and would have produced an annual supply of skins for all times. As it is, however, seals in the Antarctic regions are practically extinct, and I have given up the business as unprofitable.[4]

The whaling and sealing industries were akin to mining: go there, grab what you can and leave. The Antarctic Treaty now bans any commercial exploitation, but both whaling and sealing industries collapsed through their own short-sighted overuse of resources long before the international treaties kicked in.

Now, the only permitted commercial activity is tourism and the Peninsula is by far the most visited region of Antarctica. Some visitors are on massive cruise ships that can't fit into many of the ports, but most come on smaller vessels, with just a hundred passengers or so. These are called expeditions rather than cruises. They do not have casinos and tea dances. They are often converted research vessels and they bring people of all ages who have saved and dreamed and dared, and are looking for adventure.

There are those who say that the tourism is dangerous for Antarctica, but the self-policed rules among tourist operators are at least as stringent as those on the scientific bases. None of the ships is allowed to discharge anything in the water below 60° south. Before being allowed off the ship, you are warned sternly about not approaching the wildlife, about washing off your boots before you go, about taking nothing with you and leaving nothing behind. It is a key part of the experience. Unlike the sealers and whalers, Antarctic tourist operators have too much sense to foul their own nest.

Besides, who is to say that Antarctica belongs only to government-sponsored scientists? Some researchers have been known to grumble that the tourists get in the way of their studies and have no right to be there. The better-mannered ones are more prepared to share. One biologist even told me: 'I sometimes feel that I'm a tourist here myself.' And it's true that in the gaps between their formal research, many of the continent's scientists are just as likely to be staring in wonder at the continent's wildlife or its historic sites.

The most visited site on the continent is Port Lockroy, a refurbished British base showing what life used to be like there when it was last occupied, decades ago, with the short-wave radio still chattering against a background hiss in the comms room, and the kitchen and bunks carefully reconstructed to be exactly as they were. (It also has a modernised section bearing a gift shop and a post office.)

Port Lockroy should cheer those who fear the effects of the rising tourist tide. The base shares its home with a colony of gentoo penguins. A few years ago one half of the penguin colony was roped off and kept undisturbed. In the other, people were left free to roam at will. After five years of study, researchers investigated the difference between the two halves of the colony, those disturbed and those left in peace. They were looking for signs of changed breeding patterns, poorer feeding, less success at raising a new generation. The result? There was no difference at all.

The Peninsula also has a higher concentration of human habitations than anywhere else on the continent. It's still not exactly crowded, but some of the most accessible parts are brimming with scientific bases built by countries looking for the easiest possible ticket into the Antarctic club. And perhaps because there are so many, so close, there is a sense here of countries jockeying for position: a tug-of-war between the instinctive cooperation that pervades the continent and the desire to stake a claim on the land.

King George Island at the northernmost tip of the Peninsula is one of the first islands that you hit after crossing Drake Passage. This otherwise barren lump of volcanic rock has a host of stations sitting cheek by jowl, owned by Brazil, Ecuador, Argentina, Peru, Uruguay and Chile, as well as South Korea, Poland, China and Russia.

I went there to see the Russian base, Bellingshausen, on board the *Akademik Sergey Vavilov*, as the guest of Peregrine Adventures.[5] Though she was chartered as a tourist vessel, the ship was owned by the Russian Academy of Sciences and had a Russian crew. The previous season, the ship had carried the skeleton of a church to Bellingshausen. The church had since been built and dedicated and – having lived with its timbers and bells on the journey down – both sailing and expedition crews were curious to see how it had turned out.

There are many places of worship scattered around Antarctica. Most bases have at least one room that can be used occasionally for whatever form of service the inhabitants care to propose. The larger, or more devout, ones have a building set aside for the purpose, though they are often makeshift, based around steel containers.

The Russians had apparently decided on a different approach. Their church was a hymn to the sublime. We had already seen it from the ship. You couldn't miss it. There it stood silhouetted on a prominent headland – a glorious onion-domed structure of Siberian larch and cedar, anchored to the rock by massive chains as if it would otherwise float upwards to the heavens. It was utterly strange even by the standards of this strange continent.

The church also came with a full-time pastor. As our motorboat approached the shore, we picked out a messianic figure against the gloom. He was wearing a grey parka over a full-length black cassock; his beard was priestly in scope but red in colour; his arms were outstretched in grave greeting. This was Father Kallistrat, the continent's first, and indeed only, Russian Orthodox priest. He was twenty-nine years old. He had come to this bare outpost ready to stay for months, perhaps years at a time, serving a flock that numbered barely twenty in the height of the summer.

'It's hard to find someone,' he said as we started the hike up to his church. 'A young man might not be strong enough. An old man might find it too hard. You couldn't send a man who has a wife and children.' And why had he agreed? 'My bishop said "go", so I came.'

On a continent formally dedicated to science, in a base funded by the public purse where every person, every expenditure must be justified in triplicate, Father Kallistrat's presence was already astonishing. But that was nothing compared to his church.

It had been designed by Russia's finest architects, and paid for by ice-inspired oligarchs. The trees that supplied its structure had been hand-selected by specialist woodcutters. The entire building was created in Russia before being dismantled and transported on the *Vavilov*. It had occupied most of the stern deck, both holds and half of the main deck. Father Kallistrat had set up his altar in the ship's foyer. In full, gold-braided regalia he had conducted his services for hours with bells and candles and incense.

The sky was growing gloomier and when we reached the top of the hill the light snow turned to sleet. But even in this bleak landscape the church was beautiful. It could almost have been an elegant log cabin but for the clock tower and those extraordinary onion domes. Up in the belfry a clanging tune started out. Someone's head poked out of an upper window like a human cuckoo clock. Tourists and worshippers alike let out a ragged cheer.

Inside the church was unexpectedly small. A few members of our crew were there, lighting candles with long bent tapers. The icons were exquisite, painted – Father Kallistrat whispered – by some of Russia's greatest artists. I found myself lighting a candle of my own, and pushing some British pounds into the Russian collecting box. 'Weird enough for you?' grinned our expedition leader, David McGonigal, as I re-emerged.

Down at the base, the station manager, Oleg Sakharov, was waiting for me. Oleg was in his late forties, handsome and brusque, betraying just a hint of irritation at the invasion. He looked at a tour member photographing a lone penguin on the shore and grimaced. 'Tourists never want to come to the stations,' he grumbled. 'All they care about is wildlife, wildlife, wildlife.' He'd been coming here for nine years, he told me; this time he would be here for eighteen months at a stretch. Yes, he had a family back in Russia. How did his wife and children deal with his long absences? He shrugged. 'It's my life.'

And then he opened the door to the base. I followed and was immediately hit by the dismal smell of overcooked cabbage and a fug of stale cigarette smoke; the walls bore dull grey pictures, the lino was torn. We passed a room whose back wall contained metal shelves crammed with ancient octagonal film canisters, in dull green, brown or silver, with numbers roughly painted on the sides in white. This, Oleg told me, was the projector room where the base gathered to watch Russian films.

So far, so predictable. But then we crossed into the next building and emerged into an unexpectedly lovely lounge, with picture windows framing an exquisite scene of rock, sea and snow. My attention, however, was diverted by the huge widescreen TV showing an actress in a Chilean soap opera, wringing her hands and scrunching her beautiful face over some trauma that I couldn't follow.

And not just a TV, but a state-of-the-art entertainment system. This had nothing at all to do with the grim Soviet style of the rest of the base. Oleg smiled at my confusion. He told me this had been a gift from the South Korean government. Now I was really astonished. The South Koreans were giving gifts to the Russians? I wouldn't have thought these two countries were the most obvious bedfellows.

It turned out that, a year earlier, five Koreans from one of the many nearby bases had gone missing in a storm. Their boat had capsized and they had had to swim through appalling seas to an abandoned shore. Russian scientists from Bellingshausen had risked their own lives to go out and find them. They had rescued four of the five Koreans and brought them home alive. (The fifth man had already died of exposure.) A thank-you note had subsequently arrived from the government in Seoul by ship, along with this entertainment system. 'It was nice,' said Oleg. 'They said they were sorry they couldn't send a bigger one.'

So this was Antarctic cooperation in action again, national barriers melting under a common physical threat. I understood that. But I was still baffled by the church. Why go to so much trouble? Why build something so exquisite in such a place? Oleg sighed and trotted out what sounded like a standard response. 'Many Russians have died here in Antarctica and this way we can be respectful to their memories.'

Yes, I could see that. But why did it have to be so elaborate? The Chilean base next door had one that was much more the standard of Antarctic devotions. It was an old stainless steel container, painted bright blue, with a wooden cross on the door. If they wanted a church at Bellingshausen, why not make do and mend like everyone else?

Oleg turned and looked me directly in the eye. 'Look,' he said, 'you can close down a station, *da*? You can say "the economy is bad, the time is hard". But you can't close down a church.' Ah yes. In the past five years, several of Russia's stations had been mothballed through lack of funds. But a spectacular church like this one? No, you couldn't close that. This seemed as cynical a form of imperialism as any other claim-staking on the continent.

But maybe it wasn't as cynical as it sounded. For while I was still digesting his first comment, Oleg hit me with a burst of pure romanticism that left me reeling. 'And so,' he said, 'there will be a piece of Russia's soul in Antarctica for ever.'

Yes, indeed there would. A church sent from Russia, with love.

If the Russians had found a spiritual way to stake their claim, the Argentinians and Chileans came up with something just as evocative — but perhaps more human. In November 1977, the Argentinian authorities airlifted Silvia Morella de Palma to their base Esperanza ('Hope') on the tip of the Peninsula. Silvia, who was the wife of the base's army chief, was also seven months pregnant. On 7 January 1978 she gave birth to Emilio Marcos Palma, who is the only person in human history *known* to be the first born on any continent. And what better way to assert your ownership of a place than to have new citizens born there?

Since then seven more babies have been born at Esperanza, and three at the Chilean base on King George Island, near Bellingshausen. (The Chileans saw what the Argentinians were doing and realised they might be missing a trick.) That makes eleven young men and women who can reasonably claim to be full citizens of Antarctica.

Though the births themselves had now dried up, both bases still allowed children and families, violating the no-children rule that applied almost everywhere else in the continent. Truly it seemed these were more colonies than scientific stations. I was eager to visit Esperanza, to see for myself what an Antarctic 'colony' looked like. And I got my chance in 2008 on a voyage with the Royal Navy's HMS *Endurance*, which was supporting scientists from the British Antarctic Survey (BAS)[6]. We were passing within a short distance of Esperanza. The captain had given permission for us to fly to the base while the ship steamed ahead, and then rejoin it afterwards.

But first, our comms people had to raise the team at Esperanza and say we were on our way. So we waited, half dressed in the hot, bright orange rubber immersion suits, which were compulsory for passengers in the *Endurance*'s helicopters. (To be allowed to fly in a Royal Navy helicopter over water you also have to pass a 'helidunk' course back in the UK, which involves being packed into a model helicopter fuselage with a bunch of squaddies, dropped from a height into a swimming pool, and showing that you can swim safely out of the emergency exit. The first time, the lights are on and you stay upright; the second time, more realistically, the 'helicopter' spins upside down; the third time, the lights dim to twilight; and the fourth you are submerged and then inverted in pitch darkness. The last one was the worst. We all got out within the allotted time, but with less grace than in the previous attempts. I got some bruises in that dunking, but I gave some, too.)

This was my first direct encounter with a military operation, and I blundered around at first, trying to assimilate the bewildering array of rules. Officers could go into the Ward Room, but not into the Junior Ratings' mess. Senior Ratings could go into the Junior Ratings' mess but only if invited. Scientists didn't count – we could go more or less anywhere. But everyone had to ask before going on to the bridge, by stopping at the entrance and intoning a formula – 'Permission to enter the bridge' – to which the Officer of the Watch would reply not 'Permission granted' as you might expect but, bafflingly, 'Yes please'.

It was also odd to be on a military vessel in Antarctica, a continent formally dedicated to peace. Of course, the ship was supporting the UK's scientific efforts, and there is a long tradition of support from the military for many, perhaps most, of the Antarctic nations. But it was also there to keep an eye on Britain's ongoing interests in the region. The *Endurance*'s stated mission was not just 'supporting the global community of Antarctica', but also 'to patrol and survey the Antarctic and

South Atlantic, maintaining Sovereign Presence with Defence Diplomacy'.[7]

Nevertheless, as time went on I became drawn to these men and women: the twenty-four-year-old navigator, who steered our icebreaker through the night while we slept, and briefed us over the PA each morning with her 'sitreps' – which told us not just our current position, but what we would be eating for the daily breakfast special; the privates talking wistfully of when they could get away from this pretty but peaceful continent, and back into the war, where they belonged; the restless marines abseiling down the front of the ship to keep their hand in. (I was getting fairly restless myself by this point and the marines were very gracious about letting me join their abseiling.)

I began to enjoy being woken at 7 a.m. by a uniquely military combination of traditional and modern: a bosun's whistle, blown via a microphone and PA system into everybody's cabins, 'pee pee pee peep, pee pee pee peeeeouw'. I even learned to do this myself, bounding out of my bunk at 6:30 a.m. for the privilege of waking the rest of the ship. The trick lies in curling your fingers over the whistle's hole at just the right moment to make the dying sound of the peeeeouw. At the beginning it seemed that our military hosts were as bemused by us as we were by them, but after a few weeks' sailing down to Rothera and then back up north we had become friends.

The go-ahead finally came, and we donned our helmets and were guided into the helicopter on the back deck, literally by the scruff of our necks. (When the rotors were going, nobody on board was prepared to take any chances with the civilians.) We flew over glaciers and bergs, rocks and dark grey water, till we came to a pleasant little cove, grey-skied and streaked with snow. The buildings of Esperanza were all, or almost all, the same bright cherry-red, made of steel containers but with dark triangular roofs that made it look like a toytown.

We landed at the helipad, met the five-strong delegation that had come to greet us, and were guided down to the main building for coffee and cake. When it became obvious that neither the base commander's English nor our Spanish would serve for much beyond name, rank and serial number, someone was dispatched to fetch a young meteorologist to translate for us.

Everyone was pleasant, they were all smiling, but there was still something odd about the interpreter's questions. He was quizzing us about our reasons for being there, with a sort of polite urgency. 'Didn't the ship tell you all this when they called?' I said in the end. 'There was no call,' he replied. 'We didn't know you were coming.'

What? But we had only got permission to fly on the assumption that our radio room had finally managed to speak to theirs! Something had obviously gone wrong with the communications. We had dropped unannounced out of the sky into an Argentinian colony, territory formally disputed by our two nations, in a Royal Navy helicopter!

Britain and Argentina had a shaky record in this part of the world. Both countries, along with Chile, laid claim to this part of the continent, although all three claims were now on hold thanks to the Antarctica Treaty. Before the treaty was signed, though, we had definitely squabbled over the land. In 1943 a British expedition had hauled down the Argentinian flags that had been left on nearby Deception Island, and hoisted the Union flag instead. In 1952 a team from the British Antarctic Survey was unloading supplies here in Hope Bay from the ship *John Biscoe* when a shore party of Argentinians fired a machine gun over their heads. The respective governments later extended and graciously accepted a diplomatic apology but I'm sure that wasn't much consolation for the scientists involved.

Admittedly during the war of 1982 when Britain and Argentina fought for control of the Falkland Islands (a conflict that the writer Jorge Luis Borges memorably described as being like 'two bald men fighting over a comb'), Antarctica was reportedly the only place in the world where Argentinians and British maintained cordial relations. But this is still not a place where you would want to send in a British naval helicopter unheralded and uninvited.

And yet our hosts were nothing but charming. Maybe there is something magical about squashing human beings together in a place where humans have never been. The Arctic has long been a place of conflict. Deserts the world over are just as likely as lush grasslands to be battle zones. In the rest of our planet, bald men still fight over combs. But in Antarctica it seems that normal rules may not apply.

When we finished our coffee and our questions, the base commander, Lt Colonel Miguel Monteleone, gave us a tour. The ground was rocky, the paths and boulders dusted with snow, and the buildings stood out cheerfully against an otherwise drab backdrop. Miguel (in spite of his formidable military bearing, he told me I could call him Miguel) took us to the tiny *capilla*, the chapel, and the laboratory and infirmary. Then we passed a signpost with arrows pointing every which way, announcing the whereabouts of the port, the helipad, the canteen. And there, too, was the one sign that I had not seen anywhere else in Antarctica. *Escuela*, it said. School.

This was the building I'd been waiting for – the first sign of Esperanza's children. It comprised several containers bolted together and Miguel walked me through, pointing out the different rooms. 'This one is a playroom for all the children. Then here is the class for the children in seventh grade, the last year of primary school; in the next room there are two children for second grade, one in third and one in fourth grade. And here in the last class, kindergarten, two little kids of five or so, pre-school really.'

I stopped on the threshold of this last room. There was an adult-sized chair and desk, presumably for the teacher, and, next to it, a small square table that barely came to my knees, and two small chairs. No: they weren't just small, they were tiny. They were *miniature*. Though I knew that there had been small children and even babies here, seeing those chairs was somehow deeply shocking. And then I wondered why I was so shocked. Why did it seem so abnormal? How had I become so accustomed to the 'no children' rule that I accepted it as gospel?

'How many children are there?' I asked.

'From 12 March, when the families come, we will be fifty-one, with eight women and fourteen children.'

'What other facilities do you have on the base for the families?'

'There is a satellite dish that allows us to get four digital TV channels and another satellite dish that allows us to connect to the internet, and in the social club there is ping-pong, table football and pool. And in winter, weather permitting, we offer open-air activities.'

It sounded to me like a wonderful childhood. But this wasn't just to give a few kids a great experience.

'Esperanza is very unusual in Antarctica,' I said cautiously, 'because of the families and children. Why do you have families here?' I wasn't going to use the 'c' word, colonisation, but it seemed that Miguel had no qualms.

'*Bueno,*' he said airily. 'It was our General Pujarto who initiated the Argentine Antarctic activity on behalf of the army. One part of his plan was to colonise Antarctica with families. The aim was to put a small town with Argentinian people in the Argentinian sector of Antarctica.'

I think I must have blinked. I hadn't expected such frankness. General Hernán Pujarto had been right-hand man to President Perón back in the fifties. He had set up Argentina's Antarctic

Institute as well as its southernmost base, and he was a strong advocate of colonising the Peninsula to claim it for his country.

'Do you think there is a political aspect to having families here?' I asked. 'It's more like having a colony instead of having a scientific base?'

'Well, there is scientific activity in the base,' Miguel replied. 'The scientific work runs alongside family life and is also very important.'

Yes, of course, the 'science'. Although there was that small lab, and five scientists currently on the station, the overt aim of colonisation and occupation was more evident in Esperanza than anywhere else I'd seen in Antarctica, and the sticking plaster of doing science seemed the least convincing excuse.

And yet, and yet . . . that wasn't the whole story. Miguel was clearly serious about the science at Esperanza. And although doing research may not be his government's prime motivation, Argentine science has undoubtedly made its mark on the continent. For it was here, or very near here, that two Argentinian scientists discovered something that changed our perception of this barren, ice-ridden world.

It was January 1986, and geologists Eduardo Olivero and Roberto Scasso had landed just around the tip of the Peninsula from Esperanza, on the northern part of James Ross Island. They hiked about a mile or so south of Santa Marta Cove and started casting around for fossils. This was a good time to look. It was the height of the Antarctic summer and the top parts of the soil had briefly thawed enough to give them a chance of picking up some useful finds.

The area had once been a shallow sea, and half buried in the soil were the typical ammonites and sharks' teeth. But then the two researchers found something astonishing: a fragment of jawbone, a few teeth the shape of broad flat leaves, pieces of skull, vertebrae and limbs. They had discovered Antarctica's first ever dinosaur.

Antarctopelta oliveroi was a new species of ankylosaur, a stocky, plant-eating quadruped, stretching perhaps four metres from tip to tail. It had armoured skin and, like other ankylosaurs, its tail may have ended in a mighty club – though no trace of that has yet been found. It had a short spike protruding over its eye. It lived in the late Cretaceous Period, less than a hundred million years ago. And for some reason it died on the coast and was washed out and buried in a shallow sea.[8]

Eduardo and Roberto's finding confirmed what many scientists had already suspected: Antarctica has not always been a frozen wilderness. Although all but a tiny percentage of the land is now buried in ice, the few remaining outcrops of rocks bear many signs that its ancient past was much warmer than today.

Since *Antarctopelta*, many more dinosaurs have shown up around Antarctica. The next was *Crylophosaurus ellioti*, a twenty-foot carnivore that died with its last meal – the leg of a hapless plant-loving prosauropod – stuck in its craw. *Crylophosaurus* had an armament on its head, shaped like a Spanish comb on a flamenco dancer, or perhaps an Elvis quiff. And then there were more. Some Antarctic dinosaurs were large, some trim; one appears to have had a duckbill. But all would have lived before the ice came.[9]

There was also the vegetation to match. Near the Beardmore Glacier – which both Shackleton and Scott's polar expeditions used as their staircase up on to the plateau – researchers discovered an eerie patch of petrified forest, which would once have nourished and shaded Antarctica's dinosaurs, but was now reduced to stone stumps, their tree rings clearly visible where the trunks had been sheared off. On his journey back from the Pole, Scott himself picked up rocks on the Beardmore that had ancient fern leaves fossilised into them like a fingerprint.

Scott didn't know that the continents could drift, that Antarctica spent much of its geological history wandering around the warmer parts of the world, before the grinding of the Earth's tectonic plates took it to its current resting position at the South Pole. But we know that now. So perhaps all these fossils came from a time when the continent was basking in the warmth of the tropics.

Well, not exactly. Geologists have traced Antarctica's path through the ages, and it landed at its present position some one hundred million years ago – within the days of the James Ross ankylosaur. Even when Antarctica was sitting squarely at the Pole, it was a green continent, covered with forests and ferns and dinosaurs.[10]

The time of the dinosaurs was warm everywhere, including the poles, thanks largely to the very high levels of greenhouse gases in the air. Volcanoes had been belching out carbon dioxide for millions of years and Earth was a hothouse. But then, trees fell into those steamy swamps and were buried before they could rot, and the floors of shallow seas became carpeted with sea creatures, whose bodies, too, were buried in a rain of mud and sand. And time passed, and the carbon in the trees and the bodies of the sea creatures was buried further and cooked and squeezed and chemically transformed into coal, oil and natural gas. The Earth had found a natural mechanism to suck carbon out of the air and bury it where the sun didn't shine.

That is why the world started its cooling trajectory, and why Antarctica began to feel a chill that was helped along by the opening of Drake Passage and the forming of those swirling, isolating currents. The dinosaurs died out sixty-five million years ago, probably as a result of a colliding meteorite. But the forests and ferns eventually followed, driven away by the freezing air and the creeping ice. Antarctica has more or less been cooling ever since.[11] Or it had.

For in the past two centuries we humans have been mining down into the dark remnants of those ancient lands, extracting the fossilised fuels they contain, burning them and pouring their carbon back into the air. And inevitably the world is starting to warm back up again. In the past century the average temperature of our planet has risen by nearly 1.5°F and the effects are being felt here on the Peninsula more strongly than anywhere else. This part of the continent is warming at an extraordinary pace – three times the global average.[12] It is one of the planet's hot spots, melting visibly under the eyes of scientists and their instruments. Its shelves of ice are shattering. It is shedding icebergs like armadas. Even the animals are feeling the heat.

The Peninsula is changing, and Rothera Station lies at the heart of this change. The main headquarters of the British Antarctic Survey's operation,[13] it is seated on a rocky promontory on Adelaide Island about halfway down the west of the Peninsula. Icebergs out in the two adjoining bays gleam in the low-slanting sunlight, and chunks of ice wash up against the shore, jangling like wind chimes in the waves.

Although the facilities at Rothera are now state-of-the-art, with en-suite bedrooms, high-grade laboratories and quick flights in and out from the Falklands to minimise both the time and cost of the science, this base also has the closest, most recent connection to the past. Many of the people are drawn here by tales of the heroic age, and the older ones can still remember a time when life at the British bases echoed that of those great explorers. Until the mid-1980s, work and life here would have been comfortably recognisable by the likes of Amundsen, Shackleton and Scott.

For one thing, this was the last base on the continent to get rid of their huskies. Originally the dogs were there to work, but then as machines took over they became a recreation, a great way to go out on a Sunday and experience the Antarctica of the heroic age. But they were also a drain on resources. They had to be exercised, fed, stitched up when they got hurt in fights.

Argentina, Australia and Britain were the last nations on the continent to keep dogs and all were initially mutinous when the edict went out in 1994 that they were now to be banned. First the Australians, then the Argentinians sent their remaining dogs home. Finally, in February 1994, the last fourteen huskies on the continent of Antarctica were loaded on to a Dash-7 plane at Rothera in specially designed kennels. From then onwards the only 'alien' species permitted on the continent would be humans. And the last direct connection to the heroic age passed out of sight and into history.

But still there is that lingering regret for the old days. Though Rothera now has twenty-four-hour internet and unlimited phone calls, winterers continue to gather around the radio on 21 June to hear the traditional Midwinter Broadcast, bearing personal messages from home through the shortwave medium of the BBC World Service.

That whiff of nostalgia also remains in the food sent out from Rothera into the field. A box of 'man food' (so-called to distinguish it from 'dog food') to take out to a camp still contains the sort of rations that Scott's men would have been happy to share: powdered milk, porridge oats, tea and cocoa, 'biscuits brown' (which were called by this military-style language to distinguish them from 'biscuits fruit').

At least the boxes don't contain pemmican, that classic heroic age mix of fat and dried meat that sustained all our heroes during their epic voyages. But you sense that some people at Rothera regret its absence. Instead, in a nod to modernity there are sachets of dried, reconstituted meals of curries, stews and ragouts that are more or less indistinguishable in spite of the different ingredients listed on the packets. No other major Antarctic nation still sticks to this dreary camp food – although you are now allowed an extra 'goodies box' and some of the bigger camps have stretched to pizzas and bread-making.

Of all the changes that took place in the early nineties, the arrival of women seems to have caused the least stir. The first woman to spend a summer field season there was a scientist named Liz Morris. She had been newly appointed Head of the Ice and Climate Division at BAS, but the authorities had assumed that she would have no desire to go south. They were wrong. She was undeterred by the letters explaining that there were no hair-dressers, shops or, more darkly, 'facilities' in place to receive her, and she went to Rothera in 1987–8.[14]

To the shame of the British, this was very late when compared, say, to the Americans, but by the early 1990s more women were spending summers there, and in 1994 the first women wintered at Signy base, to the north. And then . . . to the credit of the British, mixed teams suddenly began to seem normal. When they returned to the bases in the late 1990s some of the first women were astonished by the change. Nobody was watching or judging you in any special way. You could just be yourself.

People who were at Rothera during these times of great change bring up the loss of the dogs immediately, and often then mention the arrival of the plane. But if you ask them what it was like to have women at the base and then in the field, they look perplexed for a moment, as if they've forgotten it was ever any different. Although Rothera is still far from achieving the sort of ratio found at McMurdo, and although the British programme waited longer than most to bring women south, the integration now seems complete.

With equality of opportunities comes equality of risk. On the hill at the apex of Rothera Point, amid an assortment of crosses and memorials dedicated to Britons who have lost their lives in this part of Antarctica, the newest and shiniest is dedicated to a woman named Kirsty Brown.

Though plenty of scientists go out from here to study ice and rocks, Rothera itself specialises in understanding the animals of the continent, especially those in the seas around the base. Kirsty was a marine biologist studying these sea creatures. She had short brown hair and an engaging smile, and was so full of smarts and energy that people called her 'Bang'. She was just finishing her Ph.D. at the University of Adelaide. She was also an accomplished rider and diver. And on 22 July 2003, the day the sun finally returned to Rothera after six weeks of winter darkness, she was out snorkelling. Kirsty was excited about diving among the ice – and had already stated that she would go out every day if she could. This particular day, she was swimming along with her buddy (the rules strictly forbade going alone), with two more watching from the shore.

Nobody had noticed the leopard seal in the water. Swimming was forbidden if they were around, but only so as to avoid disturbing the seals. Leopard seals are big and brutish. They can be thirteen feet long. They have thick thuggish necks and squared-off muzzles that jut aggressively. They are top predators, swaggering rulers of the Antarctic seas. Leopards are the reason that penguins hesitate nervously at the ice edge, silently egging each other on, till one jumps and the others spontaneously follow in a cascade of black and white. There's safety in numbers. Or, at least, there's less of a chance that you will be the one to be caught. Penguins and fish fear leopard seals with good reason, but they had never been known to attack humans. And yet, this one did.

Kirsty probably didn't see it coming. She barely had time to scream. Its head was the size of her entire upper torso. It must have weighed six or seven times as much as she did. Her diving knife would have been of little use even if she'd had time to wield it. The seal took her down, held her head in its mouth; it seemed to be playing. She resurfaced once then vanished again while her companions were still launching the rescue boat. By the time they got to her, it was too late. Her dive computer showed that the seal had taken her to 230 feet below the surface and held her there for six minutes before abruptly releasing her. Nobody knows why it attacked. Perhaps it thought she was a fur seal. Perhaps she accidentally disturbed it. The doctor spent an hour trying to resuscitate her. And then the shocked winter crew spent another few weeks with her body, waiting for the emergency plane that would fly in and take her back home.

Kirsty's monument on the hill at Rothera Point sits on a cairn of artlessly arranged rocks; it is a toposcope, a circle of metal explaining the view through 360°, naming the surrounding glaciers, mountains and seas. And running round the centre is an engraved tribute: 'Kirsty "Bang" Brown. In such a short time she achieved so much and lived life to the full.' She was only twenty-eight.

Rothera divers still brave the waters around here, but there is always someone watching, ready to sound the alarm. They bring their catches to Rothera's aquarium, a cold bright room filled with round tanks that are heaving with weird Antarctic sea life.

Lloyd Peck specialises in the effects of warming on the cold-blooded creatures that have made Antarctica their home. The *Endurance* had delivered me to Rothera for a brief visit, and Lloyd had offered to show me his beloved animals. He bounced enthusiastically between tanks, pulling out the ten-legged starfish that I had seen in McMurdo, and the antifreeze fish and the giant sea spiders and all those other alien adaptations by which the animals here make the most of the frigid waters.

'It's funny,' I said. 'If you mention life in Antarctica, people don't think of any of these. It's always penguins, seals and whales.'

'That's because films about Antarctica always focus on the charismatic animals,' he replied. 'But warm-blooded animals only account for less than 0.00001 per cent of species on Earth. So for a scientist, if you take a statistical approach they don't exist. They're such a small proportion of life on Earth that they don't really exist.'

Whoa. Statistically speaking warm-blooded animals, including humans, *don't really exist*?

Lloyd laughed. 'The real animals that we have to understand and know about are the ones that are the vast majority of species on Earth, the cold-blooded animals. Like the clams in this tank.'

He reached in, grabbed one and pointed it towards me. This was far bigger than any clam I had ever seen. Lloyd could barely hold it in one hand. It had a luminous pearly clamshell, hinged and cylindrical, and, at the top, a wrinkled concertina of splodgy grey muscle. 'We do a lot of work on this species,' he was saying when the animal unexpectedly launched a freezing jet of sea-water at me as if it were a schoolboy in a peeing contest. I yelped and jumped backwards. 'Yes, I forgot to say that they squirt. Sorry.' He was laughing again.

'That's why I like them. They do things you don't expect. They're the only clams that can swim by jet propulsion. They're normally buried in the sea floor and the wrinkled part is all you can see. But if they're dug up by an iceberg they have to get back down to a low point to bury themselves. So they squirt out a jet of water and take off. Of all the bivalves – molluscs, oysters, mussels – they're the only ones that can do this!'

Lloyd clearly enjoys his animals. But his research on these clams and many of the other creatures in the aquarium is yield-ing troubling news about the wildlife of the Peninsula. Although there is little now to be feared from the men with their harpoons and clubs, warming is subjecting the animals here to a new threat and it could turn out to be the worst danger yet.

'We're looking at how they cope with rising temperatures. If you pull these clams out of the sediment they have to rebury themselves to do the normal things they do in life. If you warm them up, you quickly get to a temperature where they can't do it any more. For these guys that's only about a two-degree warming.'

He knew this because he and his colleagues had done the experiment. They put some of these clams into a tank, changed the temperature of the water, and watched what happened. Antarctic sea creatures are never in a hurry. If you watched in real time, you would quickly get bored. But Lloyd showed me the speeded-up video, with twelve hours compressed into about a minute. At 32°F the clams were enthusiastic, jigging up and down like jackhammers as they forced their shells back underground. But when he heated them up by just a few degrees they simply lay there, limp, flaccid and supine. It was too darn hot.

'Why does a warmer temperature make it harder for them to bury themselves?' I asked.

'Warm-blooded animals like us set our own internal temperatures regardless of what it's like outside,' Lloyd said. 'But cold-blooded animals keep themselves at the same temperature as the environment and their metabolic rate depends on that temperature. As you warm these animals up, their metabolic rate goes up, and so does their cost of living.

'If I get you to walk upstairs you can probably hold a conversation. If I ask you to run upstairs and raise your metabolic rate it will be harder. If you eat a big meal first and try to run up the stairs you'll probably be sick because you can't get enough oxygen quickly enough to power both your muscles and your digestion. With these animals, warming them up is the equivalent of giving them a big meal and making them run upstairs. They don't have the spare capacity to do anything else.'

'What happens if they can't bury themselves?'

'They're vulnerable to predators. Also they have to be in the right position to pump water to feed and to reproduce. For them, not being able to get back in the sediment is really bad news.'

And then he showed me more of the creatures he had tested in his warming tanks. The strangest were bright yellow snails the size and shape of lemons, which had their shells on the inside, covered with soft tissue that shone with a ghostly glow. Each was glued to the side of the Perspex tank with one large yellow foot, and you could see their tentacles twitching as they 'breathed' the oxygen in the seawater.

'Aren't they amazing?' Lloyd said. 'They eat sea squirts. They exist in huge profusion in some parts of Antarctica, and apart from a handful of biologists, most people have never seen them before.'

'How vulnerable are they?' I asked.

'We know that these animals can't cope with rising temperatures. Evolutionarily speaking, the temperatures here have been very low and very constant for a long time. The animals back home in European seas are used to a seasonal change of ten, maybe twelve degrees. These guys have a temperature change of two degrees or less during the year. They've lost the ability to cope with big temperature changes. That means that as the seas warm they'll be the first ones to suffer.'[15]

Lloyd is very worried about the effect the warming already happening on the Peninsula will have on the sea creatures that, until now, have been flourishing here. His experiments have already shown that it won't take much more warming to tip them over the edge.

'We've looked at eight different species and so far they have all been sensitive to small changes. Some of these amazing creatures could disappear before most people even know they're there. And that's a crying shame.'

For the first time since I'd met him, Lloyd's face fell. He wasn't laughing now.

These animals are Lloyd's life, but why should the rest of us care? Well, you don't need to lose many species for it to make a big difference to the ecosystem as a whole. One in particular, a small, shrimp-like creature called krill, is a cornerstone for the entire food web. And it seems to be suffering, too.

Krill depend on the presence of sea ice for their livelihood. They eat the algae that grow under sea ice, and their own young also hang out under the protection of the ice in great krill nurseries. But with the recent warming has come melting. And in a study of nearly 12,000 net hauls from the krill catches of nine different countries, going all the way back to 1926, research-ers have found what they describe as a 'significant' decline in numbers.[16]

That in turn appears to be having a knock-on effect on the charismatic creatures – many seals, whales and penguins – that rely on krill for their food. Already, numbers of chinstrap and Adélie penguins are falling on the Peninsula. Their staple food-stuff is disappearing, and so are they.[17]

Of course there are winners as well as losers. But in this case, the winners moving in to take over the ecosystem are dismal creatures called salps, which are formless gelatinous blobs that are palatable to almost nobody in the higher echelons of the food web.[18] Taking out chinstrap penguins and Adélie penguins and perhaps seals and whales, too, and replacing them with salps is probably a good thing for the salps. For the rest of us? You decide.

And there's another alarming change afoot. Until recently the waters of Antarctica have been the most isolated in the world. When the ice first came to the continent tens of millions of years ago many crushing creatures – such as lobsters and crabs – became extinct, and the prohibitively long swim from warmer climes farther north means they have never been replaced. That left a host of evolutionary niches for the rest of the animals to radiate into.

But now the crabs are coming back. In 2010 researchers sent a remotely operated submarine deep down into a stretch of water just off the west coast of the Peninsula, to scout out any interesting forms of life on the seabed. To their astonishment they found a massive, teeming colony of king crabs, perhaps 1.5 million of them. The first pioneers probably washed in with a surge of warmer water from the south, and now these notorious bone-crushers are poised, ready to descend on an unsuspecting ecosystem that has lost the evolutionary ability to protect itself.[19]

It's no longer necessary to look at thermometers to know that the Peninsula is warming. Change is not just in the air here; it is in the animals, and it's also in the ice. Over the past few decades, floating shelves of ice that surround the Peninsula have been falling one by one, like dominoes. They break apart, shatter into icebergs that drift away leaving open water where before there was none. For scientists it has become imperative to discover whether this warming really is because of human activity, and, if so, to try to predict what will be next.

Antarctic ice shelves are highly impressive. You have to sail up close to them to appreciate their size and apparent solidity. The early explorers called the first one they encountered 'the Barrier' because it dwarfed their tiny ship. There was no sailing past it, no going round.

That was the Ross Ice Shelf, near McMurdo on the other side of the continent, the great expanse of floating ice the size of France where Amundsen set up base and Scott and his men perished. Another giant shelf lies almost diametrically opposite this, stretching out from the eastern side of the Peninsula, like the webbing at the base of the Peninsula's thumb. This is the Ronne

Ice Shelf, which covers about the same area as the Ross Shelf, is thicker, and is similarly fed in part by the fast-moving glaciers of West Antarctica.

Every so often, a massive slab on the seaward edge of one of these monsters will flex just a little too much; perhaps the surface crevasses will start to make their way deeper; tides work the ice up and down, making more crevasses, more cracks until, finally, the slab breaks off and sails away, forming one of those tabular icebergs, flat-topped and square-shouldered, the size of a floating city, or even a county.

There are also plenty of smaller ice shelves around the Peninsula proper. They float at the inner end of many of the region's fjords, filling them with icebergs, bergy bits, growlers and all the various debris of the world of ice. By the standards of the Ross and Ronne ice shelves, these are minor players. Anywhere else in the world they would be considered large.

And it is these shelves, on the Peninsula, that have started to alarm scientists by falling apart. The first to go was the Larsen Inlet Ice Shelf, which disappeared in 1989. Then, in 1995, the Prince Gustav Ice Shelf, which draped the narrow channel between the northern tip of the Peninsula and James Ross Island and had been retreating for decades, finally gave up the ghost.

Larsen A, the Prince Gustav's nearest remaining neighbour, was next. It was about 700 square miles and broke apart in January 1995, sending a plume of icebergs into the Weddell Sea. Researchers now looked uneasily at the next domino in the chain: Larsen B, twice as large and presumably more robust. Was it likely to shatter soon?

Larsen B lay fairly far down the eastern side of the Peninsula, and to get there meant traversing the notoriously ice-jammed Weddell Sea. The best way to watch it was by satellite. But researchers itched to get there, on the ground, and see for themselves what was happening.

One of these was Eugene Domack, a sedimentologist from Hamilton College in Clinton, New York. He knew that the Peninsula was undergoing serious change right now, but he was also ready to take the long view. It was possible that this was just some perfectly natural local warming. Perhaps the Peninsula regularly experienced hot flushes that could disappear as quickly as they came. After all, we had only been acquainted with the region for a couple of centuries. Ice shelves might have been breaking and reforming repeatedly for thousands of years, with nobody there to notice.

If he could only get up close to one of the disintegrating ice shelves, Gene thought he had a way to figure out whether the ice had a habit of breaking up like this, or if the recent events were truly as alarming as they seemed. First, he needed to test his model on one of the more accessible ice shelves, on the western coast – which is rarely choked up with pack ice. If it worked, he could then try taking it into the rather more challenging waters of the Weddell Sea.

I joined him on a trial voyage aboard one of the US National Science Foundation's two research vessels, the *Nathaniel B. Palmer*.[20] Following our crossing of Drake Passage, we had steamed straight on down the Peninsula, not stopping at any of the islands or bases, not even the Peninsula's American base, also called Palmer, which was apparently one of the loveliest on the continent, though sniffed at by the rest of the people on the programme as being too cushy. We were heading for an inlet called Lallemand Fjord, about a third of the way down the Peninsula, which bore an ice shelf that Gene had his eye on.

Gene was a man in a hurry. The operations on the *Palmer* were on an industrial scale, with massive winches and cables, and it was forbidden to go out on to the back deck without a float jacket and hard hat. If he felt he had to be out there *now*, Eugene would rush up with his clipboard and pen, grab a hard hat out of someone's hand (or, once, off somebody else's head), and cram himself into the nearest float jacket even if it announced its size as SMALL in large letters on the back.

But at least he was still prepared to go along with one of the oldest Navy traditions. The previous night, the ship had sailed past the invisible line in the sea that marks the Antarctic Circle, and those of us who were first-timers had had to undergo an initiation ceremony. Originally this only applied to crossings of the equator, during which naval 'pollywogs' (neophytes) were transformed into 'shellbacks' (veterans) by means of the sort of humiliations that would make members of a fraternity turn pale. Scientific cruises take this at least as seriously as naval vessels, and I know otherwise rational researchers who, when departing on an equator-crossing expedition, would rather forget their passports than their certificate saying they have already paid suitable obeisance to King Neptune, and don't need to do so again.

Luckily for those of us on board who were Antarctic Circle pollywogs, our local King Neptune, biologist Rob Dunbar from Stanford University, had decided to let us off lightly. Instead of the compulsory haircuts and random shavings, or ceremonial dumping into vats of rubbish, he demanded that we each write a poem demonstrating suitable deference to the king.

That evening, after handing in my ten verses of doggerel, I received a certificate stating in elegant copperplate that, at two bells of the first watch of the day, I

Did, Boldly and Without Trepidation, Cross the Antarctic Circle at 66° 33' South Latitude, 67° 36' West Longitude, aboard the Vessel Nathaniel Brown Palmer, entering the Treacherous and Unforgiving Reaches of the Antarctic Ocean. By so Doing and having Subsequently displayed proper Obeisance to King Neptune and his Faithful Lieges prior to Departing the Southern Reaches, She now Commands due Honor and Respect from all Persons, Whales, Seals, Penguins, Fishes, Crustaceans, Sponges, Insignificant Microscopic Creatures and other Denizens of the Polar Domains.

(Rob studies insignificant microscopic creatures, which is probably why they made it on to the list.)

Below all this, just above the signature of King Neptune, it added:

She bears this Distinction with Pride for it is neither Lightly Undertaken nor Easily Attained.

Certificate in hand, I watched for a while up on the bridge, but there was little to see but monotonous grey water with the occasional flash of a distant iceberg on the radar screen. Eventually I stumbled off to bed, to be woken next morning by my cabin mate, Mary, urgently shaking my shoulder. 'Get up!' she said. 'You've got to see this!' She was right. While we'd been sleeping the ship had turned into the mouth of the Lallemand Fjord and we were now about halfway along.

The scene was spectacular. All around us there was ice: the great squared-off tabular bergs that had only recently broken off; medium-sized ones with rounded edges and longer histories; and small chunks, with odder shapes. You could see what you wanted in these natural sculptures: a mermaid, a horse's head, swans with their necks entwined, dragons.

But their shapes also told real stories if you knew how to read them. With a practised eye you could see where, as they had melted from below, they had become repeatedly unstable and flipped over and then flipped again. There were shelves of ice jutting out in mid-air, where old water lines had once been, or sides rippled with lines created by bubbles of air that had once escaped from the melting ice below the water, and bobbled their way to the surface.

All of this ice had come from the land, from snow, turning to ice, turning to glaciers, spilling into the sea, floating, flexing and finally breaking off. But the water, too, was freezing. Here it was slushy with grease ice, or frazil, which slithered against the ship's hull; there it was so still that it had already begun to form pancakes, like frozen water lilies, decorated with streaks of snow. As we continued, the sea ice became more abundant, and thicker. The *Palmer*'s bow now smacked with pistol cracks as she performed a stately slalom through the pack. And overhead snow petrels wheeled, silhouetted against a slate grey sky, graceful as swallows.

At last, the ship heaved to. Ahead a cliff of ice blocked the way, standing perhaps sixty feet above the water and much more below. This was the Müller Ice Shelf, the parent of all these icebergs, the end point of the waste-disposal chute that was perpetually carrying snow from the mountains of the interior back down to the sea.

The Müller Ice Shelf was to be Gene's test case. He already knew that it had retreated and re-advanced perfectly naturally in the past, and he believed that the signature of this was there to be read, in the mud of the Lallemand Fjord's sea floor.

This mud had accumulated week by week, year by year, from a steady rain of debris through the seawater. Just as with the ice cores, looking down through the layers of this mud was like looking back in time. It contained dirt and ground-up rock carried from land by the glacier, and dead bodies and excretions of tiny sea creatures living in the water, and the relative proportions of land dirt and water creatures could show the times when the ice shelf was hanging overhead, and the times when it was gone.

But first, we had to collect the mud. The crew and science team heaved a square metal tube over the side. It was three metres long and had a heavy weight on the top and when it finally reached the sea floor it sank gently into the soft sediment, collecting a long plug, before being heaved back up and winched on to the ship.

Down below decks in the labs, the core lay out on a bench ready for its autopsy. Amy Leventer, from Colgate University in Hamilton, New York, pored over it, meticulously comparing each layer against a rock colour chart. '5Y 4/4 moderate olive brown,' she said, and a graduate student noted it down. (All of the researchers were so familiar with this chart and its arcane nomenclature that they couldn't resist practising on other objects, too. Rob Dunbar had already identified the precise shade of my coat. I'd have called it beige, but he assured me it was 'light olive grey, 5Y 5/2'.)

To my less expert eye, the top of the core was just a nondescript sludgy grey, but deeper down, where the sediments were older, it changed to a fetching olive green. There it was, the very moment that the ice had appeared, written into the core. The green colour came from microscopic sea creatures; the sludgy grey, from where the glacier had advanced out on to the water and dropped its load on the sea floor, swamping the biology with hard grey grit.

In other words, the model was working. A few thousand years ago, there was no ice shelf here. But then, in the seventeenth century, the world was hit with a global climate cooling called the Little Ice Age. Londoners built bonfires and held markets and fairs on the frozen River Thames. And in Antarctica, out of human sight, the Müller Ice Shelf began to jut out into Lallemand Fjord and make its mark in the mud.

There was one last thing to check. To be sure that the mud on the sea floor really was an accurate record of the sediment falling through the water, Gene and his team had left a mooring in the fjord the previous year. A string of four bright yellow cones was now floating somewhere in the water, anchored to the sea floor with heavy weights, their heads turned upwards to catch the falling rain of dust, sand and debris. Now all we had to do was find the mooring and retrieve the traps.

The finding part was easy enough – the mooring's long string quickly showed up on the high-frequency sonar – but retrieving it was going to be tricky. Since it had been deployed, a large iceberg had drifted up close to the mooring site, and the captain was worried. Those of us who were non-essential were banned from the back deck and had to take turns watching through the open door. It was snowing now, thick fat flakes. The crew were out there in full immersion suits, attached to safety ropes to stop them falling into the frigid fjord. As the ship trawled past the site again and again, they toiled to snag the rope with a grappling hook over the side, like a heavy engineering version of the gift-grabbing games at seaside resorts.

Once, twice, they felt the snag and hauled the hook up only to find a few bare chunks of ice. Back over the edge, try again, and then ... finally ... gotcha! And the winch kicked in to haul the mooring up. I still can't believe how much effort it took to dot the i's of this model, to do the careful additional due diligence that would gather just a few more points on the graph.

But it was all a vital part of the story. The only way to be sure – really sure – of what was happening in Antarctica now was to interpret the clues from the past, and Gene was determined to get it right. And all his care was paying off. The results from Lallemand Fjord looked good; the model was making perfect sense. Now he needed to go to the other side of the Peninsula, to see if the other, bigger ice shelves were also just coming and going perfectly naturally, or if their recent retreats were something more sinister. That, however, meant sailing into the Weddell Sea, the iciest of Antarctica's waters, and also perhaps the most perilous. Even today, few ships manage to penetrate the pack ice that builds there; and one of the first that tried – the *Endurance*'s namesake – met a horrible fate, in one of the most spectacular stories of the heroic age.

It was 1914 and Ernest Shackleton had a new plan. After turning back from his attempt to reach the South Pole five years earlier, he had decided to try a new adventure. He intended to make the first ever crossing of the continent, from sea to shining sea.

An expedition of this scale would need two ships. One, the *Aurora*, would go to the familiar Ross Sea side of the continent, while Shackleton himself would lead an expedition on a second ship, the *Endurance*. This would brave the infamous ice of the Weddell Sea, and land somewhere on the floating Ronne Ice Shelf, the mirror image of the great Barrier. Shackleton and his men would then make their way across the continent, using depots laid by the Ross Sea party. Never one to understate his case, he had named the expedition in the grandest of terms: the Imperial Transantarctic Expedition.

Of the two ships, the *Endurance* had the harder sailing task. For some reason the Weddell Sea was always far more choked with pack ice than the Ross Sea, and an earlier expedition had already lost a ship there. But at first all was well. Though it encountered ice early, the little ship made its way gamely along leads of open water, and steamed and smashed through the frozen sea ice between. On they crept through the pack, getting closer and closer to their goal. By January 1915 they were within eighty miles of the coast. They could see it. They could almost touch it. The men, heartily tired of the voyage, began to talk eagerly of how they would set up their base on land, and prepare for the expedition to come.

But then, agonisingly, the pack closed in. There were no more leads of open water, no more thin sections of ice that the ship could smash her way through. She was stuck. On 20 January 1915, *Endurance* found herself pinioned, a helpless prisoner forced to drift back north as the coast moved tantalisingly back out of sight. Shackleton had had to turn back within one hundred miles of the Pole. Now, once again, his goal was slipping away.

February passed, and March. The pack around the ship was like solid ground, enough for the men to practise sledging, exercise their dogs, play games and climb the pressure ridges that the ice threw up as it shifted and squeezed. Many were still hoping that the ship would eventually go free, but Shackleton knew better. In the privacy of his cabin he confided to Frank Worsley, captain of the *Endurance*: 'You had better make up your mind that it is only a matter of time ... What the ice gets, the ice keeps.'[21]

And the ice kept up its pressure, in visible waves that squeezed ever tighter around the ship. She listed this way and that. Her timbers creaked and groaned, and then finally cracked. On 27 October, the crew were forced to abandon ship. Shackleton gathered the men around him in front of *Endurance*'s shattered remains. 'Ship and stores have gone,' he said, 'so now we'll go home.'[22]

'I think it would be difficult to convey just what those words meant to us,' wrote one of the men, 'situated as we were, surrounded by jostling ice floes as far as the eye could reach, tired out with our efforts to save the ship, and with no idea as to what was likely to happen to us – "We'll go home".'[23]

Each man was allowed no more than two pounds of personal gear. (One of the few exceptions was a banjo belonging to one of the crew members, which Shackleton insisted on taking, saying it was 'vital mental medicine'.[24]) In such a pass, the values of the outside world were meaningless. Forced to confront what mattered most to them, men threw away money and kept photographs. Shackleton himself cast a handful of sovereigns onto the snow, and tore a page from the ship's Bible, with this memorable verse from the Book of Job:

> *Out of whose womb came the ice?*
> *And the hoary frost of Heaven, who hath gendered it?*
> *The waters are hid as with a stone,*
> *And the face of the deep is frozen.*[25]

At first the men marched, attempting to drag their two lifeboats with them over the towering pressure ridges of ice. But the hills were too high and too hard. 'The floes grind stupendously, throw up great ridges, and shatter one another mercilessly,' Shackleton wrote in his diary. 'Human effort is not futile, but man fights against the giant forces of nature in a spirit of humility.'[26]

And so they waited, and drifted, at a camp they called 'Patience' until in April 1916 they met enough open water to launch their lifeboats and sail for the nearest land. This was Elephant Island, a tiny, uninhabited and unsung patch of volcanic rock at the very tip of the Peninsula. The men set up camp on an inhospitable spit of land and contemplated their future. Nobody would come to rescue them there, for nobody knew where to look. Shackleton decided the only recourse was to equip one of the open lifeboats, the *James Caird* – which was less than twenty-five feet long – and sail it across the stormy Southern Atlantic, seeking help.

Cape Horn was the closest occupied land, about 600 miles away, but it lay in the wrong direction. The prevailing westerly winds that tore around the continent made reaching it impossible. Instead, Shackleton and the five men he chose to accompany him would have to forge out into the wide ocean, and try to reach the whaling station at South Georgia, a tiny pinprick of land more than 700 miles to the north-east, a needle in the great grey haystack of the Atlantic Ocean. If they missed it, all would be lost. The next nearest land was thousands of miles away.

To the twenty-two men left behind, and perhaps also to the six in the tiny boat, the mission must have seemed suicidal. But nobody dared say so. For Shackleton, pessimism was the only unforgivable sin, and he described optimism as 'true moral courage'. He was convinced that believing in an endeavour took you more than halfway to achieving it. And as his story shows, he may well have been right.

'We fought the seas and the winds,' Shackleton wrote. 'At times we were in dire peril . . . flung to and fro by Nature in the pride of her strength . . . So small was our boat and so great were the seas that often our sail flapped idly in the calm between the crests of two waves. Then we would climb on the next slope and catch the full fury of the gale where the wool-like whiteness of the breaking water surged around us.'[27]

The men not on watch, or bailing out the leaky craft, crawled into soaking sleeping bags in the tiny covered space that the carpenter had contrived and tried to get some rest. But the hasty construction had not been designed for comfort. 'The bags and cases seemed to be alive in the unfailing knack of presenting their most uncomfortable angles to our rest-seeking bodies,' Shackleton wrote. 'A man might imagine for a moment that he had found a position of ease, but always discovered quickly that some unyielding point was imping-ing on muscle and bone.'[28] And the makeshift cabin was also suffocating. One of the crew wrote that more than once on waking, he had the ghastly fear that he had been buried alive.[29]

But Shackleton had chosen his five companions well. Worsley wrote in his navigating book that Irish seaman McCarthy 'is the

most irrepressible optimist I've ever met. When I relieve him at
the helm, boat iced & seas pourg down yr neck, he informs me
with a happy grin "It's a grand day, sir".'[30]

And Shackleton also had Worsley himself, the captain of
Endurance, the master navigator whose task was to find South
Georgia in this wide and stormy sea. The normal procedure by
which seamen calculate courses and distances had become,
Worsley wrote, 'a merry jest of guesswork'. Instead, on the rare
occasions where the sun could be seen, Worsley knelt on the
thwart, two men holding him on either side, and tried to snap
the altitude of the sun with his sextant while the *James Caird*
bucked and heaved and rolled beneath him.

It ought to have been impossible. It *was* impossible. But fourteen days after they left Elephant Island, the men saw the cliffs of
South Georgia rearing in front of them. Worsley's handful of sextant
sightings had done the trick. They had achieved one of the greatest boat journeys ever made.

However, their ordeal was not over. Before the men could
land they were hit by a mighty storm that nearly dashed the
poor *James Caird* to pieces. Two days later, when the craft finally
limped to shore, it was on the uninhabited side of a mountainous and uncharted island. The whaling station that could bring
rescue lay ninety miles round the coast. Their boat was wrecked
and so were they.

So Shackleton took two of his companions up and over the
mountains of the interior on a forced march lasting thirty-six
hours. Typically, Shackleton led from the front. He insisted on
going ahead, breaking the trail in the snow, staying awake to
watch while he let his men sleep for five minutes at a time, and
then waking them (and pretending for their spirits' sake that they
had slept for half an hour).

And when the three men arrived at the whaling station at
Grytviken, the first humans they had seen in nearly three

weeks – two small boys – saw their filthy, battered appearance and ran away.

The manager of the whaling station took a different view. As soon as he had grasped the names, and exploits, of his guests, he shook their hands, then had them bathed, fed and feted, and their three companions rescued from the far side of the island. But winter was closing, and there were still the men on Elephant Island to reach.

Shackleton cabled the Admiralty requesting a rescue ship. But the Admiralty had never supported him; he was a merchant seaman, who was not, and never would be, one of them. The reply came that there would be nothing available until October. Too late. By then, some or even all of the men might have succumbed. Shackleton felt personally responsible for every one of his marooned men. He raced to South America from where he made two attempts to sail into the pack, on ships lent first by the Uruguayan government and then by a British shipowner. Both times the ice beat him back.

But the third time was the charm. In mid-August, Shackleton finally reached Elephant Island aboard a little steam tug, the *Yelcho*, lent to him by the Chilean government. When they saw the ship coming into the bay, the men on the island signalled frantically. They lit a fire. They raised a flag. The running gear on the flagpole wouldn't work and the flag itself was frozen solid, so they tied a Burberry jacket halfway up the flagpole, as high as they could reach.

On board the *Yelcho*, Shackleton saw the 'flag' at half-mast and was dismayed. But then he pulled out his field glasses and carefully counted the men waving on the shore. Twenty-two. All present and correct. 'He put his glasses back in their case and turned to me,' wrote Worsley, 'his face showing more emotion than I had ever known it show before.'[31]

The men on shore, meanwhile, were mystified. How was a steam tug coming to their rescue, and a Chilean one at that? But then the *Yelcho* lowered a boat. When Wild saw the unmistakable figure of Shackleton in its bow he nearly cried.

Within an hour all the men were off Elephant Island, heading for home. 'I have done it,' Shackleton wrote to his wife on arriving back at Punta Arenas. 'Damn the Admiralty ... not a life lost and we have been through Hell.'[32]

Shackleton's expedition marked the end of the heroic age. His men had left a world of Edwardian heroism and endeavour and returned to the insanity of world war, and the Somme. But though his hopes had been crushed by the ice of the Weddell Sea, Shackleton had once again made his Antarctic mark.

Apsley Cherry-Garrard, one of Scott's most loyal followers, wrote this about the merits of Antarctica's three most famous heroes: 'For a joint scientific and geographical piece of organization, give me Scott ... for a dash to the Pole and nothing else, Amundsen: and if I am in the devil of a hole and want to get out of it, give me Shackleton every time.'[33]

And before he left for home, Shackleton wrote a poem in the visitor's book of one of the local dignitaries that captures better than most the madness that keeps people returning to the ice even today:

> *We were the fools who could not rest*
> *In the dull earth we left behind*
> *But burned with passion for the South*
> *And drank strange frenzy from its wind*
> *The world where wise men sit at ease*
> *Fades from our unregretful eyes*
> *And thus across unchartered seas*
> *We stagger on our enterprise.*[34]

• • •

Following his work on Lallemand Fjord, Gene Domack was satisfied that his model was working. He could study the mud beneath a former ice shelf and learn if the shelf had a habit of breaking up, or if the recent events truly ought to be alarming.

His new target was Larsen B, the next shelf on the list for potential break-up. It was much bigger than the other ones that had recently retreated – more than 1,000 square miles in area, and 700 feet thick. So far, it had also held firm. But lately it had been shedding some large icebergs. Gene planned to go to the place where one had broken off, and examine the mud beneath.

The ice might yet hold them back. The year after the *Palmer* worked Lallemand Fjord, a British team led by glaciologist Carol Pudsey from the British Antarctic Survey had tried to get down to Larsen B, but the pack had thwarted them. Instead they made it only as far as the ex-Prince Gustav Ice Shelf at the tip of the Peninsula. They collected mud from where the ice used to be and found unmistakable signs that this shelf had disappeared before, a few thousand years ago. It seemed that it came and went perfectly naturally. The collapse of the Prince Gustav, at least, could not be put down to human climate change.[35]

That sounded like good news. But the Prince Gustav Shelf was both small and very far north. It wasn't that surprising that it might come and go. Larsen B, on the other hand, was much larger, and more southerly. If that, too, showed signs of previous collapse we humans were probably off the hook as far as the Peninsula warming was concerned. But if it didn't, that could be very bad news.

Gene, Amy and the team hit lucky. Aboard the *Nathaniel B. Palmer*, they found enough gaps in the pack ice to edge their way south into the Weddell Sea. They passed Elephant Island,

and James Ross Island and many of the landmarks that
Shackleton had noted as he and his men drifted helplessly by
on their Patience camp. In January 2002 they sailed right up to
the face of the Larsen B ice shelf, to where a berg had broken
off in 1995, and began their coring and sampling. They were
hoping to find the same sort of signals they had seen at
Lallemand Fjord – dull grey mud when the ice shelf had been
overhead, delivering its ground-up rock to swamp the seafloor
with grit, and green mud if it had ever retreated in the past, and
left open water for green living things to flourish and then sink
when they died. Gene and his team cored and collected and
stored and headed back, satisfied, across Drake Passage to Punta
Arenas.

Nobody expected what happened next. In February, just a
few weeks after Gene and the *Palmer* left the area, Larsen B
unexpectedly exploded. It became suddenly shot through with
cracks and the ice turned to rubble. Newly formed icebergs
jostled to escape. They lurched on to their sides, and crashed
into each other and rode their way out of the newly formed bay
in a gigantic plume. By the beginning of March, 500 million
tonnes of ice, an area bigger than the US state of Rhode Island,
had shattered.[36]

The opening scenes of the Hollywood climate disaster movie
The Day After Tomorrow are modelled on the break-up of Larsen
B. They show the hero working in Antarctica, camping on a
floating shelf of ice, drilling ice cores through its surface. The first
sign of impending doom comes when the ice shelf cracks, right
across the research site. In trying to save his precious ice cores,
our hero only just survives.

Most of the movie was ludicrously overplayed from a scientific
point of view. The hurricanes and tornadoes and tidal waves were
wildly exaggerated for blockbuster effect. But not the break-up
of Larsen B. If our hero had been on the real ice shelf

as it shattered, he would have had to run for his life. Larsen B's catastrophic collapse could represent the first time ever that reality was too much even for a Hollywood disaster.

Gene and the rest of the world's ice scientists were stunned. They had thought Larsen B might begin to break up some time soon, but not like this, so fast, so furiously. Could this be something new, a terrible effect of recent warming? Or were there any reassuring signs that it had happened before?

Hastily Gene sorted through his newly retrieved samples to see what the mud had to say. And what he found was as shocking as the Larsen B's almighty breakdown. As far back as the record could show him, all the way to the end of the last ice age 10,000 years ago, the ice shelf had been fully intact.[37]

The spectacular collapse of Larsen B was completely new.

This was deeply troubling news. It seemed to confirm what many meteorologists suspected – that the warming of the Peninsula really is down to our activity.[38] In the disappearing ice shelf, Gene had found concrete evidence that humans are touching the Peninsula with more than just churches and schools, or even harpoons. Our entire way of life, the cars we drive, the electricity we make, the forests we clear, all are now apparently making their mark on the Antarctic Peninsula.

There was one shred of comfort. Floating ice already displaces water, so when ice shelves disintegrate they don't make sea levels rise. But they now looked like a serious warning sign, a shot across our bows. 'The Peninsula ice shelves really are the canary in the mine,' Gene said. 'And if the canary goes, you have to be worried.'

What's more, the shelves seem to have an important effect as gigantic buttresses, holding the land ice back and preventing it from sliding into the sea. There are already signs that some of the glaciers that used to feed Larsen B, freed from its restraining influence, are now speeding up.[39] If the same thing happened

with the monster ice shelves, and the glaciers they dam, spectacular rises in sea level could be with us sooner than anyone has
imagined.

And that's the biggest worry of all. Antarctica's land-based ice
sheets contain enough ice to swamp our puny, shore-hugging
civilisations. If the Peninsula is showing this response to climate
change, could the ice sheets themselves be next?

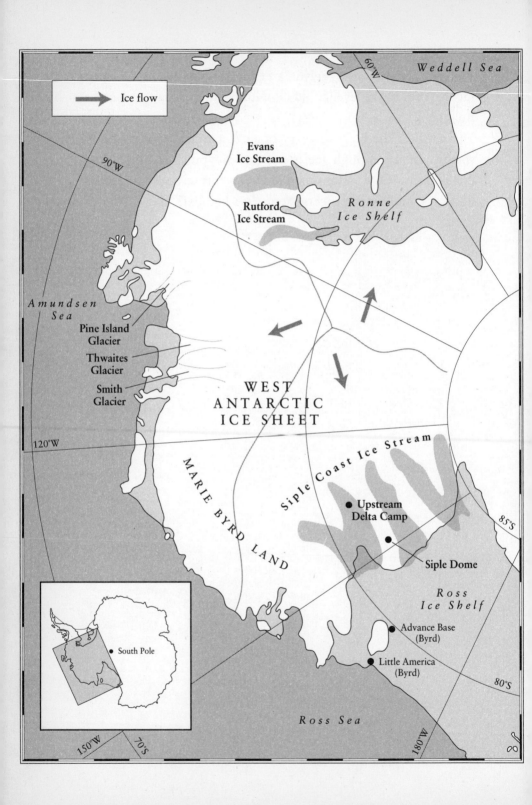

7

INTO THE WEST

One is old and cold and settled in its ways. The other is smaller but nimbler, moving quickly, connected to the oceans, looking – perhaps – to change. These are Antarctica's two great ice sheets, joined, like mismatched butterfly wings, by a backbone of mostly buried mountains running the length of the continent.

On the eastern side is the East Antarctic Ice Sheet, by far the larger of the two, a mighty behemoth that contains more than 80 per cent of all the ice on Earth. Though its average thickness is more than a mile, most of its base still rests safely on high ground and most of its ice creeps only sluggishly from the centre to the sea. It has been around for tens of millions of years.

Since its coastline tracks the Indian and Atlantic Oceans, the eastern ice sheet is relatively easy to reach by ship or plane from New Zealand, Australia, South Africa and the tip of South America, and its edges are dotted with scientific bases. Even its harsh interior is the home of the American South Pole Station, Russia's Vostok, the French-Italian Concordia.

On the west, however there is . . . nothing. The coastline of the West Antarctic Ice Sheet faces the broad, empty expanse of the Pacific Ocean. No nation can reach it simply by sailing south

and it has not one single permanent scientific station. Most of
the ice sheet lies beyond the normal reach of any existing
Antarctic operations. The west of Antarctica is truly Earth's final
frontier.

Five times smaller than its eastern sibling, it is also much more
vulnerable to change. The rock on which the West Antarctic Ice
Sheet rests isn't high like the east. Instead, almost all of it lies below
sea level, and some is ten thousand feet deep. So deep, in fact, that
if it weren't for the ice there would be nothing in the west but
ocean, and a smattering of small island archipelagos.

The only reason the western ice hasn't already floated away is
that it's currently thick enough to keep the sea at bay. But if the
glaciers that drain it speed up, and the ice sheet thins, the sea
could reclaim its ground, floating and shattering the ice in a catastrophic meltdown that would be felt in rising sea levels the
world over.[1]

There is plenty of evidence in Antarctica's climate records that
this has happened before, when temperatures were naturally
higher than they are today. Nobody knows exactly when the last
collapse happened. It could have been as recently as a hundred
thousand years ago – the last time the Earth was between ice
ages, as we are today. But it was certainly some time in the last
million years, the 'recent past' on the long timescale of ice.[2]

Scientists have known this for decades. With temperatures
now rising for reasons that appear to go far beyond natural fluc-
tuations, the question now exercising them is: how soon will it
happen again? There are already signs that, although the east
looks more or less in balance, the west is now seriously losing its
ice.[3] The high plateau of the east is where researchers look into
the past: up into space to the origins of the universe, or down
into the ice through climate layers of history. The west is where
they look to our future.

•   •   •

West Antarctica is a tough place to visit. My one and only trip there nearly didn't happen at all.

The western ice sheet divides neatly into thirds, each region acting as a separate giant conduit through which ice drains from the interior out into the sea. I wanted to get to one of these three conduits. If changes were happening anywhere, this was where to find them.

Two of the three were more or less out of bounds: one, the sector that fed the Ronne Ice Shelf, was on the far side of the continent, studied mainly by the British and Germans who did not have the spare logistics capacity to take non-essential personnel so far out into the field; one, which spilled into the Amundsen Sea right in the middle of the ice sheet, was far from everyone's logistics, shrouded in perpetual fog and studied by nobody.

But the remaining third might be reachable – just. The Siple Coast sector was just a few hours' flight from McMurdo by Hercules plane, and American researchers had been studying it for decades. There, five massive glaciers called ice streams were spilling into the far edge of the Ross Ice Shelf. They were thicker and wider and moved faster than almost any other ice on Earth. And a team from Caltech was currently drilling through one of them, hoping to reach the engine room that is driving the glacier from below.

It was remote, of course, and even the National Science Foundation's extensive logistics were stretched when they reached out that far. But still, all was looking promising until disaster struck during the camp set-up. Two months before I was due to go, the Herc that was carrying the scientists and their support team broke into a crevasse while taxiing on the snow. It didn't seem too dramatic at first; the plane just tilted from one side to the other, then stopped. But the pilots quickly realised they had opened up a snow bridge and one of the plane's skis had lurched into a hole that was about three metres wide, and very dark and deep.

The passengers had to climb out through the escape hatch on the roof, roped together by a mountaineer who was still fuming that she had not been allowed on the flight deck to advise the pilots. A Twin Otter came in to take the science team home and a new team moved in, with snow dozers and giant air bags and heavy lifting equipment.

While the rescuers toiled to fill in the crevasse and retrieve the $45 million plane, the researchers kicked their heels back at McMurdo and wondered if the season would be a bust or if they would still be able to salvage at least some of their plans. They learned to dance, and knit; they made snow sculptures, put on concerts and plays; they made a papier mâché piñata in the shape of a Hercules, with toilet paper rolls for engines, cardboard wings and lolly sticks for propellers, which they smashed open ceremonially to exorcise the evil spirits that were keeping them from their field site.

And then, in the second week of January when it was almost too late, the call finally came. The researchers raced to set up their drill rigs, and were now scrambling to do in two weeks what they had intended to do in twelve.

I had been in contact with the science team all along, and they had assured me that I was still welcome to join them. But then I hit a snag. Mactown's National Science Foundation representative, Dave Bresnahan, had decided that all visits were off. This camp had been enough trouble already. Anyone extraneous to the science was now officially banned. And that meant me.

I had wheedled and begged and argued, but the best I had managed was a reluctant offer to send me instead to Siple Dome. This was a temporary base on the tip of the western ice sheet, a few hours' flight from McMurdo. But still, it wasn't what I needed. At Siple Dome I would find a few researchers who had just finishing drilling an ice core, looking into the region's climate past. That was potentially important in its own way. But the camp I was trying to get to, which was called 'Upstream D', was right on top of one of the ice streams draining the western ice into the sea. The researchers there were investigating just how vulnerable the West Antarctic Ice Sheet was. They were looking not at the dead and gone, but at the here and now and next.

And yet . . . Siple Dome was also just a short Twin Otter flight away from the Upstream D camp. Maybe, just maybe, I could still find a way.

When I arrived at Siple Dome I headed straight for the camp manager, Sarah Grundlock. I was bearing messages for her from several of my contractor friends at McMurdo, who had also assured me that if anyone could figure out how to get me to UpD, Sarah could. And, sure enough, when I delivered my messages and then explained my mission, she took me into the Jamesway tent that served as a galley and pointed out a man sitting at a table there. He was Henry Perk, chief pilot for the Twin Otters. He was doing regular hops to resupply UpD. In fact, he was going there tomorrow. And, what's more, he made colourful watch straps to sell. 'Buy one of his watch straps,' Sarah advised. 'That will be your boarding pass.'

A couple of hours later, with a new watch strap on my wrist, I was in the Siple Dome comms tent, putting a radio call through to Dave Bresnahan back in Mactown. He couldn't hear me, so everything had to be relayed through MacOps.

'I have a ride to Upstream D,' I said. 'Henry has offered to take me. Do I have your permission to go?'

I waited for the message to be passed on. The crackly reply came:

'Will Henry pick you up on the same day or would you have to stay?'

'I'd like to stay.'

Another pause.

'He says you could be stuck there. He can't guarantee to fly you back out for maybe five days or more.'

'Fine by me.'

This time the pause between messages was longer. I waited anxiously. And then through the static came the voice of MacOps. 'He says tell her to enjoy her trip.'

The next morning Henry and I took off early. At first the ground was flat, white and featureless. But, suddenly, I saw crevasses on the surface of the ice, like score marks made by gigantic finger-nails. Here and there, the snow bridge had broken open, and that familiar vivid blue ice shone through from beneath. Then the crevasses became less regular, criss-crossing, curving, a tangled mess of scattered dips and hollows. 'We're right over the margin now,' Henry said from the cockpit.

That meant we were crossing over into the ice stream. On one side, the ice was moving perhaps several feet per year. On the other, it moved that same distance in a *day*. On the outside of the margin the ice was resting, on the inside it was racing, and the area between was being ripped apart with the strain, creating such extraordinary patterns of crevasses on the ice that the Twin Otter pilots had given the different margins fanciful sobriquets: 'The Snake', 'The Dragon', 'Valhalla'.

Until now the biggest glacier I'd witnessed was the Beard-more, the staircase that Shackleton and later Scott had used to climb up on to the polar plateau. I'd seen it on the flight to the South Pole and it was streaked with flow lines, an impressive frozen river. This one was much, much bigger, too big to take in from the air. It was thirty miles wide, a half mile thick and ran inland for hundreds of miles. The great size and fantastic speed of these ice streams meant they were all colossal superhigh-

ways, transporting ice at an extraordinary rate from the interior
to the sea. And because of this, many researchers were convinced
that they were the key to the stability – or otherwise – of the
West Antarctic Ice Sheet.

Moreover, these ice streams weren't just big and fast; they were
also dynamic, stopping and starting, writhing from one place to
another on timescales short enough to matter to humans.[4] The
neighbouring ice stream to this one[5] was scarcely moving at all.
And yet radar measurements of buried crevasses at its margin
showed that it must have been moving as quickly as all the rest,
as recently as 130 years ago.

There was something else odd about these ice streams. When
we passed the jumbled, chaotic crevasses of the margin, the ice
was completely smooth again. It was moving faster than any
other glacier I had yet seen. That ought to mean that the ice
was jumbled into crevasses as the racing glacier snagged on the
ground beneath. But there were no flow lines, no signs of
movement, nothing. Researchers had discovered that the ice
streams had no flow lines because they slid incredibly smoothly
on the base, so that there was nothing to rip, strain or distort
the ice.

There were many theories for why the motion should be both
so fast and so smooth, but now Barclay Kamb from Caltech was
leading the effort to see for himself. One by one he was visiting
as many as possible of the Siple Coast's six ice streams, drilling
holes through them to find out what was happening at the business end, the meeting point where the ice slipped over the
ground beneath.

Though I hadn't yet met Barclay, I'd read many of his papers.
He habitually described himself as a 'doubting Thomas', who
needed to see and touch before he could believe. He called it 'the
truth of the drill'. 'You can have remote-sensing data and interpretations and theories of what is down there, deep below the

surface, but until you drill down and get hold of the actual materials, you never really know.'

We landed on a bright blue Antarctic morning. Steve Zebroski,
the camp manager, had come to meet the plane and say a hasty
hello. He was pale and red-eyed through lack of sleep; the team
had been working round the clock to rescue their season. We
went together into the galley tent, which held a fully working
kitchen filled with the enticing smell of freshly baked bread.
Lesley, the camp cook, had just pulled a tray of rolls out of the
oven. She offered me one, with a cup of tea, but Steve warned
me that the team at the drill site was within about fifteen minutes
of breaking through to the base of the ice on its latest hole. I
declined the tea, stuffed a roll into my parka pocket and followed
him back out.

'You can take this skidoo,' he said, pointing to one that had a
name – *Clarence* – stencilled in duct tape on the side. It turned
out that Barclay's team always chose a theme for naming their
skidoos, and this year it was characters in the movie *It's a Wonderful
Life*. Clarence was the angel who came to show James Stewart's
failing businessman that his life wasn't so bad. I'd always found
the movie too soppy for my taste, but I was still quite pleased to
get the angel.

'How do I find the drill site?'

Steve gave me a dry look. 'There aren't many tracks around
here,' he said. 'Just don't go near any black flags.'

Ah yes. After the trouble with the Hercules, a team of mountaineers had scoured the area for any further crevasses, and had
marked the few danger spots with flags. And in any case Steve
was right. There was only one 'road', where the snow had been
churned up into a visible track. I turned on the engine, pulled
down my goggles and headed off.

Barclay came to meet my skidoo. He was tall and clean-shaven
– which was rare for men out in the field. I later discovered that

among its other amenities this camp even had a shower. True, you had to shovel your own snow to make the water, but the result was as hot and comfortable as any hotel. (As instructed, I shovelled the snow after I'd finished, so the water could be ready melted for the next person to come along. It was hot work, so I didn't register how cold the air was – until I heard a tinkling sound, which turned out to be strands of my wet hair that had quickly frozen solid.)

The set-up at the drill site involved the same sort of derrick and cable winch that I'd seen for ice coring. But unlike the ice-corers who needed to bring back samples of the stuff they were drilling through, all Barclay wanted to do was get through the ice sheet to what lay beneath. So there was no need for a complicated drill with a rotating metal head and sharp teeth. Instead, the Caltech method was much quicker and cleaner – amounting more or less to a vertically mounted fire hose. The idea was to melt a large amount of snow – which is why there were three people frantically shovelling from a bulldozed snow pile into a large vat – heat the water to about 200°F and pump it under very high pressure through the tip of a jet that looked like the head of a spear. Then you just pointed the jet downwards, pressed the right buttons, and let the combination of hot water and gravity do the rest.

Still, the ice was so thick that it took twenty-four hours to get through it. The team had started this particular hole yesterday and were just about to hit the bottom. Various graduate students and field assistants were kneeling on sheets of plywood around the hole. The derrick was holding the hose in place and one woman was feeding it down through her hands, letting it slide, feeling for the tug it would give when it hit the floor. 'Come on . . .' she said. 'Break through.'

Barclay's colleague from Caltech, Hermann Engelhardt, emerged suddenly from the Jamesway tent, as short as Barclay was tall, as hirsute as Barclay was clean-shaven. He had been monitoring the instruments and seen the shift in tension on the hose. 'That's it!' he shouted. 'Pull it out!' Two people started heaving upwards on the hose, while another dangled his weight from the cable to lend additional pulling power. I ran over and joined in, heaving until someone said: 'OK, she's safe.' Now, apparently, there was no chance of the drill sticking, though I didn't know how they knew. We let go and the winch took over, pulling the jet back up to the surface.

Barclay had ducked into the tent again with Hermann and I followed. Both were leaning over a laptop looking at a series of peaks in a graph. 'That's beautiful,' Barclay said. Things were apparently going well.

He told me that this was the fourth hole they had drilled in very rapid succession and all were testing why the ice streams could move so quickly and so smoothly. The answer was a combination of two things that you wouldn't normally expect to find under a kilometre of ice: water and mud.

Previous holes that they had drilled through other ice streams had shown that these giant carpets of ice seemed to be sliding on their own bed of water. Though this might seem surprising, it's not that hard to make water at the bottom of the ice sheet. There is always a certain amount of warmth radiating outwards from the planet's hot interior, and this geothermal heat would certainly help. Then you have the weight of the ice, and the friction caused by its scraping along the bed. Put those together and you have enough energy to melt the ice at the base of the glacier and give it a reason to slip.

But it's hard to prove, really prove, that there's water down there if you're using a hot-water drill. How could you tell if you were just seeing your own water? So for the first hole that Barclay and his team had drilled here, they had deliberately used the lowest water pressure that they could get away with. If it was lifting up the entire weight of the ice sheet to let it slide, the water down below would have to be at a very high pressure. Go in there with a lower pressure, and the water from below should surge up the hole. And that's exactly what happened. When they broke through on that first hole, they saw a spike in the pressure caused by the ice sheet's own plumbing system. There was definitely water down there, and it was definitely at a high enough pressure to lift and lubricate the ice.

In subsequent holes they had been experimenting with how interconnected the plumbing was. This time, they had seen oscillations in the pressure as water swilled up and down first one of their boreholes then another, showing that the channels under the ice really were connected. That's what had caused the peaks in the graph that Barclay was so pleased about.

There was also another factor that affected why the ice streams moved so quickly and so smoothly. Their beds were made not of rock, but of mud. It was the same sort of stuff that you find on the sea floor, and was probably left over from the last time that West Antarctica was an ice-free ocean. On hole number two, the team had managed to drill out a plug of sediment from the bottom of the hole, quickly, before the water inside it froze and the hole closed over. Barclay took a small tub off the shelf and opened it to show me. Inside was dark slate-grey mud, gritty and very sticky, and embedded with small pieces of gravel. He smeared a little on my fingertips and I rubbed them together. Now it was strong, but Barclay assured me that when it was saturated with water – a half mile below our feet – it was soft and fluid. With the help of the water, this mud was strong enough to carry an ice sheet on its back, but weak enough to deform and slip and let the ice slide.

The next day, I took my skidoo off to see the crevasse that had caused all the trouble with the Hercules. The rescuers from Mactown had half filled it with snow to retrieve their plane.

You could walk down a snow slope into it, touch the sides and wonder. Inside it was cold, much colder than the surface, and my eyelashes quickly frosted over. Close to the entrance the walls were decorated with frost fronds the size of dinner plates, sticking out from the ice like corals. But as I climbed farther in the sides became sheer, and glowed faintly with a cold, hard blue. They grew closer together until I could barely fit in the gap between. I tried to imagine what it would be like to fall and be wedged in, and shivered. Nobody knew why there was a crevasse here in the inner part of the ice stream, far away from the margins where the ice was supposed to run smooth. But perhaps there was some kind of bobble in the bed beneath, just enough to make the ice rear up a little and split. It wasn't a trap so much as a reminder that Antarctica was not built with humans in mind. We could occupy it, and study it, but it was still barely tolerating us.

That evening the light was lovely. I borrowed some skis and went out a few kilometres beyond the camp. Apparently there hadn't been much wind lately; the sastrugi were smooth and low. This was a new variant of the familiar 'flat white' of the East Antarctic plateau. Though the air here was 5°F and dry enough to scrape the skin, it was still noticeably damper than the dry desert of the east. There was moisture enough in the air to coat guy ropes with hoar frost. And the crystals on the surface were big and bold and flashy. They glinted in the slanting sunshine, as if someone had scattered handfuls of diamonds over the snow.

There was something liberating about being able to go where I pleased, with no tracks or roads to direct me. Earlier in the day, when one of the team had offered to let me drive one of the snow cats back to the camp, I had asked him nervously 'what if I crash into something?' He had turned slowly on his heels in a full circle, peering in exaggerated fashion at the flat white landscape. 'Into what?' he had said.

I had been assured that there were no hazards as long as I stayed away from the only crevasse in the neighbourhood, took a radio and kept within sight of the camp. But still I felt oddly nervous. Suddenly I felt myself falling with a mighty 'whump!'. Almost before I could register the sensation, I hit solid ground again and gasped with relief. It was a 'firn quake', in which an area of ice weakened by the attentions of the sun suddenly drops a few centimetres. Steve had warned me about them a few days ago, though I'd forgotten. 'It's shocking at first,' he had said. 'You fall three inches to your death.'

Apart from freezing to death, crevasses are the most prevalent – and romantic – danger in Antarctica. The great Antarctic heroes marched resolutely over the ice, knowing the risks, that at any moment they could plunge through a thin bridge of snow and find themselves dangling helplessly in their harnesses over a gigantic blue crack that descended all the way to oblivion. And yet although my heart was now racing from the firn quake, I still couldn't understand how it would feel to be faced with an apparently innocent landscape that was riddled with dangers. I still didn't really know crevasses at all.

Next morning, the team decided to pack up. They had done as much as they could and there was a plane coming soon to take out the first load of equipment. In eight days they had drilled six holes. They were exuberant, deservedly so. Now the people shovelling snow into the melter were preparing a hot tub, while the rest took a banana sledge and tobogganed down the snow pile, which they had unofficially christened 'The Mountain'. Wheeeee! 'Look at that,' Barclay said. 'It's the only mountain on the West Antarctic Ice Sheet.'

Barclay's work at Upstream D confirmed what he had seen before and what he, and others, would see again. Some combination of water and mud lay beneath all of the ice streams, both here on the Siple Coast feeding the Ross Ice Shelf and the ones

on the other side of the continent, which were feeding the
Ronne Ice Shelf.

Though it makes the ice streams both quick and dynamic, this
could still be good news. Some of the mechanisms that researchers have since found to explain the dynamism of the ice streams
also suggest that they may be making the ice sheet more stable,
not less.[6]

If they sped up, for instance, the ice would get thinner,
which would mean less weight pressing down, which meant
less friction, so less water, so they would slow down again. If
they ate back into a region where there was no sediment, they
would probably stop. And radar evidence from planes criss-
crossing the Siple Coast suggests that it is not losing ice; in fact
it may be thickening slightly.[7] On the other side of the continent, the streams feeding the Ronne Ice Shelf look, if anything,
even safer. They are thicker, but they run in grooves, so it is
hard for them to widen or writhe, and one of the largest – the
Rutford Ice Stream – is pegged on a high rise that keeps it in
check.[8]

So several decades of work on the ice streams feeding the Ross
Ice Shelf on one side of the continent, and those feeding the
Ronne Ice Shelf on the other, have produced this reassuring
message: for the foreseeable future, it looks as though these two-
thirds of the West Antarctic Ice Sheet are fairly stable. Even as
temperatures warm over the next few centuries, the shifting,
snaking ice streams are very unlikely to speed up enough to send
the ice sheet sliding into the sea.

But, of course, there's a twist. Because while all these scientists
were spending all this time and trouble tramping around the
front and back doors of the West Antarctic Ice Sheet, nobody was
checking the side door. The Amundsen Sea Embayment is the
third section of the West Antarctic Ice Sheet, the one that spills
out into the South Pacific, the one that's hardest to get to, that's

farthest from anyone's field of operation and has the foulest weather. The one that nobody was watching. And it turns out that this missing piece, this final third of the West Antarctic jigsaw puzzle, is the one where all the action is.

It wasn't entirely unexpected. Certain glaciologists have been worried about the Amundsen Sea Embayment for decades. First, there was the lack of ice shelves. Unlike the other two exit points for West Antarctic ice, which flow into the Ross and Ronne ice shelves, the glaciers pouring into the Amundsen Sea have no massive shelf of floating ice to buttress them. Instead, each has its own miniature ice shelf that runs for just twenty miles before it hits open water. That puts the glaciers perilously close to the ocean, with very little to hold them back.

On top of that, there were signs from expeditions made back in the 1950s that the ground deep beneath these Amundsen Sea glaciers seemed to have an unusual shape: from the coast going inland, it sloped downwards like the inside of a bowl.

This combination of warm seawater lapping up close to the glacier front, and underlying ground sloping downwards as it went inland, could be devastating. The point where the land ice goes offshore and starts to float acts like a hinge; the floating part moves up and down with the tides (and any other changes in sea level). If this hinge line started to retreat inwards, the seawater would follow it, flowing in and down the sides of the bowl beneath the land ice. This would reduce the resistance for the flowing land ice, so it would slide faster, so the hinge line would retreat further, moving inwards towards that central basin in what could be an unstoppable feedback. Back in the early 1980s, the Amundsen Sea Embayment was already being called the 'weak underbelly of Antarctica'.

And yet, there was no way to know for sure. This whole region of West Antarctica is appallingly hard to study. For one thing, it's perfectly positioned to evade scientific scrutiny. Although the Amundsen Sea Embayment is not much more than 1,000 km from the main British base on the Peninsula, that puts it just beyond the comfortable range of the British Antarctic Survey's Twin Otter aircraft. The Americans could reach that far with their ski-equipped Hercules planes, but McMurdo is further away, again just far enough to put it out of reach.

And even if it were closer to one or other of these major research centres, reaching it would still be challenging. The region's speeding glaciers – called Thwaites, Pine Island and Smith – fill the bay with icebergs and help choke it up with sea ice for eleven months of the year, deterring all but the bravest of captains from entering by ship. And the heavy snowfall that feeds these glaciers comes from clouds that sock the place in for most of the year, discouraging planes and fogging the vision of satellites that might otherwise have been able to take stock from space.

This mysterious third of the West Antarctic Ice Sheet couldn't have done a better job of keeping out of the scientific limelight if it had tried.

But then, in the 1990s, the European Space Agency launched the European Research Satellites (ERS-1 and -2). Unlike previous satellites, these carried radar instruments capable of firing radio waves through the clouds to reflect off the ice beneath. They also made two passes over the same piece of surface, about a month apart. By comparing the measurements from one pass to the next, researchers could derive a very accurate measurement not just of the height of the ice, but of changes in that height. If the ice were thinning, or if the hinge line were moving, the new satellites should be able to tell.

And they did. In the late 1990s NASA scientist Eric Rignot from the Jet Propulsion Laboratory in California put together images of the front end of Pine Island Glacier from 1992 to 1996. By looking for the places where the floating ice moved up and down with the tides, he managed to track the hinge line, the place where the glacier started to float. And he discovered that in just four years its hinge line had retreated inwards at more than a half mile per year.[9]

His paper, published in July 1998, caused a sensation. Other scientists pored over the satellite results, hastily publishing a blizzard of papers in all the best journals. And they all pointed to massive change in the Amundsen Sea Embayment: Pine Island Glacier's floating hinge line was indeed moving inland, and the grounded glacier itself was shrinking, losing nearly six feet of height per year. And it was moving faster every year. Thwaites Glacier's hinge line was also moving inland. And it was thinning, too. In fact, all the glaciers flowing into the Amundsen Sea were thinning. And Thwaites was getting steadily wider. And every year, more and more of the West Antarctic Ice Sheet was rushing out through that unwatched side door and tipping into the Amundsen Sea.[10]

If only one of the glaciers had been affected, it could have been something local – a particularly soft bed to slide on, or extra heat coming from below. But this synchronised thinning needed something more general, something from the outside. Eric suspected the oceans. He teamed up with two British scientists, Andy Shepherd and Duncan Wingham, to look at the satellite data from those small floating ice shelves just off shore.[11] They found that all three shelves in the bay showed that they had been getting thinner, by an impressive eighteen feet per decade.[12]

Marine geologist Stan Jacobs thought he knew why. Most of the seawater around Antarctica is very cold. The freezing air sucks warmth out of the surface waters, taking it close to 28°F, the point at which salty seawater can freeze. But deeper down is a band of warmer water, protected from that cold air, that hovers at a relatively toasty 34°F.

This warm deep water doesn't usually get a chance to approach the ice too closely. It is held back by a gigantic underwater shelf that skirts the entire continent. But in the Amundsen Sea there were a few weak points in this natural defence, channels gouged out in the sea floor in the past, when the ice sheet was bigger and the glaciers stretched out much farther than they do today. Back in 1994, Stan had managed to battle his way into Pine Island Bay by ship, and get up to the front of the Pine Island floating shelf. There he found that warm water had crept up through these channels and was lapping right up against the shelf, where it had no right to be.

Perhaps, then, it was this unusually warm water that was doing the damage. Still, the data from the 1994 cruise gave just one snapshot in time. In January 2009 Stan decided to go back, in the National Science Foundation's icebreaker, the *Nathaniel B. Palmer*. This time, he found the water near the shelf was warmer still, and the shelf was melting even more dramatically. Stan calculated that the melting rate had increased by 50 per cent in just fifteen years. But why?

With him on the ship was Adrian Jenkins from the British Antarctic Survey, who had already tried several times to get into Pine Island Bay. He was desperate to look underneath the ice with a specially designed autonomous submarine, Autosub3. This clever beast is twenty feet long, does not need to be tethered, and can go for more than thirty hours before having to return to the ship. It sends out sound waves to scan the ice above and the sea floor below. It can look into the darkest, murkiest, most inaccessible corners of the ocean beneath the ice, see things that no other instrument can see, and still come back when called. It is the hunting dog of the submarine world. And although nobody actually lives in it, it is also pleasingly yellow.

Dealing in autonomous subs is risky. They are unattached and beyond a couple of miles you have no way of speaking to them.

The Autosub engineers had already lost a previous prototype under a small ice shelf.

But if you want a true picture of what's going on under these ice shelves, you have to take the risk. The technicians from the National Oceanography Centre in Southampton, UK, who had lovingly designed and built this and the previous machines, could only give it instructions, release it from the ship – and hope.

At first the missions went well. The little yellow submarine sank below the waves, headed off to the Pine Island Ice Shelf, and chose a careful path underneath the ice, mapping the sea floor on the way out and the ice's underbelly on the way back. Three times it went, each time penetrating twenty miles – which was halfway along the shelf.

On 24 January came the final mission, the big one. In this, Autosub3 was to go as far as it could get, mapping the shelf all the way to the hinge line where the glacier started to float. This trip would be the most dangerous. The sub would have to decide for itself how far was too far, and turn back before the water was so shallow that it would be trapped. The researchers released it into the water, and for the next thirty-six hours they waited.

Autosub3 hummed along in the semi-darkness, broadcasting its sound waves, picking up and storing the echoes, making careful adjustments to stay a safe distance from both ice above and sea floor. Now it was beyond twenty miles, in uncharted waters, heading towards that hinge line where ice met water met mud. Closer it drew, broadcasting and receiving all the way, keeping a weather eye on the depth, until its instruments warned it that the water was only 650 feet deep. Time to turn. The sub safely rotated and rose up towards the ice to begin its journey home. Going out it had mapped the sea floor. Now it was supposed to study the underside of the ice shelf. That was OK. It knew how to stay safely 300 feet below the ice, how to keep out of trouble.

But something was wrong. Its collision avoidance system detected an obstacle ahead. Again, the sub knew what to do: retreat about a kilometre, adjust its direction slightly, and try a different route to avoid the obstacle. Back it motored and BANG! There was something behind. Collision avoidance needed. Move forward. CRASH! Backwards, forwards, the submarine barged helplessly, trapped inside a narrow ice fissure that its sonar hadn't detected and its brain couldn't understand. It was getting battered now, its fibreglass casings scratched, its aluminium wings bent and twisted. BANG! CRASH!

And then, something else kicked in. Luckily the engineers had programmed one last piece of wise advice into the Autosub's mental circuitry: 'If something isn't working, stop trying.' The sub finally admitted to itself that the collision avoidance strategy had hopelessly failed. It dropped deeper down into the water, and headed for home.[13]

The first the researchers knew of this drama was when they lifted the sub out of the water and saw how battered and bruised it was. But the data it contained was intact. And when put together with the data from the other missions, it showed something fascinating about the Pine Island Glacier Ice Shelf, something that would help explain why it was melting at such an astonishing rate.

There was a ridge. About halfway into the shelf a mound of sea floor, running parallel to the shelf front, rose up to within a few hundred metres of the overhead ice. When Stan rushed back and looked at satellite pictures from the 1970s of the ice shelf from above, he found a lump on the ice in exactly the same place. *But the lump wasn't there now.* The shelf must have been stuck on this ridge, pinned there, until the warm deep waters that had crept into the bay had melted enough of it away that it could float free. Now the warm water was unchecked. It had rushed into the far side of the shelf, right up to the hinge line, and was hollowing out a huge cavity, like a rotten tooth. No wonder the ice was melting and the hinge line receding.[14]

This is all very troubling. It's the first time ever that melting of ice on land has been directly connected to something in the outside world that we know is changing. As the world warms, the deep water around the fringes of Antarctica is already getting noticeably warmer, and models predict this will continue.[15] And the warmer the water, the more effectively it can eat away at the hinge lines of the Amundsen Sea glaciers, lowering the resistance of the ice shelves, and allowing the land ice behind them to accelerate into the sea.

So the seas are eating away at the Amundsen Sea glaciers from the coast. Now we need to know how far this can go. That depends on what's happening underneath the glaciers themselves. If the land beneath them really does slope downwards all the way to the interior then there would be nothing to stop this process eating all the way into the heart of the West Antarctic Ice Sheet.

Two research groups – one from the UK and one from the US – have recently shed light on this question, and the news is both good and bad. Veteran Antarctic glaciologists David Vaughan from the British Antarctic Survey and Don Blankenship from the University of Texas at Austin have long been studying their respective sides of the West Antarctic Ice Sheet. David probably knows more than anyone alive about the activities of the ice streams feeding the Ronne Ice Shelf, and Don has been studying the Siple Coast for decades. When they realised the problems with the Amundsen Sea Embayment, the two decided to join forces. Both had survey planes, bristling with instruments, capable of criss-crossing a body of ice and measuring its height, its thickness and what lies beneath. They would take the two planes to the inland part of the Thwaites/Pine Island area. David would study Pine Island Glacier. Don would study Thwaites. And they would put the answers together.

Since their camps were fairly far from the coast, the weather wasn't too bad, but the operation still stretched the resources of both Rothera and McMurdo. But the results justified the effort. The good news came from Pine Island. Though David discovered that the ground beneath this glacier did indeed slope downwards as it went inland, there was a natural limit. At a certain point, the land rose into a ridge. That meant the meltdown of the glacier could only go so far before geography would intervene. He calculated loss of all the ice in the vulnerable basin would lead to a global sea level rise of about eleven inches, which would be serious but not necessarily catastrophic. Moreover, the trunk of the glacier was confined to a trough, stopping it from getting any wider.[16]

However, the news from Don's investigations of the Thwaites Glacier wasn't quite so good. He found that there was nothing to stop Thwaites going all the way. Moreover, there was no trough beneath Thwaites, which means that it wasn't nearly as confined. Melting there could spill over, allowing seawater to flood into the apparently safe upper basin of the Pine Island Glacier, and even perhaps over to the ice streams on the Siple Coast.[17]

If the whole region collapsed in this way, we're now talking a sea level rise of about five feet. That's not as bad as the twelve feet originally feared. But when added to the sea level rise expected from melting ice in Greenland it would still be enough to cause death and destruction, particularly among the many millions living on low-lying deltas in the developing world.[18]

All this is very new and fresh and there is a lot left to learn. It matters, of course, how long the melting might take. If the world's seas rose by five feet within a few decades, that could be devastating. If it took centuries, we might be able to adapt. However, the news from Antarctica's weak underbelly is that change is defi-

nitely happening, and at a rate that otherwise conservative researchers find alarming.

The fate of the Amundsen Sea glaciers has become the hottest
topic in Antarctic research, tied up as it could be with the fate of
us all. And as we digest its implications, we could do well to
remember the experiences of the man who first flew over and
named this empty terrain more than seventy years ago. He had
his own way of assessing his adventures. I would summarise them
in this way: 'Learn what you can from Antarctica, but don't ever
underestimate it.'

Admiral Richard Byrd, soldier, aviator and explorer, was already
a hero in America when he arrived in Antarctica on 17 January
1934. He came from a proud Virginian family, and at the age of
twelve had travelled alone around the world, stopping to visit
family friends in outlandish outposts. As an adult he had fought
bravely in the First World War, flown across the Atlantic – just
barely scooped by Charles Lindbergh from being the first – and
flown to the North Pole.

Then he had come south where, on his previous expedition,
he had flown to the South Pole, and had flown over and mapped
much of West Antarctica. (He named the western part of the ice
sheet Marie Byrd Land in honour of his wife. It is so remote that
in spite of the attempts at land grabs by various nations before
the Antarctic Treaty came into force, nobody wanted this part,
and it remains the largest unclaimed territory on Earth.)

Byrd's plan this time was to spend the winter on the Ross Ice
Shelf, where he could sail in with his supplies yet still be within
flying distance of West Antarctica; when summer came he would
then continue exploring this great empty western ice sheet.

Most of his men were to pass the winter at a well-established
base that he called Little America, close to the coast. But Byrd
became consumed by the idea of establishing a small outpost a

hundred miles inland, where we now know that the Siple Coast ice streams spill out on to the shelf. Scientifically, he wanted to measure the inland weather through an Antarctic winter, and see if this could help explain the weather patterns at the coast. Personally, he was captivated by the idea of establishing the first inland wintering station on the continent.

So, he sent a tractor train limping south over the ice from Little America, skirting crevasse fields and feeling its way into the heart of the Barrier. They stopped about 130 miles from Little America, dug a great hole and sunk a prefabricated hut deep into the snow. But when the trip was delayed, making it impossible to do a second supply journey to equip the hut for the three occupants Byrd had originally envisaged, he promptly decided to be dropped off by plane and spend the winter there himself – alone.

Even today, it is hard to find yourself alone anywhere on the continent. For safety's sake the stations that I visited refused to let anyone out of sight of the camp without a companion. In Byrd's time, when there could be no possible hope of rescue if anything went wrong during the long polar night, his decision was extraordinary. Perhaps he was tired of all the effort and the adulation, the necessities of glad-handing and fundraising and being a society darling for rent the moment one expedition finished and he needed to pay off its debts and start planning the next.

He wrote:

> Out there on the South Polar barrier, in cold and darkness . . . I should have time to catch up, to study and think and listen to the phonograph; and for maybe seven months . . . I should be able to live exactly as I chose, obedient to no necessities but those imposed by wind and night and cold, and to no man's laws but my own. [19]

In the first few days, his only complaint was that he had forgotten to bring a cookbook. Never having had to cook anything for himself before, he was hamstrung. He wrote in his diary about the 'Corn Meal Incident' in which he overdid the amount of corn meal in a pan and induced a volcanic reaction. 'It oozed over the stove. It spattered the ceiling. It covered me from head to foot. If I hadn't acted resolutely, I might have been drowned in corn meal.' He grabbed the pan, rushed it to one of the storage tunnels and slammed it down, where it continued to spew until it froze.

Byrd recounted these incidents insouciantly to the men back in Little America on his thrice-weekly radio calls. He could hear their actual voices but he had to reply laboriously, spelling out his messages with the dots and dashes of Morse code. His men teased him about his incompetence with the code, especially when he was asked to broadcast a message live to the Chicago World's Fair, to be relayed via Little America and then somehow translated into a firework display. 'If the fireworks are supposed to spell out what you send,' his friend Charlie Murphy told him over the radio, 'then Chicago is in for the wildest display since the fire.'

Byrd and his men had a deal. If he missed more than one of the scheduled calls, they would try to reach him daily, and then start to worry. But there was surely nothing to worry about. Each day he would push open the wooden hatch of his shack and go up on to the Barrier to measure the temperature and winds. The first darkness had begun to come and go, with its stars and auroras, and sunsets. On 5 May, spellbound by one particular sunset, he wrote: 'I watched the sky a long time, concluding that such beauty was reserved for distant, dangerous places, and that nature has good reason for exacting her own special sacrifices from those determined to witness them.' He had no idea, then, of the sacrifice that he would be forced to make.

At first it was the near misses that began to alarm him. The time when he put his foot through a snow bridge near his radio antenna, and miraculously managed to throw himself the right way and avoid plummeting into a hidden crevasse; the time when he was absent-mindedly enjoying the sky and went beyond the edge of his flag lines, and just barely managed to find his way back to the hut; the time when he went up aloft in a blizzard and the hatch jammed behind him so that he had to work it desperately for an hour before he could make his way back to warmth, and safety.

And always he knew that if something went wrong there was no hope of rescue. Nobody would know there was a problem unless he missed several of his radio calls. Even if the tractors could then make it through the cold of the polar night, which was doubtful, they would certainly be too late to save him – and he had expressly forbidden his men from risking their lives in any such attempt.

But still Byrd must have thought that luck and the gods were with him, until he began to feel an insidious creeping depression, which came with an endless ache behind the eyes, and a sense of hopelessness that he couldn't shake. He wrote of how the loss of all the distractions of civilisation had been more of a wrench than he expected. He dragged himself through his tasks, all insouciance now gone.

Byrd didn't know it yet, but he was being poisoned. A last-minute adaptation of his stove to burn oil, rather than the coal it was designed for, meant that it was slowly leaking fumes of colourless, odourless, deadly carbon monoxide. The temperature up above frequently fell to -70°F. He needed his stove and insulated shack to survive. The stove was his enemy, but he could not live without it.

Soon, he was passing out, unable to swallow dribbles of hot milk without spewing it back up again, and lying on his bunk, too exhausted to clean up the mess. Somehow he managed to keep up his radio calls, cranking up the transmitter with the last of his strength, painfully spelling out jokes in Morse code in the hope that his friends back in Little America wouldn't notice the difference.

It was not even midwinter. The sun was three months away. In the past when he had been ill, he had wanted to be left by himself, but now he craved companionship and comfort. But he could not ask his friends for remote radio solace without arousing their suspicions and tempting them to risk themselves in a foolhardy attempt at rescue. Unlike Mawson, who had found himself without companions in a summer race against death because of unforeseen disaster, Byrd had chosen to be alone in the black heart of an Antarctic winter. He was very painfully aware of this: 'You asked for it, the small voice inside me said, and here it is.'[20]

He couldn't even convince himself that it had been worth it for the sake of the science. Who knew what those rolls of paper and lines of meteorological figures were worth? He berated himself for his hubris. By the middle of June, this once proud Virginian lay sobbing in his bunk, all strength and hope dissipated, his face turned to the wall. Now his only fear was for his men, for the fate of his expedition, and for his family back at home. He wrote last letters to them all.

But still he continued to drag himself up, still tried to force food down. He had figured out that the stove must be to blame and was doing without it for as long as possible each day. The pools of vomit on the floor now froze. Frost started creeping up the walls of his shack. And yet he cranked up his transmitter, sent coded messages to his men, tried to pretend for their sake, if not for his.

They knew him far too well to be fooled. At the end of June, one of his men told him they had been refurbishing the tractors and airily suggested that they could make a night journey to make measurements of meteorites after the weather had warmed a little, but before the sun returned to spoil the view. They could perhaps come his way, and use his shack for shelter before the return journey. Byrd was torn. Suddenly this held out the possibility of rescue, but how could he allow his men to risk their own lives to save his?

In the end he authorised the journey, to be started in the middle of July, though they had to turn back if there was any trouble finding the trail, or if the weather blew in. The hope revitalised Byrd, but twice this hope was crushed as he dragged himself up aloft to light beacons for the men. Several times he thought he saw an answering flash on the horizon, but it was always a star, or a mirage. After the second of these attempts he wrote in his diary how he had lit a magnesium flare 'making a tremendous blue hole in the night. It burned for about ten minutes. Then the darkness rushed in, and I was sensible of the ultimate meaning of loneliness.'[21] For each time he dragged himself back down again, it was only to hear on the radio that the men had had to turn back.

The third time, the word from Little America was good, and the tractors seemed to be getting through. For the last 30 miles, Byrd lost all contact, and with it most of his hope. But he continued to light the beacons, and then, at last, at long long last, there was an answering light that did not disappear; and a rumbling sound to break the silence of the Antarctic night; and the shadowy shape of a tractor; and three men who climbed out and solemnly shook his hand. 'Come on below,' Byrd said, 'I have a bowl of hot soup waiting for you.' Then he climbed down the ladder and collapsed.[22]

It was another two months before Byrd was strong enough to make the return journey to Little America. And some time after that before he trusted himself to resume flying over West

Antarctica to continue charting that unknown territory that even today remains both a mystery and a threat.

Byrd had learned his lesson – he would never again underestimate Antarctica. But it's not yet clear that we have learned ours. For as we belatedly scramble to understand the complex mechanisms driving the glaciers of West Antarctica, the continent has one more wild card to throw on to the table: not ice, but a huge reservoir of ready-melted, squirting, spouting water.[23]

Slawek Tulaczyk had never seen an ice stream in the flesh, let alone stood on one. He did all his analysis in his office, back home at the University of California, Santa Cruz. But after ten years of studying these great glaciers from afar he knew how they were supposed to behave. And something was definitely wrong. First there was the data from flights over two of the Siple Coast ice streams in 1998 and again in 2000. The planes had been firing lasers to measure the height of the ice. And for some reason the ice in 2000 seemed to be thirteen feet higher than in 1998. That was far too much to be explained by a bit of extra snowfall. Something had to be lifting the ice up from below.

Then some satellite data came in, showing ice heights and speeds in the same region in 1997. The satellite had made a couple of passes. And when he compared the data from 26 September with another twenty-four days later, Slawek found that some parts of the ice had slumped downwards by about half a metre, while other parts on a nearby stream had moved either up or down. 'You look at that and ask yourself why? How can you change the ice surface so fast?' he says. There was only one explanation that either he or anyone else could think of.

Water. It had to be water, squirting beneath the ice streams, filling up hollows and emptying them again, lifting the ice like a jack beneath a car, then allowing it to fall as the water moved on.[24]

How could that be? Close to its surface, much of the ice sheet is colder than -58°F. Beneath this hard outermost face could there really be so much water squirting and lifting and pouring?

Slawek's idea might have seemed crazy, but for a parallel set of discoveries that had been taking place ever since the 1960s. Beneath Antarctica's mantle, in the deep dark places where ice met rock, it seemed that there were entire districts of hidden, liquid lakes. Nobody had ever seen or touched one of these lakes; they were buried under miles of ice and hadn't seen daylight for hundreds of thousands, perhaps millions of years. But researchers knew they were there thanks to the way ice can't help but betray its roots.

The surface of ice always shows a little of the topography that it is resting on. If there's a mountain down below, the ice surface will reveal its presence with a bump. If there's a valley, the surface will have a dip. And if there's a lake, there will be no topography at all. The lake water will be flat, and so will the ice floating above it. To find a hidden lake, you just need to find a large surface patch of completely flat ice.

And researchers have now found hundreds of them. Perhaps it shouldn't have been surprising. After all, the pressure of the overhead ice, and the heat coming from inside the Earth were together enough to take the ice to its melting point. All you then need is a suitable hollow or basin in the rock for the water to collect in and you have your lake. But still, the sheer number of these lakes has changed the way many researchers view the continent.

The current tally is nearly four hundred under-ice lakes, some of them huge.[25] The first showed up back in the 1960s and as satellite data replaced laborious local flights more are showing up all the time. There are several under Concordia Station, at least one near the South Pole, and the crown jewel is beneath Vostok

Station – a body of water the area of Lake Ontario but twice as deep, making it the seventh largest freshwater lake in the world.[26]

All this was intriguing enough, and many scientists had been itching to drill down into these lakes and see if they might contain some form of life. But nobody had thought they might be interconnected. Or at least, not until now.

It could have been a one-off. But then Duncan Wingham, who was using satellite data to measure the height of Pine Island Ice Shelf, noticed that a patch of ice in East Antarctica seemed to have lurched downwards by three metres. At the same time, several lakes nearby seemed to be filling up, each by about a metre. Duncan tracked the satellite data for more than a year as an invisible river the size of the Thames drained one lake and filled two more.[27]

And then in May 2006, just after Duncan's paper was published, Helen Amanda Fricker from Scripps Institute of Oceanography found that over a two-year period part of the Siple Coast ice had dropped by *thirty feet*. What's more, the region that had fallen was also flat. She had discovered a new lake, and the lake was emptying. Now she mapped the rest of the Siple Coast and found fourteen more areas where the ice was falling or rising, as water shifted beneath.[28]

This was happening everywhere! All over the continent it seemed that hidden lakes were filling and emptying and water was sloshing about with abandon. It was presumably moving for the same sorts of reasons that water moves around on the Earth's surface: one lake would fill to overflowing and the water would spill 'down' to the next one. But 'down' didn't necessarily mean the same thing here. Because of the intense pressure it exerts, the ice sheet overhead counts for far more than local hills and valleys when it comes to deciding where water should flow. So in the wacky world of Antarctica's underside there were lakes sloping down mountainsides, and waterfalls squirting uphill.

But what really shocked glaciologists was the speed of it all. Nothing beneath the ice was supposed to be able to change that quickly. Don Blankenship summed up the mood of the moment: 'This thing that takes millions of years to change is being tickled by a process that happens on a timescale of months. I don't think anyone has yet been able to swallow what that means.'

And it's not just lakes. A student of Don's, Sasha Carter, has now discovered a whole new set of almost-lakes that he thinks may be marshes or wetlands. They are flat like the lakes, but their surfaces are rough. He calls them 'fuzzy' lakes and thinks they could have patches of land poking through the water to prevent them being smooth. These under-ice wetlands could be regularly flooded by overflows from the regular lakes, and then pass the water on down the line.[29]

In fact, the latest calculations suggest that all the water in under-ice marshes could make the underside of Antarctica the world's largest wetland. If the numbers are right, there is more water trapped in sediments beneath the ice than in all the rivers, lakes, ponds and puddles on the rest of the planet.[30]

That's astonishing, but it should also be worrying. 'Remember, this is the lubricant that's moving around,' says Don. 'If it's down there it's slippery, and we don't know where the ice sheet's ticklish spots are.'

For instance, Leigh Stearns from the University of Maine has found that Byrd Glacier in East Antarctica speeded up for a year, and that its acceleration coincided exactly with the draining of a nearby under-ice lake.[31] And Robin Bell from Lamont Doherty Earth Observatory in New York found several lakes at the onset of one of the fast-moving ice streams in East Antarctica – the Recovery Glacier, which flows out into the Weddell Sea. She believes the presence of the lakes has set the glacier sliding so quickly, by providing the sediments beneath with the water they need.[32]

'Antarctica has two faces,' Robin says. 'It has the face it shows to the world and it has the one on the inside. And the inside face could be the one that really matters.'

I still can't get my head around this. This continent that is so forbidding, and cold, and dry, and slow, has a soft warm heart? While nothing changes on the outside, down below is a vital world of rise and fall, give and take, water slipping and sliding from place to place, perhaps taking the ice with it. The implications for us might be grave. Perhaps the ice is more vulnerable than we realised. Perhaps this vibrant inner life will boost our own activities and help send the ice sliding into the sea.

Of course that's troubling. But I can't help being intrigued. What would it be like to see that hidden face? To be down in the dark among the lakes and wetlands and floods and uphill waterfalls?

It turns out that there is one place where Antarctica's icy mask has slipped, back in the Dry Valleys of Antarctica, the home of Lake Hoare and Beacon Valley, and Battleship Promontory. This is the landscape so otherworldly that NASA scientists go there to imagine Mars; and where the life has found such extreme ways to survive – under lake ice, inside rocks, in holes on the tops of glaciers – that biologists use it to study what alien life might be like. But this dry and ancient terrain also bears the signs of something much closer to home.

'Do you see these channels? Do you see them? That big channel coming down there, and those scooped-out benches, and the ripples on top where the water went over. That's a huge empty waterfall. You're standing at the top of a Niagara Falls!'

George Denton, from the University of Maine, is a veteran of veterans when it comes to Antarctica. His expertise is interpreting glacial landscapes, picking up clues like a forensic scientist, deducing what has gone before. He has been doing this for decades, and he knows the Dry Valleys probably better than he knows his own hand.

He worked long ago with Dave Marchant – whom I met in Beacon Valley looking for ancient ice and ash layers to date. In fact, George *taught* him how to do it back in the days when Dave was a fresh-faced student and George was his Ph.D. adviser. Dave and George are both now convinced that the Dry Valleys were once not nearly as dry as they are today. And on a late, late January night, when sensible people back in McMurdo were in bed, and the shadows were low and long, George had brought me out here to the valleys by helicopter to show me why.

It was a spectacular journey. From our refuelling stop at Marble Point, just across the Sound from McMurdo, we passed over the flat grey ice of Lake Fryxel, and climbed up Canada Glacier with its smooth snow and tumbled blue crevasses. And then we were high in the Asgard Range, turning and weaving between the rows of chocolate-coloured peaks. George was in the co-pilot seat, taking photograph after photograph through the helicopter's bulbous windows. I was sitting behind, holding on, when the voice of Gregg Leibert, the pilot, came into my headphones:

'Don't worry. I'm not going to fly into a mountain.'

'Please don't.'

'I never like doing that.'

And then on we went, skimming above this gigantic landscape with its sepia-toned mountains and valleys and ice. We crossed the Olympus Range,[33] and the vast expanse of Mackay Glacier, before stopping here on the great sandstone cliffs of Battleship Promontory.

This was where Chris McKay found his green streaks of life, hidden inside the rocks. But the surfaces of these rocks hid another secret, on a much grander scale. George had brought me to see the carved signature of a massive, almost unimaginable, under-ice flood.

The pale sandstone cliff that we were standing on disappeared in a precipitous edge a few metres away. I craned my neck to see where the dry rock plunged down more than 3,000 feet.

'I wouldn't like to go over this in a barrel,' I said.

'Can you see?' George said eagerly. 'Can you see how it's a waterfall? You see what's over the edge here? All the potholes at the bottom? And the ripples leading off from it? And all those conical hills down there? There's a big huge rippled terrain that goes all the way down to the sea. Shhhrrrrooom!'

And then he gave a satisfied sigh. 'Spectacular isn't it? It looks like it's been bombed by B52s.'

It was certainly dramatic. And, yes, even to my inexpert eyes those bombed-out potholes were clear as day. 'How do they form?' I asked. 'From the water,' George said. 'Water has come along those channels, right behind where the helicopter is, and it's spilled over and formed a plunge pool and another plunge pool and it just keeps on going. And there are thousands of them in these mountains.'

We walked to the other side of the cliff where the drop looked more like a scree slope, leading to yet more gigantic pits and potholes. 'See how it looks like the Washington State scablands,' said George, 'like Dry Falls, and the Grand Coulee.'

I hadn't seen the scablands but I knew about them. A vast area of Washington State in the US has terrain that baffled geologists for decades. It looks, apparently, as if some frenzied giant had scooped out chunks of land and flung them around. We now know that the scablands formed during the last ice age, when a finger of the ice sheet that covered much of Canada crept round and dammed a gigantic lake formed from meltwater. The lake built up and built up until eventually it burst through in a catastrophic flood. That, believed George, was more or less what happened here.

'A landscape eroded by floods looks just like this. It has scoop-like features all over, it has ripples in the top, it has lots of potholes and channel systems, it has coulees like this, it has conical hills like you see right at the end. None of those are typical of glaciated landscapes. This is completely different.'

'OK,' I said. 'I can see that it looks like it was made by water. But how do you know the water was under ice?'

'We can trace these channels a long way,' George replied. 'We've tracked individual ones with helicopters and they don't just go down. They go up over mountains that are two thousand metres high. Ice is the only explanation we have for how to force water up over a mountain range.'

So here it was. The dried-out cataract I was standing beside wasn't just an ex-Niagara. It was part of a network of waterfalls that were forced uphill by the weight of a massive overhead ice sheet, churning and rushing and carving out the landscape as they ran. This was Antarctica's hidden face, laid bare.

We had maybe half an hour of ground time here so the three of us headed off to the side of the scree slope and started to scramble down the ex-waterfall. As usual in Antarctica the distances were deceptive. These potholes were huge: a hundred feet deep, with sheer cylindrical sides. I could see now that they usually occurred where channels crossed; the confluence must have created huge whirlpools, focusing the water's energy and making it rip into the rock.

From the size of the channel, and of the lumps it ripped out of the rock, Dave Marchant has calculated that the water must have been travelling at up to 30 mph. And there must have been a lot of it. A few years ago people might have been sceptical, asking where the water could have come from. But we know now, of course, that there is plenty of water to be had beneath Antarctica's frozen exterior. It would only have taken a flood from one Lake Vostok, or perhaps one and a half, to carve out the channels scattered through these mountains.

There were other signs that there must have been ice overhead when the water ran here. In some places a channel stopped abruptly as if it had run out of steam. That could happen if racing, rushing water met a place where the ice was frozen to the bedrock. The water wouldn't be stopped; it would force open cracks in the ice and spurt up into the overhead glacier. In other places there were 'hanging tributaries', where water had been pirated away from a channel, leaving it high and dry while the others eroded around it. It was one of the most spectacular landscapes I had ever seen.

On the way home, we flew over another dramatic signature of past flooding here: the Labyrinth, at the head of Wright Valley. To the south was the gleaming white edge of the polar plateau, held back for the most part by mountainous cliffs; just one wide strand of ice had managed to spill over the precipitous drop and spread its skirts to form Wright Upper Glacier. Long thin channels of ice radiated out from the sides of this glacier, like scars against the brown dolorite rock of the valley floor. And beyond those lay the Labyrinth itself, a tortuous landscape of yet more interlocking channels, the raised parts glowing golden brown in the midnight sun, the hollows in shadow. 'Look down here,' George told me through the headphones, though I was already looking. 'Can you see the cataracts and potholes? Just imagine the waterfalls cascading down.'

Dave Marchant has been working hard on the Labyrinth, tracing its complex interrelationships and peeling back its layers of history. He and George have carefully charted different parts of the channel systems in the Dry Valleys. They have worked out which cuts through what, separated out the older features from the younger, used volcanic ashes to date different layers and figure out what happened when. They agree that this landscape is incredibly old. There was probably a series of floods, but the last one took place somewhere between twelve and fourteen million years ago, and almost nothing has happened since.[34]

That fits the history of this mighty ice sheet. The cut-off came just about the time when the tundra was disappearing from the land, and the ice sheet was making its transition from one that was warm and wet and temperate to one that was frozen to the rock. It was also, probably, larger than it is today, over-reaching itself before settling back. And as parts of it froze to the bed, that could have been what dammed the shifting water beneath until it was powerful enough to burst out of its prison.

Floods like this wouldn't happen often, but, when they did, they would make themselves felt. Beyond carving out the rock, one of these mega floods wouldn't have raised global sea levels by much when it finally spilled into the Ross Sea. Perhaps it would have added a centimetre or two. But according to Dave, it might nonetheless have tweaked a sensitive spot when it comes to climate.

That's because the Ross Sea is one of the key parts of the global conveyor belt, an interdependent set of ocean currents that carries heat around the planet in a complex pattern that evens out some of the imbalances between the overheated tropics and the frozen poles. As sea ice forms here, the remaining water becomes saltier, and heavier, and sinks down to set the conveyor in motion. Throw in a sudden lens of freshwater on the top and you could jeopardise the whole thing. And though Dave can't prove it, he noticed that there were a few uncomfortable climate shifts that took place just around the time that the Dry Valley cataracts were being carved.

Luckily for us, this hasn't happened for at least twelve million years, and is unlikely to happen again any time soon. But there is one final twist to this story. Marine geologist John Anderson has found another Labyrinth-like feature in the ocean floor. And is it in a sensitive spot? John's underwater labyrinth is right in the middle of . . . Pine Island Bay, the place where, thanks in part to our own human ways of making and using energy, the warming water is eating away at the ice – and potentially opening the floodgates.

We don't know if or when there will be another mega flood around the coast of this mysterious continent, though researchers are learning more about it every day. Nor have we yet decided whether we humans will act to help the melting ice or hinder it. What we do know is that this icy landscape hasn't always been so listless and lifeless. And now it seems the warmth is coming back. Of course, there is a very long way to go before Antarctica will be steamy and tropical again, but that is the path we are currently taking.[35] The Peninsula is already warming much more quickly than it should, and there are now the first signs that the rest of the continent is warming, too, with a signal that researchers have identified as both unnatural, and human.[36]

Thanks to the efforts of science we know a lot about how the continent is today. If you are reading this book in the northern summer, male emperor penguins are now huddling together somewhere in the lee of an ice cliff, taking turns to protect their fellows from the wind, taking care to keep each egg safely balanced on their feet, waiting for the return of the sunlight, and their mates, and the chance to eat again.

If you are reading in the northern winter, the sun is now shining over the continent. Snow petrels are jealously fighting for their rocky nests. Adélies are busily rushing through their short summer window for reproducing themselves, and scientists are just as busily making their pinprick marks on the vast continent, gleaning what they can from the ice.

And on the Peninsula, the ice is melting, the shelves weakening, while warming water laps perilously at the West Antarctic Ice Sheet's soft underside.

But what about the future? To some extent that's down to us.

Though the whaling industry will never return on any scale, if some great new opportunity came up to exploit the continent, the treaty accords might well disintegrate, leaving everyone to revert to being very much for themselves.

This scenario is unlikely, though, because Antarctica itself would make it so very hard. Less than 1 per cent of the continent is free of ice. If oil grew scarce enough in the rest of the world that seeking it in Antarctica became attractive, it might be possible to drill offshore – though the icebergs would always be a threat. Onshore, the challenge would be all but insurmountable.

And even if you could drill here, the power of Antarctica to change people's mentalities might still prevail. It was in Antarctica that British scientists discovered the hole in our protective ozone layer, which led first to denial and confusion, but then to spectacular international cooperation as the chemicals doing the damage were globally banned and the hole began to recover.

Perhaps the steadying influence of this inhuman continent will help us all to tip the balance from smash and grab to human solidarity. I hope so. Because if we continue to pour out the gases that are warming our world, the melting will continue, and the seas will rise. If we stop, we can probably avert some or all of this danger. Our choice.

Two of the men the ice took to the edge, and who recorded their experience, discovered something important in the final analysis. When Richard Byrd lay sobbing in his bunk, and then wrote what he thought would be his last letter to his wife, he suddenly remembered the final entry in Scott's diary, which had been scrawled over the rest: 'For God's sake, look after our people!' Byrd had thought about this before, but only intellectually. Now he understood completely. He wrote: 'It seemed a pity that men must undergo a cataclysmic experience to perceive this simplest of truths.'[37]

Jake Speed, the South Pole winterer, said that, too. After I met him, he spent a season up in the north in Greenland, and found himself trapped out in a storm with no survival gear. Jake made it through three days of hell before he was rescued. He lost both legs and one arm. He says he survived by thinking of his new wife and family and friends.[38] In the end, what really matters to us is our people.

So there it is. You go to the end of the Earth and you find . . . a mirror, a truism, something you should have known all along; or perhaps you did know it the way Richard Byrd knew it, intellectually. But now, after Antarctica, it's in your gut.

And when I think of all the things the people there told me, I realise that the other lessons that Antarctica has thrown up all point this same way: it is only when you are forced to rely overtly on the people around you – and people in far-off bases who you'll never meet – that you remember how fully we rely on each other back in the real world. It can take being in pure emptiness to remind you to let go of your hubris; and it can take being blocked by the power of nature to remind you how precarious our existence is and how tenuous and temporary our mastery.

Some find this frightening, but I take a strange kind of comfort from knowing that this patient and implacable continent doesn't care what we think or do. It will yield warnings if we seek them. We can avert human catastrophe if we act on them. But Antarctica itself is under no threat.

That, in the end, is what I love most about it. Antarctica is bigger than all of us, bigger than our technologies, our human strengths and weaknesses, our eagerness to build and our capacity to destroy. Enough ice could slide into the sea to turn West Antarctica into an island archipelago, and to raise the sea to heights that would swamp coastal cities, without causing so much as a flutter in the continent's cool white heart.

And even when all of the ice finally does melt that will not be the end of Antarctica. The Sun is naturally warming as it ages, and some distant day, perhaps millions of years in the future, the white continent will turn green again no matter what we do. When this happens, as it must, we humans will probably not be there to witness it. But someone or something else surely will.

TIMELINE

100 million years ago: Antarctica drifts over the South Pole and settles there, as part of a massive supercontinent, which is already breaking apart. Concentrations of greenhouse gases in the atmosphere are much higher than those of today, and the Earth is about 18°F warmer.

66 million years ago: dinosaurs become extinct following a massive asteroid strike, and mammals take over Antarctica's lush forests. Atmospheric levels of greenhouse gases are falling, and the Earth is gradually cooling.

40–35 million years ago: Australia and South America are the last pieces of the supercontinent to break away from Antarctica. The continent is now isolated by circular oceanic currents, which encourage further cooling.

34 million years ago: the first large ice sheets appear on the continent.

14 million years ago: following yet more cooling, the ice sheets become extensive and permanent. From now on, in the interior of the Dry Valleys, time stands still.

1773: Captain James Cook and his crew cross the Antarctic Circle.

1820: Russian naval officer Captain Fabian Gottlieb von

Bellingshausen and his expedition crews aboard the *Vostok* ('East') and the *Mirny* ('Peaceful') see the first Antarctic land.

1821: sealer Captain John Davis is the first person to set foot on the continent.

1898: Belgian naval officer Baron Adrien de Gerlache and his crew survive the first Antarctic winter on their trapped ship, the *Belgica*. On board is a young Norwegian explorer named Roald Amundsen, who will later return to the continent to lead the first team to the South Pole.

1899: Anglo-Norwegian explorer Carsten Egeberg Borchgrevink leads the first expedition to winter on the continental mainland. His glowing report of the endeavour does not match the secretly kept diaries of some of his discontented team members, who write in sarcastic terms of his leadership abilities. The expedition ends in acrimony.

1901–2: British team comprising Captain Robert Scott, Edward Wilson and the Anglo-Irish explorer Ernest Shackleton makes the first attempt to walk to the South Pole, but reaches only 82°17' S.

1909: Shackleton and three other men are the first to climb up on to the Antarctica plateau and reach a new farthest south, but are forced to turn back through lack of food just a hundred miles from the Pole.

December 1911: Amundsen and four companions become the first men to reach the South Pole.

January 1912: Scott and his three companions reach the South Pole, having come second in the race.

February–March 1912: all five members of Scott's polar party die on their way back to the coast.

1912: Australian geologist and explorer Douglas Mawson leads a scientific expedition to Terre Adélie Land, which becomes the first to establish radio contact between Antarctica and another continent, and the first to find an Antarctic meteorite. During a sledging journey to the far east of the base, Mawson's two companions die, one of them by falling into a crevasse that also swallows most of the food and equipment. In a spectacular feat of endurance Mawson manages to survive and return to base, only to see his ship disappearing over the horizon, leaving him stranded on the continent for another winter.

1915–16: Shackleton makes a new attempt on an Antarctic record, this time hoping to be the first to cross the continent on foot. However, his ship, the *Endurance*, is crushed in the Weddell Sea. Shackleton's men end up trapped on Elephant Island, while he and five others successfully sail to South Georgia in a small open boat to seek help – achieving one of the greatest boat journeys ever made. Shackleton then leads the rescue of all the remaining stranded men.

1929: US Admiral Richard Byrd and three companions are the first to fly over the South Pole.

1934: Byrd sets up a small inland base on the Ross Ice Shelf for meteorological studies, which he mans alone for the entire winter. He nearly dies from carbon monoxide poisoning, and although he tries to keep his illness secret from the team at the coast, they eventually rescue him just before the return of the sun.

1935: Caroline Mikkelsen, the wife of a Norwegian whaling captain, goes ashore briefly and becomes the first woman to set foot on the continent.

1947–8: Jennie Darlington and Edith (Jackie) Ronne, both wives of explorers, become the first women to spend a winter on the continent.

1954: Australian Mawson base is established – now the oldest continuously occupied station south of the Antarctic Circle.

1956: US station McMurdo founded on Ross Island, beside the site of Scott's first hut.

1957–8: International Geophysical Year, a scientific project involving all major countries with the exception of China, triggers intense scientific interest in Antarctica. This is the dawn of the age of science on the continent. The Russian Vostok and American South Pole stations are both founded on the high plateau of the East Antarctic Ice Sheet. During this period, the British Commonwealth Transantarctic expedition led by Vivian Fuchs finally succeeds in crossing the continent from the Weddell Sea to the Ross Sea, via the Pole, more than forty years after Shackleton made his abortive attempt.

1961: the Antarctic Treaty, initially signed by twelve nations, comes into force. The treaty puts all existing claims for land on hold, and pledges to use Antarctica only for scientific studies and peaceful purposes.

1969: American researchers discover antifreeze in the blood of Antarctic fish. This is also the year that six women who have just been allowed into the American programme are flown from the coast to the South Pole for a photo opportunity. Stepping off the plane, they link arms so that all six of them become the 'first' women there.

1978: Emilio Marcos Palma is the first baby to be born on the continent, at Argentine station Esperanza on the Antarctic Peninsula.

1979: the first Martian meteorite is found on the continent – though it is not initially recognised as such.

1981: the first lunar meteorite anywhere in the world is discovered on the continent. Until now, scientists had not believed that rocks could arrive on Earth from other large planetary bodies. This find triggers a re-evaluation of previous ones the world over, revealing that a whole category of previously unidentified meteorites have in fact come to us from the planet Mars.

1985: British scientists working at Halley Station on the Ronne Ice Shelf report a hole in the ozone layer over Antarctica.

1986: the first dinosaur in Antarctica is found by Argentine scientists on James Ross Island.

1994: the last dogs leave the continent. From now, in accordance with the Antarctic Treaty, the only non-native species permitted on the continent are humans.

1995: American researchers report the discovery of buried ice in the Dry Valleys that is at least eight million years old and yet is still frozen solid.

1996: Russian drillers at Vostok Station halt their ice core at a depth of 12,000 feet, to avoid contaminating the lake beneath. The longest ice core ever drilled – until it was surpassed in 2010 by the West Antarctic Ice Sheet core – Vostok contains the records of four full ice ages and shows a very tight correlation between temperature and greenhouse gases such as carbon dioxide.

1998: American researchers report satellite results showing that ice in the Amundsen Sea sector of the West Antarctic Ice Sheet is retreating at an alarming rate. A blizzard of papers follows, showing that this large area of the continent is indeed the 'weak underbelly of Antarctica'.

2002: the Larsen B Ice Shelf, an area of ice the size of the US state of Rhode Island, shatters in spectacular fashion, triggering fears that the Antarctic ice is responding to global warming. American researchers find that this has not happened for at least 10,000 years.

2004: European consortium EPICA halts its ice core drilling at Dome C. Though the core is slightly shorter than that of Vostok, it goes back farther, through eight complete ice age cycles. Tiny bubbles of ancient air trapped in the core confirm the tight connection between higher levels of greenhouse gases and higher temperatures, and show that levels of CO_2 in the atmosphere today are higher than they have been for at least 800,000 years. This is also the year that contract worker Jake Speed becomes the first person to spend five winters at the South Pole. Though his record has since been surpassed, he remains the only person to have spent five successive winters there.

2005: French-Italian Concordia Station is occupied for its first winter. Concordia becomes the first new wintering station on the polar plateau in almost fifty years. Separately, American researchers discover that the continent has a hidden face. They find that the hundreds of lakes underlying the Antarctic ice are not isolated, but are interconnected by channels and waterfalls; many of the lakes appear to be continually filling and emptying, with rushes of water that could destabilise large parts of the ice sheet.

2005: temperature records from many stations confirm that the Antarctic Peninsula has warmed by nearly 5°F over the previous fifty years, which is more than three times the global average.

2009: China establishes a summer-only station called Kunlun at Dome A in the Antarctic interior, with the intention of drilling a new ice core to probe even further into Antarctica's buried climate records.

2011: the American WAIS Divide project retrieves the continent's deepest ever ice core, and one of the few from the West Antarctic Ice Sheet. They hope it will reveal much more about the history and likely fate of this highly vulnerable ice sheet.

GLOSSARY

ANSMET: the Antarctic Search for Meteorites, a programme for seeking meteorites on the continent.

Antarctic 10: a person of the opposite sex who would rate a 5 back in the real world.

Antarctic Treaty: a treaty regulating ownership and use of the entire Antarctic continent, which came into force in 1961, and has now been signed by forty-nine nations. The treaty sets aside the continent as a scientific preserve and bans commercial exploitation and military activity.

Barrier: early explorers' name for the Ross Ice Shelf.

Boomerang: a flight from New Zealand to McMurdo Station that has to turn around at the Point of Safe Return because of poor weather at the landing site.

Bunny boots: large white (or sometimes blue) boots that look like space boots and are adapted with layers of insulation for extremely cold weather.

Cat or snow cat: snow dozer or tractor with caterpillar tracks.

Comms: communications – a central part of Antarctic operations.

Cosmic Microwave Background (CMB): the faint afterglow of the birth of the Universe, the Big Bang, which is invisible to human eyes but still pervades the sky.

DDU: Dumont d'Urville, the main French base on the Adélie coast.

EPICA: European Project for Ice Coring in Antarctica, involving two deep ice cores, one at Dome C and one in Dronning Maud Land.

Fingee: the pronunciation of 'FNG', which stands for 'fucking new guy (girl)'.

Freshies: fresh fruit and vegetables – which are worth more than gold in Antarctica.

Galley: common name for dining area in bases and camps, derived from early naval logistics support on the continent.

Helo: helicopter.

Herc or Hercules: C-130 military transport aircraft used extensively by the US programme in Antarctica for long-distance flights. Other operations use Hercs to fly on to the continent using wheels on sea-ice runways, but only the United States has the technology to attach skis to the planes, and therefore to use Hercs in the interior.

Ice sheet: a thick layer of ice covering a very extensive area of land; currently the only remaining large ice sheets in the world are the three that lie on Greenland, East Antarctica and West Antarctica. If any or all of these melt substantially they would dump very large amounts of water into the oceans, raising sea levels significantly around the world.

Ice shelf: a region of floating ice, where a glacier has spilled out into the sea but not yet broken up to form icebergs. Antarctica has large numbers of smaller ice shelves, and two very large ones – the Ross Ice Shelf (also known as the Barrier) and the Ronne Ice Shelf, which are each approximately the same size as France.

Ice stream: very large and wide glaciers, typically more than a kilometre deep and up to 50 km wide, which move extremely quickly and drain ice from the centre of the ice sheets down to the sea.

Jamesway: long half-cylindrical tent with two layers of tarpaulin and a wooden floor, usually heated with stoves. This is often used as a communal space in larger camps, or as sleeping accommodation.

Knots: a nautical measure of speed for winds or ship travel. One knot is equivalent to 1.85 kmph.

Mactown: a nickname for McMurdo Station, the US headquarters in Antarctica.

Mattrack: a strange-looking Antarctic vehicle that resembles a pick-up truck but has triangular wheels with caterpillar tracks that grip on to sea ice.

Medevac: contraction of 'medical evacuation': an emergency flight out for someone who is gravely ill or injured.

Ob Hill: Observation Hill, a volcanic cinder cone overlooking McMurdo Station.

Pack or pack ice: tightly packed sea ice.

Sastrugi (sing. sastruga): wave-like ridges of snow built up by the wind.

Scott tent: pyramid-shaped tent based on Captain Robert Falcon Scott's original design, usually intended to accommodate two people plus a stove for cooking.

Sea ice: frozen ocean, usually much thinner and more fragile than land ice.

Skidoo: a common means of individual transportation on snow, which looks like a motorbike on skis. It can also be used to tow sledges.

Snow dozer: like a bulldozer, but for snow.

300 Club: to belong to this, you need to have passed, naked, through a temperature change of 300°F (149°C). Typically, you start in a sauna at 200°F (93°C) before going outside wearing only bunny boots and a mask and walking a set distance in -100°F (-73°C). This is only possible while wintering in the coldest parts of the continent − principally the South Pole − and it's a very exclusive club.

'Toast': Antarctic slang for the mental instability that affects most people who spend the winter there, as in 'going toast' or being 'toasty'.

Twin Otter (or 'Otter'): a twin-engine, propeller aircraft famous for its rugged construction, reliability and ability to take off and land on short runways. Designed for remote environments, Twin Otters can be equipped with skis or wheels, and can get into Antarctic field sites that larger planes only dream of.

Winter-over: to spend the entire winter on the continent.

NOTES

Introduction

1. https://www.comnap.aq/facilities/antarctic_stations
2. Jonathan L. Bamber, Riccardo E. M. Riva, Bert L. A. Vermeersen and Anne M. LeBroq, 'Reassessment of the Potential Sea-Level Rise from a Collapse of the West Antarctic Ice Sheet', *Science*, vol. 324, 2009, pp. 901–3.

1. Welcome to Mactown

1. This vehicle has its name 'Ivan the Terra Bus' stencilled on the side. Nobody in Antarctica seems to be able to resist puns.
2. Huntford, *Race to the South Pole*, p. 39.
3. http://www.nsf.gov/dir/index.jsp?org=OPP
4. Sam has an excellent website describing his work at http://www.bowserlab.org/antarctica/
5. There's a spectacular, though disturbing, BBC video of ribbon worms feeding on a dead seal in McMurdo Sound: http://news.bbc.co.uk/earth/hi/earth_news/newsid_8378000/8378512.stm
6. Named after the great Australian scientist and explorer Douglas Mawson.
7. Stephanie B. Suhr, Stephen P. Alexander, Andrew J. Gooday, David W. Pond and Samuel S. Bowser, 'Trophic modes of large Antarctic foraminifera: roles of carnivory, omnivory, and detritivory', *Marine Ecology Progress Series*, vol. 371, 2008, pp. 155–64.
8. From the US Antarctic Program newspaper, the *Antarctic Sun,* available at http://antarcticsun.usap.gov/features/contenthandler.cfm?id=1946
9. You can hear some of these sounds here: http://www.antarctica.gov.au/about-antarctica/fact-files/animals/sounds-of-antarctic-wildlife
10. K. M. Proffitt, J. J. Rotella and R. A. Garrott, 'Effects of pup age, maternal

age, and birth date on pre-weaning survival rates of Weddell seals in Erebus Bay, Antarctica', *Oikos*, vol. 119, 2010, pp. 1255–64.

11. K. M. Proffitt, R. A. Garrott and J. J. Rotella, 'Long-term evaluation of body mass at weaning and postweaning survival rates of Weddell seals in Erebus Bay, Antarctica', *Marine Mammal Science*, vol. 24, 2008, pp. 677–89.

12. Gillian Louise Hadley, *Recruitment Probabilities and Reproductive Costs for Weddell Seals in Erebus Bay, Antarctica*, Ph.D. Thesis, Montana State University, Montana, April 2006. Available at: http://etd.lib.montana.edu/etd/2006/hadley/HadleyG0506.pdf. See also Kelly Michelle Proffitt, *Mass Dynamics of Weddell Seals in Erebus Bay, Antarctica*, Ph.D. Thesis, Montana State University, Montana, March 2008. Available at http://etd.lib.montana.edu/etd/2008/proffitt/ProffittK0508.pdf

2. The March of the Penguins

1. David has an excellent website describing his penguin work, at http://www.penguinscience.com/

2. The letter B signifies that the berg broke off between 90°W and 180°W, it was the fifteenth named that year, and it was called 'a' because the original B15 then broke up into fragments of which this one was the largest.

3. Riffenburgh, *Nimrod*, p. 25.

4. Ibid., p. 226.

5. Ibid., p. 226.

6. Ibid., p. 260.

7. Ibid., p. 107.

8. One website offered a reward for anyone who could track this original advert down. You can follow the results here: http://www.antarctic-circle.org/advert.htm

9. Apsley Cherry-Garrard, *The Worst Journey in the World*, p. 281.

10. Ibid., p. 240.

11. Ibid., p. 246.

12. Ibid., p. 242.

13. Ibid., p. 251.

14. C. W. Parsons, *Zoology*, vol. 4, 1934, p. 253. See also Gabrielle Walker, 'The Emperor's Eggs', *New Scientist*, 17 April 1999, p. 42.

15. Apsley Cherry-Garrard, *The Worst Journey in the World*, p. 234.

16. Ibid., p. 274.

17. P. J. Ponganis, T. K. Stockard, J. U. Meir, C. L. Williams, K. V. Ponganis, R. P. van Dam and R. Howard, 'Returning on empty: extreme blood O2 depletion underlies dive capacity of emperor penguins', *Journal of Experimental Biology*, vol. 210, 2007, pp. 4279–85.

18. Frenchman Guillaume Dargaud wrote a lovely review of his contrasting experiences of alcohol at McMurdo and DDU for the website Big Dead Place: http://www.bigdeadplace.com/alcoholreview.html

19. C. Gilbert, Y. Le Maho, M. Perret and A. Ancel, 'Body temperature changes induced by huddling in breeding male emperor penguins" *American Journal of Physiology*, vol. 292, 2007, pp. 176-85.

20. Unlike for seals, the researchers had discovered that flipper tags impeded the penguins so did not use them: Claire Saraux et al., 'Reliability of flipper-banded penguins as indicators of climate change', *Nature*, vol. 469, 13 January 2011, pp. 203–6.

21. C. Gilbert, G. Robertson, I. Le Maho, Y. Naito and A. Ancel, 'Huddling behavior in emperor penguins: Dynamics of huddling', *Physiology & Behaviour*, vol. 88, 2006, pp. 479–88.

22. C. Gilbert, S. Blanc, Y. Le Maho and A. Ancel, 'Energy saving process in huddling emperor penguins: From experiments to theory', *Journal of Experimental Biology*, vol. 211, 2007, pp. 1–8.

23. Mawson, *Home of the Blizzard*, p. 77.

24. Ibid., p. 83.

25. Riffenburgh, *Race with Death*, p. 71.

26. Ibid., p. 118.

27. Ibid., p. 141.

28. To be safe, Thierry told me, they never keep a captive animal under the lowest weight they have measured in a wild male, which is 3.3 kg. If any bird hit that weight, even if they weren't moving about and digesting proteins, they got their freedom.

29. Thierry and his group have since discovered that corticosterone is indeed key. See M. Spee, L. Marchal, A. M. Thierry, O. Chastel, M. Enstipp, Y. Le Maho, M. Beaulieu and T. Raclot, 'Exogenous corticosterone mimics a late fasting stage in captive Adelie penguins (*Pygoscelis adeliae*)', *American Journal of Physiology: AJP Regulatory Integrative and Comparative Physiology*, vol. 300, 2011, pp. R1241–9.

30. Olivier and his colleagues have since confirmed this. See Aurélie Goutte, Marion Kriloff, Henri Weimerskirch and Olivier Chastel, 'Why do some adult birds skip breeding? A hormonal investigation in a long-lived bird', *Biol. Lett.* vol.7, 2011, pp. 790-2; A. Goutte, E. Antoine, H. Weimerskirch, and O. Chastel, 'Age and the timing of breeding in a long-lived bird: a role for stress hormones?' *Funct. Ecol.* vol. 24, 2010, pp. 1007–16; F. Angelier, B. Moe, H. Weimerskirch and O. Chastel, 'Age-specific reproductive success in a long-lived bird: do older parents resist stress better?', *Journal of Animal Ecology*, vol. 76, 2007, pp. 1181–91.

3. Mars on Earth

1. There is a nice short summary of the evidence for water on Mars together with the latest tantalising findings suggesting that there could even have been liquid water there in the geologically recent past. Richard Kerr, 'A Roller-Coaster Plunge Into Martian Water – and Life?', *Science*, vol. 330, no. 6011, 17 December 2010, p. 1617.

2. Gabrielle Walker, 'Antarctic Landscape is Testbed for Mars', *New Scientist*, 17 April 1999, p. 48.
3. http://geology.cwru.edu/~ansmet/
4. Cassidy, *Meteorites, Ice and Antarctica*, pp. 64–7.
5. In May 2011, Ralph's University, Case Western Reserve, awarded John an honorary doctorate. His friends have now taken to calling him 'Dr Johnny Alpine'.
6. Gabrielle Walker, 'Meteorite Heaven', *New Scientist*, 17 April 1999, p. 30.
7. Cassidy, *Meteorites, Ice and Antarctica*, p. 147.
8. http://curator.jsc.nasa.gov/antmet/lmc/F2%20ALHA81005.pdf
9. http://www.lpi.usra.edu/publications/slidesets/marslife/slide_12.html
10. NASA's Jet Propulsion Laboratory has an excellent website about the Martian meteorites at: http://www2.jpl.nasa.gov/snc/index.html
11. Sean C. Solomon et al., 'New Perspectives on Ancient Mars', *Science*, vol. 307, 25 February 2005, no. 5713, pp. 1214–20.
12. D. S. McKay et al., 'Search for Past Life on Mars: Possible Relic Biogenic Activity in Martian Meteorite ALH84001', *Science*, vol. 273, no. 5277, 16 August 1996.
13. http://www2.jpl.nasa.gov/snc/clinton.html
14. http://people.bu.edu/marchant/
15. D. R. Marchant and J. W. Head, 'Antarctic Dry Valleys: Microclimate zonation, variable geomorphic processes, and implications for assessing climate change on Mars', *Icarus*, vol. 192, 2007, pp. 187–222.
16. The astronauts named part of the landing site 'Head Valley' in Jim's honour. See the Apollo 15 flight journal at http://history.nasa.gov/ap15fj/20day10_science.htm
17. J. S. Levy, J. W. Head, D. R. Marchant, J. L. Dickson and G. A. Morgan, 'Geologically recent gully-polygon relationships on Mars: Insights from the Antarctic Dry Valleys on the roles of permafrost, microclimates, and water sources for surface flow', *Icarus,* vol. 201, 2009, pp. 113–26; J. S. Levy, J. W. Head and D. R. Marchant, 'Cold and Dry Processes in the Martian Arctic: Geomorphic Observations at the Phoenix Landing Site and Comparisons with Terrestrial Cold Desert Landforms', *Geophysical Research Letters*, vol. 36, 2009, p. L21203.
18. D. E. Sugden, D. R. Marchant, N. Potter, R. A. Souchez, G. H. Denton, C. C. Swisher, and J. L. Tison, 'Preservation of Miocene Glacier Ice in East Antarctica', *Nature*, vol. 376, 1995, pp. 412-14.

4. The South Pole

1. Huntford, *Race for the South Pole*, p. 184.
2. Cherry-Garrard, *The Worst Journey in the World*, p. 525.
3. There are two excellent websites about South Pole station. http://www. southpolestation.com/ is especially good on 'trivia', including stories about past occupants of the station. The official National Science Foundation site is also full of great images and videos, including an

excellent virtual tour of the new station: http://www.nsf.gov/news/special_reports/livingsouthpole/index.jsp

4. Huntford, *Shackleton*, p. 408.

5. http://www.polarconservation.org/information/evacuations/2002-russian

6. Johnson, *Big Dead Place*, p. 78.

7. Martin Pomerantz was an American scientist who realised the potential of the South Pole for astronomy, back in the 1960s.

8. A. A. Stark, C. L. Martin, W. M. Walsh, K. Xiao, A. P. Lane and C. K. Walker, 'Gas Density, Stability, and Starbursts near the Inner Lindblad Resonance of the Milky Way', *Astrophysical Journal Letters*, vol. 614, 2004, pp. L41–4.

9. There is a superb video construction of this, based on Tony Stark's work, at http://easylink.playstream.com/nsf/video/milky_way.rm

10. At first they made only hydrogen and helium, but then these elements were processed through generations of stars to create the suite of complex elements that make up humans.

11. Jeff Peterson, 'Universe in the Balance', *New Scientist*, 16 December 2000, pp. 26–9.

12. http://www.amanda.uci.edu/collaboration.html

13. http://icecube.wisc.edu/

14. Luckily for us, and everything else made of atoms, neutrons stay intact when they are bound inside atoms.

15. Both men have nonetheless documented their many seasons in websites. Robert's in particular shows some truly breathtaking images. For Robert's page see http://www.antarctic-adventures.de/ and for Steffen's, http://www.adventure-antarctica.de/

16. Being a telescope nanny means dressing and undressing many times a day. For making your commute, you start with a basic layer of thermal T-shirt and long johns. Perhaps add long trousers before pulling on your thermally insulated Carhartt overalls, usually in a sickly mustard shade. A thick fleece jacket comes next, followed by the trusty green polar parka. You'll need a hat and balaclava to go under your parka hood. And everyone adds their own little touches. Robert Schwarz improvised a rubber mask and tube, bowdlerised from the fire-breathing apparatus, which sat under his balaclava. It made him look like an android, but it stopped his breath from fogging up his goggles.

17. Following the inconclusive inquest, there were many articles about Rodney Marks's death. Two of the best are Jeff Mervis, 'A Death in Antarctica', *Science*, 2 January 2009, pp. 32–5, and Will Cockrell, 'A Mysterious Death at the South Pole', *Men's Journal*, available at http://www.mensjournal.com/death-at-the-south-pole

18. Johnson, *Big Dead Place*, p. 92.

19. Though at the time this was the most winters anyone had spent there, that particular record has now been exceeded. At the time of writing,

Robert Schwarz has spent seven winters there, and Steffen Richter shares the current record of eight winters with a man named Johan Booth. However, Jake's record still stands for the most consecutive winters. For the latest on this and other South Pole wintering statistics, see http://www.southpolestation.com/trivia/wo.html

20. Here is a blog from someone who actually did this: http://nathantift. com/southpole/journal/journal28.htm

21. See, for example, Lawrence Palinkas, 'Psychological effects of polar expeditions', *The Lancet*, vol. 371, 12 January 2008, pp. 153–63. DOI: 10.1016/ S0140-6736(07)61056-3.

22. http://www.bigdeadplace.com/welcome.html

23. http://www.pnra.it/

24. http://www.esrl.noaa.gov/gmd/obop/spo/observatory.html

25. http://www.iris.edu/hq/programs/gsn

26. Spufford, *I May Be Some Time*, p. 173.

27. Solomon, *The Coldest March*.

28. Gabrielle Walker, 'In From the Cold', *New Scientist*, 13 October 2001.

5. Concordia

1. EPICA was funded to the tune of more than €7 million by the European Commission, Belgium, Denmark, France, Germany, Italy, the Netherlands, Norway, Sweden, Switzerland and the United Kingdom. The project involved a second core at Dronning Maud Land near the coast, which was drilled after the one at Dome C was finished. See the European Science Foundation EPICA website at http://www.esf.org/ index.php?id=855

2. http://www.institut-polaire.fr/

3. The lowest reliably measured temperature on Earth, −89.2°C, was recorded at Vostok on 21 July 1983.

4. One of the meteorologists, Guillaume Dargaud, recorded the experience in an excellent blog: http://www.gdargaud.net/Antarctica/ WinterDC.html. In fact the record low was -78.6°C. The rest of Guillaume's site is full of fascinating information about Concordia and Dumont d'Urville, as well as Antarctica in general.

5. The same experiment was deployed at the South Pole in 2002 within earshot of the station. It 'mysteriously' failed at the beginning of winter.

6. The answer turned out to be complex, but fascinating. See Gabrielle Walker, 'Antarctic astronomy: Seeing in the dark', *Nature*, vol. 438, 24 November 2005, pp. 414–15.

7. Although Vostok was deeper than the EPICA core, the thicker ice there insulated the base more, making it harder for the slight heat radiating from the inside of the Earth to escape. Thus, the oldest layers have melted away and turned into a giant under-ice lake.

8. J. R. Petit et al., 'Climate and atmospheric history of the past 420,000 years from the Vostok ice core, Antarctica', *Nature*, vol. 399, 1999, pp. 429–36.

9. EPICA Community Members, 'Eight glacial cycles from an Antarctic ice core', *Nature*, vol. 429, 2004, pp. 623–8.

10. James White, 'Do I Hear A Million?', *Science*, vol. 304, 11 June 2004, no. 5677, pp. 1609–10, but see also Edward Brook, 'Tiny Bubbles Tell All', *Science*, vol. 310, November 2005, no. 5752, pp. 1285–7.

11. D. Lüthi, et al., 'High-resolution carbon dioxide concentration record 650,000–800,000 years before present', *Nature*, vol. 453, 2008, pp. 379–82.

12. The Chinese have already begun testing for suitable ice core sites. See Xiao Cunde et al., 'Surface characteristics at Dome A, Antarctica: first measurements and a guide to future ice-coring sites', *Annals of Glaciology*, vol. 48, 2008, pp. 82–7. They are also planning to do astronomy there. See Richard Stone, 'In Ground-Based Astronomy's Final Frontier, China Aims for New Heights', *Science*, vol. 329, no. 5996, 3 September 2010, p. 1136.

13. U. Siegenthaler et al., 'Stable carbon cycle–climate relationship during the Late Pleistocene', *Science,* vol. 310, 2005, pp. 1313–17.

14. Though she initially refused all food there, she was tricked by Hades into eating some pomegranate seeds, which was enough to connect her to the underworld for all time.

15. http://www.atmos.washington.edu/~brandt/

16. Stephen G. Warren, Richard E. Brandt and Thomas C. Grenfell, 'Visible and near-ultraviolet absorption spectrum of ice from transmission of solar radiation into snow', *Applied Optics,* vol. 45, issue 21, 2006, pp. 5320–34.

17. D. Six, M. Fily, S. Alvain, P. Henry and J. P. Benoist, 'Surface characterisation of the Dome Concordia area (Antarctica) as a potential satellite calibration site, using Spot4/Vegetation instrument', *Remote Sensing of Environment*, 89(1), 2004, pp. 83–94.

6. A Human Touch

1. http://iaato.org/tourism_stats.html

2. Translated by Peter Oxford.

3. I have made three return trips to the Peninsula by ship, once on the US National Science Foundation's *Nathaniel B. Palmer,* once on the *Akademik Sergey Vavilov*, a Russian research ship chartered for tourist trips by Peregrine Adventures, and once aboard the Royal Navy icebreaker HMS *Endurance*, which was supporting the scientific activities of the British Antarctic Survey. That makes six crossings in total. And every time, Drake Passage has been as flat as a mirror. It can't be a coincidence. I am clearly some kind of charm – lucky or unlucky depending on what you wish for. If you decide to make this trip and you're worried about seasickness I suggest you take me with you. But if you want the full experience – the romance of some heavy winds to write home about – make sure I'm not on board.

4. Jeff Rubin, *Lonely Planet: Antarctica,* pp. 29–30.

5. www.peregrineadventures.com/antarctica

6. http://www.antarctica.ac.uk/

7. Sadly, the HMS *Endurance* is now out of commission. Owing to a problem with her valves she came close to sinking in the waters of South America in 2009; though she was returned to the UK, the repair bill would have been too great and she has now been scrapped, to be replaced with a Norwegian icebreaker.

8. The first report of this dinosaur was: E. Olivero, R. Scasso and C. Rinaldi, 'Revision del Grupo Marambio en la Isla James Ross – Antartida', *Contribución del Instituto Antártico Argentino,* 331, 1986, pp. 1–30; however, it took more than a decade to assemble all the available pieces, and the new species was not named until 2006, in Leonardo Salgado and Zulma Gasparini, 'Reappraisal of an ankylosaurian dinosaur from the Upper Cretaceous of James Ross Island (Antarctica), *Geodiversitas,* vol. 28, 2006, p. 119.

9. For an overview of Antarctic dinosaurs and references for the finds, see http://antarcticvp.com/education.html

10. Dominic Hodgson et al., 'Antarctic climate and environment history in the pre-instrumental period', in *Antarctic Climate Change and the Environment,* Scientific Committee on Antarctic Research, pp. 119–23, Victoire Press, Cambridge, 2009.

11. The cooling happened in fits and starts, and ice ages were, of course, generally colder than intervening warm periods such as the one we have today. But the overall trajectory has been securely downwards. See, for example, Hodgson et al., 'Antarctic climate and environment history in the pre-instrumental period', p. 123.

12. John Turner, Steve Colwell, Gareth Marshall, Tom Lachlan-Cope, Andrew Carleton, Phil Jones, Victor Lagun, Phil Reid and Svetlana Iagovkina, 'Antarctic climate change during the last 50 years' *International Journal of Climatology,* vol. 25, 2005, pp. 279-294.

13. The British Antarctic Survey has a very good website, with information about its own scientific activities as well as a host of material about Antarctica more generally: http://www.antarctica.ac.uk/

14. Felicity Ashton, 'Women of the white continent', *Geographical* (Campion Interactive Publishing), vol. 77 Issue 9, September 2005, p. 26.

15. L. S. Peck, K. E. Webb and D. M. Bailey, 'Extreme sensitivity of biological function to temperature in Antarctic marine species', *Functional Ecology,* vol. 18, 2004, pp. 625–30.

16. Mark A. Moline, Hervé Claustre, Thomas K. Frazer, Oscar Schofield and Maria Vernet, 'Alteration of the Food Web Along the Antarctic Peninsula in Response to a Regional Warming Trend', *Global Change Biology,* vol. 10.12, 2004, pp. 1973–80.

17. W. Z. Trivelpiece et al., 'Variability in krill biomass links harvesting and climate warming to penguin population changes in Antarctica', *Proceed-*

ings of the National Academy of Sciences 2011, vol. 108, 3 May 2011, pp. 7625–8.

18. Angus Atkinson, Volker Siegel, Evgeny Pakhomov and Peter Rothery, 'Long-term decline in krill stock and increase in salps within the Southern Ocean', *Nature*, vol. 432, 2004, pp. 100–103.

19. Craig R. Smith, Laura J. Grange, David L. Honig, Lieven Naudts, Bruce Huber, Lionel Guidi and Eugene Domack, "A large population of king crabs in Palmer Deep on the west Antarctic Peninsula shelf and potential invasive impacts", *Proceedings of the Royal Society B*, Published online before print 7 September, 2011, doi: 10.1098/rspb.2011.1496

20. Gabrielle Walker, 'Southern Exposure", *New Scientist*, 14 August 1999, p. 42.

21. Huntford, *Shackleton*, p. 432.

22. Ibid., p. 455.

23. Ibid.

24. Ibid., p. 473.

25. Shackleton, *South*, p. 83.

26. Ibid., p. 81.

27. Ibid., p. 168.

28. Ibid., p. 167.

29. Huntford, *Shackleton*, p. 555.

30. Alexander, *The Endurance*, p. 148.

31. Ibid., p. 183.

32. Ibid., p. 185.

33. Apsley Cherry-Garrard, *The Worst Journey in the World*, Constable and Company, 1922, vol. 1, p. viii.

34. http://www.shackletoncentenary.org/the-team/-henry-worsley-writes.php. Note that this is a deliberate misquotation of a sixteenth-century poem called *Ship of Fools*. The original wording read '… burned with passion for the West'.

35. C. J. Pudsey and J. Evans, 'First survey of Antarctic sub-ice shelf sediments reveals mid-Holocene ice shelf retreat', *Geology*, vol. 29, 2001, pp. 787–90.

36. T. Scambos, C. Hulbe and M. A. Fahnestock, 'Climate-induced ice shelf disintegration in the Antarctic Peninsula', *Antarctic Research Series*, vol. 79, 2003, pp. 79-92.

37. Eugene Domack et al., 'Stability of the Larsen B ice shelf on the Antarctic Peninsula during the Holocene epoch', *Nature*, vol. 436, 2005, pp. 681–5.

38. Scientists think the warming on the Peninsula comes from a combination of the rise in greenhouse gases (from our human burning of coal, oil, gas and trees) and a nasty side effect of the loss of the ozone layer (from our human creation and use of ozone-destroying chemicals). See, for example, J. Perlwitz, S. Pawson, R. L. Fogt, J. E. Nielsen and W. D. Neff, 'Impact of stratospheric ozone hole recovery on Antarctic climate', *Geophysical Research Letters*, vol. 35, 2008, p. L08714.

39. H. DeAngelis and P. Skvarca, 'Glacier surge after ice shelf collapse', *Science*, vol. 299, 2003, pp. 1560–2.

7. Into the West

1. Jonathan L. Bamber, Riccardo E. M. Riva, Bert L. A. Vermeersen and Anne M. LeBroq, 'Reassessment of the Potential Sea-Level Rise from a Collapse of the West Antarctic Ice Sheet', *Science*, vol. 324, 2009, pp. 901–3.

2. See, for example, Robin Bell et al., 'Large subglacial lakes in East Antarctica at the onset of fast-flowing ice streams', *Nature*, vol. 445, 22 February 2007, pp. 904–7, and R. P. Scherer, 'Did the West Antarctic Ice Sheet collapse during late Pleistocene interglacials: A reassessment', *Geophysical Research Abstracts*, vol. 11, 2009, EGU2009–5895.

3. Eric Rignot et al., 'Recent Antarctic ice mass loss from radar interferometry and regional climate modeling', *Nature Geoscience*, vol. 1, 2008, pp. 106–10.

4. Ian Joughin and Richard B. Alley, 'Stability of the West Antarctic ice sheet in a warming world', *Nature Geoscience,* vol. 4, 2011, p. 506.

5. This was first labelled 'Ice Stream C' and has now been renamed Kamb Ice Stream in honour of Barclay.

6. Ian Joughin and Richard B. Alley, 'Stability of the West Antarctic ice sheet in a warming world', *Nature Geoscience,* vol. 4, 2011, p. 506.

7. I. Joughin and S. Tulaczyk, 'Positive Mass Balance of the Ross Ice Streams, West Antarctic', *Science*, vol. 295, 2002, pp. 476–80.

8. David G. Vaughan, 'West Antarctic Ice Sheet collapse – the fall and rise of a paradigm', *Climate Change*, vol. 91, 2008, p. 65.

9. E. Rignot, 'Fast recession of a West Antarctic glacier', *Science*, vol. 281, 1998, pp. 549–51.

10. A. Shepherd, D. J. Wingham, J. A. D. Mansley and H. F. J. Corr, 'Inland thinning of Pine Island Glacier, West Antarctica', *Science*, vol. 291, 2001, pp. 862–4; A. Shepherd, D. J. Wingham and J. A. D. Mansley, 'Inland thinning of the Amundsen Sea sector, West Antarctica', *Geophysical Research Letters*, vol. 29, 2002, p. 1364; E. Rignot, D. G. Vaughan, M. Schmeltz, T. Dupont and D. MacAyeal, 'Acceleration of Pine Island and Thwaites Glaciers, West Antarctica', *Annals of Glaciology*, vol. 34, 2002, pp. 189–94.

11. A. Shepherd, D. Wingham and E. Rignot, 'Warm ocean is eroding West Antarctic Ice Sheet', *Geophysical Research Letters*, 31, 2004, p. L23402.

12. Since the shelves are floating, lower doesn't necessarily mean thinner. The sea level could have dropped locally for some reason, taking the ice down with it, or less snow could have fallen on the surface. But the researchers checked and rechecked and none of these explanations fitted. Any variations in sea level or snowfall were far too small to explain the drop they were seeing. The shelves had to be melting away from their undersides.

13. Stephen D. McPhail et al., 'Exploring beneath the PIG Ice Shelf with the Autosub3 AUV', in *Oceans 09 IEEE Bremen – Balancing Technology with Future Needs,* IEEE, Piscataway, New Jersey, 2009.

14. Stanley S. Jacobs, Adrian Jenkins, Claudia F. Giulivi and Pierre Dutrieux,

'Stronger ocean circulation and increased melting under Pine Island Glacier ice shelf', *Nature Geoscience*, vol. 4, 2011, pp. 519–23; Adrian Jenkins et al.,'Observations beneath Pine Island Glacier in West Antarctica and implications for its retreat', *Nature Geoscience*, vol. 3, 2010, pp. 468–71.

15. Nathan P. Gillett, Vivek K. Arora, Kirsten Zickfeld, Shawn J. Marshall and William J. Merryfield, 'Ongoing climate change following a complete cessation of carbon dioxide emissions', *Nature Geoscience*, vol. 4, 9 January 2011, pp. 83–7.

16. D. G. Vaughan et al., 'New boundary conditions for the West Antarctic ice sheet: Subglacial topography beneath Pine Island Glacier', *Geophysical Research Letters*, vol. 33, 2006, p. L09501.

17. J. W. Holt et al., 'New boundary conditions for the West Antarctic Ice Sheet: Subglacial topography of the Thwaites and Smith glacier catchments', *Geophysical Research Letters*, vol. 33, 2006, p. L09502.

18. Because of ocean currents and the way the Earth spins, dumping ice into the ocean in Antarctica doesn't raise sea levels everywhere by the same amount. Researchers calculate that water from melting ice in West Antarctica would be particularly focused in the Indian Ocean, and on both east and west coasts of the United States.

19. Byrd, *Alone*, p. 7.

20. Ibid., p. 214.

21. Ibid., p. 262.

22. Ibid., p. 293.

23. Gabrielle Walker, 'Hidden Antarctica: Terra Incognita', *New Scientist*, 29 November 2006, pp. 30–35.

24. L. Gray et al., 'Evidence for subglacial water transport in the West Antarctic Ice Sheet through three-dimensional satellite radar interferometry', *Geophysical Research Letters*, vol. 32, 2005, p. L03501.

25. At the latest count there were 397. See A. Wright and M. J. Siegert,'The identification and physiographical setting of Antarctic subglacial lakes: An update based on recent discoveries', in *Antarctic Subglacial Aquatic Environments, Geophysics Monograph Series*, vol. 192, 2011, edited by M. J. Siegert, M. C. Kennicutt II and R. A. Bindschadler, pp. 9–26, AGU, Washington, DC.

26. A. P. Kapitsa, J. K. Ridley, G. de Q. Robin, M. J. Siegert and I. A. Zotikov, 'Large deep freshwater lake beneath the ice of central East Antarctica', *Nature*, vol. 381, 1996, pp. 684–6; M. J. Siegert, S. Carter, I. Tabacco, S. Popov and D. Blankenship, 'A revised inventory of Antarctic subglacial lakes', *Antarctic Science*, vol. 17, 2005, pp. 453–60.

27. D. J. Wingham, M. J. Siegert, A. Shepherd and A. S. Muir,'Rapid discharge connects Antarctic subglacial lakes', *Nature*, vol. 440, 2006, pp. 1033–6.

28. H. A. Fricker, T. Scambos, R. Bindschadler and L. Padman, 'An active subglacial water system in West Antarctica mapped from space', *Science*, vol. 315, 2007, pp. 1544–8.

29. S. P. Carter et al.,'Radar-based subglacial lake classification in Antarctica', *Geochemistry Geophysics Geosystems*, vol. 8, 2007, p. Q03016.

30. J. C. Priscu et al., 'Antarctic subglacial water: Origin, evolution and ecology', in *Polar Lakes and Rivers*, p. 119, W. Vincent and J. Laybourn-Parry, eds, Oxford University Press, 2008.

31. L. A. Stearns, B. E. Smith and G. S. Hamilton, 'Increased flow speed on a large East Antarctic outlet glacier caused by subglacial floods', *Nature Geoscience*, vol. 1, 2008, pp. 827–31; Helen Amanda Fricker, 'Water Slide', *Nature Geoscience*, vol. 1, 2008, pp. 809–16. DOI: 10.1038/ngeo367.

32. Robin Bell et al., 'Large subglacial lakes in East Antarctica at the onset of fast-flowing ice streams', *Nature*, vol. 445, 22 February 2007, pp. 904–7.

33. I found out later that this contains a feature called 'Liebert Cirque', which is not far as the helicopter flies from 'Denton Glacier'.

34. Adam R. Lewis, David R. Marchant, Douglas E. Kowalewski, Suzanne L. Baldwin and Laura E. Webb, 'The age and origin of the Labyrinth, western dry valleys, Antarctica; evidence for extensive middle Miocene subglacial floods and freshwater discharge to the Southern Ocean', *Geology*, vol. 34, July 2006, pp. 513–16; D. R. Marchant, S. S. R. Jamieson and D. E. Sugden, 'The geomorphic signature of massive subglacial floods in Victoria Land, Antarctica', in *Antarctic Subglacial Aquatic Environments*, Martin J. Siegert, Mahlon C. Kennicutt II and Robert A. Bindschadler, eds, *Geophysical Monograph Series*, vol. 192, 2011.

35. Dominic Hodgson et al., 'Antarctic climate and environment history in the pre-instrumental period', in *Antarctic Climate Change and the Environment,* Scientific Committee on Antarctic Research, p. 123, Victoire Press, Cambridge, 2009.

36. N. P. Gillett et al., 'Attribution of polar warming to human influence', *Nature Geoscience*, vol. 1, 2008, pp. 750–4; Eric J. Steig et al., 'Warming of the Antarctic ice-sheet surface since the 1957 International Geophysical Year', *Nature*, vol. 457, 2009, pp. 459–62.

37. Byrd, *Alone*, p. 181.

38. Jake's friends at the South Pole set up a page dedicated to him, which you can see here: http://www.southpolestation.com/trivia/00s/jake/jakespeed.html. There is also an interview with him on New Zealand TV, shortly after the accident, in which he is exactly the same thoughtful, funny and irrepressible person I met at the South Pole, proudly demonstrating the use of his new claw hand, and talking about his plans to go surfing – which he then did: http://tvnz.co.nz/close-up/stranded-in-middle-ice-2901536/video.

SUGGESTIONS FOR FURTHER READING

Alexander, Caroline, *The Endurance*, Alfred A. Knopf, New York, 1999

Amundsen, Roald, *The South Pole*, Hurst & Co, London, 2001

Bainbridge, Beryl, *The Birthday Boys*, Carroll and Graf, New York, 1991

Byrd, Admiral Richard E, *Alone*, Kodansha International, New York, 1995

Cassidy, William, *Meteorites, Ice and Antarctica*, Cambridge University Press, Cambridge, 2003

Cherry-Garrard, Apsley, *The Worst Journey in the World*, Picador, London, 1994

Crawford, Janet, *That First Antarctic Winter*, Caxton Press, Christchurch, 1998

Gosnell, Mariana, *Ice*, Alfred A. Knopf, New York, 2005

Griffiths, Tom, *Slicing the Silence*, Harvard University Press, Cambridge, 2007

Huntford, Roland, *Race for the South Pole – The Expedition Diaries of Scott and Amundsen*, Continuum, London, 2010

Huntford, Roland, *Scott and Shackleton*, Hodder & Stoughton, London, 1979

Huntford, Roland, *Shackleton*, Abacus, London, 1985

Johnson, Nicholas, *Big Dead Place – Inside the Strange and Menacing World of Antarctica*, Feral House, Los Angeles, 2005

Riffenburgh, Beau, *Nimrod*, Bloomsbury, London, 2004

Riffenburgh, Beau, *Racing with Death*, Bloomsbury, London, 2008

Robinson, Kim Stanley, *Antarctica*, Bantam Books, New York, 1999

Rubin, Jeff, *Lonely Planet: Antarctica*, Lonely Planet, 2008

Mawson, Douglas, *The Home of the Blizzard*, St Martin's Press, New York, 1998

Pyne, Stephen J, *The Ice – A Journey to Antarctica*, University of Washington Press, Seattle and London, 1998

Scott, Robert F, *Scott's Last Expedition*, Smith, Elder & Co, London, 1913

Shackleton, Ernest, *South*, Robinson, London, 1998

Solomon, Susan, *The Coldest March*, Yale University Press, New Haven and London, 2001

Spufford, Francis, *I May Be Some Time: Ice and the English Imagination*, Faber and Faber, 2003

Spufford, Francis, ed., 'The Antarctic' in *The Ends of the Earth*, Granta Books, London, 2007

Tyler-Lewis, Kelly, *The Lost Men*, Bloomsbury, London, 2006

Wheeler, Sara, *Terra Incognita – Travels in Antarctica*, Vintage, London, 1997

ACKNOWLEDGEMENTS

This book has been more than ten years in the making, and many people have helped both in the gathering of information and the process of writing.

My visits to Antarctica were only possible because of generous grants and programme awards from the British Antarctic Survey, the US National Science Foundation's Office of Polar Programs, the French Institut Paul-Emile Victor, the Italian Programma Nazionale di Ricerche in Antartide, and Peregrine Voyages. Thanks in particular to Nino Cucinotta, Karl Erb, Gerard Jugie, David McGonigal, Nick Owens and Chris Rapley, and for logistical help to Dave Bresnahan, Linda Capper, Athena Dinar, Patrice Godon, Guy Guthridge and Elaine Hood. Thanks also to Jeremy Webb, for commissioning me to make my first, fateful trip to the continent.

As well as the people mentioned in the book who I spent time with on the ice, thanks in the US programme to 'computer whisperer' Holly Troy, my McMurdo roommate Elizabeth 'E. T.' Traver, and my fellow 'Artists and Writers' Elena Glasberg, Susan Fox Rogers and Connie Samaras. At Concordia thanks to Gilles Balada, Guillaume Dargaud, Michel Munot and Hubert Sinardet, and to Laurent Augustin for permission to quote from his personal diary. On board the *Nathaniel B. Palmer*, thanks to my cabin mate Mary Roach, and on the HMS *Endurance*, thanks also to Athena Dinar and Martin Redfern.

As well as the scientists mentioned in the book, who generously shared their research and in many case also their field sites and camps, thanks are due to Richard Alley, Sridhar Anandakrishnan, Michael Bender, Bob Bindschadler, Mike Castellini, Jérôme Chappellaz, Pete Convey, Henry Kaiser, Karl Kreutz, Berry Lyons, Doug MacAyeal, Phil Leat, Robert Mulvaney, Dean Peterson, Dominique Raynaud, Julian Scott, Andy Smith and Eric Wolff.

Thanks to Simon Marr for support during my longest trip, and to Eileen Cywinski and her class at St Clare's whose enthusiasm, engagement and brilliant questions sustained us through six weeks of slog aboard the HMS *Endurance*. Thanks are also due to Captain Bob Tarrant and the *Endurance*'s crew, to the crew and expedition staff of the *Akademik Sergey Vavilov*, and to the crew and scientists aboard the *Nathaniel B. Palmer*.

The following people read all or part of the manuscript: David Ainley, Anita Anand, Kent Anderson, Fred Barron, Don Blankenship, David Bodanis, Sam Bowser, Richard Brandt, Olivier Chastel, Gene Domack, Peter Doran, Julian Dowdeswell, Michael Evans, Bob Garrot, Caroline Gilbert, Ralph Harvey, Elaine Hood, Karen Howell, Rosa Malloy, Damian Malloy, Dave Marchant, Darran Messem, Rob Mulvaney, Thierry Raclot, Martin Redfern, Larry Rickard, Sara Russell, Leslie Sage, Leon Tayler, John Vandecar and David Vaughan. Their comments and suggestions improved the manuscript considerably; any remaining errors are, of course, my own.

Thanks to all my colleagues at Xyntéo for their unfailing support, especially Osvald Bjelland and Phil Harrison. Thanks also to my friends who have supported me with tolerance and cheer throughout this long process, especially Anita Anand, Jeanne Barron, Dave Barrows, Stephen Battersby, Romy Brandeis, Natalie deWitt, Alex Eccleston, Karen and Wayne Howell, Lucy Legg, Donna Lieberman, Dominick McIntyre, Darran Messem, Adrienne Schure, Simon Singh, Billy Stampur, John Vandecar and Jeff and Jeany Wolf. Thanks also to my friends at Paragon, especially Hazel Gale, Lisa Kent, Stuart Lawson, Keith Morris, Jonathan Smith and Mark Walker, for helping me to clear my head when I most needed it.

Extra special thanks are due to five people: Jill Ashley, Fred Barron, David Bodanis, Martin Redfern and Leon Tayler. Without their encouragement and timely interventions, this book could not have been written.

Thanks to the splendid efforts of my agent, Michael Carlisle, I have been blessed all along with two of the best editors in the business. Andrea Schulz from Harcourt believed in this book before there was even a proposal to show for it and has never wavered in her support. Bill Swainson from Bloomsbury has gone far beyond the call of duty in helping me find my way through the blizzard. I certainly could not have done this without him.

Thanks to my wonderful family: Rosa, Helen, Ed, Christian, Sarah, Damian, Jayne, Niall and Shannon, Felix and Ella. And finally thanks to all the foolishly brave men and women who have been drawn to the white continent over the scant few centuries that we have known of its existence. They have paved the way to a new understanding not just of Antarctica, but ultimately, of course, of ourselves.

• • •

Journey in the World by Apsley Cherry-Garrard (Picador, 1994), by permission of the Scott Polar Research Institute, University of Cambridge; pp. 74–5, from *Racing with Death: Douglas Mawson – Antarctic Explorer* by Beau Riffenburgh (Bloomsbury, 2008). Reproduced with permission of the author and the Mawson Centre at the South Australian Museum; pp. 116–17, from *Meteorites, Ice and Antarctica* by William Cassidy (Cambridge University Press, 2003); p.264 from *Lonely Planet: Antarctica* by Jeff Rubin (Lonely Planet, 2008). Reproduced with permission; pp. 156 and 174, from *Big Dead Place – Inside the Strange and Menacing World of Antarctica* by Nicholas Johnson (Feral House, 2005). Reproduced with permission; p. 298, from *Shackleton* by Roland Huntford (Abacus, 1985); pp.300–01 and 302, from *The Endurance: Shackleton's Legendary Antarctic Expedition* by Caroline Alexander (Alfred A. Knopf, 1999). Reproduced with permission; pp. 332, 333, 335 and 336, from *Alone: The Classic Polar Adventure* by Admiral Richard E. Byrd. Copyright © 1938 by Richard E. Byrd, renewed 1966 Marie A. Byrd, Afterword Copyright ©2003 by Kieran Mulvaney, *Alone* was originally published G.P. Putnam's Sons. Original text design by Paul Johnson. Reproduced by permission of Island Press, Washington, D.C.

INDEX

A NOTE ON THE AUTHOR

Gabrielle Walker has a PhD in natural sciences from Cambridge University and has taught at both Cambridge and Princeton universities. She is Chief Scientist of strategic advisory firm Xyntéo, a consultant to *New Scientist*, contributes frequently to BBC radio and writes for many newspapers and magazines. In 2009 and 2011 respectively she presented the *Planet Earth Under Threat* series and *Thin Air* for BBC Radio 4, and in 2011 she presented *The Secret Life of Ice* for BBC4. She lives in London.

A NOTE ON THE TYPE

The text of this book is set in Bembo. This type was first used in 1495 by the Venetian printer Aldus Manutius for Cardinal Bembo's *De Aetna*, and was cut for Manutius by Francesco Griffo. It was one of the types used by Claude Garamond (1480–1561) as a model for his Romain de L'Université, and so it was the forerunner of what became standard European type for the following two centuries. Its modern form follows the original types and was designed for Monotype in 1929.